# EMPIRE'S TWIN

A volume in the series

## The United States in the World

edited by Mark Philip Bradley, David C. Engerman, Amy S. Greenberg, and Paul A. Kramer

*A list of titles in this series is available at www.cornellpress.cornell.edu.*

# EMPIRE'S TWIN

## U.S. Anti-imperialism from the Founding Era to the Age of Terrorism

**Edited by Ian Tyrrell and Jay Sexton**

Cornell University Press
Ithaca and London

First published 2015 by Cornell University Press

First printing, Cornell Paperbacks, 2015

Printed in the United States of America

Library of Congress Cataloging-in-Publication Data

Empire's twin : U.S. anti-imperialism from the founding era to the age of
    terrorism / edited by Ian Tyrrell and Jay Sexton.
        pages cm — (United States in the world)
    Includes bibliographical references and index.
    ISBN 978-0-8014-5255-0 (cloth : alk. paper) —
    ISBN 978-0-8014-7919-9 (pbk. : alk. paper)
    1. Anti-imperialist movements—United States—History. I. Tyrrell, Ian R.,
editor. II. Sexton, Jay, 1978– editor. III. Onuf, Peter S. Imperialism and
nationalism in the early American republic. IV. Series: United States in
the world.
    E183.7.E475    2015
    325'.320973—dc23          2014027816

Cornell University Press strives to use environmentally responsible
suppliers and materials to the fullest extent possible in the publishing
of its books. Such materials include vegetable-based, low-VOC inks
and acid-free papers that are recycled, totally chlorine-free, or partly
composed of nonwood fibers. For further information, visit our
website at www.cornellpress.cornell.edu.

Cloth printing          10 9 8 7 6 5 4 3 2 1
Paperback printing      10 9 8 7 6 5 4 3 2 1

# Contents

# Acknowledgments

In the course of editing this book, we have incurred the usual debts and then some. We would first like to thank the Rothermere American Institute at Oxford University, which hosted the 2011 conference that launched this project. Without the support of Nigel Bowles, Jane Rawson, and Laura Harvey, the conference, and hence this book, would not have been possible. Further thanks are due to the Oxford Fell Fund and the Oxford History Faculty, both of which generously provided funding. Logistical support came from Queens College and Corpus Christi College. Thanks must also go to the benefactors of the Harold Vyvyan Harmsworth Chair in American History at Oxford, a position that Ian Tyrrell occupied for the academic year 2010–11.

This book is much more than a revised set of conference papers. Several individuals were unable for a variety of reasons to proceed to the final volume; and we have included chapters by new contributors Jeffrey Ostler and Laura Belmonte, both of whom have been outstanding in their timely collaboration with us. We have, ourselves, also written a final chapter dealing synoptically with post-1945 American anti-imperialism. All the contributors to this volume have been tireless in their efforts to improve the final product and in the collective endeavor to rewrite and extend the original papers. We also extend our thanks to Elizabeth Borgwardt, Amy Kaplan, Francis Shor, and Frank Ninkovich, all of whom made important contributions to this project. The project was enriched by the comments of Gareth Davies, John Thompson, Nicholas Guyatt, and Dan Scroop. Steve Tuffnell provided tireless assistance for the conference and book, for which we are grateful. Thanks also goes to Skye Montgomery for producing the index. The editors of the series "The United States in the World" and the anonymous readers for Cornell University Press have made this volume possible with their insightful critiques and encouragement, as has Cornell University Press's Michael McGandy.

Our partners Diane Collins and Julie Wood played personal roles without which any of our work would be impossible or unthinkable.

# EMPIRE'S TWIN

# Introduction

IAN TYRRELL AND JAY SEXTON

The year was 1900, and the American acquisition of the Philippines, Guam, Puerto Rico, Hawaii, and Samoa was less than two years old. A bloody war of resistance against U.S. rule was already under way in the Philippines, and at home a presidential election loomed. The "Great Commoner" William Jennings Bryan ran as the Democratic Party candidate for president. At the brand-spanking-new Convention Hall of Kansas City, the silver-tongued orator spoke in stirring tones at the party's national convention, drawing on a historical tradition of anti-imperialism that still has resonance.

If the Republicans are prepared to censure all who have used language calculated to make the Filipinos hate foreign domination, let them condemn the speech of Patrick Henry. When he uttered that passionate appeal, "Give me liberty or give me death," he expressed a sentiment which still echoes in the hearts of men. Let them censure Jefferson; of all the statesmen of history none have used words so offensive to those who would hold their fellows in political bondage. Let them censure Washington, who declared that the colonists must choose between liberty and slavery. Or, if the statute of limitations has run against the sins of Henry and Jefferson and Washington, let them censure Lincoln, whose Gettysburg speech will be quoted in defense of popular government when the present advocates of force and conquest are forgotten.[1]

Bryan's speech was as much a history lesson as a political ploy. It evoked a long tradition, one that told of the nation's anti-imperial roots in the faith of the "founding fathers," roots that Bryan believed were continually reaffirmed in the course of the Republic's first century. In his view, these principles were in dire danger.

Bryan's position was replete with the complexities and contradictions of American anti-imperialism. He had not opposed the Spanish-American War to "free" Cuba, and the platform of the Democratic Party did not oppose "expansion"—a euphemism also used by Republicans—but only overseas island possessions taken against the will of the inhabitants. Not a word did the platform mention about the questionable annexation of Hawaii, and Democrats announced: "We are not opposed to territorial expansion when it takes in desirable territory which can be erected into States in the Union, and whose people are willing and fit to become American citizens." The party also favored "trade expansion by every peaceful and legitimate means." Democrats opposed only "seizing or purchasing distant islands to be governed outside the Constitution, and whose people can never become citizens."[2] Anti-imperialism was clearly selective, geographically, racially, and constitutionally. Bryan was against formal empire, and against grabbing lands where nonwhite people remained in a majority, but he was implicitly willing to accept the vast nineteenth-century annexation of land from Indians and Mexicans as perfectly legitimate.

Another tension stemmed from the statement in the Democratic platform on the universality of anti-imperialism. This was not just an American tradition. If it "were possible to obliterate every word written or spoken in defense of the principles set forth in the Declaration of Independence, a war of conquest would still leave its legacy of perpetual hatred, for it was God Himself who placed in every human heart the love of liberty. He never made a race of people so low in the scale of civilization or intelligence that it would welcome a foreign master."[3] Self-government was a matter of human rights, not just American rights. These human rights could be a reason for nonintervention in the affairs of others, including nonwhites, but they could also be construed by imperialists to require U.S. intrusion to help along the processes of universal freedom. That, ironically, could lead to an imperialist form of anti-imperialism.

Bryan lost the election, and his anti-imperialism is remembered as the statement of a defeated minority of Americans. Yet, paradoxically, his policies soon prevailed in public sentiment and even in government action, in the sense—and to the degree—that Americans and their governments quickly became uncomfortable with formal colonies. The anti-imperialist forces had wrought their political and cultural effects. Scholars would come to call the acquisition of the island empire a "great aberration" in U.S. diplomatic history.[4] Generations of schoolchildren would grow up being taught that the United States was fundamentally an anti-imperialist nation. By the mid-twentieth century, anti-imperialism had become a functional and foundational part of American exceptionalism. The conditions had been created to allow Donald Rumsfeld, the irascible secretary of defense during another imperial "adventure" a century after the Philippines war, to blithely state: "We don't seek empires. We're not imperialistic. We never have been."[5]

In historiography, however, the tide had already turned, in part because of the very actions that Rumsfeld sought to justify. Gone was the dominance of the "great aberration" thesis. In its place came an avalanche of scholarship that made clear the centrality of imperialism in American history.[6] Some conservatives such as Niall Ferguson and Max Boot urged Americans to accept the implications of their actions and their preponderant power and use the term "empire" unabashedly.[7] From the Left, too, the "empire" word is now so regularly applied that the epithet is no longer shocking or even very controversial.

As the historiographical stocks of empire have risen, those of anti-imperialism have fallen. Whereas over the course of American history until the 1990s it was empire that was so often erased from memory, now it is the tradition of anti-imperialism that scholars are more likely to overlook. This is not to say that there are no studies of American anti-imperialism. It is not surprising that scholarly interest in the topic has tended to coincide with periods of dissent over foreign policy. The 1920s and '30s witnessed the first modern wave of anti-imperial scholarship, which included works ranging from the political history of Fred Harvey Harrington to the radical critiques of American empire in a series published by Vanguard Press.[8] Another flourish of works appeared in the wake of the Vietnam War, examining mostly political anti-imperialism and focusing on the period 1898–1920.[9]

In more recent times, most scholars interested in anti-imperialism have approached it from the perspective of those outside the American

Anti-Imperialist League or the political establishment more generally.[10] Important work has been produced on anti-imperialism in relation to feminism and suffrage.[11] Historians such as Judith Stein and Gerald Horne have explored African American anti-imperialism in work covering W. E. B. Du Bois, Marcus Garvey, and Pan-Africanism. African Americans have been "among the vanguard of American anti-imperialism," Gerald Horne writes, though some historians have "scandalously" neglected them. For the mid-twentieth century, Penny Von Eschen has explored how African American activists linked the struggle for civil rights at home to the breakdown of the old colonial order in Africa and Asia.[12] Richard Seymour has brought these themes together in a synthetic history of American anti-imperialism that ties its development to the political Left.[13]

These works focus on social protest movements or individuals, and they concern relatively marginalized groups and their allies fighting against discrimination at home while opposing imperialism abroad. They are in line with what might be called an "anti-imperial tradition" of minority protest against the mainstream of power politics and institutions. This work has had an important political purpose—indeed, the scholarship itself reflects Bryan's approach of mobilizing a line of opinion in support of contemporary political debates. Readers on anti-imperialism, for example, give students access to the classic texts and ideas of the anti-imperialists, exposing them to the rich vein of foreign-policy dissent in American history.[14] Recent scholarship also has had a crucial historiographical function: by examining the views of those outside the political establishment, it has brought to light the central role in anti-imperial thought played by dissenting minorities.

There is a need to build upon this work, particularly by expanding its parameters to include anti-imperial dissenters in U.S. colonial possessions. Equally, however, there is a need to step back and assess just how widespread and deeply woven into American culture anti-imperialism has been. A striking and paradoxical feature of the American critique of empire is that it has emerged not just from the oppressed, but also from within the corridors of power.[15] Whereas few American statesmen would have labeled themselves "imperialists," almost all would proclaim themselves to be "anti-imperialists." The critique of empire produced by elite political actors certainly differed from that of dissenters and activists, but it was nonetheless a form of anti-imperialism. This is not to suggest that the United States has been a consistent anti-imperial power, but rather to raise the question of how and why anti-imperialism became something of a shared lens through which a wide spectrum of Americans—including those who were the architects of American empire—viewed the world around them.[16] Recent scholarship on the British Empire has wrestled with similar issues and attempted to bring the fields of anti-imperialism and imperialism together in fruitful analytical relationships.[17] What has become apparent in the British case might hold even truer in that of the United States: anti-imperialism and empire cannot be easily separated, and their fortunes have been symbiotic, waxing and waning in a myriad of ways. It is time to reconsider that anti-imperialist tradition in all its permutations, not least because anti-imperialism has deeply affected the kind of empire the United States has been. Anti-imperialism was, in short, empire's twin.

This volume is premised on a catholic definition of anti-imperialism. Anti-imperialism has been both a strand of political thought and a form of social and political action. It has been a foreign policy, a versatile language, and a political cause that animates groups such as the Anti-Imperialist League. It also has been a cultural formation, a form of subaltern resistance, and a type of historiography. The meaning of anti-imperialism is contingent upon historical context. For much of the nineteenth century, for example, there was no such thing as "anti-imperialism" in the sense that this term did not exist. Yet there was "anti-imperialism" in the broader sense that the projection of power of one nation or people over another was contested and resisted. The language and symbolism of anti-imperialism have varied across time and space: anti-monarchism, Anglophobia, religious revivalism, self-determination, and anti-Americanism, to name a few, have been forms of anti-imperialism. These various vocabularies and formations have been both historically contingent and diachronically connected. The challenge confronting the historian of anti-imperialism—and the aim of this volume—is to keep in view the particularism of specific anti-imperialisms, while also tracking the evolutionary and interconnected story of the *longue durée*.

Taken as a whole, the following chapters make clear the significance of anti-imperialism in American history and the engagement of the United States with the wider world. Rather than attempt to provide a comprehensive or linear history of American anti-imperialism, the purpose of this volume is to highlight its diverse manifestations, as well as to showcase the different ways that historians can approach it. The agenda is threefold: first, to broaden our conception of anti-imperialist actors, ideas, and actions; second, to chart this story across the range of American history, from the Revolution to our own era; and third, to open up transnational and global dimensions of American anti-imperialism.

## Varieties of Anti-imperialism

We take as our starting point the diversity of historians' conception of empire. Empire is not a single "thing" but a complex and ever-changing set of unequal relationships. There are different manifestations of empire, though one should not draw too sharp a distinction between formal and informal imperialism, given that they share traits and often serve similar functions. Furthermore, "formal" and "informal" are themselves not discrete categories, since U.S. power has been exerted to different degrees in different areas of informal control, and at different times. If historians have at times overstated the significance of the formal/informal divide, they have been correct to emphasize the various forms empire has taken in American history: white settlement of continental North America, wars of conquest against Native Americans and Mexico, the forcible annexation of foreign lands such as the Philippines, the establishment of unequal economic relationships and regimes, the use of political and economic institutions to compel weaker states and peoples to comport with U.S. demands—all of these and more can be seen as "imperialist," even though they differ from one another in many ways.

The very range of imperialism, in short, ensures that its mirror image of anti-imperialism is similarly diverse. Its versatility and evolution present a challenge to historians, not least because many of its proponents did not find it necessary to come up with a strict definition of what they took "anti-imperialism" to mean. In some cases, it might best be labeled "anticolonialism," on the grounds that what was being opposed was formal colonialism, not the more general projection of imperial power. To further complicate matters, when critiquing other empires (the British in the nineteenth century or the "evil empire" of the Soviets in more recent times) Americans have tended to apply standards different from those they have applied to their own empire. As many of the essays in this volume make clear, there has been no small amount of hypocrisy in Americans' "do as I say, not as I do" denunciations of foreign empires. The task of telling the story of anti-imperialism is made even more difficult by historical actors, like Rumsfeld himself, who have seized upon the language of anti-imperialism as part of a pitch for covertly imperialist policies of foreign intervention, or perhaps even out of the belief that their actions were aligned with anti-imperial traditions.

Rather than focusing on sterile definitional history, a debate that is ultimately not resolvable, this volume's emphasis is on the historical actors that generated anti-imperial critiques. This volume does not impose a fixed definition on them but instead seeks to follow their own attempts to wrestle with what constitutes imperialism, why they thought it wrong, and what actions those beliefs led them to take. This approach expands the cast of characters and ideas that merit consideration as anti-imperial. Chapters in this volume reexamine those who traditionally have been labeled anti-imperialist (the revolutionaries of 1776, Woodrow Wilson), as well as those who have not often been considered as such by historians, though imagined themselves as part of an anti-imperial lineage (Southern secessionists, Cold War propagandists). The objective of this volume is not to determine which groups were the most authentic carriers of an imagined anti-imperial tradition, but rather to examine how, why, and to what effect such a range of historical actors developed and articulated critiques of empire.

In seeking to capture the range and variations of anti-imperialism it may be useful to note how historians have treated other "anti" movements or intellectual currents. Antislavery is a similar phenomenon in that it is negatively framed, yet elastic and contingent in historiographical treatment. No one now writes of antislavery as if it were a single and consistent thing. Rather, historians have written much on its genesis and evolution over time, as well as the various (and at times contradictory) policies that it became identified with—colonization and deportation, free-soil, gradual and compensated emancipation, immediatism and racial equality. Antislavery thought also must be viewed in relation to the evolution of its alter ego, pro-slavery thought. Finally, antislavery ideas took on different forms—political, cultural, literary, and moral, to name the most obvious. This volume seeks to explore anti-imperialism in a similar way. Investigation of the topic should not be limited to historical actors who were card-carrying members of the Anti-Imperialist League, any more than the study of antislavery should be limited to those belonging to abolitionist societies.

Instead of merely a road not taken or a social/political group that lost battles to determine policy, U.S. anti-imperialism, this volume contends, was an important shaper of American empire. The essays here build upon the insight of the New Left that anti-imperialists, far from opposing all forms of empire, were inextricably bound up in imperialist processes and structures.[18] This theme plays out in many different ways in the chapters that follow. First, some actors were anti-imperialist on some issues, while imperialist on others. There is no better example here than the founding fathers themselves, who broke the imperial bond with Britain in part to advance their aim of westward colonization. Second, and related, many Americans were anti-imperial when it came to opposing illiberal Old World empires while imperialist when it came to advocating what they viewed as their new, more moral, "empire of liberty." This attitude can be found across U.S. history, from the promoters of westward expansion in the nineteenth century to those that trumpeted the forcible promotion of democracy abroad in more recent times. Third, many of the critics of imperialism within the U.S. empire called for its reform rather than its demolition. This was the case with a range of actors, including missionaries, dissenters within the post–1898 possessions, and even U.S. grand strategists whose realpolitik led them to repudiate costly and counterproductive imperialist policies.

Anti-imperialism traditionally has been seen as mirroring *external* empire, but its domestic or internal applications, particularly in the nineteenth century, should not be neglected. Many of the most powerful anti-imperial critiques in American history have focused on the danger of imperialism within the United States, normally in the form of an aggressive central government trampling upon the rights of individuals, states, or social groups. A variation of this theme can also be seen in the anti-imperialism of Native Americans who resisted the dispossession of their lands by white colonizers supported by federal power. Revealingly, the word "imperialism" itself appears initially to have been used in the United States in relation to domestic matters, not foreign ones. Historians long have credited Victorian critics of British prime minister Benjamin Disraeli's embrace of foreign adventurism for coining the word in the 1870s.[19] Yet Charles Sumner used "imperialism" as a description for Radical Reconstruction at home in 1867 (in this case, as a positive description: "Call it imperialism, if you please; it is simply the imperialism of the Declaration of Independence, with all its promises fulfilled."[20]) The first usage of "imperialism" in the United States pertained to internal politics and the power of the federal government, not overseas expansion.

White Southerners squirmed at this Yankee imperialism, calling instead for the restoration of internal anti-imperialism in the form of "home rule" and "states' rights." Even in the early twenty-first century, this brand of internal anti-imperialism could still be detected. The "Tea Party" identification of federal power as a threat to individual and state liberty is but a modern reincarnation of this old anti-imperial critique. Some conservatives and libertarians expanded this critique of federal power in the domestic realm into a broader anti-imperial vision of U.S. foreign policy. Just as contemporary leftists claim the mantle of anti-imperialism, so too have some on the political Right who see the policies of an interventionist president like George W. Bush as a betrayal of "middle-American anti-imperialism," as a conservative commentator has recently put it.[21]

Though in many cases anti-imperialism has been a reactionary impulse, this need not mean that American anti-imperialists were consistently negative, narrow, or bigoted in their outlook. Though, by its very nature, anti-imperialism is negatively framed, its proponents invariably face the question of what should replace the imperialism that they denounce. Just as recent work has made the case for a positive agenda among isolationists,[22] the essays here argue that anti-imperialism was more than just a negative and reactionary movement. For colonial peoples, this agenda obviously began with the notions of self-determination and nation building. For Americans, social reform, peace agitation, civil liberties, and equality for women were often linked with anti-imperialism and isolationism in the decades from the 1890s to the 1920s, and associated with names such as Jane Addams.[23] Among the policy-making elite, anti-imperialism can be seen to have shaped their worldview and diplomatic agenda, at times mitigating interventionist impulses or leading statesmen to consider the costs of expansionist policies.

## Anti-imperialism across Time

Our most important intervention is to chart anti-imperialism across time and space. In part, this is a story of continuity, of the development of an anti-imperial tradition. There are recurring symbols, texts, and ideas from 1776 to the present. One of the most important is the memory of 1776 itself that Bryan invoked. Subsequent generations of Americans came to see the Revolution as the genesis of anti-imperialism, the beginning of a new and enlightened world order. The Revolution's utility lay in its extraordinary versatility: nearly all major anti-imperial groups and movements have imagined themselves as carriers of the tradition of 1776. The memory of the American Revolution also has had purchase outside the United States among anticolonial nationalists both within and without the American empire. The Declaration of Independence, David Armitage has made clear, circulated around the globe, serving as a malleable template through which peoples could make their case for self-determination.[24]

Though the anti-imperial critique shows much continuity across time, countless differences and points of contestation are also manifest, not least because imperialism itself is a moving target. The very ubiquity of the American Revolution in anti-imperial thought ensured that its meaning and legacy were contested. Rather than attempt to construct a linear history of American anti-imperialism, the chapters that follow uncover what it has meant in different historical contexts. The vocabulary, meaning, and action of anti-imperialism have varied greatly. Anachronism is the great danger in a study of this nature: it is all too easy to project back in time modern forms and ideas of anti-imperialism, not least because anti-imperial movements have constructed linear and ahistorical narratives to legitimate their contemporary positions. A related danger concerns that of romantic nostalgia, or the tendency to see anti-imperialists as being on the "right" side of important questions. No doubt many anti-imperial positions in American history harmonize with the values of contemporary historians. But reducing anti-imperialism to those historical actors that anticipated today's norms flattens its diverse forms that this volume seeks to uncover.

Part one of this volume, "Conquest and Anticolonialism in the Nineteenth Century," explores the symbiotic, if paradoxical, relationship between the conquest of the North American continent and the development of a powerful tradition of American anti-imperialism. We begin with Peter Onuf's examination of how the roots of American anti-imperialism lay in a particular critique of the British Empire. From the beginning, the denunciation of the British Empire was fused with the imperialist project of settler expansion on the North American continent. As the nineteenth century progressed, Americans constructed an imagined memory of their Revolution as a highly principled and singular anticolonial revolt against an interfering and distant empire. The language of anti-imperialism for much of this period was that of Anglophobia and anti-monarchism, and its political applications were as often internal (against domestic political opponents) as external. Anti-imperialism was further fueled by the growing Irish-Catholic immigration to the United States whose memories of English landlords and the Great Famine of 1845–48 stoked anti-imperialist indignation. This proto-anti-imperial critique proved to be versatile and malleable, even being deployed as justification for U.S. territorial expansion on the grounds that it weakened the position of Old World empires in North America. It was appropriated and reconfigured by a variety of actors, including Native Americans. In an essay that spans the nineteenth century, Jeffrey Ostler examines the diverse forms of Native American anti-imperialism, giving particular emphasis to religious revivalism. Some white Americans struggled to square their imagined anti-imperial tradition with the policies and processes of their era, not least their dispossession of Indian lands and the war of conquest against Mexico. No issue attracted more political debate on the meaning of the American Revolution, however, than did the mid-nineteenth-century crisis of the Union and the Civil War. Jay Sexton's essay explores the ways in which Southerners and Northerners alike understood their respective causes in relation to the imagined tradition of anti-imperialism.

Part two, "Anti-imperialism and the New American Empire," explores the evolution, expansion, and foreign appropriation of anti-imperialism in the new context of American colonial and global power at the turn of the century. By 1900, the period of "high" European colonialism in which Bryan operated saw imperialists come out to repudiate anti-imperialism and proclaim the long-standing nature of American empire, as Senator Albert Beveridge did in his speeches on the annexation of the Philippines. Many Americans waxed lyrical on the rise of a "Greater America" that encompassed the island territories, and scoffed at anti-imperialists, while others sought to adapt an imagined national tradition of anti-imperialism to the new political context. But, as Julian Go's essay makes clear, the conversation on American empire was never a purely internal one, and as the American use of force outside the continental United States increased in the years 1898–1934, anti-imperialists throughout the new American empire and beyond themselves reworked and adapted to their own purposes the nineteenth-century American traditions of the Declaration of Independence and the Constitution.

Early twentieth-century anti-imperialism was a diverse and contested phenomenon. Alan Knight's essay on the U.S. response to the Mexican Revolution shows the wide range of policies and interest groups that sought to advance some form of anti-imperialism. His survey of U.S. policy finds that what might be considered anti-imperial—the eventual rejection of coercive and annexationist policies in favor of a policy of engagement and collaboration—nonetheless sought the imperialist objectives of the advancement of U.S. economic, political, and strategic interests. U.S. policy toward Mexico in this period thus portended the informal imperialism characteristic of the later post-1945 American empire. Ussama Makdisi engages with similar themes in his essay on the American presence in the Middle East in the nineteenth and early twentieth centuries. The hostility of American missionaries to the European and Ottoman empires found political expression in the King-Crane commission of 1919. Yet, as in Mexico, Americans' aversion to formal empire in the Middle East was wedded to paternalistic assumptions that many Arabs were unprepared for self-government and required the tutelage of the United States. Ironically, the legacy of American anti-imperialism in the Middle East was that the liberal ideas propagated by missionaries in time became the basis for the anti-American critiques of the post-1945 era.

Part three, "The Extent and Limits of Anti-imperialism," begins with Erez Manela's essay examining how World War I gave new prominence to anti-imperialism at home and abroad. The rise of Bolshevism and the Wilsonian alternative of the Fourteen Points strengthened the position of anti-imperialism internationally—indeed, Manela contends that this period witnessed the birth of anti-imperialism as a principle for the restructuring of global order. The sheer carnage of World War I, a war widely thought to be the result of imperialist intrigues, and the disillusionment over the failure of the Versailles Treaty to supply a viable long-term settlement, meant that anti-imperialism in the United States now became aligned with opposition to American involvement in foreign wars. The spread of Communist internationalism, too, had its effects on American anti-imperialism, as formerly Progressive reform anti-imperialists were radicalized into opponents of financial imperialism, particularly as it came to be practiced in the name of dollar diplomacy in the Caribbean basin.[25] The Communist International organized the All-American Anti-Imperialist League, which operated across Latin America as well as in the United States. As Roger Baldwin of the American Civil Liberties Union noted, the U.S. affiliate was "inspired by our Communist friends" but had "both a membership and an appeal outside the Communist movement."[26]

Spurred by the forces of nationalism and international socialism, anti-imperialism became by the mid-twentieth century a global political force and predominant culture extending far beyond the United States and its areas of influence. The ascendancy of anti-imperialism by that time did not rule out the pursuit of American empire, particularly when advanced informally. Indeed, decolonization was, the New Left argued long ago, a way of prying open the protected colonial markets of the former European empires. Thus Franklin D. Roosevelt and others who spoke against European empires in World War II framed their approach as anticolonial rather than in the broader language of anti-imperialism.[27]

If anti-imperialism picked up steam globally in the first half of the twentieth century, it was not without its limits, particularly in the United States. In a conceptual essay, Patricia Schechter examines the limits of anti-imperialism in the history and historiography of turn-of-the-century feminism. She suggests that the concept of the "decolonial" has greater explanatory potential for understanding feminist encounters with empire than does anti-imperialism. Ian Tyrrell's essay approaches the limits of American anti-imperialism by looking at recent international critiques of globalization from an environmental point of view, and through critical environmental histories that find anti-imperialism and conservation connected. He asks why the connection between anti-imperialism and environmental concerns is relatively underdeveloped in the American context.

The final section, "Anti-imperialism in the Age of American Power," considers the nature of anti-imperialism in an era of U.S. ascendancy. American anti-imperialism in the years since World War II became complicated by how the decolonization of European empires related to the struggle against communism and the division of the world into "free" and "enslaved," a point explored in Laura Belmonte's essay on U.S. and Soviet propaganda during the Cold War. From the American point of view, this anticommunist crusade aimed to liberate the world from the oppression of the Soviet Union's "evil empire," or at least to hold the line against it, thus legitimating assertive and interventionist policies in the Third World. That Western European countries to varying degrees invited U.S. participation in their struggle to survive—that the American empire was "an empire by invitation"[28]—gave further weight to the conception of U.S. Cold War policy as an outgrowth of anti-imperial traditions.

But as Soviet propagandists stated, interventionist U.S. policies sat uneasily beside American professions of anti-imperialism. Furthermore, domestic objections to U.S. imperialism abroad reappeared with great force again in the 1960s. An early example can be seen in the opposition to U.S. interference in Cuba, as in the Fair Play for Cuba Committee that became infamous through its association with Lee Harvey Oswald. More than Cuba, anti–Vietnam War protests spurred the resurgence in the idea of the American empire among what became known as the New Left, and certain radical antiwar groups defined their agitation as anti-imperialist.[29] A rich historiography illuminates the extent of the opposition to the war and that opposition's anti-imperialist connections. But some of these connections were prominent within the American political system as representatives of the Democratic and Republican parties.[30] Robert Buzzanco's essay adds to this picture, showing that in the case of dissent at home during the Vietnam War era, some of the most powerful calls to draw back from imperial entanglements in the post–World War II period originated from within the military-industrial complex.

An important subtheme running through the essays concerns how anti-imperialism grew as an ideal in the twentieth century within the American imagination, and within global society. This is not to suggest that the

United States was the only source of global anti-imperialism, nor that for-eigners who took up American anti-imperialist symbols did so uncritically. In fact, foreigners repeatedly adapted these symbols to their own purposes. In this volume, the American-centered part of this global story is developed empirically by following certain symbols and texts as they took root among ever larger groups of peoples: especially the Declaration of Independence or the anticolonial appropriation of Wilson's Fourteen Points. The global development of ideas of anti-imperialism can also be linked in part to the rise of the United States as a global force (which indirectly made American symbols of anti-imperialism of greater political importance nationally and internationally as U.S. power increased). The revulsion against World War I along with the rise, after World War II, of antiracism, antifascism, and human rights agitation that propelled opposition to colonialism in Africa and Asia helps to explain the shift. The final chapter, coauthored by Ian Tyrrell and Jay Sexton, tracks anti-imperialism in this decolonizing and postcolonial era, when imperialism took new and often less visible forms.

## Transnational Connections

Though anti-imperialism clearly crossed national boundaries, historio-graphical debates within the United States have only begun to consider such contexts. A complete survey of such matters is beyond the scope of this book and requires a host of local studies tracing national anti-imperial reactions to U.S. global and regional power. Our focus here has been prin-cipally on anti-imperialism within the United States but also extends to representative places that had intimate and long relationships with Ameri-can power: Mexico, Puerto Rico, the Philippines, and the Middle East. In these cases, the direction of anti-imperial traffic moved both ways. First, the United States projected anti-imperialism outward, as we have seen. Symbols such as the Declaration of Independence or Wilson's speeches circulated around the globe to be appropriated by foreign peoples, as well as by those within an expanding U.S. empire. It should not be forgotten that the rise of American formal and informal empire was, in general, a disrup-tive force for Europeans. American missionaries, for example, frequently critiqued the imperialism of European countries but found American anti-imperialism could be turned against American practice when the "pure" anti-imperialism that white American elites imagined as the heritage of the nation became both an inspiration for colonial peoples and a mirror to hold up to the United States in the countless instances in which it did not live up to this ideal.[31]

The second aspect of transnational connection concerns the reciprocal traffic in anti-imperialism back into the United States. In some instances, foreign actors sought to influence U.S. policy by a complex circulation of ideas that actually originated in the United States. They deployed the language and symbols of American anti-imperialism for their own purposes against American conceptions of regional and global power, a point Alan Knight develops in relation to Mexican diplomats during the revolutionary period of 1910–40. In other instances the traffic of anti-imperialist ideas stemmed from non-American sources. American Marxists of the 1920s who drew upon the ideas of the Soviet Communist International and orthodox Marxist conceptions of imperialism provide one case. But there are others. Anti-imperialists within the U.S. empire, such as those in Puerto Rico examined by Go, drew from recipients of British imperial power to critique the United States, using mostly the experience of Irish nationalists. The same processes apply for the forms of anti-imperialism that have flourished in the era of "new globalization" since the 1980s.[32]

Given the cross-fertilization that can be easily shown between empires, it is hardly surprising that the opposition to empire is cross-"national" in these ways. The most obvious examples come from the international reaction to Wilson's anti-imperialism examined by Manela, but there are many other possible cases. Clearly the American anti-imperialists of the later nineteenth century lived in the world of the Anglo-American rapprochement in which reciprocal transatlantic reform influences were marked, as Daniel Rodgers has shown.[33] These transatlantic dimensions extend to American anti-imperialism. M. Patrick Cullinane has pointed out that after Bryan's defeat in 1900, many anti-imperialists turned to the cultural realm, seeking the broadest possible field of agitation and critique. They campaigned against the Boer War, a cause not directly implicating the United States, but involving the Anglophobic element of American anti-imperialism, in which Boers were turned into freedom fighters against the perfidious power of Britain along the model of the American Revolution.[34]

This book places U.S. anti-imperialism firmly within American political and cultural traditions, but it also indicates the need to situate U.S. anti-imperialism in a wider and ultimately global context. Many opportunities for the further study of anti-imperialism are thereby revealed. Ostler's examination of Native American anti-imperialism suggests the need for future comparative studies with indigenous resistance to settler colonization in other places. The essays on the early U.S. Republic by Onuf and Sexton raise questions concerning the transnational history of Anglophobia. Did the American language of Anglophobic anti-imperialism catch on outside its borders? How did other traditions of Anglophobia—one thinks here of the Irish, Quebecois, and other discontents within Britain's empire, as well as France and its overseas dominions—relate to the American incarnation? And, to pose a conceptual rather than empirical question, was Anglophobia the transnational vocabulary of anti-imperialism before there was an international consciousness of what became known as anticolonial nationalism?

Future research should examine the lost cosmopolitanism of anti-imperialist adherents in the late nineteenth and early twentieth centuries. The classic moment of U.S. anti-imperialism of 1898–1920 was also a formative one outside the United States, as Manela, Go, and Knight make clear. No study exists, for example, that has looked at the influence on U.S. anti-imperialism of Englishman J. A. Hobson, the author of the classic work *Imperialism* (1902), even though Hobson is well known for his influence upon V. I. Lenin's mutation of Marxism that made imperialism the "highest stage" of financial capitalism.[35] Yet, as Hobson biographer Michael Schneider has noted, "Between 1902 and 1905 John Hobson made a series of long visits to the United States and Canada, lecturing to universities, clubs and to more popular audiences."[36] He influenced Thorstein Veblen, who reviewed his *Imperialism* volume,[37] and even exchanged views on political economy with William Jennings Bryan and socialized with the Great Commoner.[38]

Another point for future research raised in this volume is anti-imperialist currents within the great outpouring of American mission and other civil society action abroad since the late nineteenth century. Though these phenomena have typically been seen as agents of imperialism, the missionaries' role as critics of empire and as brokers between imperial power and those subject to that power has not been studied nearly as intensively or as extensively as desirable. Ussama Makdisi's contribution shows how sympathetic missionaries were toward the subordinated peoples of the Ottoman Empire, and how hostile to the idea that any European imperial regime should take the place of the Ottoman in the Arab world at the end of World War I. The problem is that the anti-imperialist missionaries were on some occasions hostile to non–American empire, yet, when the United States acquired territories, they often sought to reform that empire rather than overthrow it. Nevertheless, it is clear that the experience of being a missionary was sufficient to bring out the gap between American ideals, especially regarding race, and the reality of hierarchy within American empire.[39]

Little is known within U.S. historiography about the diversity and scope of anti-imperialism directed against American power in a variety of foreign countries. Future studies might well be part of the project for internationalizing American history by drawing attention to how American ideas "travel" and how foreign peoples have responded. Many countries have felt the impact of American power in the nineteenth and twentieth centuries, producing both anti-American and anti-imperial manifestations. Yet scholarly work that brings U.S. actions and those of critics and collaborators of empire abroad together in either a comparative or a transnational framework is rare. One promising topic for investigation involves the relationship between immigrant and refugee diasporas within the United States and opposition to U.S. foreign policy. Examples of this kind of transnational anti-imperialism can be found across time, from the Irish who called for a more assertive anti-British U.S. foreign policy in the nineteenth century to the Central American refugees who opposed Reagan-era policies toward their homelands.[40] Since U.S. anti-imperialism existed within a wider framework of reactions to the spread of formal and informal empires, it is also worth asking what formal comparison can tell us, by both similarities and absences, about the nature of American anti-imperialism. Thus far, only episodic and fragmentary comparisons of this sort have been made between different anti-imperialist traditions of modern empires, for example Britain versus the United States.[41]

A further possible set of topics takes us to the present and to contemporary history. Historians have written much about the current political conjuncture in world politics and the changing role of the United States since the collapse of the Soviet Union, the Gulf War (1991), and the events of 9/11. But, as the concluding chapter suggests, a rich story remains to be told concerning domestic and foreign opposition to this latest phase of American empire. Scholars should further explore how recent manifestations of anti-imperialism around the globe relate to earlier anti-imperial forms and movements. Furthermore, historians could reflect upon how their mostly anti-imperialist assumptions are shaping historical scholarship today. To what extent and to what effect is the recent outpouring of studies on empire in American history itself a form of anti-imperialism?

Anti-imperialist social movements did not end with the Vietnam War and the antiglobalization and antinuclear protests of the 1980s. They continue to be a part of political life. The radical African American group Black Is Back joined the Occupy Wall Street campaign in late 2011 and combined antiracism with opposition to the Iraq and Afghanistan wars.

This was one of a host of small groups that have kept alive the language of anti-imperialism, drawing, in the case of black protest, from W. E. B. Du Bois and Pan-African anticolonialism. They demanded "an end to the wars throughout the Middle East, Africa, Latin America and against oppressed communities inside the U.S.," which, these groups say, "are driven by Wall Street interests."[42] At the other end of the spectrum, the U.S. government, having learned from the domestic and international criticism that followed the wars in Iraq and Afghanistan, anxiously avoided taking a leading and highly visible military role in the 2011 U.N. action in Libya. "America is not the crude stereotype of a self-interested empire," Barack Obama asserted in his 2009 Cairo speech. "We were born out of revolution against an empire."[43] Yet such rhetoric has not convinced many critics of the United States in the Arab world, who continue to point to the gap between American words and actions. Anti-imperialism is not dead on the streets, nor in the government, nor in wider public policy, and it remains an integral part of American and global affairs.

PART I

# CONQUEST AND ANTICOLONIALISM
# IN THE NINETEENTH CENTURY

Chapter 1

# Imperialism and Nationalism in the Early American Republic

PETER S. ONUF

In the early United States, the concepts of "empire" and "nation" were inextricably linked. In the original and still conventional understanding, the relationship is dialectical and sequential: in the process of overthrowing the British Empire, rebellious colonists became a nation. As they killed the king, these self-designated "Americans" recognized themselves and each other as countrymen, patriots who proclaimed their right to a "continent" that their ancestors had conquered, cultivated, and civilized. Independent Americans set a precedent for anti-imperial nation making, boldly proclaiming to the world a new standard of legitimacy: the "consent" of a sovereign people to its own government.[1]

It is the contention of this chapter that the sequence of empire and nation on which the American national narrative pivots is fundamentally mistaken and misleading. If this is so, anti-imperialism—the opposition to putatively "imperial" tendencies in the new national regime—would necessarily have an equally tangled and complicated history. Our challenge is to distinguish the protean idea of "empire" from the British Empire as patriots came to understand it through the imperial crisis and Revolutionary War. Colonists mobilized on behalf of their understanding of what they thought the empire was or should be, rallying in defense of colonial "constitutions" and the constitution of the empire that protected them. If, as exponents of parliamentary sovereignty argued and the Declaratory Act of 1766 made explicit, there was no such thing as an imperial constitution, then it was incumbent on enlightened statesmen on both sides of the Atlantic to negotiate one and thus to forge "a more perfect union." Before they belatedly realized, in the midst of violent resistance, that they were a distinct "people" and that their goal was independence, patriots could only be described as—and understand themselves to be—"imperialists."

The patriots' idea of empire did not disappear with independence. If the British king and the empire over which he reigned epitomized all that was evil and despotic in the old regime, an "empire for liberty" now extended across the former colonies. That the term would *not* be contaminated by associations with Britain was testimony to the powerful hold of the imperial idea in the American political imagination. A corrupt king and administration had betrayed the empire: arguably, *they* were the real anti-imperialists, not the Americans. "Nation" was a similarly protean concept. Colonists' strong identification with the empire and persistent allegiance to George III reflected a broader process of Anglicization that was fueled by the consumer revolution and their closer integration in commercial and cultural networks.[2] Americans' national identity clearly betrayed a British genealogy, for it was only by imagining themselves as Britons—and proclaiming their English rights—that they could transcend the narrowly provincial identities that historically divided them and threatened to subvert their common cause. As Jefferson plaintively told fellow Britons in the metropolis in his original draft of the Declaration, "we might have been a free and a great people together; but a communication of grandeur & of freedom it seems is below their dignity."[3] Now Americans would have to transform themselves into the "free and great people" they could not be in the British Empire. Nation and empire thus were hardly incompatible terms for revolutionary Americans: indeed, nationhood was meaningless outside the context of empire, as colonial Americans understood it, or of the federal union, its successor.[4]

## American Exceptionalism

Focusing on a reluctantly exercised right of revolution, patriots were the first "idealists," brandishing universally applicable principles of self-determination to a "candid world." Their self-understanding became the

"American creed," an inspiring conception of the new nation's exalted role in world history that was most memorably expressed by Abraham Lincoln in his Gettysburg Address: "we here highly resolve that these dead shall not have died in vain—that this nation, under God, shall have a new birth of freedom—and that government of the people, by the people, for the people, shall not perish from the earth."[5] This creedal nationalism has defined a dynamic, demographically diverse people across more than two centuries. Projected across time and space, the American nation has become indistinguishable from "democracy," the fundamental character or ethos of a regime that, as Thomas Jefferson wrote at the end of his life, was "opening . . . all eyes" to "the rights of man."[6] In America, the right of national self-determination had overcome the might of a great empire.

"Realists" offer a complementary counter-narrative, emphasizing interests over ideas but also insisting on the fundamental principle of self-determination. Harking back to the first settlers' conquest of the wilderness, they celebrated a history of self-sufficiency, self-government, and continuous improvement. The empire had always been an empty shell, incapable of enforcing edicts that seriously compromised the vital interests of a rights-conscious settler population. The challenge for patriots was to alert their countrymen to immanent threats and overcome the habitual loyalties of lightly governed, enterprising subjects with better things to do: "our ancestors," as Jefferson wrote in 1774, "were farmers, not lawyers."[7] The moment for lawyers like Jefferson would come with the imperial crisis. They spoke "common sense" and "self-evident" principles to a mobilized people, aroused from their slumbers and newly conscious of their collective power. The author of the Declaration of Independence later acknowledged that these were not "new principles, or new arguments, never before thought of," but rather "the common sense of the subject."[8]

Idealists and realists, then and now, offer variations on the exceptionalist theme. They differ on the relative importance or primacy of ideas and material interests in explaining patriot intentions, and therefore on the exportability and universality of republican principles. At one extreme, a realist might argue that the facts on the ground in British America were unique (or exceptional) and would never be replicated elsewhere: the role of patriot propaganda was to alert their fellow colonists to their endangered interests and arouse them in their defense. The Revolution was nothing more or less than a tax revolt, and the Declaration was therefore "a merely revolutionary document" of local significance.[9] The invocations of natural rights were, as Lincoln quoted his opponents, "glittering generalities" and "self evident lies"; the promise of nationhood was extended by Americans to themselves: "it meant nobody else."[10] Lincoln positioned himself at the other, idealist extreme with Jefferson, who had introduced "an abstract truth" into the Declaration, "applicable to all men and all times, and so to embalm it there, that to-day, and in all coming days, it shall be a rebuke and a stumbling-block to the very harbingers of re-appearing tyranny and oppression."[11] But even in their most polarized positions, idealists and realists embraced the logic of nationhood, cherishing their independence and disentanglement from European alliances and imagining a glorious future. The new nation's ascendancy might be realized *in* history, as realists imagined, with the United States extending its influence and promoting its interests on the continent, through the hemisphere, and around the world; or it might take place at the *"end* of history," when all the nations of the world embraced the liberal democracy that the new nation first modeled to the world.[12]

Historians have long argued about whether the American Revolution was "radical" or "conservative." Controversy revolves around the putative character of regime change: how sharp was the break between provincial and republican America, the British Empire and the new federal republic? Following the lead of the revolutionaries themselves, exceptionalists of all stripes accentuate discontinuities, differing on when, why, and how colonists became alienated from the mother country and therefore conscious of their distinctive collective identity.

A conservative, "consensus" interpretation looks for Revolutionary causation in the distant past, as colonies set forth on largely autonomous trajectories and adapted English institutions to novel American conditions. When imperial reformers challenged this benign status quo, patriotic colonists mobilized against change in order to defend their liberty and property. Americans were pragmatic conservatives, "born liberal" in an environment that fostered enterprise and self-sufficiency.[13] By contrast, the now dominant ideological interpretation, most fully and eloquently developed by Bernard Bailyn and Gordon S. Wood, rises above material interests and focuses instead on questions of identity that came to the fore with the imperial crisis. The Revolution's most momentous, radical changes were enacted in the "minds" of British colonists who *became* Americans.[14] The ideological interpretation coincided with an emerging historiography that depicted the British colonies as far-flung fragments—or "marchlands"—of early modern Europe. The "Europeanization"—and Anglicization—of early American history set the stage for reimagining the Revolution as a radical *ideological* transformation: colonists had to overcome a deep-seated sense of cultural inferiority and dependence in order to recognize themselves as Americans and declare themselves an independent people.

Both "conservative" and "radical" approaches to Revolutionary causation are exceptionalist, Whiggishly assuming the irresistible and inevitable emergence of a new nation destined for greatness. Revisionists might question whether this is a good thing, emphasizing the human and environmental costs of expansion and reflexively indicting the United States as a latter-day imperial hegemon, but they take the nation's ascendancy for granted; like Lincoln, they take their bearings from Jefferson's Declaration, hoping for a course correction that will one day redeem the revolutionaries' "promissory note" to the American people and to the peoples of the world.[15] Whether they emphasize nation-making material interests or nation-defining ideals, whether they are patriotic celebrants or revisionist critics, exceptionalists assume a fundamental opposition between empire and nation, Old World from New. As legal historian Christopher Tomlins writes, "American historical orthodoxy has long seized upon the social and political modernity colonizing made possible and has lashed it to an idealized temporality of progress that leaves . . . the pre-modern in its wake."[16] Like the revolutionaries, whose ultimate success depended on demonstrating that the rupture between the metropolis and its erstwhile provinces was complete, exceptionalists deny and suppress continuities: phoenix-like, the new nation rose from the ashes of Revolutionary battlefields where the empire died.

Recent trends in historiography suggest that the powerful hold of the exceptionalist paradigm may be waning. As exceptionalism wanes, the legacies of imperial practices as well as ideas about empire in the early American republic come more clearly into view. The long shadow of empire shaped a protean, Anglophobic anti-imperialist, nationalist discourse. Succeeding generations of American partisan patriots remembered and refought the Revolution, projecting aristocratic and monarchical ambitions onto electoral opponents. Yet as they did so, these anti-imperialists projected more benign, republicanized images of "empire" across the continent. Independent Americans thus turned the old empire inside out, demolishing the structures of transatlantic governance while they unleashed the energies of colonizing settlers, land speculators, and slaveholders. If they would "consecrate their union," James Madison promised in *Federalist* 14, Americans across the continent would remain "fellow citizens of one great respectable and flourishing empire."[17]

The protean character of the terms "empire" and "nation" and their inextricable relation confused contemporaries and confuses us still. To the extent independent Anglophobic Americans identified "empire" with the insidious influence and power of the former metropolis, they could see themselves as anti-imperialists: from this perspective, imperialism—the quest for "universal monarchy"—was a leading pathology of the old regime, characteristic of all the great powers in their never-ending struggle for advantage. But the focus on the metropolis and the exaggerated opposition between monarchical and republican America obscured fundamental continuities between old regime and new. Americans broke with Britain in order to preserve the cherished liberties that a progressive and enlightened empire was supposed to have secured; they were also determined to sustain the colonizing impulses that the British Empire had—before the imperial crisis—so vigorously promoted.

## Languages of Empire

Republican revolutionaries saw the break with Britain and the rejection of monarchical government as a decisive turning point in their own histories and in the progress of political civilization. Yet their greatest achievement, the construction of a federal union that would secure provincial liberties (or state rights) and the rights of Englishmen (or the civil rights of citizens), harked back to an idealized version of the old empire: federalism was a republicanized version of imperialism. As a result, the "languages of empire" that David Armitage, Jack Greene, and other scholars have been reconstructing remained salient in the new United States long after independence.

Armitage links an emerging "ideology" of empire in mid-eighteenth-century Britain and its overseas provinces with the broader development of British nationalism. The British Empire was depicted as "Protestant, commercial, maritime and free," a formulation that avoided hard questions about imperial governance and the identity or status of Anglo-Americans.[18] As Kathleen Wilson has written, this broadly appealing, "nationalistic" vision was "rose colored and self-serving, mystifying and obscuring the brutal and violent processes of 'trade' and colonization."[19] That Anglicizing Americans should find this conception of empire attractive is hardly surprising, for it helped suppress less flattering and widely shared images of creole barbarism and degeneracy that underscored differences between metropolitan and provincial Britons. In Armitage's terms, the *ideology* of British imperial grandeur enabled provincials to imagine that they shared an *identity* with their metropolitan counterparts. But that imperial ideology was contestable, and would be demolished during the imperial crisis.

Greene offers the fullest account of the various "languages of empire" circulating in the Anglophone world during the colonial and Revolutionary period.[20] Languages of commerce and liberty simultaneously fostered provincial attachments and imperial patriotism: before the imperial crisis, creoles experienced little cognitive dissonance in reconciling local and cosmopolitan identities.[21] Quite the contrary, participating in a metropolitan culture of politeness and civility enabled creoles to overcome their civilizational deficit and to imagine their provinces as civil—British—places. But other ways of talking about empire were more problematic. The "language of national grandeur" that emerged with the triumph of British arms in the Seven Years' War was broadly appealing to Anglo-Americans, particularly as they looked to an expanding hinterland, now freed from the incubus of French power, and dilated on the "westward course of empire." Yet, at the same time, Greene writes, metropolitan observers attributed the war's glorious outcome to the imperial government's "fiscal and military exertions." "British fame and power no longer appeared to be the virtually spontaneous and largely self-sustaining products of settler initiative and industry," but rather the happy result of "Britain's own commercial, political, maritime, and military genius."[22]

The language of national grandeur exposed a widening rift in conceptions of empire. The British "nation" or people did not necessarily include Anglo-American subjects of imperial administration. Parliamentary sovereignty claims mapped neatly onto a new geography of empire, centered on the metropolis, with Britain consolidating its dominant position in a European state system. As Britain shouldered the burdens of empire—including a staggeringly large national debt—it also claimed the benefits. Liberty did *not* move westward with empire, as Anglo-American provincials had long supposed: they should instead recognize, in Massachusetts governor Thomas Hutchinson's blunt language, that "there must be an abridgement of what are called English liberties" on the frontiers of empire.[23] The empire was "British" because it buttressed the power and promoted the wealth of the island nation, not because its overseas subjects were Britons.

This more narrowly circumscribed conception of the nation prompted Adam Smith in 1776 to urge British policy makers either to acknowledge the colonists' independence or incorporate them on equal terms into the nation: for too long British rulers had been deluded by a "golden dream" of an empire that "hitherto has existed in imagination only," not an actual empire, "but the project of an empire."[24] This delusory empire was *not* the empire of commerce and liberty that had promoted the prosperity of Britons on both sides of the Atlantic, but rather an empire of conquest that would only come into existence with the subjugation of rebellious American subjects. For deluded nationalist-imperialists, conquering the rebels would restore the colonies to their original conquered condition, as outposts of empire seized from indigenous sovereigns or other imperial powers. This narrative of empire-making directly challenged the creole counter-narrative of self-created settler societies. "America was not conquered by William the Norman," Jefferson wrote in 1774: "her settlements [were] made, and firmly established, at the expence of individuals, and not of the British public." If metropolitan and provincial Britons did not constitute a "free and a great people together"—the premise that animated American resistance to misguided, unconstitutional imperial reforms—it followed that they must be two distinct, disunited peoples. If British ministries persisted in their efforts to suppress the resistance movement and deprive Americans of their liberties, it would only "too plainly prove a deliberate and systematical plan of reducing us to slavery."[25]

Jefferson and like-minded patriots were reluctant to embrace the idea that Americans and Britons were distinct peoples, as foreign to each other as masters and slaves. But metropolitan Britons had ample warrant in the idioms of empire that Greene analyzes for distinguishing themselves from their transatlantic cousins. The "entrenched view of the inhabitants of the colonies as unworthy to call themselves Britons and the social entities they had created as distorted and inferior versions" of metropolitan society gained a powerful new impetus from growing humanitarian revulsion with slavery and the slave trade.[26] At a time when Anglicizing provincials were anxiously asserting their equal rights and identity as Englishmen, metropolitan critics were increasingly inclined to characterize them by their despotic treatment of their human property. Their taunts hit home. As Jefferson and other enlightened creoles conceded, slavery had a barbarizing effect on masters as well as slaves: "the whole commerce between master and slave is a perpetual exercise of the most boisterous passions, the most unremitting despotism on the one part, and degrading submissions on the other."[27] Jefferson did not need Samuel Johnson's devastating question (why do "we hear the loudest yelps for liberty among the drivers of negroes?") to recognize the disturbing parallels.[28] Mastering slaves—and mating with them—debauched and degraded creoles' "manners," making them barbarous, un-English "others."

Metropolitan revulsion against the brutal treatment of enslaved Africans and indigenous peoples underscored the distinction between imperial center and creole periphery. As colonizers and colonized merged in the metropolitan imagination, an emerging humanitarian sensibility made it easier to identify with the victims of what Adam Smith characteristically called "the savage injustice of the Europeans."[29] Anglo-Americans were imaginatively cast "beyond the line" of civility and legality, making the need for enlightened imperial administration increasingly conspicuous.[30] Not surprisingly, a metropolitan public sensitized to creole lawlessness and violence was reflexively hostile to provincial patriots' increasingly aggressive claims to autonomy and self-government under a customary imperial constitution. The boorish behavior of creoles who came "home" to the metropolis to flaunt their wealth reinforced metropolitan disdain.[31] Far from being plausible replicas of Britain, the American "plantations" were seen by metropolitan critics as sites of savage exploitation and degradation.

Radically conflicting understandings of empire coalesced along the fault lines of emerging national identities in the period leading up to the American Revolution. The reconfiguration of languages of empire in the metropolis shaped more familiar debates on constitutional questions. Imperial reform efforts constituted a massive assault on traditional provincial liberties, calling into question the very existence of a transatlantic imperial political community within which Anglo-Americans could assert and defend their rights. As metropolitan Britons became more acutely conscious of its benefits and burdens, "empire" was increasingly understood in insular, nationalistic terms as the projection of British power against imperial rivals. The languages of commerce and liberty that had made provincials' claims to equal rights seem plausible receded in relative importance.

Metropolitan policy makers and pundits recognized the importance of colonial staple production and markets for metropolitan prosperity and power, and therefore defended slavery and the slave trade against humanitarian critics. But the prudent arguments of political economists only accentuated the humanitarian concerns that cast creoles in an increasingly unflattering light. In effect, economists argued, entanglement in a barbarous trade and institution was the price Britain had to pay to sustain national grandeur and defend its liberties against powerful foreign enemies. Moralists who asserted that the price was too steep were equally insular in orientation, focusing on Britain's national character and the state of its soul. Their agitation would gain traction in the wake of the Revolution, as Britons began to incorporate opposition to slavery into a more exalted, moralistic conception of their national identity.[32]

Metropolitan Britons talked about empire in ways that distanced them from—and alienated—provincial Anglo-Americans. In response, American patriots invoked "traditional" conceptions of empire, emphasizing the equal rights of overseas settlers under the imperial "constitution."[33] If the language of resistance was anti-imperialist, it was only so in the narrow sense of opposition to a corrupt and despotic imperial administration that "unconstitutionally" served Britain's insular interests at the expense of the American continent. The increasingly nationalistic inflection of metropolitan imperial discourse—epitomized in parliamentary sovereignty claims—forced Anglo-Americans to think in national terms as well. As they did so, Thomas Paine's argument in *Common Sense* became increasingly compelling: "there is something very absurd, in supposing a continent to be perpetually governed by an island."[34] The metropolis had no right to "govern" the American provinces at all, if that meant Americans were to be stripped of their rights and thus of their identities as Britons. If Britain succeeded in suppressing the resistance movement, Americans would *become* the conquered people misguided ministries already assumed them to be: they would then be "slaves," subject to the despotic will of their British masters, not freeborn Britons. To vindicate their British rights, patriots had to overthrow British rule. Then they could reconstitute the empire according to the enlightened principles and practices that the British government had so egregiously betrayed.

## Empire to Union

One of the most striking continuities across the Revolutionary divide was the persistence of a broad distribution of power in a plurality of autonomous jurisdictions under the coordinating and protective authority of a superintending central government. Building on the seminal work of Andrew C. McLaughlin, Jack P. Greene emphasizes ongoing tensions and negotiations along a vertical axis—between metropolitan and provincial, or state and federal governments—before and after independence.[35] Revolutionaries themselves exaggerated the novelty of their "new order for the ages" in order to justify killing the king, and the imperatives of mobilization and collective action required them to minimize provincial differences and embrace an "American" identity. During the imperial crisis, the ambiguous dual identities of Anglo-Americans—patriotic provincials who were loyal subjects of the British king—had proven highly unstable and ultimately unsustainable. Independence did not resolve the dissonance. To the contrary, the emergence of congressional government on a continental scale provided a new arena for articulating the conflicting interests of states and sections. Center-periphery tensions were thus conspicuous from the outset, and local loyalties coexisted with—and were inextricable from—loyalty to the "common cause." Union would thus prove to be as problematic after independence as before. It remained to be seen whether the formal negotiation and ratification of a continental constitution could sustain a postimperial federal balance.

The focus on federalism gives us a much clearer sense of the challenges faced by British imperial reformers and their American successors as they sought to impose some degree of uniformity and distribute equitable tax burdens on recalcitrant and disunited colonies and states. It is hardly surprising that the Philadelphia founders "invented federalism," though we might reverse the formulation and suggest that federalism—the institutional and ideological realities of broadly distributed authority—"invented the founders." But this is not to say that nothing happened or that, despite their world-changing pretensions, American revolutionaries were "conservative." There was nothing inevitable, and indeed something almost miraculous, about saving, much less perfecting, the union in 1787. Americans imagined and anticipated a wide range of outcomes throughout the Revolutionary era, from the union's dismemberment and the emergence of distinct and hostile regional unions to an anarchic state of nature that would prepare the way for a new, consolidated despotism. All these scenarios were rehearsed during the imperial crisis as patriots contemplated the subversion of their provincial and civil liberties and their own ultimate "enslavement."[36]

To restore an imperial status quo that had never been formally recognized—if it had ever existed—and to translate that idealized balance into constitutional and institutional reality would be an extraordinary achievement. Political philosophers and statesmen had long sought to achieve that balance, avoiding the extremes of "universal monarchy" on one hand and anarchy on the other. Because of its broad distribution of authority and institutional capacity the United States seemed to offer its political architects the opportunity to construct a regime, secured by balances within and among governments, that avoided these extremes. European Enlightenment fantasies of political perfection could be projected across the Atlantic and embraced by Americans precisely because the "New World" was *not* a blank slate, but had already progressed—under the aegis of British imperial rule—to an advanced state of political civilization.[37]

The great French philosopher Montesquieu provided one influential script for the founders in his *Spirit of the Laws* (1748). Significantly Montesquieu, like the Anglo-American patriots of a later generation, celebrated Britain's constitution and the expansion of its commercial empire: Britain was the "one nation in the world whose constitution has political liberty for its direct purpose"; by extending its benign rule across the Atlantic, such a "government would carry prosperity with it, one would see the formation of great peoples, even in the forests to which it had sent inhabitants." Montesquieu did not predict the empire's collapse, but he did presciently advocate the creation of a "federal republic" for independent political societies: "ultimately men would have been obliged to live forever under the government of one alone"—a despotic George III and his successors—"if they had not devised the kind of constitution that has all the internal advantages of republican government and the external force of monarchy." The great achievement of the Declaration, Jefferson later recalled, was to reconstitute the empire along republican lines: it was "the fundamental act of union of these States."[38] And the promise of the Declaration was fulfilled by the framers at Philadelphia when, in Montesquieu's words, they created a "society of societies that make a new one, which can be enlarged by new associates that unite with it."[39]

Montesquieu's *Spirit of the Laws* was the most authoritative "political science" textbook in the founding era. For Revolutionary Americans, the French philosopher's celebration of Britain's mixed constitution was sufficiently abstracted from the corrupt, unconstitutional British government they had overthrown to provide a template for their own new state constitutions. At the same time, Montesquieu's neo-Aristotelian typology of regime types broke mixed government down into constituent elements—monarchy, aristocracy, and republic—that could be recombined in their postimperial federal union. State-republics depended on the "virtue" of engaged citizens, while a new continental government would guarantee collective security by grounding aristocratic and monarchical elements in a broad representation of states and people.

In the years leading up to independence, American patriots assumed that an imperial constitution extended across the Atlantic, securing their provincial liberties as well as their rights as Englishmen. As exponents of parliamentary sovereignty invoked the irresistible logic of *imperium in imperio* and demolished that assumption, revolutionaries began to conceptualize federalism as "multi-layered sovereignty" while improvising new forms of union among their self-constituted independent states. The new logic of federalism would only be fully articulated and applied on a continental level, as Alison LaCroix has shown, when the peoples of the respective states constitutionalized the union by making the United States a federal republic.[40] American federalism may have been continuous with British imperial experience. But effective union outside the empire did not therefore come easily, as the tortuous, frequently frustrated, and nearly failed progress of nation building and constitutional reform between 1776 and 1789 demonstrated. And the federal union they did create proved far from perfect, collapsing in the Civil War of 1861–65.

## Colonization

The survival of the union depended on its capacity to add "new associates," thus preempting security threats on its expanding borders and opening new territories for speculation and development. By privatizing public lands, organizing territorial governments, and providing for the admission of new states, the federal Constitution enabled Americans to resume and perpetuate the colonization of the continent. As Christopher Tomlins convincingly argues, the "technology" of law furnished "the institutional capacities" to promote and regulate overseas settlement, channeling people and capital into "the concrete realization of jurisdiction" in "new commonwealths."[41] Far from being the spontaneous product of enterprising settlers with a genius for self-government, the establishment of new colonies in North America depended on the "interdependent processes" of "manning, planting, and keeping," all requiring "long-term investment" under effective jurisdictions.[42]

The colonial charters articulated a "discourse of territorial appropriation, occupation, and improvement," Tomlins writes, that was embraced everywhere in Anglo-America, most notably by settlers themselves.[43] When, during the run-up to Revolution, American patriots invoked their charters—even those, like Virginia's, that had long been vacated or superseded—as "constitutions," they reaffirmed their fealty to the fundamental principles of the empire's colonizing regime. Indeed, it could be argued, colonists' anxieties about how imperial reform efforts might restrain future colonization—by curbing land acquisition, protecting indigenous clients, and perhaps even by threatening planters' property in slaves—drove them *out* of the British Empire. Imagining a postcolonial empire that would subvert their liberties and constitutional rights *as colonizers*, Anglo-Americans declared their independence in order to sustain colonization.[44]

Metropolitan observers who complained about colonists' lawlessness and unruliness failed to recognize that the real problem was too much law, not too little. The "local contextualizing of legal processes" gave rise to a plurality of loosely coordinated legal regimes in British North America.[45] Parliamentary sovereignty claims jeopardized the autonomy and effective capacity of provincial legal systems that promoted colonization by distributing land and creating new jurisdictions. The perceived assault on provincial liberties led patriots to invoke and exploit a broad popular attachment to the "rights of Englishmen" that imaginatively bridged the growing rift between British metropolis and American provinces. But patriots mobilized in defense of those rights in order to preserve the multiple legalities of a decentralized empire, not to dissolve them.[46] In rejecting imperial reform efforts, Americans insisted on their fidelity to imperial and colonial constitutions that had authorized and promoted colonization. British efforts to curb colonization after the Seven Years' War by protecting Indians from settler encroachments by the Proclamation of 1763 or by extending Quebec's jurisdiction to the Ohio country in 1774 made the implications of parliamentary sovereignty all too clear. For patriots who mobilized in defense of property rights, colonization was constitutional.[47]

The new federal union restored an idealized imperial regime that promoted colonization through the technology of law. State constitutions consolidated the local legal authority of postcolonial regimes, and new state advocates sought congressional recognition for their own colonizing projects. The conventional explanation for this constitutional efflorescence is that revolutionaries had to justify the break with Britain by expeditiously filling a vacuum of legitimate authority. Yet again, however, it was less the absence than a surfeit of legalities that jeopardized the Revolution's success. Given the centrality of law to the history of American colonization, lawyers naturally assumed a dominant role in the destruction of the old regime and the founding of a new one. Their great achievement was to sustain a fundamental continuity across a period of potentially radical and disruptive regime change. As they rejected the British Empire, independent Americans perpetuated the old empire's colonization project, creating a new federal constitutional structure that guaranteed the rights of member states and the equality of new members.

American revolutionaries were convinced that the British government meant to destroy the old empire. As parliamentary sovereignty claims and the new language of national grandeur indicated, the ministry's animating spirit was narrowly "national," focusing on metropolitan prosperity and power, not inclusively "imperial." Patriots glimpsed an emerging British state that would incorporate far-flung provinces into a unitary, "consolidated" whole, subject to the sovereign command of central administration. As a result, the term "national" had a more equivocal valence in Revolutionary discourse than "empire," particularly when linked to the embryonic structures of continental governance. Americans collectively might think of themselves as a nation or people that shared common principles and joined in a "common cause" that vindicated British or natural rights, but they reflexively resisted the kind of "national" government that Britain sought to establish over its wayward colonists.

For Jeffersonian Republicans, "national" was a synonym for "metropolitan," evoking images of court corruption and the perversion of republican government. Good Republicans pointedly eschewed the language of national "grandeur" even as they looked westward to an expanding "empire for liberty."[48] In his first inaugural address, Jefferson thus pledged that his would be "a wise and frugal Government," the very antithesis of the strong national government Anglophile Federalist administrations had sought to erect on the ruins of American liberty. Yet he did not hesitate to celebrate the American people's imperial prospects, congratulating his countrymen on "possessing a chosen country, with room enough for our descendants to the thousandth and thousandth generation."[49] This was the colonizer's ultimate fantasy, a vision of boundlessness that would be echoed repeatedly by neo imperial expansionists in subsequent decades.

## Anti-imperialism

In the spirit of their colonizing forebears, Jeffersonian Republicans fostered a broad and inclusive national identity by projecting settlement westward and imagining a glorious American future. This was the "constitutional" imperialism that provincial Anglo-Americans so fervently embraced, an empire without a dominant center or despotic sovereign that built on the solid foundations of the colonizing people's power. Federalists, by contrast, were Anglophile nationalists who looked at Britain as the exemplary modern fiscal-military state. Pursuing the policy initiatives of their British

imperial predecessors, Hamilton and fellow advocates of "energetic" government sought to circumscribe states' rights, curb expansion, and protect
Indian clients: they expanded conventional state capacity in order to sustain
the new nation's authority over a vast and vulnerable hinterland. In opposition, Republicans saw Federalists as the enemies of American independence, avatars of the monarchical empire that British reformers had failed
to establish *over* the Anglo-American provinces.

Republican imperialists drew sustenance from the Revolutionary legacy of 1776, invoking the evil British Empire and its continuing, hostile
presence in their world. Anglophobic Republicans thus railed against *the*
empire even as they promoted the new nation's manifest—and manifestly
imperial—destiny. Old World empires, most notably Britain's, threatened
American security and prosperity. Patriotic Republicans characterized
*those* empires by their despotic, unconstitutional regimes, conflating the
oppression of their subjects at home with subjection and exploitation of
their overseas colonies. Americans would not exercise *this* kind of imperial
authority over fellow citizens on their expanding frontier.

The genius of the new territorial system established under the Northwest Ordinance of 1787 and the federal Constitution was anticolonial: as
they passed successive population thresholds, settlers would begin to govern
themselves, ultimately claiming full and equal membership in the union of
state-republics.[50] Anticolonial did not mean anti-colonizing. Quite to the
contrary, the founders constitutionalized colonization, guaranteeing that
colonizers themselves would never be reduced to the level of colonized
subjects. Settlement thus would proceed under the aegis of the rule of law,
and embryonic frontier "commonwealths" would replicate the histories of
their Anglo-American predecessors—up to the point when the metropolis had jettisoned the imperial constitution and sought to rule American
subjects without their consent. The American territorial system may have
epitomized the enlightened statecraft of the founding generation, but it also
vindicated and perpetuated the historical experience of Anglo-American
colonization that Tomlins has so brilliantly illuminated.[51]

The Republicans' embrace of "constitutional colonization" necessarily
entailed a broadening of the electorate and therefore of the political nation. That nation was inclusively defined against the metropolitan "other,"
the evil empire that had betrayed its historic libertarian legacy, as well as
against a neo-metropolitan phalanx of "aristocrats" and "monocrats" intent on transforming the federal union into a European-style nation-state.
External and internal threats were conflated in the Jeffersonian image of

"Anglomen" seduced by British influence and all too eager to recolonize themselves as British subjects. Anglophobic Republicans—and their Democratic successors—thus infused their nationalistic appeals with a powerful strain of anti-imperialism, focusing obsessively and, as threats from other sources subsided, exclusively on Britain. This version of anti-imperialism harked back to the "languages of empire" that circulated through the Anglophone world before the Revolution, inverting the negative stereotypes of colonial barbarism, degeneracy, and alterity that reinforced metropolitan claims to cultural superiority and political sovereignty. The republican revolution revealed that the empire was a sham: British claims to civility and constitutional government could not disguise a savage lust for world domination. The French threat of "universal monarchy" that liberty-loving Britons on both sides of the Atlantic had so long resisted now emerged in a new and insidious form in Britain itself, beginning with its failed effort to conquer the American colonies. For patriotic Republicans, the French Revolution completed this transvaluation of values, with "aristocratic" Britain in the counterrevolutionary vanguard against "democratic" France and its "sister republic," the United States.

Anglophobic anti-imperialism retained a powerful hold over the American political imagination for many decades.[52] Yet the field was never uncontested. Hamiltonian "nationalists" enjoyed the upper hand under Federalist administrations, and it was the success of their federal state-building enterprise that made Republican mobilization and its ideological appeals to discontented patriots seem so imperative. The excesses of the French Revolution—ironically culminating in the emperor Napoleon's bid for universal monarchy—generated a popular reaction that gave British-style nationalism a powerful new lease on life. Federalists argued effectively that the limited capacity of the federal state constituted its greatest vulnerability, particularly in wartime. The government's poor performance in the War of 1812 gave rise to a neo-Hamiltonian National Republicanism that guaranteed the obsolescence of Federalism but proceeded to open a widening rift among Jefferson's Republican progeny

Though anti-expansionists could not halt the ongoing progress of state-sponsored colonization, the spread of chattel slavery, or the appropriation of Indian lands, they crafted a moralistic anti-imperialist discourse that continues to resonate to this day. This more familiar, self-critical version of anti-imperialism reversed the outward thrust of Anglophobic anti-imperialism. Discounting the global significance of revolutionary regime change, these early revisionists resuscitated Enlightenment critiques of colonization to condemn slavery and the slave power, "savage injustices" to native peoples, and their fellow Americans' betrayal of the natural rights principles on which the nation was supposedly founded. The impact of such revisionism was to puncture and deflate Americans' complacent sense of moral superiority and to minimize Anglo-American differences. If anything, Britain's widely touted leadership in the global crusade against slavery and other relics of barbarism turned the tables on revolutionary republicans who believed that the destruction of the old regime would promote the progress of civility and morality. Perhaps, American reformers suggested, monarchical Britain, not republican America, was showing the way toward the new millennium.

Alternative anti-imperialisms in the early United States developed in dialectical fashion, building on languages of empire that circulated in the old British Empire. Debate centered on the nature of American experience in the empire. Expansionist anti-imperialists focused on the process of colonization that had created the original American commonwealths but was interrupted by misguided British reform efforts that threatened to deprive colonists of their liberty and property. Radical regime change—the destruction of monarchy and the reconstitution of governments grounded in the sovereignty of the people—was absolutely essential to the defense of American rights. Yet the Revolution was not simply "conservative" in this familiar sense, but was more fundamentally continuous with the interdependent processes of colonization that the British imperial state had authorized and sponsored. Of course, as critics hastened to emphasize, the animating spirit of this form of Anglophobic anti-imperialism was itself imperialistic.

The moralistic anti-imperialism that emerged in opposition to Jefferson's expanding "empire for liberty" could also trace its genealogy to the pre-Revolutionary period. As they moralized about creole barbarism and inhumanity, metropolitan critics exposed the dark side—and human costs—of Britain's imperial project: their indictment of colonization called into question the very character and constitution of the empire. At first, reform-minded Britons were inclined to take American patriots at their word and so support the Revolution: perhaps slavery was an archaic survival, propped up by the imperial old regime, and self-governing Americans would find a way toward emancipation. But as the union expanded and slavery flourished it was increasingly hard to take this promise seriously. American critics joined a British-led chorus of condemnation, reviving and expanding on earlier analyses of the pathologies of colonization.

Anti-imperialist discourses were linked to conflicting and dynamic conceptions of national identity. It would be a mistake, however, to make too much of differences that contemporary ideologists were bound to exaggerate. Whatever their emphases—and whatever purposes they served—polemicists insistently proclaimed their own patriotism even as they disparaged that of their opponents. And the positions they staked out inevitably shaped their opponents' positions. Latter-day Republicans and Democrats became "nationalists" in a more conventional sense, exulting in the power and prosperity of their "great nation" and vigorously promoting its expansion with the instruments of state power. For their part, the Whig and Republican heirs of Federalists and National Republicans sought to promote economic development in ways that would secure genuine American independence and counter the hegemony of Britain's "free trade empire."[53] These nationalists were no longer necessarily "conservative," nor did their admiration for Britain—the great power of the age—necessarily compromise their patriotism. For the United States to hold its own in the world, they argued, it would have to compete effectively against Britain, if necessary by following its lead. The great weakness of the democracy, Whig nationalists argued, was the supine posture free-trading export producers assumed in the face of British commercial domination. Southern cotton planters were the great advocates of a slave-based, resource-stripping colonization regime that inevitably would weaken the United States and reduce it to neocolonial dependency.

The continuity between British Empire and American federal union and the resumption of colonization after independence call into question the fundamental premises of American exceptionalism. The postcolonial United States was one of many places around the world where expanding frontiers of settlement promoted the prosperity and power of the British metropolis: what made the new nation "exceptional" was that it played this role *outside* the empire, thus eliminating the overhead costs of imperial administration.[54] It was thus no coincidence that so many Loyalist refugees from the American Revolution should be in the vanguard of the new wave of settler-driven imperial expansion. These "Americans" had a genius for colonization.[55]

American patriots who broke with the British Empire and metaphorically killed their king were, of course, disinclined to acknowledge their crucial role in British empire-building after 1776. Revolutionary republicans exaggerated the significance of regime change, imagining—as successive generations of Americans have imagined ever since—that they had initiated an epochal transformation in the history of the modern world. Americans' Anglophobia fostered a kind of false consciousness, obscuring continuities across the Revolutionary divide. American national identity was predicated on a self-deluding anti-imperialism—the reverse image of Adam Smith's empire of the "imagination," a "project" for the liberation of benighted peoples bursting the shackles of despotic monarchical regimes. If Smith's empire was really a nation, the American nation was really an empire.

Yet a different sort of nationalism, focused on state capacity and economic development, provided a critical counterpoint to the Republican imperialism that culminated in manifest destiny. State-building advocates of protection and internal improvements were better able to resist British domination of the new nation's neocolonial economy *because* they were Anglophiles who could recognize the sources and implications of the mother country's continuing power and influence. Their arguments gained traction as popular Anglophobia subsided in the late antebellum period. With the British "other" receding, Northern Whig-Republican nationalists could articulate an anti-imperialist discourse that focused increasingly on the pathologies of colonization, most conspicuously in the "empire for slavery" that Southerners sought to perpetuate and expand.[56]

Lincoln's inspiring formulation of the American creed, identifying the nation with liberty, equality, and union, and secession with the Slave Power's regressive imperial ambitions, reaffirmed unionists' conception of national purpose. This was the essence of American exceptionalism, the apotheosis of the great democratic nation that defines itself against empire and opposes despotism wherever it appears, at home or abroad.[57]

Chapter 2

# Native Americans against Empire and Colonial Rule

JEFFREY OSTLER

In 1776, when the signers of the Declaration of Independence denounced George III, among their indictments was that he had "endeav-
oured to bring on the inhabitants of our frontiers, the merciless Indian
Savages." As Peter Onuf points out, the colonists' grievances against the
British Empire did not entail a rejection of imperialism. Rather, the national identity Americans would craft was linked to ambitions to create an
"empire for liberty."[1] But what of the "merciless Indian Savages" inhabiting
lands that would be coveted by speculators, yeomen, and planters? Far from
being pawns of British tyranny, as represented in the Declaration, Native
Americans were prepared to contest and critique the U.S. project of constructing a neo-European empire in their lands.

More than most varieties of anti-imperialism, Native American opposition to the U.S. project of building a continental empire has seldom been
recognized for what it was. In part, this is because of a failure to confront
the fact that Native Americans have been subject to imperialism in the first
place. American studies scholars have challenged American exceptionalism
and recognized empire's embeddedness in American culture, but the emphasis has been on overseas imperialism, not on Native America.[2] Specialists
on Native America have been more likely to recognize "western expansion" as imperialism and have written on Indian resistance to the United

States manifest in prophetic movements like the one associated with Tecumseh in the early 1800s and the Ghost Dance at the end of the century, opposition to removal in the 1830s, the post–Civil War militancy of Plains Indians, and critical commentary by indigenous writers. Often, however, associations of Indians with the primitive have encouraged anthropological description at the expense of recognizing Native American movement building, sustained strategic action, and systemic critique. Native American resistance has seldom been considered as a form of anti-imperialism.

This chapter offers an overview of Indians' opposition to U.S. empire-building from the time of the American Revolution to the consolidation of continental empire in the early 1900s. Defining key terms for this case presents unique problems. The process of building the U.S. continental empire can clearly be categorized as a case of imperialism, though the relationship between imperialism and colonialism is less clear. A recent focus on the distinctive discursive operations of settler colonialism, particularly its demands for Indian elimination and its strategies of disavowal, suggest a convergence between settler colonial ideology and the project of continental empire-building.[3] Yet, two distinct (though overlapping) phases can be identified in U.S. empire-building: the subjugation of autonomous Indian nations by military and pseudo-legal means, and rule over subjugated Indian nations, conceived by settler colonial discourse as invisible or disappearing, but nonetheless actually existing, and thus similar to non-eliminationist forms of colonialism. With this in mind, I will refer to indigenous expressions opposing or critiquing U.S. empire-building under conditions in which Indian people retained substantial political and economic autonomy as anti-imperialism and those from conditions of subordination as anticolonialism.

This chapter identifies a variety of oppositional orientations. The most radical of these took the form of prophet-inspired multi-tribal millenarian movements (sometimes overtly militant, sometimes not) that drew on distinctively native religious traditions while at the same time appropriating Christianity. These movements sometimes developed a comprehensive, historically grounded critique of European Americans while at the same time denouncing Indians who pursued accommodationist strategies. A related orientation was that of single tribes and alliances that took up arms to defend their lands and ways of life. In recorded statements, militants more often targeted factions within their own nations seeking compromise with Americans as the best route to survival rather than U.S. imperialism per se, though their actions obviously implied a rejection of empire. Anticolonialism was also visible in efforts by tribes with an educated leadership articulating nationalist aspirations to sovereignty within space controlled by the United States, often invoking the moral authority of Christianity and U.S. political traditions. Finally, individual Native Americans educated in mission or secular institutions published anticolonial critiques and proposed reforms, again appealing to Americans on their own terms. They did not necessarily call for the end of colonialism, but their positions carried the possibility of preserving or opening meaningful space under colonial rule.

When the Revolutionary War began, Indian nations generally sought neutrality. As the conflict progressed, some Indian nations (or factions within them) allied with the United States. More, though, sided with Britain and criticized the revolutionaries, ironically drawing on earlier arguments against British imperialism articulated by a multi-tribal confederation that emerged at the close of the Seven Years' War. Grounded in the prophetic teachings of Neolin (a Delaware) and Pontiac (an Ottawa), this confederation contended that the British had damaged Indians by making them dependent on alcohol and other trade goods, destroying game, and encroaching on their lands. In 1763, Indians launched a series of attacks against British posts, igniting Pontiac's War.[4]

If the 1763 confederacy's anti-British stance suggested that Indians might support a colonial revolution, settler aggressions in the late 1760s and 1770s led many Indians to regard Americans as their most serious threat. In April 1776 a delegation of Shawnees, Delawares, Mohawks, Nanticokes, and Ottawas traveled to Cherokee country to build an anti-American alliance. An unnamed Shawnee indicted the colonists, saying they have "taken away all their lands and cruelly and treacherously treated some of their people" and "unjustly brought war upon their nation and destroyed many of their people." As the Revolutionary War progressed, Indians opposed to the colonists penned no formal manifestos, though observers caught occasional glimpses into Native American thought. One British agent reported that the Mohawk leader Joseph Brant, in calling on Iroquois warriors to fight the Americans, alleged that they "began this Rebellion to be sole Masters of this Continent."[5]

John Heckewelder, a Moravian missionary with long experience in the Ohio country, provided an unusually thorough account of anti-American thought among Indians in that region after the Revolutionary War. According to Heckewelder, Indians objected to the "highly offensive" treaties imposed on them after the war, protesting that U.S. officials spoke to them as people who "*must* . . . submit to the dictates of a proud conqueror."

Indians also indicted Americans for a Pennsylvania militia's slaughter of Christian Indians in March 1782 at Gnadenhütten in eastern Ohio: "[T]hey did kill upwards of one hundred of our people, who never took up a single weapon against them but remained quiet at home, planting corn and vegetables." Ohio Indians did not regard this massacre as an outlier but rather as manifesting designs evident since the advent of Europeans. "[O]ur forefathers received the white people with kindness," Heckewelder quoted them as saying. "[T]hey gave them Land to live, and plant upon," but Europeans had never been "satisfied with this," always saying they "must have more Land; and if we are not quick in giving it to them, they take it, saying we will have it." Given this history, Indians alleged, Americans would not rest until "they have extirpated us entirely; and have the *whole* of our Land!"[6]

By the late 1780s, Indians throughout the west had formed a confederacy consisting of Shawnees, Delawares, Mingoes, Wyandots, Miamis, Ottawas, Ojibwes, Potawatomies, Creeks, and Cherokees to resist further U.S. encroachment. Gregory Dowd emphasizes that uniting people from dozens of distinct communities involved political work: creative argumentation, intricate diplomacy between tribal communities, management of internal dissent, and strategic planning. It also entailed the revival of "nativist" religious practices such as the Green Corn Ceremony and consumption of an emetic known as the black drink, which ritually enacted purification from European ways of life. Prophecy was central to the movement. One prophet, a Mohawk woman named Coocoochee, spoke of the "first landing of the 'pale-faces' from their monstrous canoes with their great white wings" and of their "increasing strength and power, their insatiable avarice, and their continued encroachments on the red men." This history led her to predict that the "Long Knives . . . would not be satisfied until they had crowded the Indians to the extreme north to perish on the great ice lake; or to the far west until, pushing those who should escape from their rifles into the great waters, all would at length be exterminated."[7]

Confederationists repelled U.S. military expeditions in 1790 and 1791, but eventually the seemingly limitless capacity of the United States to sustain offensive war undermined resistance. In 1794, an expedition commanded by General Anthony Wayne struck the confederacy's headquarters at the Glaize in northwestern Ohio and defeated the confederation army at Fallen Timbers. Key militants, notably the Shawnee Blue Jacket, calculated that the costs of resistance were too high and agreed to the 1795 Fort Greenville Treaty, which ceded most of what would become the state of Ohio.[8]

In the first years of the nineteenth century, facing game shortages, indebtedness to traders, and relentless pressure on their lands, Indians began to build a new anti-imperial movement. In 1805 a disreputable Shawnee known as Lalawethika (Noisemaker) changed his name to Tenskwatawa (Open Door) and began relating a series of visions in which the Master of Life instructed him to exhort Indians to abstain from alcohol, reject European trade goods and technology, disavow acquisitiveness, return to pre-European modes of dress and consumption, and renew religious ritual. In one of his visions, Tenskwatawa saw "a great ugly crab that had crawled from the sea, its claws full of mud and seaweed." This crab, the Master of Life explained, "comes from Boston and brings with it part of the land in that vicinity. If you Indians do everything which I have told you, I will overturn the land, so that all the white people will be covered and you alone shall inhabit the land."[9]

The message of Tenskwatawa and similar prophets resonated with substantial numbers of Delawares, Kickapoos, Potawatomies, Ottawas, Ojibwes, Menominees, Ho-Chunks, Sacs, Foxes, and Iowas, who joined a revived western confederacy. Tenskwatawa strongly criticized leaders who cooperated with the United States and charged chiefs who had signed the Fort Greenville Treaty with witchcraft. In this instance, then, the immediate target of an anti-imperialist movement was not the imperial power; it was those perceived to be collaborating with it.[10]

Settler land hunger soon led the confederacy to directly confront the United States. After William Henry Harrison used bribery and threats to pressure accommodationist leaders into agreeing to yet another land cession in the 1809 Fort Wayne Treaty, Tecumseh met with Harrison and delivered a speech offering a strong critique of U.S. imperialism. After reviewing "the treachery of the British" toward Indians, Tecumseh reminded Harrison that "their new fathers the Americans . . . told us they would treat us well." Yet the Americans' murder of "men women and children" at Gnadenhütten in 1782 and other acts of unprovoked violence since showed how far from the truth these words had been. Not only were Americans untrustworthy—a point Tecumseh drove home by asking how Indians could have "confidence in the white people when Jesus Christ came upon the earth [and] you kill'd and nail'd him on a cross"—but violence was linked to the general design of the United States to take Indians' lands. "You are continually driving the red people," Tecumseh said, "when at last you will drive them into the great lake."[11]

To strengthen the confederacy, Tecumseh traveled widely over the next several months, seeking British support in Canada and recruiting Great Lakes Indians, and then traveling south to visit Chickasaws, Choctaws, and Creeks. From Prophetstown, the confederacy's headquarters in Indiana, Tenskwatawa dispatched messengers to tribes west of the Mississippi and to Mohawks in Ontario and conducted diplomacy with U.S. emissaries. Committed to acquiring all Indian lands east of the Mississippi River, the United States was bound to use force to subjugate a movement contesting this objective. In fall 1811 Harrison led a military expedition against Prophetstown. Although the battle of Tippecanoe was not the decisive victory Harrison claimed it was, it contributed to the movement's demoralization. In the early phases of the War of 1812, a briefly resurgent confederacy allied with the British against the United States and achieved some military successes in the Northwest, but at the battle of the Thames in October 1813 U.S. troops routed British and Indian forces, killing Tecumseh as he tried to rally his men. Six months later, to the south, Andrew Jackson led troops against the Creek Red Sticks, killing over eight hundred at Horseshoe Bend.[12]

The battles of the Thames and Horseshoe Bend can be seen as marking the defeat of a string of interrelated anti-imperial movements that had waxed and waned for over fifty years. At their strongest moments, these movements had adherents in scores of Indian communities from the Gulf of Mexico to the Great Lakes and posed a serious threat to U.S. imperial ambitions. Initiated and guided by "prophets of rebellion," to use Michael Adas's term for similar prophets that opposed European imperialism in Africa, Asia, and New Zealand, these movements were vehicles for religious and cultural "revitalization."[13] They also created new forms of political organization and identity, positing a polygenetic theory of human origins, a separate creation and correspondingly different ways of life for "red" and "white" people.[14] Though placing "red" people in a superior moral position, the confederationists' theory of racial division was pluralistic, as it held that the Creator had given each people specific technologies and separate lands, rather than hierarchical, as in European and U.S. racial theory, which regarded "civilization" as inherently superior to "savagery." The confederationists also articulated a systemic critique of European and U.S. imperialism. Prophets not only received visions and preached moral regeneration and the revival of ritual; they developed a historically and empirically informed analysis of imperial interests and strategies and used this analysis to mobilize supporters, assess current conditions, and forecast future possibilities. Although the anti-imperialist confederationists developed the most robust oppositional ideology of any Indians in the early nineteenth century, critiques emerged from communities that had already been colonized. Until the 1830s, however, oppressive conditions generally worked against openly anticolonial articulations.

If any native people could have hoped to find a secure place within the United States, it might have been those in the Northeast who had adopted the colonizers' religion. In the 1730s and 1740s, beset by population decline, loss of resources, and constantly shrinking lands, many Indians converted to Christianity, hoping that through the spiritual power it promised and the selective adoption of European ways of life they would be able to survive. During the Revolutionary War, most Christian Indians supported the colonists, enlisting (and dying) in significant numbers. Yet support for the Americans afforded Indians little protection against dispossession. At the "praying town" of Stockbridge, Massachusetts, for example, Christian Indians were forced to sell off most of their remaining holdings to satisfy creditors.[15]

Although the Stockbridge and other Christian Indians established new communities on Oneida lands in the 1780s and were momentarily optimistic, they soon faced new reasons for demoralization: settlers gnawing at their lands, traders plying them with alcohol, material deprivation, and racial discrimination. As David Silverman shows, Christian Indians believed that Americans' actions were a central cause of their misery, a belief reflected in Timothy Pickering's observation that "*White Man* is, among many of them, but another name for *Liar*." Yet, instead of moving toward an anticolonial position, Christian Indians concluded that God must be punishing them for the sins of their ancestors. As Samson Occom, a Mohegan minister, expressed it, Indians "are under great Judgment and Curse from God."[16] Despite such fatalism, in the early 1800s many Christian Indians looked to Indiana and Wisconsin as places far enough west to establish viable new communities. At the same time, small Indian communities, increasingly intermarried with people of European and African descent, persisted in New England.

From this beleaguered Native American space emerged William Apess, a Pequot minister and, in Arnold Krupat's words, "the earliest producer of Native American writing in resistance to colonialism." In an 1833 essay, "An Indian's Looking-Glass for the White Man," Apess challenged European Americans' pretensions to superiority. Was the "white man, being one in fifteen or sixteen" of the world's population, he asked, truly "the only

beloved images of God?" Should the "crimes" of the world's nations be
written on each nation's skin, he continued, "which skin . . . would have
the greatest?" To answer that question, he asked two more that indicted
whites for their treatment of Indians and African Americans: "Can you
charge the Indians with robbing a nation almost of their whole continent,
and murdering their women and children, and then depriving the remain-
der of their lawful rights, that nature and God require them to have? And
to cap the climax, rob another nation to till their grounds and welter out
their days under the lash with hunger and fatigue under the scorching rays
of a burning sun?"[17]

Three years later, Apess furthered his anticolonial critique in a speech
delivered in Boston and later published as *Eulogy on King Philip*. Here, Apess
provided a revisionist account of New England history beginning when
the Pilgrims landed at Plymouth. As the newcomers began to act imperi-
ously, "the Indians (though many were dissatisfied), without the shedding of
blood or imprisoning anyone, bore it." But despite their "kindness and res-
ignation toward the whites," Apess continued, Indians "were called savages
and made by God on purpose for them to destroy." After decades of abuse,
in the 1670s, King Philip (Metacom), "the greatest man that ever lived upon
the American shores," called on his people to take up arms in "protecting
and defending their rights." In addition to justifying Philip's cause, Apess
summoned a prophecy Philip had supposedly made at the beginning of the
war, that "these people from the unknown world will cut down our groves,
spoil our hunting and planting grounds, and drive us and our children from
the graves of our fathers, and our council fires, and enslave our women and
children." All of this had been fulfilled, Apess said, though, in contrast to
widespread perceptions that Indians had disappeared from New England,
they had survived, as Apess's own presence in Boston proved. Apess's invocation of Philip's prophecy showed the continued relevance for a Christian
minister of non-Christian Indian religious practices; at the same time, he
drew on Christianity to indict non-Indians for their hypocritical treatment
of Indians and to call on them to repent. Given the radicalism of Apess's
historical analysis of colonialism, his concluding appeal for equal treatment
under a single law to promote shared citizenship may seem a capitulation
to settler colonialism's demand for assimilation. Yet, as Jean O'Brien argues,
Apess was moving toward articulating a position of "dual citizenship," insisting on equal treatment within the U.S. polity while also recognizing a
unique right of self-determination for Indian communities.[18]

Other Indians writing at this time, notably Cherokees, were less confrontational. In the 1820s and 1830s, Cherokees embarked on a project of nation building that entailed the adoption of institutions and ways of life that would be legible to U.S. Americans as indisputable signs of "civilization." This, combined with treaties previously negotiated, would require U.S. recognition of the Cherokees as a sovereign nation and prevent removal. Reflecting their commitment to a discourse of civilization and the sanctity of treaties, Cherokees' analyses of the history of U.S.-Indian relations were less comprehensive and systemic than those of Apess or the confederationists. Nonetheless, they offered critical perspectives on U.S. colonialism.

In "An Address to the Whites," initially delivered on a speaking tour of eastern cities and subsequently published in 1826, Elias Boudinot, a Cherokee educated at a mission school, disclaimed the necessity to "darken these walls with deeds at which humanity must shudder," giving as examples "the scenes of Muskingum Sahta-goo" (yet another reference to Gnadenhütten) and "the crimes of the bloody Cortes." Rather, he wished to detail Cherokee progress toward civilization. After accomplishing this central task, Boudinot appealed to the "mercy" of his audience to allow Cherokees to avoid the common fate of "the poor aborigines [to] melt away before the white population." Boudinot's skirting of sustained criticism was typical of Cherokee political writing during the removal period. As Andrew Denson points out, Cherokee histories often "recall[ed] times when white America had treated them with kindness" and then related how recent U.S. actions had betrayed a long-standing friendship. At the same time, in gesturing toward an earlier history of destructive acts toward American Indians and criticizing current policies, Boudinot's writings signaled what Maureen Konkel characterizes as "an emerging oppositional critique."[19]

As the removal crisis intensified, Cherokees offered more forceful criticisms. Once it became clear that pro-removal President Andrew Jackson would not enforce the U.S. Supreme Court's ruling in *Worcester v. Georgia* (1832), which held that Georgia laws undermining Cherokee sovereignty were unconstitutional, Cherokees became deeply divided. A minority favored removal as the only practical means of national preservation, while a majority predicted dire consequences. One anti-removal petition to Congress declared that "[o]ur property may be plundered before our eyes; violence may be committed on our persons; even our lives may be taken away . . . and there is none to regard our complaints. We are denationalized; we are disfranchised. We are deprived of membership in the human family!"[20] U.S. officials were unmoved by such appeals and forced the Cherokees west in 1837–38 at the cost of great suffering and loss of life.

Like most movements challenging colonialism in the nineteenth century, Cherokee resistance involved compromise, contradiction, and ambivalence. Cherokees to some extent emulated the colonial power and, to draw on Kevin Bruyneel's perspective, appealed to it to live up to its professed principles "to gain the fullest possible expression of political identity, agency, and autonomy." In this way Cherokee leaders were similar to moderate nationalists in India who appealed to Britain to extend its mission of furthering civilization by helping prepare India for eventual self-government.[21] Further, although Cherokees emphasized their uniqueness, their resistance had broader implications. By persuading the U.S. Supreme Court to recognize tribal sovereignty, if only in the compromised "domestic dependent nations" formulation in *Cherokee Nation v. Georgia* (1831), Cherokee political work was crucial in shaping the legal doctrine upon which hundreds of Indian nations today contest colonialism's boundaries.

By the end of the 1840s, although many small Indian communities remained east of the Mississippi River, the United States had accomplished what genocide studies scholar Ben Kiernan terms the ethnic cleansing of that region.[22] Under the banner of manifest destiny, the United States had also acquired northern Mexico by war and most of the Oregon country through bluster and diplomacy. Within the European imperial system, the boundaries of the U.S. continental empire were now mostly complete. It would take decades, however, to subjugate western Indians and confine them to reservations.

In the Pacific Northwest, prophets began warning about European imperialism as early as the 1810s when a Kutenai woman turned man named Kauxuma-nupika (Gone to the Spirits) told Indians along the Columbia River that "the Small Pox . . . was coming with the white Men & that 2 Men of enormous Size" would "overturn the Ground," thus "burying all the Villages and Lodges underneath it." When settlers began flooding into Oregon, other prophets emerged. In 1854 Leschi, a Nisqually from the Puget Sound area, traveled to southwestern Oregon, the site of a massive gold rush, to tell of a vision of settlers' intentions "to take all the Indians, where the sun never shone, and where they would be damned to live out their days in a cold, dark, barren world." Leschi was attempting to organize a regional multinational movement of resistance, but the processes of U.S. empire-building in the Pacific Northwest unfolded too rapidly to create alliances among diverse communities. Objecting to the Medicine Creek Treaty, which ceded Indian lands in the Puget Sound area, Leschi organized a force of a few hundred Indians and attacked some settlements, including Seattle, but most Indians did not support this movement.[23]

Resistance to the United States was stronger east of the Cascade Mountains. In 1855 U.S. officials summoned Yakamas, Walla Wallas, Umatillas, Cayuses, Wascoes, and Nez Perces to agree to a major land cession. Indians were already suspicious of U.S. intentions. Eight years earlier, Cayuses had killed missionaries Marcus and Narcissa Whitman, holding them responsible for inflicting disease and promoting settlers' efforts to take over their country. During the treaty negotiations, some Indians voiced opposition to selling land. Owhi, a Yakama leader, explained that "God made our bodies from the earth as if they were different from the whites" and then asked, "Shall I give my lands that are a part of my body and leave myself poor and destitute?" His answer: "I love my life, is the reason why I do not give my lands away," adding in an apparently strategic use of Christian doctrine that if he sold the land, "I am afraid I would be sent to hell."[24]

As settlement increased, Columbia Plateau Indians divided. Some moved to reservations and (partially) adopted Americans' ways of life, while others took a more confrontational position. From the late 1850s through the 1870s, opposition was articulated mainly through the Dreamer religion. Above all, the Dreamers emphasized the sanctity of the earth. The best known of them, a Wanapam named Smohalla, opposed plowing, asking "Shall I take a knife and tear my mother's bosom?" The Dreamers had a clear sense of history. In the 1880s Smohalla explained to a military officer that his father told him that the "first white people that came into this country . . . were few in number and almost naked and starving." His people could have killed the newcomers, Smohalla related, but instead they "fed them and took care of them." As additional settlers arrived, Indians continued to be generous, but "the white men fenced up their springs and would not let the Indians water their ponies there." Smohalla further indicted whites for inflicting disease on Indians, as when Marcus Whitman, having obtained "a bottle of poison," uncorked it "and all the air was poisoned." The result was that Indians "are now so few and weak we can offer no resistance."[25]

With these historical trends in mind, Dreamers forecast various futures. Some, like Skamia, who by some accounts predicted the building of the dam that destroyed Celilo Falls in 1957, pointed to increasingly dismal prospects. Others, however, indicated that Indians' fortunes might improve. Unlike the prophetic movements from the 1760s through the 1810s, the Dreamers did not consider militant resistance and looked solely to spiritual sources for world renewal. If they remained true to traditional ways, including revived ritual, Indians who had died would return to life, a cataclysmic event would remove European Americans, and the earth would be renewed.[26]

Although the Dreamers generally opposed violence, some Nez Perces took up arms in 1877. This happened when the government attempted to force non-treaty Nez Perces onto a reservation. At first, Nez Perces refused to comply, with Toohoolhoolzote invoking a central tenet of the Dreamer religion, insisting that he "belonged to the land out of which he came." Eventually, most leaders decided that they had no choice but to move; but when a few young men attacked settlers, the leaders decided they must fight to defend themselves against U.S. retaliation. For months, as they moved toward Canada, the Nez Perces held off U.S. troops. When they approached the border and its promise of refuge, the army finally cornered them. What Elliott West terms "the last Indian War" concluded when most Nez Perce leaders agreed to live on their Idaho reservation. Rather than sending them there, however, U.S. officials decided to punish them by banishing them to exile in Indian Territory (Oklahoma), something they regarded as "the foulest betrayal."[27]

Conditions for sustained armed resistance to U.S. empire-building were the most favorable on the Great Plains, where Lakotas, Cheyennes, Arapahoes, Kiowas, and Comanches defended their lands and independence from the 1850s into the 1870s, when the near-extinction of the bison undermined their economic independence. Plains Indians' resistance is appreciated for its heroism, though it is often seen as atavistic and pre-political. Yet Plains Indians who fought against the United States not only undertook military organization, training, and planning; they engaged in political work: building unity within tribal polities, conducting diplomacy and forming alliances with other tribes, and negotiating with U.S. officials. Plains militants' anti-imperialism produced few written manifestos, but their actions made their intent clear enough, most famously when Lakotas and Cheyennes defeated Custer's Seventh Cavalry at the Little Bighorn in 1876, but in many other instances as well. Like the Zulus, who defeated British forces at Isandlwana in 1879, Plains Indians, in their militancy, spoke clearly of a desire to preserve lands and independence in the face of aggressive expansion and destruction of vital resources (bison in North America; cattle in South Africa).[28]

To the extent that expressions of Plains militants' anti-imperialism were recorded, they often took an indirect form of criticizing Indians who accommodated to the United States. Sitting Bull, for example, told Assiniboines, "You are fools to make yourselves slaves to a piece of fat bacon, some hard-tack, and a little sugar and coffee," while the Comanche prophet Isatai, attempting to unite all Comanches and recruit Kiowas, Cheyennes, and Arapahoes in 1873, argued that the Caddos and Wichitas on reservations were "going down hill fast." Plains Indians also made specific charges against Americans. One Arapahoe lamented the coming of whites into his country, accusing them of destroying and scaring away the game, while a Cheyenne recalled the horrific Sand Creek massacre and accused U.S. troops of continuing to make unwarranted attacks upon his people. Diplomatic considerations frequently led Plains militants to profess friendship and a desire for peace, though on their own terms. Kiowa leader Satanta informed a treaty commission in 1867, "I love the land and the buffalo" and "I don't want any of these medicine homes [churches] built in the country; I want the papooses brought up exactly as I am." On *that* basis, Satanta said, there could be a "long and lasting" peace. Overall, Plains militants' anti-imperialism, then, at least as reflected in the historical sources, was expressed less as a comprehensive ideology than through specific critique.[29]

Armed resistance achieved military and even political success. Favorable provisions in the 1868 treaty with the Lakotas, for example, reflect a U.S. need to make concessions to powerful militants. Nonetheless, material deprivation caused by the destruction of game, along with a growing recognition that Americans had the will and resources for never-ending war, eventually led militants to lay aside their arms and relocate to reservations.

U.S. policy-makers never imagined Indian reservations to be permanent. Instead, they envisioned them as a kind of halfway house on the road from "savagery" to "civilization." Eventually, consistent with the logic of settler colonial ideology described by Patrick Wolfe as one of elimination, Indians would either expire through contact with a superior race or be absorbed into the dominant culture. In the 1880s, policy makers hoped to achieve rapid assimilation. They moved aggressively to stamp out native religious and cultural practices, established a system of education, designed, in the words of one of its chief architects, Richard Pratt, to "kill the Indian . . . and save the man," and attempted to privatize tribal lands through allotting them to nuclear families.[30] Although these policies envisioned the extinction of Indian people and their lands, their implementation nonetheless established formal rule over subject populations and employed methods common to colonial regimes elsewhere: indirect rule through indigenous leaders, the establishment of native police forces, the imposition of an external legal regime, and the legibility of subject populations through censuses and other mechanisms. Because U.S. officials conceived of exercises of colonial authority as temporary, they did not acknowledge them for what they were, thus preserving a sense of American exceptionalism that continues to affect scholarly and public historical understandings.

The imposition of colonial authority provoked strenuous resistance. In a few instances, Indians used violence, as in 1887 when a Crow named Sword Bearer led a group of young men in an attack on reservation headquarters, or in 1898 when Leech Lake Ojibwes "shocked the United States by declaring themselves at war."[31] More often, however, Indians used nonviolent tactics. In opposition to government efforts, authorized by the 1887 Dawes Act, to privatize (allot) tribal lands, Cherokees employed methods similar to those they had used to resist removal decades before, appealing to U.S. Americans in their own terms. The *Cherokee Advocate*, for example, drew on the contemporaneous perspectives of the Populists to contend that within the United States, "[t]he wealth of the few has become more and more enormous—the poverty of the many, more widespread and hopeless, since the famous declaration was made by Jefferson that all men are created free and equal." By contrast, under the Cherokee Constitution, all Cherokees were able to benefit from "the gifts of the Creator, common to all." In the late 1890s, after unrelenting pressure, most Cherokees finally agreed to allotment, though even then the Nighthawk Keetoowahs revived traditional Cherokee religious and cultural practices in an effort to retain tribal lands.[32]

The largest anticolonial movement of the late nineteenth century, the Ghost Dance, was initiated by another prophet of rebellion, a Paiute in Nevada named Wovoka. Like earlier prophets, Wovoka forecast a cataclysmic event in which some or all non-Indians would either be destroyed or removed from Indian America. The world would be renewed, with animals returning in their former abundance and deceased ancestors coming back to life. World renewal would be contingent on adherence to moral reform and performance of a dance in which participants lost consciousness and saw visions of the new world to come. Wovoka's teachings differed from the confederationist prophets in his opposition to armed resistance; in this sense, he was more like Smohalla.

Indians from dozens of western tribes visited Wovoka and heard his teachings in 1889 and 1890. Many reported that he claimed to be the Christian Messiah. Although the precise nature of Wovoka's claims remains unclear (Wovoka later denied saying he was the Messiah), it is evident that he and his followers engaged Christianity not so much to create a blend of Christianity and Indian religion as to turn Christianity's contradictions to Indian advantage. As the Lakota Ghost Dancer Good Thunder reported, when the Messiah "appeared to the white people, [they] scorned him and finally killed him. Now he came to red men only. He said their crying sounded loud in his ears. They were dying of starvation and disease." In appropriating Christianity in this way, the Ghost Dance was similar to millenarian movements elsewhere in the world. In a move almost identical to Good Thunder's, leaders of the Xhosa Cattle-Killing movement in southern Africa declared that whites were ineligible for salvation because they had killed Christ, while Te Au Haumene, a Maori prophet in New Zealand, saw his people as descendants of the Israelites regaining a stolen land of Canaan.[33]

By early 1890, the Ghost Dance movement had taken root on dozens of Indian reservations throughout the American West. Because the movement presented an ideological challenge to colonial authority, and because Ghost Dancers' actions violated reservation decrees against native religion, withdrawing children from schools, and neglecting crops, civilian officials who managed reservations saw it as a threat to colonial order. Some adopted a noninterventionist policy of allowing the movement to run its course, calculating that adherents would eventually abandon the Ghost Dance when the apocalypse failed to occur. Other officials used more aggressive methods to suppress the movement, cutting off rations, deploying native police forces, and in some instances calling on limited military support. These tactics were generally effective, but in November 1890 the army decided to employ massive military force against Ghost Dancers at the Lakota reservations.

Army officers hoped that surrounding the Lakota reservations with thousands of soldiers would provide sufficient shock and awe to induce the Ghost Dancers to abandon the movement. By late December, however, army officers had grown frustrated by their inability to persuade all Ghost Dancers—by now terrified—to surrender. All along army officers had criminalized the Ghost Dancers. When they intercepted a band of Ghost Dancers under a chief named Big Foot at Wounded Knee Creek, they decided, for punitive rather than tactical reasons, to disarm them. This provocative act led to a shot being fired. General firing then broke out. Although Big Foot's people had a few weapons, U.S. troops had an overwhelming firepower advantage, including four Hotchkiss guns. When the slaughter finally ended, the army had killed at least 240 Lakotas—the majority women and children.[34]

Native writers at the turn of the century distanced themselves from the Ghost Dance. Charles Eastman, a Dakota Christian with a medical degree from Boston University, who was the government physician on the Lakotas' Pine Ridge reservation in 1890, characterized the Ghost Dance as a "craze . . . foreign to Indian philosophy," an indication that "my people were groping blindly after spiritual relief in their bewilderment and misery." The Paiute Sarah Winnemucca, author of the first book written by a Native American woman, dismissed her tribesman Wovoka's teachings as "nonsense."[35] Eastman's and Winnemucca's attitudes toward the Ghost Dance followed from their outlook on the necessity for Indians to adapt to the modern world. While this orientation sometimes made them appear to endorse assimilation, their writings contained sharp critiques of the United States and an effort to create space for an indigenous modernity.

Sarah Winnemucca learned English as a girl in the home of a Nevada settler family and worked for the government as a schoolteacher and translator on various Great Basin reservations. In the 1880s she traveled to the East to lecture on the difficulties facing Indians; in 1884 she published her autobiography, *My Life among the Piutes*. Siobahn Senier observes that although Winnemucca has often been read as "a voice for assimilation," her writings were at times "fiercely oppositional." In her autobiography, for example, she included a historical overview of European American treatment of Indians. Like William Apess, Winnemucca invoked Plymouth Rock, asking those who had "covenant[ed] with God to make this land the home of the free and the brave" to consider the contrast between the "welcoming hands of those who are the owners of the land" and "your so-called civilization sweep[ing] inland . . . leaving its pathway marked by crimson lines of blood." Winnemucca's account of the early history of settlement in Nevada and California—in Ned Blackhawk's words, "anchored in articulation of indigenous trauma"—provided several details to support her indictment of civilization's bloody path, documenting the pervasiveness of racism and genocidal language among early settlers and narrating assaults on her family, including an attempted rape of her older sister.[36]

For Charles Eastman, Wounded Knee revealed a sharp contrast between civilization as preached and practiced. As Heather Cox Richardson suggests, the massacre led him to a more critical perspective on the United States. In recounting the "Ghost Dance War," Eastman related that "all of this was a severe ordeal for one who had so lately put all his faith in the

Christian love and lofty ideals of the white man." Eastman continued to adhere to Christianity, but he advanced the radical proposition that "Christianity and modern civilization are opposed and irreconcilable." In a move ironically parallel to the Ghost Dancers', Eastman claimed Christianity for Indians, writing that "the spirit of Christianity" was "essentially the same" as that of Indians' "ancient religion."[37]

Like Winnemucca, Eastman did not contest the deeper structures of colonialism. Instead, he worked for moderate reforms in reservation management. Along with other Indian intellectuals like Carlos Montezuma and Gertrude Bonnin (Zitkala Ša), who formed the Society of American Indians in 1911, Eastman ultimately hoped that the United States would recognize indigenous citizenship. This, however, did not entail accepting a "gift" on U.S. terms. In Eastman's view, a U.S. *recognition* of Native American citizenship would not lead to Indians being absorbed into the larger culture. Rather, it would facilitate a modern identity for distinctively Indian people.[38]

As the contrast between the Ghost Dancers on the one hand and Eastman and Winnemucca on the other reveals, Indian expressions of anticolonialism differed significantly in the late 1800s and early 1900s. For some Indians, it remained possible to imagine the restoration of a precolonial world. For others, coercive policies constricted available space for imagining possibilities. In both instances, however, Native Americans, in contrast to many colonized peoples in other parts of the world during the same period of time, rejected armed resistance. Obviously, many factors are relevant for explaining this difference, though a comparison to the 1906 Bambatha Rebellion in which Zulus took up arms in protest of a tax designed to proletarianize Zulus by forcing them from their lands suggests the importance of demographics. Zulus, with a population of close to a million, were by far the majority population in Natal and KwaZulu. By contrast Native American nations had much smaller populations and were vastly outnumbered by surrounding settler populations.[39]

This chapter's stopping point in the early twentieth century should not be taken to mean that U.S. rule over Indian nations ended then or that Native Americans ceased contesting colonial conditions. On the contrary, colonialism has remained a reality, one Indians have consistently challenged as they have worked to achieve their aspirations for sovereignty and community well-being. Native Americans are certainly aware of a long history of imperialism and colonialism, referred to on the eve of the Columbus quincentenary by Wilma Mankiller, Principal Chief of the Cherokee Nation, as five hundred years of "utter devastation among our people." At the same time, however, the success of their ongoing struggles, struggles informed by the legacy of anti-imperialism and anticolonialism explored in this chapter, allow them to say, as Mankiller continued, "we are very hopeful."[40]

Chapter 3

# "The Imperialism of the Declaration of Independence" in the Civil War Era

JAY SEXTON

The Civil War rarely features in the history of U.S. anti-imperialism. The standard narrative of the mid-nineteenth century focuses on those who opposed Jacksonian Indian removal, the war against Mexico, and the annexationist schemes in the Caribbean in the 1850s. The story then jumps to the postwar opponents of the annexation of Alaska and Santo Domingo, the discussion of which sets the stage for the emergence of the Anti-Imperialist League of 1898.[1]

That the epochal event of nineteenth-century America has little place in the discussion of a core political tradition of the same era is in part the result of how historians have defined anti-imperialism. Scholars typically view it through the prism of 1898. An anti-imperialist, in this formulation, was one who opposed expansionist policies such as those outlined above. This brand of anti-imperialism certainly existed during the Civil War era, though opposition to expansion more often was derivative of the slavery issue rather than an anti-imperial ideology. The most prominent form of anti-imperialism in this period, however, pertained to what we now consider the domestic political question of the rights and powers of the federal government in relation to the states and sections of the Union.

The language and concept of empire in the Civil War era was as versatile as it was ubiquitous. Nearly every major political player advanced some vision of American empire. The most vocal promoters of empire were Democrats like Stephen Douglas, whose "manifest destiny" program drew from Jefferson's old formulation of an "empire of liberty." But this idea of empire did not preclude other variations: Southern slavers sought an "empire for slavery" in the western territories, if not also the Caribbean; statesmen of the "great game" variety such as William H. Seward spoke of "the commerce of the world, which is the empire of the world"; even Lincoln proclaimed in 1856 that "we are a great empire."[2] What exactly was meant by "empire," of course, depended upon who was speaking. The case is similar when one turns to anti-imperialism. Both sides of the Jacksonian Indian removal debate, to take a well-known example, saw themselves as opponents of imperialism. Theodore Frelinghuysen opposed removal on moral and constitutional grounds, portending the position of the 1898 anti-imperialists. Jackson and his supporters, on the other hand, objected to the use of federal power to set limits on the actions of the state of Georgia and the white settlers who sought Cherokee land, an exercise of central authority that to them resembled the 1763 proclamation line the British foisted upon the colonists.

Far from a fixed political or diplomatic blueprint, anti-imperialism was an adaptable language and malleable set of ideas. Its applications were not restricted to the engagement with foreign states and peoples—indeed, most anti-imperial tracts of the mid-nineteenth century continued to conceive of imperialism in terms of the traditional Jeffersonian fear that central authority, now in Washington rather than London, would infringe upon the liberties of white citizens. It is worth emphasizing that Americans in this period did not use the term "anti-imperial." Rather, the mid-nineteenth-century conception and vocabulary of anti-imperialism was rooted in memories of the American Revolution, as well as the ongoing, if often imagined, struggle against persistent British power, which menaced the American Union in the international sphere and, many feared, threatened to infiltrate and corrupt it from within.

The Civil War era witnessed one section of the United States mobilize and deploy overwhelming force to subdue a rival section and then impose upon it a new set of political and economic structures, thus subverting the old Jeffersonian model of an "empire of liberty" examined in Peter Onuf's chapter in this volume. Yet if the Northern victory forever destroyed the limited union of the early Republic, it did not change old ways of thinking, nor old political structures, overnight. "The right of each state to control its own local affairs," Frederick Douglass lamented in 1866, was "more deeply rooted in the minds of men of all sections of the country than perhaps any other political idea."[3] This persistent aversion to central authority presented Radical Republicans such as Douglass with a great challenge as they attempted to transform the defeated South and defend the civil and political rights of all U.S. citizens, including the freedmen. If recalcitrant Southerners and conservative Northerners opposed this program, Radical Republicans would have no choice but to shove it down their throats anyway. "Call it imperialism, if you please," Charles Sumner conceded in 1867; "it is simply the imperialism of the Declaration of Independence, with all its promises fulfilled."[4]

The objective of this chapter is to explore this paradoxical "imperialism of the Declaration of Independence" in the Civil War era. It argues that traditional notions and vocabularies of anti-imperialism shaped Americans' understanding of the sectional conflict. Even as nationalist statesmen like Lincoln constructed a new central-state apparatus powerful enough to wage a war of conquest against the South, they conceived of the Civil War in the anti-imperial terms of consolidating the achievements of the American Revolution. In its functionality, as well, the Union war effort drew from traditions of decentralization and popular mobilization, though directed now by a newly powerful federal government and nationalized structures of civil society. Anti-imperial ideas and structures, it will be argued, facilitated some imperial projects of the Civil War era, while limiting others. The chapter will conclude with a brief examination of the significance abroad of American anti-imperialism in this age of liberal nationalism.

Lincoln regarded the Declaration of Independence as the sacred foundation of the American Union. "I have never had a feeling politically that did not spring from the sentiments embodied in the Declaration of Independence," he declared in February 1861.[5] The genius of the U.S. political system, he argued, lay in the fact that its objective was the self-improvement of its constituents, not the self-aggrandizement of the ruling elite. Like many of his compatriots, Lincoln believed that the moral and material benefits of this political system would ensure its spread across the world. He certainly agreed with John Quincy Adams's prediction that the Declaration "was the corner stone of a new fabric, destined to cover the surface of the globe."[6] But, in contrast to expansionists in the Democratic Party, Lincoln opposed aggressive and interventionist foreign policies. America's role in the global

progress of republican liberty was as an exemplar. Lincoln applauded revolutionary movements in Latin America and Europe, but did so from the
sidelines and with respect to the principle of nonintervention, that "sacred
principle of the international law."[7] His views on foreign policy place him
within what historians would now consider the anti-imperial camp: he
questioned the war of conquest against Mexico; he firmly opposed expansionist policies in the Caribbean; his rhetoric was notable for the absence of
the jingoism employed by his great rival, Stephen Douglas.[8]

It is a great irony that this advocate of anti-imperialism and nonintervention outside the United States would preside over a war of conquest and
liberation within it. But Lincoln would not have considered his domestic
and foreign policies as contradictory, for he contended that the cause of the
Union during the Civil War was the cause of the Declaration, as well as
the subsequent Constitution of 1787. Such thinking was premised upon
his moral abhorrence of slavery as well as the constitutional thought he
developed in the antebellum years. Not only was slavery a "monstrous
injustice" that contradicted the ideals of 1776, but Lincoln deplored it "because it deprives our republican example of its just influence in the world."
The Kansas–Nebraska Act of 1854 ignited Lincoln's profound objection
to slavery. "The spirit of seventy-six and the spirit of Nebraska, are utter
antagonisms" he averred in his 1854 Peoria speech. "Let us re-adopt the
Declaration of Independence, and with it, the practices, and policy, which
harmonize with it."[9]

Lincoln's arguments rested upon the proposition that to open federal
territories to slavery would be to betray the founding fathers' vision for
the United States. He pointed out that the founders blamed Britain for
"not preventing slavery from coming amongst us." In Lincoln's estimation,
the policy of the Democrats who voted for Kansas–Nebraska placed "this
government in the attitude then occupied by the government of Great
Britain" by further enabling the spread of slavery.[10] Rather than argue that
the prohibition of slavery in the territories necessitated constitutional innovation or new powers for the federal government, Lincoln contended
that it harmonized with what he called "the proper division of local from
federal authority." He further argued that precedent for federal prohibition
of slavery in the territories could be found in the policies of the founders
themselves.[11] Lincoln nonetheless carefully circumscribed federal authority
on the slavery issue, which he made clear was limited to the territories.
Indeed, in order to salvage the Union without resorting to war, Lincoln
stated in his March 1861 inaugural address that he was prepared to sign

an un-amendable amendment to the Constitution prohibiting the federal government from interfering with slavery within the states in which it existed.[12] "Mr. Jefferson did not mean to say, nor do I, that the power of emancipation is in the Federal Government," Lincoln asserted in 1860. "He spoke of Virginia; and, as to the power of emancipation, I speak of the slaveholding States only."[13] In the first years of the war, President Lincoln clung to this belief, hoping that emancipation could be achieved through gradualist and federally supported methods undertaken at the state level.

It is a sign of the extent of the antistatist political culture in nineteenth-century America that Lincoln's moderate and carefully calibrated views on how to balance federal and local authority were seen as a blueprint for central tyranny. Stephen Douglas contended that federal control of the slavery issue in the territories repudiated America's tradition of self-government and replicated the corrupt methods of the British Empire. "Mr. Lincoln proposes to govern the territories without giving the people a representation, and calls on Congress to pass laws controlling their property and domestic concerns without their consent and against their will," Douglas declared in the famous 1858 debates. "Thus, he asserts for his party the identical principle asserted by George III and the Tories of the Revolution."[14] Douglas's crusade for "popular sovereignty" drew from traditional anti-imperial ideas by seeking to resolve national tensions over slavery by taking the matter out of the hands of politicians in Washington and devolving it to white settlers on the periphery. Even after the *Dred Scott* decision, Douglas hoped to delegate the slavery issue to local communities through the "Freeport Doctrine" of empowering municipal officials to address the slavery issue as they saw fit.[15]

South of the Mason-Dixon Line, Southern slavers developed their own interpretation of anti-imperialism and the founding documents of the United States. In their eyes Lincoln and his Yankee Republican bands threatened to enslave them and trample upon their liberties just as the British had done back in the late eighteenth century. "The Southern States now stand exactly in the same position towards Northern States that our ancestors in *the colonies* did towards Great Britain," asserted the South Carolina secession convention.[16] Southerners proclaimed the sanctity of "states' rights" and promulgated a "compact theory" of the Constitution that allowed secession, the ultimate political act of internal anti-imperialism. Yet for all the antistatist talk about limiting the power of the metropole, the very Southerners who invoked America's revolutionary inheritance during the debate over slavery had sought not to destroy central power, but to mobilize it on behalf of their particular objectives. Their cries for the protection of "states' rights" were accompanied by demands for a federal slave code, a draconian national fugitive slave act, a pro-slavery foreign policy, and a pro-slavery interpretation of the Constitution.[17] Even as they made the states' rights case for secession, forward-looking Southerners formulated plans for how a new metropolitan government in the South would advance the interests of the nascent slaveholding nation.[18]

Northern Republicans were not immune from this paradox. After all, the objective of the Republicans was not the restoration of a limited federal government free from the "slave power," but rather the application of federal authority to antislavery ends such as the restriction of slavery from the territories, as well as long-sought-after objectives such as the erection of protectionist tariffs. Even Democrats like Stephen Douglas, who lost no opportunity to tar Republicans with the George III label, nonetheless embraced an active federal government for the settlement and development of the West. America's revolutionary and anti-imperial founding was thus a versatile political instrument and language, not an ideological straitjacket. As in the period of the early Republic, national symbols such as the Declaration and Constitution remained politicized and deployed on behalf of divergent policy objectives.[19]

This is not to suggest that the many invocations of the Revolution in the run-up to civil war should be dismissed as mere domestic politicking. Many Americans believed that the struggle to free themselves from the webs of the British Empire was not complete, particularly in economic and cultural regards. As late as 1883, Henry Cabot Lodge wrote of "colonialism in the United States," referring not to American expansion or policy toward Native Americans, but to the persistence of British cultural hegemony in America.[20] British power remained an unavoidable reality in the mid-nineteenth century: nearly half the national debt was held abroad, chiefly in Britain; English novels took up most of the space on American bookshelves; the might of the Royal Navy might be turned against American commercial interests, as it had in the run-up to the War of 1812. American opposition to Britain was intensified in the mid-nineteenth century by the great migration that resulted from the Irish famine of the 1840s. Irish migrants brought with them a rich tradition of Anglophobic anti-imperialism, helping make opposition to Britain ubiquitous in the politics of the period. The roots of American anti-imperialism were thus both internal (arising from memories of the American Revolution) and external (from the arrival of

European revolutionary exiles, particularly after the failed 1848 revolution, and, most of all, Irish migrants).

To be sure, many of these alarmist mid-nineteenth-century fears of persistent British imperialism were imagined, not least in the sense that Britain did not stand in the way of the fulfillment of America's "manifest destiny" in the 1840s (indeed, by helping to finance U.S. development and sheltering the New World from European intervention, British power actually enabled U.S. expansion). Furthermore, American politicians of all sections and persuasions were adept at exploiting the British threat to appeal to an Anglophobic electorate, as well as to garner domestic support for divisive policies such as the annexation of new territories or the erection of protectionist tariffs. But whether real or imagined, British power loomed large in the minds of mid-nineteenth-century Americans.[21]

The prominence of Anglophobia in antebellum American political culture conditioned the way in which Americans perceived internal threats. The commonplace fear that one's political enemies were plotting to recreate British tyranny on American soil had a long pedigree that reached back to the creation of the first party system in the 1790s. It also drew from the dreaded overlap of internal and external threats that was central to the nineteenth-century conception of national security.[22] An ominous development in the sectional crisis occurred when both sides of the debate over slavery came to see the other in the light of the British threat. Pro-slavery Southerners viewed the antislavery forces in the Northern states as pawns of the powerful British abolitionists. Meanwhile, the new Northern Republican Party interpreted slaveholding Southerners as an un-American elite, a "slave power" that mimicked the aristocracy of old England and whose fantasies of "King Cotton" sitting upon the throne of free trade masked the reality of neocolonial dependence upon the hated British. Both sides feared that the potentially powerful federal government had been hijacked by their opponents who planned to reestablish British tyranny on American soil: the Republican "slave power" concept articulated this theme, and after Lincoln's election, Southern secessionists feared that the floodgates of antislavery into the South would be opened via the government's vast patronage networks of customhouses and post offices.

Situating the sectional conflict within memories of the Revolution and the ongoing struggle against British power allowed both sides to conceive of their cause as defensive and in harmony with an imagined anti-imperial tradition. For Southerners, the sectional crisis was a reenactment of 1776.

"We recur to the principles upon which our Government was founded," Jefferson Davis declared in early 1861, "and when you deny them . . . we but tread in the path of our fathers when we proclaim our independence, and take the hazard."[23] Lincoln faced a greater challenge in linking offensive military operations to the imagined struggle of 1776. The new president expressed hope in his inaugural address that the anti-imperial nationalism of 1776 would once again unite the Republic: "The mystic chords of memory, stretching from every battlefield and patriot grave to every living heart and hearthstone all over this broad land, will yet swell the chorus of the Union."[24] But once the war came, Lincoln invoked 1776 in a different way: the struggle for the Union was now a continuation of the American Revolution. The sectional conflict, Lincoln asserted in an address to Congress on July 4, 1861, "presents to the whole family of man, the question, whether a constitutional republic, or a democracy—a government of the people, by the same people—can, or cannot, maintain its territorial integrity, against its own domestic foes." The issues at stake in 1861 were of as great importance as those of 1776, and the implications extended beyond the Union itself. "Surely each man has as strong a motive *now*, to *preserve* our liberties, as each had *then*, to *establish* them," Lincoln asserted.[25]

The international context further led Northerners to see themselves as the guardians of the principles of 1776. An independent Confederacy might be sucked into the orbit of the British Empire, not least because of the powerful bonds of the transatlantic cotton trade. The long-feared introduction of European balance-of-power politics in the North American continent would be the inevitable result. "Our country, after having expelled all European powers from the continent," William H. Seward lamented, "would relapse into an aggravated form of its colonial experience, and, like Italy, Turkey, India, and China, become the theater of transatlantic intervention and rapacity."[26] The French intervention in Mexico, which aimed to install a European puppet monarch onto the newly created Mexican throne, was the source of further concerns. Many in the North viewed it as interlinked with secession. "The French invasion of Mexico," Union general Phillip Sheridan asserted, "was so closely related to the Rebellion as to be essentially part of it."[27] Republicans used the common language of conspiracy to describe both occurrences: they attributed secession to a corrupt "slave power" and understood the intervention in Mexico as an extension of the "papal power" of Catholic France and the "money power" of European banking houses. Just as the "slave power" sought to undermine the true meaning of the Declaration of Independence, French imperialists took aim at the Monroe Doctrine, which proclaimed U.S. opposition to European imperial expansion in the New World. "The final success of the whole program," Ohio Republican Joshua Leavitt asserted, "hinges upon the result of the first step, the breaking up of the American Union."[28]

It was in this context that Lincoln conceived of the conflict as "a People's contest." "On the side of the Union," he declared in his July 4, 1861, address, "it is a struggle for maintaining in the world, that form, and substance of government, whose leading object is, to elevate the condition of men— to lift artificial weights from all shoulders—to clear the paths of laudable pursuit for all—to afford all, an unfettered start, and a fair chance, in the race of life." But though the war was waged in the name of the people, Lincoln left open the possibility that "partial, and temporary departures" from the practice of limited central authority might be pursued out of "necessity."[29] The will of the people, in other words, would need to be harnessed—and in some cases suppressed—by a newly powerful central state, which would levy high taxes, transform banking and currency, confiscate private property, implement conscription, suspend habeas corpus, and infringe upon civil liberties. Not surprisingly, these actions triggered objections on the home front from Northern Democrats, who deployed the language of anti-imperialism and invoked analogies to the Revolution in the bare-knuckled politics of the war years. "A most remarkable similarity exists in the actions of this Administration toward the people of the North and those that were perpetrated by the Mother Country against the colonies," asserted Pennsylvania Democrat Samuel Randall in 1863.[30]

Yet for all the controversy that surrounded the increased powers of the central state, the Union war effort should not be seen as the product of some new central command structure, for it deeply drew from traditions of decentralized government and volunteerism, which were products of the antistatist political culture of the early Republic. The secret to the success of the Union war effort was not simply the growth of the federal government, but its synergy with a nationalizing and patriotic civil society— voluntary associations like the U.S. Sanitary Commission, grassroots political networks and Union Leagues, newspapers, and evangelical churches.[31] Lincoln's political genius lay not simply in how he managed a cabinet of rivals, but in his capacity to mobilize the pulpit on behalf of his aims, coax support out of skeptical editors, appeal directly to the people through his addresses and public letters, and, not to be forgotten, harness the power of state governments.[32] A comparison with the Confederacy is illuminating in this regard. One explanation historians have given for why the Confederate state became more centralized than its Washington counterpart—this despite the stronger antistatist tradition in the South—is that its civil society networks and structures were less developed than those of the North.[33]

In terms of political economy, as well, the key development in the war years was not simply the increased role played by central authority, but rather the relationships forged between Republican politicians and a newly powerful class of Wall Street capitalists. The genius of the financial legislation of the Thirty-Seventh Congress was how it fused the interests of capital and nation by incentivizing investment in the war effort and federating the major private banks of the North. The funding of the Union war effort—two-thirds of which came from borrowing—perhaps best illustrates the bonds forged between government, finance, and civil society. With the London money market skeptical of the Union's creditworthiness, the federal government turned inward, empowering a new class of financiers, such as Jay Cooke, to market bond issues to the wider public. Enthusiastic buyers, many of whom had never before entered the securities market, invested their savings in small-denomination bonds to the profit of bankers like Cooke, who worked on commission, and to the benefit of the larger Union cause. The bonds of finance and the shared interests of profit thus fused together government, capital, and citizen in the Union war effort.[34]

Lincoln's moderate vision of reconstruction also demonstrated a continued preference for decentralization and the devolution of political power. Conquest would destroy secession, but collaboration and negotiation would bring the South back into the Union. "To send a parcel of Northern men [to Washington], as representatives, elected as would be understood, (and perhaps really so,) at the point of the bayonet, would be disgusting and outrageous," he wrote in late 1862.[35] Rather than conceiving of reconstruction as a proto-nation-building project directed from Washington, Lincoln more likely had in mind a model resembling the construction of the Republican Party in the 1850s. What had fused the various anti-Nebraska and anti-immigrant factions together in the antebellum North was not just shared principles of antislavery, but also a political methodology: negotiation and compromise among different interests; synergy between local, state, and national structures; elastic frameworks that allowed, indeed encouraged, local or regional variation.[36] Lincoln argued that such a political process was necessary for the restoration of the Union and the establishment of a Southern branch of the Republican Party. And just as Lincoln had no clear timetable in the 1850s for achieving his party's antislavery platform, his vision for reconstruction was gradualist and incremental.[37]

Lincoln's views on reconstruction, of course, were not shared by all. The Radical Republican alternative, outlined in the Wade-Davis bill of 1864 and elaborated upon thereafter, aimed to use the powers of the Republican-dominated Congress to achieve a fundamental transformation of the South. That Radical Republicans gave a nod to traditional anti-imperialism by condemning unchecked executive power should not blind us to the radical nature of their political vision. They demanded that the South be treated by central authority as "conquered provinces," in the phrase of Thaddeus Stevens.[38] They denounced the Southern state governments formed under Andrew Johnson's lenient Reconstruction policy and instead called for an open-ended military occupation of ex-Confederate states, the enfranchisement of the freedmen, and the establishment of strict conditions for reentry into the Union. What the South needed, George Julian argued, was "the strong arm of power, outstretched from the central authority here in Washington, making it safe for the freedman of the South, safe for her loyal white men . . . safe for Northern capital and labor, Northern energy and enterprise, and Northern ideas to set up their habitation in peace, and thus found a Christian civilization and a living democracy amid the ruins of the past."[39]

The radicals' embrace of vigorous central authority reignited in the United States a debate about the extent to which national power should be centralized. This was a common dilemma around the world in the era of mid-nineteenth-century liberal nationalism. The radicalism of Radical Republicans is evinced in the fact that their policies raised concerns among natural allies abroad. Though an advocate of the Union cause, Mazzini in Italy expressed ambivalence about the Northern conquest of the South on the grounds that it looked rather like the authoritarian actions of the old regimes in Europe that had crushed the people's bid for self-determination back in 1848.[40] Some British liberals, such as William Gladstone, questioned the Northern effort on similar grounds. British journals could not help but note the irony that the government that had long called for Irish "home rule" was now preventing the South from enjoying the same during Radical Reconstruction. It is revealing to contrast the 1867 Reconstruction Acts, which divided the South into five districts under military control, to the British North American Act of the same year, which signaled Britain's military withdrawal from Canada and united its provinces into the new Canadian Dominion that enjoyed almost complete "home rule."

The radical vision played a key role in the central achievements of Reconstruction, particularly the passage of constitutional amendments that accorded to the national government the responsibility of protecting individual rights. New institutions such as the Freedmen's Bureau similarly pointed toward a more active central state. Yet the very novelty of this conception of the federal government as custodian of individual liberty limited its accomplishments. White Southern Democrats, of course, soon coupled the reinvigorated language of "home rule" with the force of paramilitary organizations to oppose the dictates of the Republican Party. Old Confederate leaders like Alexander Stephens rose again to denounce the new "centralized empire" that the old Union had become.[41] Opposition from this quarter comes as little surprise. But even within the ranks of Northern Republicans lurked a powerful group of "moderates" who narrowly interpreted the federal government's newfound role as guardian of individual rights and equal protection under the law. These moderate Republicans viewed the Reconstruction amendments and legislation as necessary to address the specific problems confronted in the postwar South, not as harbingers of a revolutionary change in the role of the federal government. They rejected radical proposals for land redistribution. This limited conception of federal power can be seen elsewhere: in court rulings such as the *Slaughterhouse* cases that narrowly interpreted the federal government's responsibilities under the Fourteenth Amendment, as well as in the Liberal Republican movement of the early 1870s.[42]

The retreat from Reconstruction is perhaps best evinced in the eagerness with which many Republicans reverted to the old embrace of limited central authority when they made the case for constitutional innovation. "The political system of this Republic rests upon the right of the people to control their local concerns in their several states," declared Carl Schurz in support to the Fourteenth Amendment. "This system was not to be changed in the work of reconstruction."[43] Similar arguments were advanced on behalf of the Fifteenth Amendment, which was presented as inaugurating the federal government's withdrawal from the Southern states on the grounds that it empowered African Americans to participate in the political sphere. Such logic inexorably led Republicans in the Grant years to backpedal from their commitments in the South. Federal power had subdued the rebellion and, during congressional Reconstruction, had established a Northern bridgehead within the South in the form of the tenuous Republican Party comprising African Americans, "carpetbagger" Northern migrants, and "scalawag" Southern whites. With these accomplishments in

hand, the majority of Republicans in Washington bid adieu to their counterparts in the South and advocated military withdrawal under the banners
of retrenchment and local self-government. The fate of Reconstruction
thereafter hinged upon the ability of the fragile coalition of Southern Republicans to secure and extend their vulnerable bridgehead in the face of
attacks from the Southern white majority. In these circumstances it is no
surprise that the Northern "imperial" project was left unfinished.

The point here is not to deny the revolutionary implications of the
Civil War, but rather to highlight the persistence of old understandings of
federalism and limited government, which helped make possible Southern "redemption" and, later, the implementation of Jim Crow segregation.
A similar point can be made about the staying power of the traditional language of anti-imperialism in the domestic sphere. It is often argued that one
barometer for measuring the new nationalism ushered in during the Civil
War was the replacement in the American vocabulary of "union," which
invoked limited federal authority and the old compact theory, with "nation," which implied unity under the direction of a more powerful central
state.[44] Yet an examination of digitized newspapers revealed that in most
years until the 1880s "union" was more often used than "nation."[45] Indeed,
the old vocabulary of "states' rights" and "local self-government" remained
in wide usage in the decades after the Civil War. The meaning of these
terms, of course, changed insofar as nullification and secession were no
longer in the cards. But this vocabulary nonetheless legitimated the political
actions that restored white supremacy and effective Southern "home rule."

Even where the roots of the new structures established under Republican
auspices during the war ran deepest—in political economy and finance—
the implications were not clear cut. The conquest of the South and the
imposition of nationalist measures of political economy upon it certainly
brought the region more firmly into the national market. Yet this new
political economy paradoxically limited the advancement of the nationalist
project in the Reconstruction South. The newly created masters of Wall
Street came to oppose the project of "northernizing" the South because
it necessitated high taxes, the postponement of a return to the gold standard, the potential confiscation and redistribution of private property (in
the form of land reform in the South), and the empowerment of African
Americans through state-supported institutions such as the Freedmen's Bureau. All these measures sat uncomfortably beside prevailing laissez-faire
doctrines, devotion to the sanctity of the gold standard, and free-labor ideology.[46] The new financial elite would do more than just oppose Radical

Reconstruction: it soon would deploy the languages of antistatism and anti-imperialism against the very central authority that had been midwife to its birth, denouncing any attempt by federal authorities to regulate its activities. But for all its antistatist talk, finance happily embraced federal power when it was used to bolster its interests, as frequently became the case in the Gilded Age.

If the structures of political economy created during the war proved self-limiting during Reconstruction, they accelerated the other great imperialist project of the era: the conquest and colonization of the West. The federal government was better suited to the task faced in the West (facilitating white settlement and environmental exploitation) than to the challenges in the postwar South (imposing new forms of government and race relations upon an intransigent white population). No longer paralyzed by the question of slavery in the territories, the Republican federal government supported private individuals and corporations who sought fortunes from the exploitation of the nation's vast western territories. The nexus between individual citizens, the central state, and an emergent Wall Street that had been instrumental to the Union's victory in the Civil War also turned its attention to the West, even in the midst of the great conflict. Legislation such as the Homestead Act and the Pacific Railroad Act (both of 1862), as well as the use of military force to subdue the resistance of the Great Plains Indians, extended federal support to the migrants and capitalists who settled and exploited the nation's vast western territories.

There can be no question that the "winning of the West" marked the apogee of nineteenth-century U.S. imperialism, even if it occurred within the nation's borders. By the turn of the century, U.S. imperialists would see it as such: "We have a record of conquest, colonization, and territorial expansion unequalled by any people in the nineteenth century," boasted Henry Cabot Lodge.[47] Yet many Americans in the Civil War era conceived of the conquest of the West as the fulfillment of the nation's anti-imperial destiny, the culmination of its struggle against the ascribed social and political hierarchies of the Old World. Westward colonization was often presented in the traditional terms of the peopling of an "empire of liberty" that was a magnet for foreign migrants. As Lincoln put it in his 1858 debates with Douglas, the West was "an outlet for *free white people everywhere*, the world over—in which Hans and Baptiste and Patrick, and all other men from all the world, may find new homes and better their conditions in life."[48]

The tension between the imperial reality and the anti-imperial imaginary can be seen in much contemporary discussion of the West. Those
who viewed the "winning of the West" as anti-imperial in nature could
do so only because they erased from view the Native American inhabitants of western territories and the manner in which Mexican territory
had been acquired. For these contemporaries, the anti-imperial nature of
westward colonization was evinced in the fact that the old process of the
Northwest Ordinance remained the political roadmap to statehood that
promised eventual self-government to white settlers. Yet even in this limited conception, anti-imperialism could serve as the basis for a critique of
the territorial system. Statehood was so long in coming in some places (not
until 1912 in New Mexico) that anti-imperial rhetoric was deployed by
white settlers whose patience wore thin. As one resident of the Montana
Territory put it, federal rule "is the most infamous system of colonial government that was ever seen on the face of the globe."[49] As in earlier periods,
the dispossession and conquest of Native American lands sat uneasily beside
professions of a U.S. "empire of liberty." Critics like Lydia Maria Child
pulled no punches in highlighting the savagery of white treatment of the
Indians.[50] But rather than view Native American resistance as anti-imperial
in nature, most white Americans viewed the subjugation of native peoples
as a civilizing process overseen not by a corrupt European-style "colonial
office," but by allegedly enlightened private actors and missionaries who
were empowered in Grant's so-called peace policy.

A similar paradox emerges when one turns to postwar foreign policy.
Generations of historians have made clear that the roots of the imperial
outburst of 1898 lay in the decades after the Civil War.[51] If a few forward-
looking strategists at the time welcomed this, most Americans continued
to imagine themselves as proponents of an unalloyed anti-imperial foreign
policy. This was partly because of the failure of expansionist schemes in this
period. The years after the Civil War are more notable for the failure of
expansionist foreign policies (in Cuba, Santo Domingo, the Danish West
Indies, and the Central American isthmus) than they are for the success of
them (in Midway and Alaska). The largely passive response of the United
States to the Cuban rebellion of the 1860s and '70s contrasts to the interventionism and imperialism that the instability in Cuba precipitated in
the 1890s. It is revealing that some of the loudest advocates of an active
policy in Cuba in the 1870s were Radical Republicans who contended
that central power could and should transform the South. Similarly, some
of the most ardent advocates of the annexation of Santo Domingo, such as

Frederick Douglass, were former abolitionists who hoped the move would contribute to the transformation of the South.[52]

If the possible annexation of overseas territory triggered political conflict at home, opposition to European imperial expansion did not. Indeed, it was in the Civil War era that Americans transformed Monroe's prosaic 1823 message into a national "doctrine" of foreign policy. Contingent events help account for this development. Republicans could reinvent a national tradition of unalloyed anti-imperialism by attributing the recent conquest of northern Mexico and expansionist schemes in the Caribbean to the defeated and un-American "slave power." Furthermore, the 1860s witnessed the revival of the European threat in the New World—most obviously the French invasion of Mexico and Britain's contemplation of intervention in the U.S. Civil War, but also actions such as Spain's re-colonization of Santo Domingo and the Chincha Islands. The failure of these European ventures reinforced old views in America that outright colonial expansion was not only contrary to the universal principles of the Declaration of Independence, but also ineffective. It is revealing that many of the "anti-imperialists" of 1898 who argued that colonial annexation betrayed national principles and traditions were old-timers from the Civil War generation.[53]

Yet this opposition to European imperialism was inextricably linked to evolving ideas and practices of U.S. empire. The form of U.S. imperialism shifted in this period from the outright land-grabs and conquests of the Jacksonian era to the informal projection of commercial, political, and cultural power, particularly in neighboring Mexico, Central America, and the Caribbean. The Monroe Doctrine, Republican John Kasson asserted in 1881, "is a question now of commercial rivalry and commercial advantages."[54] Americans at the time did not see this informal imperialism as a betrayal of anti-imperial traditions. Indeed, America's anti-imperial symbols more often were deployed in support of the non-colonial projection of its power abroad. Joshua Leavitt's 1863 pamphlet *The Monroe Doctrine* is one such example. An evangelical who had authored one of the best-selling hymns of the era, Leavitt viewed the French intervention in Mexico as a papist plot to extend the control of the Catholic Church. He advocated a hemispheric unity to counter this scenario. But his idea of inter-American solidarity was premised upon U.S. dominance, not the equality of the states of the New World. Leavitt's chief objective was the destruction of Catholicism in Latin America through U.S. missionary activity.[55]

In the coming decades, U.S. policy toward Latin America became increasingly assertive and interventionist, even as it continued to be packaged in the language of the Monroe Doctrine's opposition to European imperialism. The pan-American vision in the United States, particularly as espoused by James Blaine, also drew from lingering anti-British sentiment by calling for an "America for Americans" free from British free-trade imperialism.[56] The Blainite vision of "imperial anticolonialism" (as William Appleman Williams called it) revealed the extent to which opposition to European colonial expansion had become yoked with American imperialism.[57]

The U.S. Civil War was one of many instances of violent national consolidation in the mid-nineteenth-century world. It both reflected and contributed to the global rise of nationalism. When approaching the U.S. Civil War in global context, historians thus tend to view it through the prism of nation-state formation. The posthumous global celebrity of Lincoln, for example, can be attributed to the inspirational role he played in an era of rising liberal nationalism and economic development.

Yet the nationalist project was one that was inextricably intertwined with questions of imperialism and anti-imperialism. The U.S. Civil War thus contributed, if indirectly, to the global rise of anti-imperialism. It should come as no surprise, for example, to find in the papers of William Seward a letter from an early proto-nationalist in India who counted the American Union as an inspiration in his critique of British rule.[58] Cuban nationalist José Martí considered Lincoln a hero and inspiration for those struggling for self-government against foreign colonialism. Yet Martí invoked Lincoln not only to buttress Cuba's case against Spain, but also to remind U.S. statesmen that their increasingly aggressive policies in the Caribbean betrayed their nation's anti-imperial tradition.[59] Here is an early example of the transnational circulation and exploitation of the myth of American anti-imperialism, which would become ever more common in the coming century.

The Civil War was perhaps most significant to the international history of anti-imperialism in terms of geopolitics. The conflict constituted a final phase of America's liberation from the British Empire, as well as a central event in the emergence of its own empire. By determining the political, economic, and labor arrangements that would emerge from an internally contentious postcolonial period, the Civil War consolidated the Revolution. The Union triumph in 1865 cemented the bonds between the states, foreclosing the possibility of foreign intervention within the Union. The ascendancy of Northern Republicans also inaugurated the "golden era of American protectionism" that insulated the United States from British commercial power.[60] When British capitalists shied away from funding the Union war effort, the result was the development of homegrown structures of finance centered in Wall Street that in time would supplant those in London. These economic developments decreased reliance on British capital and commerce, while also creating powerful interests that would promote U.S. overseas commercial expansion after the war.

The decade of the 1860s witnessed the preservation of the American Union. It also saw the failure of the French intervention in Mexico, the devolution of British power through the establishment of confederated home rule in Canada, and a rebellion in Cuba beginning in 1868 that portended the ultimate collapse of Spanish rule. In short, it was a crucial moment in what might be called the decolonization of North America. Yet if the U.S. Civil War can be seen as culmination of the Revolution, it also laid the foundations of the U.S. imperial expansion of the coming decades. It comes as no small irony, for instance, that home rule and Canadian confederation were in part devised to fend off absorption into the traditionally expansionist American Republic. In Mexico and Cuba, traditional New World anti-imperialism empowered the opponents of Old World colonialism, while at the same time it cleared the way for the emergence of the U.S. neocolonialism of the late nineteenth century. In such ways the "imperialism of the Declaration of Independence" began to play out beyond the borders of the new American nation.

PART II

# ANTI-IMPERIALISM AND THE NEW AMERICAN EMPIRE

Chapter 4

# Anti-imperialism in the U.S. Territories after 1898

JULIAN GO

Many Americans in the early twentieth century beamed with pride at America's new overseas empire. W. E. B. Du Bois was not of them. He saw it as an extension of the color line to the world, thus rendering futile Booker T. Washington's dream of racial refuge abroad for African Americans. "[N]oth-ing has more effectually made this programme [of Washington's] seem hope-less," he wrote in 1903, "than the recent course of the United States toward weaker and darker peoples in the West Indies, Hawaii, and the Philippines,— for where in the world may we go and be safe from lying and brute force?"[1] Du Bois subsequently suggested that "Negro and Filipino, Indian and Porto Rican, Cuban and Hawaiian, all must stand united under the stars and stripes for an America that knows no color line in the freedom of its opportunities."[2]

Much later, in 1945, Du Bois had opportunity to work with some of these "weaker and darker peoples" around the world to end the global color line once and for all. In that year, he helped organize a meeting in New York in anticipation of the first United Nations conference to be held in San Francisco. Attendees at Du Bois's meeting included representatives from territories and colonized countries around the globe, such as Uganda, Jamaica, the Gold Coast, India, and Puerto Rico. By the end of the meeting they had issued a statement declaring unequivocally: "Colonialism Must Go." They then agreed to present it to the UN Assembly in San Francisco.

But they needed an official delegate from an independent nation to present it. They found their ally in Carlos P. Romulo of the Philippines, a country just emerging from more than four decades of U.S. occupation.[3]

We now know that the effort in 1945 failed. The colonial powers, including the United States, refused to make decolonization an official objective of the UN. Instead, they made independence an objective only for UN trustee territories. But the effort is worthy of note here because it encapsulates the main themes of the present chapter.

The first theme is American empire and resistance to it. Du Bois's critiques of imperialism are known by now; the aim of this chapter is to unearth the anti-imperial practices of colonial subjects overseas. Specifically, this chapter tracks the ways in which Filipinos, Puerto Ricans, and Chamorros of Guam challenged or contested American colonialism, even if they did not overthrow it.[4] It attends to the languages and forms of their resistance. It also tracks their goals. While anti-imperialism could mean different things, this chapter will show that, within America's colonial empire, anti-imperialism oscillated between movements for independence and political integration—both of which, depending upon the time and place, ran against the grain of American imperial interests.

The other theme has to do with global, as in trans-imperial and intra-imperial, collaborations, convergences, and crossings. Present at the New York meetings led by Du Bois were not only anticolonial leaders like Kwame Nkrumah of the Gold Coast but also Julio Pinto Gandía, representing the Puerto Rican Nationalist Party. In the alliance between Du Bois, Romulo, and Pinto Gandía, therefore, we see the convergence of African American, Filipino, and Puerto Rican resistances to empire. But there were other instances of cross-colonial alliance, as well as other moments of collaboration across empires. These entailed flows of ideas and inspiration as well as the sharing of tactics and mutual support. While this chapter cannot exhaust all these cross-imperial and inter-imperial workings, it aims to shed light on at least some of them, thereby illuminating how America's colonial peoples crossed empire in more ways than one.

But let us begin in 1950, in Washington, D.C., where an attempted murder was under way.

## From Washington to Jayuya

On November 1, 1950, two men walked down Pennsylvania Avenue in Washington, D.C. They stopped outside Blair House, at 1651 Pennsylvania

Avenue, just down the road from the White House. President Harry Truman was in the Blair House, temporarily residing there with his wife, Bess, while the White House residence underwent renovation. The two men approached the house. They each pulled out German automatic pistols and started firing. Their aim was to assassinate Truman, but what ensued instead was a quick gunfight that lasted thirty-eight seconds and left two dead: Griselio Torresola, one of the two would-be assassins, and Leslie Coffelt, a member of the U.S. Secret Service defending Truman.[5]

Torresola and his accomplice, Oscar Collazo, were members of the Puerto Rican Nationalist Party. One of their leaders was the famed and fiery Pedro Albizu Campos, a Harvard graduate who had come to embrace national independence as the only political solution for Puerto Rico. Another was Julio Pinto Gandía, who had, five years earlier, worked with Du Bois and Romulo to insert a decolonization clause into the UN program. Torresola and Collazo were carrying out an uprising that Albizu Campos and his party comrades had been planning for at least a year. The plan involved assassinations as well as armed revolution across Puerto Rico. In fact, on October 30, 1950, two days before the assassination attempt on Truman, the uprising had begun. Nationalists revolted in Jayuya (the headquarters of the revolt, where Albizu Campos had been storing arms) and other towns, including Ponce, Utuado, and San Juan. In Jayuya, the Nationalists seized the town square and raised the Puerto Rican flag (which had been outlawed by the United States since 1898). They declared Puerto Rico to be a free republic.

The uprising failed. After Washington declared martial law, it deployed the National Guard, bomber planes, and artillery to crush the revolt. The assassination attempt on Truman failed too. Collazo was apprehended and sent to prison. But four years later, the Nationalists staged another violent reproach. On March 1, four Nationalists entered the Capitol building in Washington and proceeded to the gallery area overlooking the chambers of the U.S. Congress. They unfurled a Puerto Rican flag, yelled "Que viva Puerto Rico libre" and opened fire. Thirty rounds of ammunition were spent. Five U.S. congressmen lay wounded. The culprits (Lolita Lebrón, Rafael Cancel Miranda, Andres Figueroa Cordero, and Irving Flores) were apprehended and sentenced to life in prison.

This was one mode of anti-imperialism in the U.S. empire: direct violence in the form of armed resistance or terrorism. It was not entirely uncommon. The Nationalist Party had been engaged in anticolonial violence for decades. In 1938, a Nationalist student attempted to assassinate Governor Blanton Winship. This was in retaliation for the "Ponce Massacre" of 1936 when nineteen people were killed by the Insular Police during a Nationalist demonstration in the city.[6] Prior to that, Nationalists had made other assassination attempts on U.S. federal judges. They had even killed the chief of the Insular Police, while others in their ranks were jailed for various conspiratorial plots.

Acts of violence in the name of national independence were not new, but what *was* new was the very goal of national independence. Initially, most islanders had welcomed U.S. occupation. In 1898, as soon as the U.S. military had ousted Spanish forces during the Spanish-American War, the towns of the island opened their welcome arms. Locals insisted that they were not Spanish but American, telling journalists: "No, Español, [we are] Porto-Rican Americano."[7] A flurry of letters, petitions, and delegations were sent to U.S. authorities and to Washington, D.C., affirming Puerto Rico's desire for U.S. occupation.

In some ways this welcome was a continuation of their preexisting political struggle with Madrid. Unlike their Cuban or Filipino counterparts in the Spanish empire, Puerto Rican politicians had not demanded independence from Madrid but rather closer integration. They had sought "autonomy" within an idealized Spanish federal system, making Puerto Rico a province akin to other Spanish territories on the mainland. This was known as the Autonomist movement. Accordingly, as the United States replaced Spain, these very same leaders hoped for integration into the United States. Prominent politicians such as Luis Muñoz Rivera, José de Diego, and Matienzo Cintrón organized new political parties and issued platforms declaring loyalty to the new American empire. When President Theodore Roosevelt visited Puerto Rico in 1906, landing in the southern city of Ponce, he was greeted not with bullets but flowers and cries of "Viva el presidente!" All the while the people proclaimed their loyalty.[8]

So what happened? Why was there a warm welcome in the early twentieth century but armed anti-imperialism later? Addressing this question will help us see some of the other modes and tactics of anti-imperialism in the U.S. empire while helping us better understand Puerto Rican nationalism.

## From Statehood to Nationalism

Despite the initial welcome to U.S. occupation, all was not well beneath the surface. Part of the problem was that Puerto Rican leaders did not want just any form of U.S. occupation; they wanted a U.S. occupation that would lead to eventual statehood in the union. Unfortunately for them, the Puerto Rican leadership had believed in American exceptionalism. They believed that the United States, unlike tyrannical European empires that repressed freedom, was a unique "empire of liberty" that incorporated new territory into its fold as fully fledged states. They had listened attentively when American forces first arrived to the island, promising that U.S. rule would "promote your prosperity and bestow upon you the guarantees and blessings of the liberal institutions of our Government" (as General Nelson A. Miles had promised upon landing in Ponce in 1898).[9] They had also learned about U.S. westward expansion, incorporating and transforming colonies into equal states, "just like California or Nebraska"—as their leader Luis Muñoz Rivera put it.[10]

The political demands of the first political parties, such as Muñoz Rivera's Federal Party, followed directly. They requested that Puerto Rico be admitted as a "Territory in the Union, with all the rights of a State, except sending Senators or representatives to Congress and instead having, like other Territories, a Delegate with a voice but no vote." They then wanted Puerto Rico, just like other prior territories in the union, to become, "in the future, a State without any restrictions, just like the other States in the Federation."[11] It is for this reason that Muñoz Rivera's party had changed its name during the transition from Spanish rule to U.S. sovereignty. They saw U.S. federalism as akin to Spanish imperial federalism and wanted from the latter the same as the former. No longer the Autonomist party that had sought to become an equal "autonomous" province within the Spanish empire, they changed their party name to the *Federal* Party, thus preparing themselves for incorporation into the American system of federalism. Muñoz Rivera stated at the Federal Party's convention: "Upon meeting today, the old liberals conform their hopes and look for a name that corresponds to the methods and traditions of the federation [of the United States]. . . . And they want to be called the FEDERAL PARTY, because they continue believing in their autonomist ideal, and because there does not exist on the planet an autonomy so ample and so indestructible as that created when the patriarchs of the America of the North wrote their laws for its states and territories."[12]

While the Puerto Rican leaders' touching faith in American exceptionalism led them to welcome U.S. imperialism, it was the racialized resistance of the latter that set the grounds for nationalist anti-imperialism. The United States did not make Puerto Rico an equal state in the union. Nor did it even make it an incorporated territory. By the Foraker Act of

1900, it turned Puerto Rico into a dependent colony. Puerto Ricans did not receive citizenship, a full bill of rights, or equal representation in the metropolis. They instead faced a colonial government legislated by the U.S. Congress and run by U.S. officials appointed by the president. Puerto Ricans were allowed to hold office, form parties, and vote, but they could only vote for and hold local offices. They were given a House of Delegates, a sort of lower legislative chamber, but this chamber was overseen by a higher body, the Executive Council, consisting of a majority of presidentially appointed Americans, including the governor. The Supreme Court declared the island to be an "unincorporated territory" unworthy of statehood. This inferior status starkly disclosed the dismal limits of Jefferson's empire of liberty.[13]

Two different paths of anti-imperialism were thus paved. One was marked by renewed attempts by many Puerto Rican political leaders to obtain local political power and autonomy for Puerto Ricans with an eye toward eventual statehood. This was the route of cautious hope, likely empowered by Hawaii's status as an "incorporated" territory and anti-imperialist forces in the metropolis. The strategy employed was to plead and if necessary protest, appealing to the new imperial master for *justicia*. While internal dissensions and local party politics initially plagued the movement, a new political party emerged as a unifying force. In 1904, the Unionist Party became the dominant party in the island for the next decade and more. Throughout, the overarching tactic of the party was to mobilize in the island and in the metropolis (with informal headquarters set up in New York) and use the political language of the master to make the case. Though only a handful of the political leaders had been educated or lived in the United States, many others mined American history, political documents, and laws, took up English, and astutely redeployed American political discourse. One common target was the Foraker Act and its associated provisions for colonial government. Unionist leader Cayetano Coll Cuchí wrote an entire book in 1903, *La ley Foraker*, that assaulted nearly every section of the act by reference to American political thought. The Foraker Act, Coll Cuchí concluded, violated America's own "Republican doctrines" and was "an offense to the memory of the fathers of the American Constitution."[14] These kinds of critiques animated much of the pro-statehood Unionist Party cause. In 1907, for instance, the Unionist-led House of Delegates petitioned President Theodore Roosevelt for a new law that would remove legislative functions from the Executive Council, thereby maintaining a separation of powers. The petition pleaded:

The United States which was born of democracy in the remote regions of its Anglo-Saxon culture; which preached democracy through William Penn and Lord Delaware; which through democracy is strong and powerful; which subsists in democracy and which owes its democracy its greatness, will not trample under foot the principles on which its existence and its prominent in the world are based. [. . .] The people of Puerto Rico desire and ask two legislative chambers elected by their votes deposited in the urns. [. . .] This, Sir, is the reform that we demand with frankness. And this will solve our problem, until such time as the Congress of the United States may resolve that we shall enter as a new State in the Union. . . . Mr. President: The day on which the stars of your flag shall shed their light on this land . . . the day on which Puerto Rico shall be truly American . . . on that day you shall be greeted by a chorus of blessings which, spreading through the hundred islands of the Caribbean Sea, will reach the Capitol of Washington, surrounding it with the dazzling nimbus of love and gratitude.[15]

This was only one among many other similar petitions, letters, and pleas.[16] Some were more defiant in tone. In 1909, having faced continued resistance to their requests, the House of Delegates staged a protest by refusing to pass the annual appropriations bill. This stopped the colonial state machinery in its tracks. The House declared: "Our people are not in sympathy with the tyrannical organic law or Foraker Act, and we ask that the law be struck from existence or at least amended to the extent that all the legislative Assembly might be popularly elected. If we were a numerous people we might win our liberty in the same way your people won yours."[17]

Amid the protest, party leaders declared that they were simply enacting the "same principles genuinely proclaimed by the People of the United States in the course of their history and in their governmental practice."[18] But the subsequent row with local authorities summoned only angry responses from Washington. President William H. Taft, familiar with colonial affairs from his time as governor of the Philippines, resorted to stereotype, insisting that the protest further proved that Puerto Ricans should not receive autonomy or statehood. Their impetuous protest proved their "unfitness" and their "ingratitude" to the United States.[19] The delegation of Union Party leaders to Washington (which included Muñoz Rivera and Coll Cuchí) only faced further resistance. When Coll Cuchí tried to convince U.S. congressmen that the Puerto Ricans' protest was honorable and in line with American traditions, one congressman replied: "Young man, you should not try to give lessons to the Congress of the United States about what is liberty and what is tyranny!"[20]

The continued condescension and racial resistance of the U.S. imperial state sparked a new round of indignation, igniting the other path of anti-imperialism: nationalist resistance. Soon after the 1909 appropriations protest by the House of Delegates, Muñoz Rivera publicly declared that the goal of statehood was unattainable. The party needed alternatives.[21] His colleague Rosendo Matienzo Cintrón denounced his original plan for statehood and declared U.S. occupation to be "false Americanization." Shattering the myth of American exceptionalism, he declared that the American flag no longer represented an empire of liberty but instead "represents . . . the same as the flag of King George in the eighteenth century! . . . What a degeneration!"[22] He soon declared that the only solution was national independence. Coll Cuchí, having returned from being scolded in Washington, later helped to form the Nationalist Association of Puerto Rico, which sowed the seeds for the Nationalist Party.[23] In 1922, the Puerto Rican Nationalist Party was officially announced, joining various political actors together under the same political umbrella.

## Boston to Dublin and Back to San Juan

The nationalist anticolonial movement in Puerto Rico was born from the frustrations engendered by American imperialism's own contradictions. But its direction and persistent power derived from other sources. The older generation of Muñoz Rivera, Coll Cuchí, and Cintrón had initially found sources for their protest in America's own traditions and history, but the younger nationalist leader Pedro Albizu Campos—who became the Nationalist Party's president in 1930—looked elsewhere and beyond. In the 1910s he had studied at Harvard University. Across the river from Harvard lay Boston's Irish districts; Albizu Campos there became inspired by the Irish Republican movement Sinn Féin.[24] In Boston he met the Irish leader Eamon de Valera. He also met the Indian patriot philosopher Rabindranath Tagore.[25] Later, in the 1920s, not long before becoming the Nationalist Party's president, he visited the Dominican Republic, which had only just seen the end of American military occupation (1916–24) a few years earlier. There he met Federico Enríquez Carvajal, an intellectual and nationalist who had been president of the Dominican Republic before being replaced by the U.S. military government. Enríquez Carvajal soon became an ally of

Puerto Rican independence. Albizu Campos also traveled to Mexico, Peru, Panama, and Haiti, where he met Haiti's nationalist leaders Pierre Paulie and Jolibois Fils. He went to Venezuela, meeting leaders of the opposition movement against the dictatorial regime of Juan Vicente Gómez. Albizu Campos went to Cuba, where he joined forces with the movement against General Gerardo Machado's dictatorship. In Cuba he also attended the Latin Press Conference of Havana that attracted delegations from around Latin America and from Portugal and Spain. At that conference he gave a speech castigating U.S. imperialism and calling for an immediate end to the U.S. presence in Puerto Rico, Haiti, and the Philippines.[26]

Though Albizu Campos organized with allies across Latin America and the Caribbean, summoning a regional revolutionary tradition that reached back to José Martí and Simón Bolívar, he was also inspired by the Irish. His ideal of national independence for a small island like Puerto Rico, for instance, was partly rooted in the Irish nationalist ideal.[27] So were some of his tactics. In 1932, the Nationalists under Albizu Campos's leadership created their guerrilla army, called the Army of Liberation (or Cadetés de la República). Bearing wooden rifles and donning white trousers and black shirts to "symbolize the nation's mourning over its colonial captivity," the army was modeled after the Irish Citizen Army.[28] And duplicating the Irish socialist James Connolly's plan of issuing bonds in the name of the Republic of Ireland, the party issued bonds to be redeemed upon independence.[29] As the Americans' own discourse had proved a miserable foundation upon which to mount an effective anti-imperialism, Albizu Campos looked elsewhere.

## "Panahon Na!" and the Rising Sun

In 1945, Albizu Campos lay in hospital. He wanted to attend Du Bois's meeting in New York, but his colleague Pinto Gandía went instead. The subsequent collaboration among Pinto Gandía and the others at Du Bois's meeting, including the Philippine delegate to the UN, Carlos Romulo, reminds us of another history of anti-imperialism in the American empire: the history of nationalist resistance in the Philippines. The reason the Philippines had a delegate to the United Nations in the first place was that it had just been granted independence by the United States.

But independence had been hard-won. It is a common myth in the narrative of American imperial exceptionalism that the United States was all too eager to grant independence to the Philippine archipelago, with its seven thousand islands and nine million inhabitants. For, unlike the Puerto Ricans' welcome, the Filipinos' reception to the arrival of the U.S. military during the Spanish-American War had been hostile. A group of landowners, merchants, and urban workers based in Luzon had already joined others around the archipelago to revolt against Spain by the time Admiral George Dewey entered Manila Bay in 1898. Led by General Emilio Aguinaldo, they had declared an independent Philippine Republic with its own constitution and legislature at the town of Malolos. The sudden arrival of the Americans during the Spanish-American War was not a welcome contingency. The result was a war for national liberation. For the Americans, it was another war of conquest. Many of the U.S. soldiers had come from fighting Native Americans on the western frontier. Atrocities proliferated. The U.S. military deployed torturing techniques that would later resurface in Vietnam and Iraq. The primary one was the "water cure." A. F. Miller of the Thirty-Second Volunteer Infantry Regiment explained it: "Now, this is the way we give them the water cure. Lay them on their backs, a man standing on each hand and each foot, then put a round stick in the mouth and pour a pail of water in the mouth and nose, and if they don't give up pour in another pail. They swell up like toads. I'll tell you it's a terrible torture."[30]

By 1902, the Americans officially declared that the war was over. Mission accomplished. But the war had cost some four hundred thousand Filipino lives and the lives of four thousand U.S. soldiers.[31] The atrocities received widespread attention in the United States. Members of the Anti-Imperialist League learned about the use of the water cure from letters that soldiers wrote to family and friends, and subsequently had them published in newspapers.[32] According to the standard narrative, the war and the atrocities flattened Americans' initial taste for overseas colonialism. While the United States maintained sovereignty, the idea of granting independence sooner rather than later took solid root.[33] This narrative also underpins the related tale of American imperial reluctance—namely, while the United States acquired an empire in 1898, it soon gave up and swiftly "gave it away," returning thus to its true anticolonial values.[34] But all of this speaks of only partial truths. Political leaders in the United States, as well as many in the American public, were not always as eager to simply cut and run. While the Democratic Party had since 1912 given lip service to the idea of independence, it too often faced resistance from within as well as without. When soon-to-be president Harding was chairman of the Senate Committee on Territories and Insular Possessions in 1916, he insisted that the

United States could not withdraw from the Philippines.[35] As late as 1922, Franklin Roosevelt wrote: "The vast majority of people in this country, I have always been certain, understand that complete independence for all these peoples is not to be thought of for many years to come."[36] These resistances to independence persisted in various forms throughout the 1920s and even the 1930s. Gallup polls in 1938 showed that 76 percent were against granting independence to the Philippines.[37]

As in Puerto Rico, therefore, local resistance to American colonialism in the Philippines persisted in various forms even after the Philippine-American War officially ended in 1902. One route of anti-imperialism converged with the Puerto Ricans' efforts for statehood. From the outset of U.S. occupation, a small group of Hispanicized, educated, and wealthy merchants in Manila supported annexation to the United States in the form of a fully fledged state.[38] These elites, led by the wealthy doctor and merchant Trinidad Pardo de Tavera, were politically noticeably distinct from the revolutionaries in the countryside. They quickly collaborated with American occupation under the impression that statehood was a real possibility. Some revolutionaries even came to join them after dropping their arms. They formed a political party called the Federal Party, which declared its expectations: "Inspired by the American spirit, adopting the English language, reading and thinking as Americas, the universal belief is that it will be demonstrated to the Republic of the United States, sooner or later, that the Filipinos are worthy and able to form a part of their federation."[39] The Puerto Rican Federal Party took notice of their Filipino counterparts, declaring that they were their natural allies in the statehood cause.[40] In fact, the Filipinos were directly copying their Caribbean colleagues. They first named their party the "Autonomists," borrowing the name from the Puerto Rican elites' political party during Spanish rule (and the anti-monarchical Autonomist movement within Spain). Then, after their Puerto Rican counterparts changed their name to the Federal Party, so too did they.

There was another similarity: the Filipinos' bid for statehood failed, just as the Puerto Ricans' had. For Americans, the racial menace posed by the Philippines was too much. Thus, after many failed attempts, and after some of them experienced the racism of their colonial masters firsthand at the St. Louis Exposition of 1904, the Federals' calls for statehood quieted.[41] The limits of America's empire of liberty became as palpable to them as it was to their pro-annexation Puerto Rican counterparts.

For Filipino anti-imperialists, national independence remained the only route out of imperialism. But even then, there were different steps to take

and interests to follow. The privileged, educated, and wealthy political leaders danced between collaboration and resistance. On the one hand, many
gave up their arms to receive amnesty after the war. They soon found that
proclaiming loyalty to the United States had its privileges. Some were economic. As many of them were landowners or allied with the landed class,
they found the North American market of some value. Other privileges
were political: the new colonial state offered a wealth of positions, all the
way up to national legislator in the Philippine Assembly. On the other
hand, these leaders maintained among themselves that ultimate independence was their goal and, in the meantime, worked tirelessly to obtain more
political autonomy within the imperial apparatus. Colonial politics became
a constant battle between the Filipino political elite and American authorities over local political control, resources, and privileges.[42] Meanwhile the
Filipinos sent independence missions to Washington. In 1919, 1922, 1923,
1924, and 1925 emissaries were sent, however to no avail.[43]

A different series of steps—along with an alternative vision of what
independence would mean—was taken by peasants in the province, the
urban proletariat, and their middle-class allies. These groups continued the
war for national liberation by other means. Some were theatrical. While
the anti-sedition law of 1901 had made talk of Philippine independence
or separation from the United States punishable by death or imprison-
ment, underground plays by Filipino nationalists were staged nonetheless,
narrating final redemption through national independence.[44] Protests and
public demonstrations also proliferated despite the repression. Notably, they
typically took place in August—the month in 1896 when fiery nationalist
Andrés Bonifacio had made his "Cry of Balintawak" against Spanish rule,
initiating the Philippine Revolution against Spain. One such demonstration occurred in 1911, when thirty-five to forty thousand people descended
upon the area north of Manila known as Balintawak. The demonstrators
wore native shirts and red trousers—thus copying the dress of the original
Philippine revolutionary group known as the Katipunan—and marched
to the newly constructed statue of Bonifacio. "Rich and poor, men and
women, old people and children" (as the police report read) cried repeatedly: "Panahon na!" (The time has come). For Tagalogs, the more precise message was clear: Independence now![45] Such demonstrations struck
fear into the constabulary, as well as high American officials, who worried about the so-called "mobs" of "ignorant and uneducated" protesters.
The demonstrations obviously summoned the specter of revolution, or at
least of riot. Each year as August or other important dates approached, the

constabulary had to step up its monitoring of secret societies, while rumors of uprisings circulated among the populace.[46]

The concerns of American authorities were well-founded. Not only was the war fresh in people's minds, but various Filipinos in the countryside were continuing the struggle from underground. As astutely analyzed by Reynaldo Ileto, what the American authorities referred to as criminality or the activity of "fanatic" religious cults was but the war for national liberation carried on by peasants and workers.[47] Continuing the millenarian strands that had been evident during the Philippine-American War, these revolutionary movements articulated a vehement anticolonial nationalism with Spanish Catholicism and Malay-influenced animism. One of them, the Santa Iglesia "cult," was led by Felipe Salvador, a former village chief during Spanish rule and then colonel in General Aguinaldo's revolutionary army. Salvador had fled to the hills after Aguinaldo's capture by American forces and from there upended the complacency of the U.S. regime until his capture and death in 1910. Reminding American forces that their mission had not yet been accomplished, Salvador led an underground revolutionary guerrilla army of at least three hundred men and one hundred rifles and enjoyed an additional fifty thousand followers. He rallied them with visions of a great flood or fire that would wipe out the unfaithful and herald Philippine independence. With independence, land and property would be redistributed. Gold and jewels would fall from the sky. The appearance of Halley's Comet in 1910 heightened the expectation among his followers that independence was near. It was a sign. In the end, though, Salvador was captured and sentenced to death.[48] Later the revolutionary leader Luis Taruc of the guerrilla Huk movement would be rumored to be Salvador's reincarnation.[49] Salvador had returned.

These and many other underground revolutionary movements drew upon local sources: a rich religious and political history of Spanish domination and indigenization. But they were also animated within a global inter-imperial field that included not only the United States but also Japan. Filipinos had a history of reaching out to Japan. During late Spanish rule, major political figures like José Rizal had visited Japan, and others found refuge in Tokyo after fleeing from persecution by Spanish officials. The Katipunan revolutionary movement against Spain had looked to Japan as the most likely champion of Asian liberation against Europe.[50] Accordingly, the Katipunan collaborated with Japanese officials to purchase arms, first during the war against Spain and then against the United States, and Japanese officers advised Aguinaldo's revolutionary government.[51] The connections continued in different guises as U.S. rule proceeded. The victory of Japan over Russia in 1905 was monumental, confirming to Filipinos Japan's status as a great power and animating rumors of a coming war between Japan and the United States. The United States was the "Russia of the Orient," fated to suffer the same fate Russia had suffered in 1905. The fall of the United States would mean an independent Philippines.

Felipe Salvador's uprising in 1910 was fueled not only by the appearance of Halley's Comet; Salvador had been prophesying a war between Japan and America and predicting that arms were on their way from Japan.[52] Even after Salvador's capture, the idea of salvation by way of the Japanese persisted. During the 1910s, peasants in the provinces whispered rumors that Artemio Ricarte, the former revolutionary general (who had been hiding in Hong Kong), was plotting with Tokyo to return to the archipelago with the emperor's armies. The people murmured about all manner of signs, from "the appearance of strange warships off the coasts" to "Japanese spies masquerading as gardeners, peddlers and the like." The Japanese emblem of the rising sun, in Tagalog conception, portrayed a "light in the east" (*liwanag*) and the coming of a redeemer—a narrative that fit well into preexisting millenarian scripts animating local uprisings.[53]

Later, during World War II, the United States would purport to liberate the Philippines from Japan by the valiant return of General Douglas MacArthur. But just a few decades before, in the eyes of revolutionary Filipinos, it was Japan that was to liberate the islands from the United States. In other words, it was Japan that was to end a conquest that had begun with MacArthur's father, General Arthur C. MacArthur, Jr., who had fought in the Philippine-American War, served as military governor-general of the Philippines in 1900, and also sent Filipino revolutionaries to exile in another site visited by the hand of U.S. imperialism: Guam.

## "Neither as Citizens nor as Aliens"

The United States did not only liberate the Philippines from the Japanese empire. In 1944, marines recaptured Guam. Guam had been part of America's Pacific security circuit, which is why the United States had seized it from Spain in 1898. Guam had also been important to Filipino revolutionaries, though for other reasons. In 1901, a key figure of the Philippine revolution, Apolinario Mabini, was deported to Guam for refusing to take the oath of allegiance to the United States. Drafter of the Philippine constitution and foreign minister in Aguinaldo's revolutionary government in 1899, Mabini had been captured and then deported to Guam by none other than General Arthur C. MacArthur, Jr. Other revolutionaries who refused to take the oath were exiled there as well, including General Artemio Ricarte, who, as just seen, would later, in 1911, be rumored to plot with Tokyo to liberate the Philippines from the American yoke. "Take the Oath, or go to Guam" was the mantra in Manila circles at this time.[54]

While in Guam, Mabini remained undeterred, refusing to proclaim allegiance to the United States. And though the Chamorros on whose island he sat did not always present such resistance, they nonetheless engaged in their own form of anti-imperialism. One of the challenges they faced was the peculiar form of colonial government that the United States constructed. Unlike Puerto Rico and the Philippines, Guam became subject to a long period of military rule whereby the U.S. commander of the naval base on the island functioned as colonial governor. This was akin to U.S. military rule over Puerto Rico and the Philippines during the first years of occupation (1898–1900). But whereas Congress gave those colonies organic legislation and hence civil government, Congress deliberately did nothing for Guam, thereby leaving it under the direct control of the navy.[55] It was not until 1950 that Congress legislated an organic act for Guam and gave it a civilian administration—meaning that, from 1898 to 1950, the island was subject to presidential executive order and hence to military rule, a continual transitional state akin to a state of exception. It is in this sense fitting that, in 1946, the United Nations declared navy rule in Guam to be "colonial" and a departure from the "principles of a democratic nation."[56]

In his first instructions to naval officials in Guam, President William McKinley had told them to "win the confidence, respect, and affection of the inhabitants of the Island of Guam" (who numbered over eleven thousand at the time).[57] But what Guam saw instead was direct naval rule whereby colonial governors / naval commanders maintained control autocratically, concentrating legislative, executive, and judicial functions into their own hands and ruling by decree, order, and command. Unlike in Puerto Rico and the Philippines, there were no local political parties or elections—no elective offices whatsoever. The rule of the naval commander was unfettered, leading to multiple directives and laws that regulated religious practices, subsistence production, and land sales (such as forbidding the sale of land without consent of the naval station).[58] The local leadership of Hispanicized Chamorros, some whom had been educated during Spanish rule, were displeased. They initiated movements for reform. One was a petition in 1901 signed by thirty-two Chamorros residing in Agaña. Addressed to the U.S. Congress, it requested that the military government end and be replaced with a "permanent" government. Military government, it said, "is distasteful and highly repugnant to the fundamental principles of civilized government. . . . We believe ourselves fully justified in asking relief from a system of government that subjects a thoroughly loyal people to the absolute rule of a single person." It also asked for representatives of the Congress to come as an investigative commission to ultimately present recommendations to Congress for a "permanent government" that would "enable us to mold our institutions to the American standard, and prepare ourselves and our children for the obligations and the enjoyment of the rights and privileges to which, as loyal subjects of the United States, we feel ourselves rightfully entitled."[59] Many islanders also requested U.S. citizenship. Governor Seaton Schroeder reported to Washington that "admission to United States' citizenship is the desire of a number of persons permanently domiciled in the Island."[60]

But the U.S. Congress did not respond to the petition or the requests, as any congressional action on Guam's status might upset its function as a naval base accountable only to the U.S. president. While the Treaty of Paris specified that Congress should decide on territorial status, it never specified *when* it had to do so. As long as Congress remained silent, military occupation under the direction of the U.S. president could proceed undeterred, and indefinitely. And it did. Meanwhile, younger leaders were cultivating new skills as clerks in the colonial bureaucracy or avid students of the English language. After the early petitions, therefore, agitation started anew. Beginning in 1917, members of the Guam Congress, an appointed advisory body with no legislative power, renewed demands that the U.S. Congress take action on Guam's status. Their campaign revealed a new cosmopolitan outlook. For example, they typically redeployed the Americans' discourse, turning America's history, traditions, and ideas against their rulers. Their 1917 plea to a gathering of naval officers and the governor beseeched an end to "servitor" status:

> The Chamorro people only desire, not their independence, but the reform of their lawful rights . . . and that their Government be adjusted to the principle established by the immortal Washington, liberator of the great nation that now rules our destinies in this Island. [. . .] It is high time that there be granted to the people, respectful, loyal and devoted to the great American nation, the same rights have been granted to the different States,

territories and possessions. [. . .] That is to say, the defining of the status of Chamorro people, in a word, that we may know whether we are to be members of the American people or their servitors, that the principles established in this Island, and that the redemption promised in the proclamation of the immortal President McKinley and the first Governor of this Island be fulfilled. [. . .] We heartily acclaim the great American Republic, our President Wilson, the imperishable memory of Washington, Monroe, Lincoln and McKinley, our beloved and esteemed Governor Smith, the American Colony in this Island and the Chamorro people rescued by America from the bonds of servitude.[61]

Their reference here to the rights of America's "different States, territories and possessions" was precisely motivated. Guam congressmen were aware of America's other possessions and that Congress had legislated for them. If for them, why not for us? This was the other characteristic of their anti-imperial agitation: the Chamorros were often inspired by and drew upon their colonial counterparts' statuses.

To be sure, a year later, another petition was penned by Guam congressmen requesting that "His Excellency the President and the Honorable Congress of the United States . . . define and resolve definitely the civil status and political inhabitants of Guam, by issuing an adequate law . . . equally to that of the Philippine Islands and Porto Rico [sic]."[62] The Guam congressmen also seized upon the fact that the United States had acquired the Virgin Islands and had quickly enacted organic legislation for the new colony. When a party of visiting U.S. congressmen landed on Guam in 1925 during their Pacific tour of inspection, Don Atanasio T. Perez, a member of the Guam Congress who had also been a clerk in the governor's office for more than twenty years, referred to the Virgin Islands to ask not only for organic legislation but also for citizenship: "The Chamorros are neither citizens nor aliens—they are truly without a country. When the United States acquired sovereignty over the Virgin Islands, citizenship was immediately conferred on the inhabitants, but Guam, for 26 years an American possession, has not yet been granted that privilege."[63] Meanwhile, another member of the Guam Congress, Ramon Sablan—who had been one of the few students sent to the United States—made appeals to Uncle Sam's wider imperial system. "It is our fervent and constant prayer that the American Congress will enact some legislation by which, we trust, we may come nearer to Uncle Sam, to understand him more, and to appreciate him more, and that we may partake of his bountiful generosity that he has so unselfishly and nobly extended to his other possessions."[64] In the case of Guam, therefore, anti-imperialism meant demands for *more* imperialism. The initial request was only that U.S. Congress legislate a colonial government rather than keep the island in a perpetual state of military emergency ruled by military power alone. It says something about the power of U.S. imperialism that the Chamorros' request was only for the very sort of colonial government Puerto Ricans and Filipinos had been fighting against for decades. But it also says something about the possible varieties of anti-imperialism and the crossing of empires.

Chapter 5

# U.S. Anti-imperialism and the Mexican Revolution

ALAN KNIGHT

This chapter analyses U.S. anti-imperialism in the context of the Mexican Revolution: it starts with a quick synopsis of U.S.-Mexican relations in the period (1910–40); addresses what "anti-imperialism" involves; and evaluates the role of "anti-imperialism" in that relationship.[1]

In 1911 the long-standing dictatorship of Porfirio Díaz—the Porfiriato—fell victim to a popular rebellion that signaled the start of the Mexican Revolution, a major "social" revolution worthy of comparison with the "great" revolutions of world history. The revolution comprised a decade of armed conflict, followed by twenty years of state building and social reform, during which Mexico changed substantially. However, from the 1940s, revolutionary momentum stalled; a new political generation took power, committed to new policies of urbanization, industrialization, and capital accumulation, which were in no sense "revolutionary." So, the revolution was the project—radical, reformist, and nationalist—of a generation, 1910–40. As such, it presented challenges to the United States, which in the same period graduated from being a regional power (committed, at least since 1898, to an expansionist policy in the Americas and beyond) to achieve the status of a global power, economically dominant and, by 1940, on the brink of global hegemony. In Mexico, the United States faced a politically, economically, and culturally very different neighbor, with which it shared a porous two-thousand-mile border. By 1910 over a billion dollars had been invested in Mexico; some fifty thousand Americans lived there; and Mexico figured prominently in U.S. geopolitical thinking. During the Díaz dictatorship relations had been good; once the regime consolidated (receiving the imprimatur of U.S. recognition in 1878), American investment, both direct and indirect, flowed south; and the southern flank of the United States seemed both stable and secure. As Archibald Cary Coolidge oleaginously observed in 1908, Mexico "is in a peaceful, prosperous condition and on excellent terms with her northern sister."[2] Or, we could say, the Porfiriato afforded a congenial context for foreign trade and investment, meshing foreign and Mexican (elite) interests to mutual advantage; indeed, anti-imperialists, like Carl Schurz, eager to be rid of the Philippines, praised the Porfiriato as a potential model for the insular possessions of the United States—since it offered stability and profit without the burden of formal empire.[3]

The revolution changed all that. Prolonged civil war threatened U.S. interests (both lives and property) and jeopardized the security of the border. Coinciding with the First World War, the revolution also stimulated fears of European and Japanese involvement (no matter that those fears were often exaggerated).[4] And, as the new revolutionary regime assumed power, it posed a nationalist challenge to U.S. economic interests. Indeed, Robert Freeman Smith qualifies the revolution as "the first important challenge to the world of the industrial-creditor, and capitalistic, nations made by an underdeveloped nation trying to assert control over its economy and reform its internal system."[5] While allegations of rampant anti-American xenophobia have been much exaggerated (by both hyperbolic observers and gullible historians), the new regime, wedded to the radical constitution of 1917, set about reformulating Mexico's relationship with foreign interests, rewriting the generous terms on which the Porfirian "collaborating elite" had struck mutually beneficial bargains with those interests.[6] The constitution redefined property rights, depriving foreign investors of their ownership of subsoil assets (minerals and hydrocarbons), while mandating a sweeping land reform, which affected both foreign and Mexican landowners. Land reform peaked in the 1930s, a decade that also witnessed the nationalization of the Anglo-American petroleum companies. At the same time, oil and mining taxes rose. The revolution also spawned a militant labor movement, which confronted foreign enterprises; while, to the consternation of American Catholics, revolutionary anticlericalism targeted Mexico's mighty Catholic Church; and revolutionary nationalism more broadly asserted Mexican values in reaction against the supposed *malinchismo* of the Porfirian old regime (and its "collaborating elite").[7]

After 1920, therefore, the United States faced a Mexico that was less violent and unstable, but more nationalistic and reformist; rowdy neighbors had been replaced by worrisome radicals, whom some Americans—including Secretaries of State Lansing and Hull—saw as a nest of Bolshevism in the Americas;[8] and such fears were exacerbated by Mexico's supposed export of the communist contagion elsewhere in the hemisphere, chiefly Central America.[9] Of course, those traits that conservatives and businessmen deplored also appealed to American radicals, who flocked to Mexico, drawn by the country's political and cultural experimentation.[10] "Mexico becomes a cult," Hubert Herring noted; "Greenwich Village moves to Taxco."[11] Mexico in the 1920s thus prefigured Cuba in the 1960s and Nicaragua in the 1980s. If Mexico offered the first radical Third World challenge to First World capitalist hegemony, it also became the first major Third World destination of radical-chic political tourists.[12]

The revolution thus polarized informed opinion in the United States, provoking strong views both for and against. Some U.S. actors advocated "imperialist" policies toward Mexico, while some were vocally "anti-imperialist." But what did these labels and attitudes denote? "Anti-imperialism," of course, is negatively defined—by what it is against.[13] It may also be associated with certain positive goals and values, such as democracy, self-determination, pacifism, and international solidarity, as well as isolationism, racial superiority, and (in this case, Protestant) Christianity. So, as I note in conclusion, discursive explanations of imperialism and anti-imperialism—which stress the autonomous power of ideas—are plainly inadequate, since much the same ideas (such as race, Providence, and the civilizing mission) can be found on both sides of the imperialist/anti-imperialist divide.

If, therefore, we are to address (negative) "anti-imperialism," we have to consider the (positive) imperialism it opposed. And, in both cases, we should distinguish between those actors, ideas, programs, movements that proudly display the "anti-imperialist" label (or something very like it), and those to which we, as historians, may apply the label retrospectively, even if the historical actors defined themselves otherwise.[14] There is little point concentrating solely on the (self-styled) "Anti-Imperialist League," which went into terminal decline in the 1900s and by the time of the Mexican Revolution was all but defunct.[15] To do so would be to reproduce the myopic perspective of Samuel F. Bemis, for whom American imperialism was a "great aberration," confined to a few short years after 1898;[16] from which we would conclude that anti-imperialism too was comparably brief, unless it lumbered on, laboring under some kind of illusory "false consciousness."

A broader and better perspective would embrace later phases of U.S. imperialism and, logically, the anti-imperialism that they prompted, even if terminology differed and no self-styled "anti-imperialist" movement occurred.[17] Indeed, we could posit a spectrum of "anti-imperialism," ranging from movements that are explicitly "anti-imperialist" (that being their self-styled raison d'être), through those that adopt different, but closely comparable, stances,[18] to those that have "anti-imperialist" consequences, without adopting any explicit program that can be so described (an extreme example would be the Ku Klux Klan, which, viscerally hostile to the Catholic Church, aligned with the "anti-imperialist," pro-Mexican lobby of the later 1920s).[19] Indeed, we could go beyond "movements" altogether and identify those structural *circumstances* that inhibited imperialist ventures (for example: military calculation, global geopolitics, business trends, and electoral considerations). Such circumstances are particularly important if (like me) you think that historical processes are often structurally determined—by "grand impersonal forces," if you like—and that notions of "agency," though fashionable, are often exaggerated. Anti-imperialism, in this perspective, is the product of compelling circumstance rather than collective agency.

*Contra* Bemis, many analyses of imperialism correctly cast the analytical net wider than formal colonies, addressing a vast range of informal relations that replicate characteristics of formal colonialism without involving the legality and/or longevity of colonial rule.[20] When U.S. forces occupied Mexico's main port of Veracruz in 1914, they did not create a formal colony, but they behaved much like "colonists" (as they did for longer in Cuba, Haiti, Nicaragua, Panama, and the Dominican Republic; and, in one case—Puerto Rico—a form of colonialism was permanently established). A similar intervention occurred in 1916–17, when Pershing's forces fruitlessly pursued Pancho Villa through the hills of Chihuahua for a year. In both cases, the United States committed sizable forces to an armed intervention that brought a chunk of Mexican territory under de facto U.S. control, even if it did not lead to permanent colonial rule. Unlike, for example, U.S. belligerence in World Wars I and II (which stemmed from great-power geopolitics), these were unilateral coercive interventions by a great power in the affairs of a weaker power, which could not reciprocate.

Furthermore, these interventions were designed not to counter an existential threat to the United States (again, compare 1941), but rather to achieve political change in Mexico: to overthrow President Huerta in 1914, and to eliminate a troublesome armed faction in 1916. Needless to say, Mexico entertained no ambitions of unseating President Wilson, nor did it consider sending troops into Texas to halt the wholesale lynching of Mexicans in 1915.[21] As General Hugh L. Scott, a major player in U.S.-Mexican diplomacy, observed: the United States would not allow a foreign army to go "sloshing around in our country three hundred miles from the border."[22] But, like the Melians of 416 BC, the Mexicans of AD 1916 had little or no choice.[23] The marked inequality of the bilateral relationship—a hallmark of imperialism—is obvious, although, like some "obvious" features of history, it is occasionally overlooked.

Apart from coercion, powerful nations, or their citizens, can exert pressure on weaker nations by diplomatic pressure (for example, by offering recognition conditional on nonreciprocal concessions: as the United States did to Huerta in 1913, to Carranza in 1915, and to Obregón in 1923); by controlling access to arms (again, a policy adopted toward Huerta, Carranza, and Obregón); by offering or denying credit, market access, or foreign investment;[24] and by supporting—sometimes with direct subventions—preferred political clients. While the first two methods are limited to sovereign states (in this case, the United States), the third and fourth can also be deployed by powerful private interests; thus, the U.S. oil companies—apart from pressuring the U.S. government to adopt preferred policies—also flexed their economic muscles and, in the case of Manuel Peláez, funded a regional warlord in opposition to an uncongenial central government.[25] Again, the bilateral relationship was highly unequal, an example, perhaps, of structural dependency. After all, Mexico could not deploy economic sanctions against the United States, nor did Mexico fund armed factions in the United States[26]—though it did, I shall note, engage in effective political lobbying.

This distinction between, on the one hand, direct and coercive imperialism and, on the other, indirect and pacific/noncoercive imperialism is pertinent to Wilson's foreign policy.[27] It is also relevant to revolutionary Mexico, which experienced both forms of imperialism at the hands of the United States, roughly following the chronological pattern already outlined: during the armed revolution (1910–20) both forms were apparent, including two serious armed interventions, Veracruz in 1914 and the Pershing Expedition in 1916–17; after 1920 armed intervention ceased (although the threat remained until 1927), but indirect, pacific intervention became more significant—and, indeed, more effective. For, in Mexico (and

elsewhere), armed interventions in revolutions are risky and counterproductive, since revolutions are highly fluid, unpredictable, and uncontrollable; in contrast, the indirect and pacific exercise of power—the carrot
rather than the stick, collaborative liaisons, "empire by invitation"[28]—can
be more successful and durable. One reason is that armed intervention
excites strong opposition, both at home and abroad, while the deployment
of indirect pacific power—bribes, investment, commercial incentives, even
the creation of client factions and states—is more reliable and less offensive.
Cuba, for example, swapped U.S. imperialism (1898–1934) for U.S. hegemony (1934–59);[29] arguably, the second was less costly and more conducive
to U.S. national interests. In Mexico, a similar transition occurred, as the
coercive interventions of the 1910s gave way to the more pacific policies
of the 1920s and 1930s, especially following 1927, when Dwight Morrow became U.S. ambassador. In one sense, Morrow was the archetypal
dollar-diplomacy diplomat—a banker who skillfully deployed American
"soft power" to bend Mexico to American wishes[30]—but in another he was
an effective *anti*-imperialist, since he eschewed the use of force, relying on
the carrot rather than the stick, thus prefiguring the Good Neighbor Policy
of the 1930s.[31] Of course, Morrow upheld both U.S. national interests and
the broad structures of North American capitalism (of which he was a
pillar); in this sense, he was an exemplary agent of U.S. imperialism.[32] But
his methods, being "soft" and noncoercive, were very different from those
espoused by red-blooded exponents of U.S. imperialism (such as Theodore
Roosevelt or Morrow's immediate predecessor, James Sheffield).

Both variants of "imperialism" can provoke anti-imperialism (in the
"imperialist" country—i.e., the United States).[33] But coercive interventions
tend to be more provocative; they are obvious, they hog the headlines,[34]
and they involve the sacrifice of both blood and treasure. Public opinion
is more likely to be aroused when major crises occur, especially crises that
carry the risk of war—thus of casualties and even conscription.[35] Noncoercive interventions are more discreet (they involve underlying structural "dependency" rather than bloody conjunctural conflicts); they do not
usually claim (American) lives or incur obvious material losses; they are
more easily normalized and naturalized. Anti-imperialist opposition may
still surface—in opposition to financial and diplomatic arm-twisting, or to
political clientelism—but it is likely to be less strident and effective. Thus,
the character and impact of anti-imperialism depend crucially on the kind
of imperialism being opposed. And, in the Mexican case, both kinds were
evident: coercive interventions during 1910–20, noncoercive after 1920.

First, therefore, the armed revolution: Veracruz (1914) and the Punitive Expedition (1916–17). The Veracruz occupation was an unusual case, which produced unusual responses. It was undertaken for "progressive" reasons:[36] Woodrow Wilson, having concluded that Mexico's counter-revolutionary dictator, Victoriano Huerta—"a desperate brute" leading a "government of butchers," as Wilson put it[37]—had to be removed, grew impatient at the slow progress of the anti-Huerta rebels, led by Venustiano Carranza. Wilson's stance alarmed big business, which favored Huerta, the "iron hand" that Mexico, a mongrel nation descending the slippery slope of anarchy, desperately needed.[38] Wilson's impatience was fanned by the biased reports of "special representative" John Lind, who underestimated the capacity of the rebels, while overestimating both Huerta's strength and the connivance of the British with the Huerta regime.[39] Wilson took casuistical advantage of a supposed insult to the American flag to order the occupation of Veracruz, naively assuming that the landing would be unopposed; in fact, it cost 19 American lives and 126 Mexican. Thus chastened,[40] Wilson reined in his more belligerent—but, I repeat, *progressively* belligerent—instincts and ordered the U.S. forces to sit in Veracruz, where they behaved like model colonial rulers, cleaning up the fetid port, and evicting the large vulture population.[41] There would be no advance on Mexico City, as jingoistic critics advocated.[42]

Wilson's decision made eminent sense: the rebels were now clearly winning (though not thanks to the American occupation, which may even have been counterproductive);[43] and he had no intention of yielding to critics who advocated a full-scale invasion, a repeat of 1846–48. Thus, Veracruz was a very limited intervention, undertaken for progressive, pro-revolutionary motives. Hence, the public reaction was mixed and confused. Outright pacifists and anti-imperialists, who deplored any deployment of U.S. armed force overseas, opposed the occupation, and were relieved when Wilson called a halt. Now, pacifist and anti-imperialist opinion swung behind the president, who was berated by jingoistic critics favoring a more aggressive policy, an American occupation, a rerun of Polk's war of aggression.[44] The chief advocates of such a policy were either doctrinaire imperialists (such as Roosevelt) or barons of the yellow press (such as Hearst); they were not, by and large, U.S. businesses with interests in Mexico, for whom an armed intervention by the United States was seriously risky.[45]

These reactions followed political, ideological, and sectional lines. Wilson's cabinet was divided, but—for the time being—Mexican policy was chiefly determined by the president, who, suspicious of State Department professionals he considered too tied to big business and the old diplomacy, bypassed normal channels and relied on "special emissaries" to report on Mexico.[46] A key element was the effective lobbying of the revolutionaries themselves, who formed a discreetly influential component of the anti-imperialist—what could be called the "hands-off-Mexico"—coalition. Mexico had a long history of lobbying in the United States, and it tended to be more successful than the kind of lobbying—often including arm-twisting and hectoring—that American diplomatic representatives under-took in Mexico (consider the long history from Poinsett through Trist and Henry Lane Wilson to John Gavin and, just recently, Carlos Pascual).[47]

There were three reasons for this. First, as the dominant power, the United States was disposed to bully, while the Mexicans knew they had to coax and cajole. Second, recurrent U.S. bullying heightened Mexican sen-sibilities, such that U.S. ambassadors often came to Mexico trailing baggage of which they were scarcely aware: the classic case was Josephus Daniels, appointed ambassador by FDR in 1933, and who, nineteen years previously, had served as secretary of the navy at the time of the Veracruz invasion.[48] The Mexicans, of course, remembered this; FDR—president in 1933 and undersecretary of the navy in 1914—appears to have forgotten it.[49] We have here a variety of Chalmers Johnson's "blowback"—a delayed and, for the Americans, unforeseen reaction to previous imperialist interventions.[50] Third, Mexican knowledge of the United States exceeded U.S. knowledge about Mexico (this imbalance is now a structural feature of the two popu-lations, not just a quirk of their elites). As the old adage of Archilochus (famously recycled by Isaiah Berlin) puts it: "the fox knows many things, the hedgehog knows one big thing."[51] The one big thing that Mexico knew was that it had to deal with the United States; and, since armed confrontation with the *coloso del norte* could be only a desperate last re-sort, diplomacy and politicking were vital.[52] Mexico's representatives in the United States were well chosen (for example: Luis Cabrera, Alberto Pani, Ramón Beteta, Francisco Castillo Nájera). The United States, on the other hand, knew many things—it was an emergent global power with growing commitments not just in the Americas but also Europe and Asia—hence it lacked focus; or it focused, as President Wilson did after 1914, on events far from Mexico. Furthermore, Mexico was not at the top of U.S. diplomatic postings. At least two ambassadors in the "revolutionary" period—Henry Wilson (1910–13) and Sheffield (1924–27)—were disastrous: Wilson con-nived at the overthrow and killing of President Madero, winning himself a privileged place in the pantheon of Mexican historical villains; Sheffield, an obtuse racist (even by the lax standards of the 1920s), bullied and blustered until he was finally removed in disgrace.[53]

At the critical juncture of 1913–14, as President Wilson wrestled with the dilemma of the revolution, the revolutionaries sent Luis Cabrera to put their case in Washington.[54] As a corporate lawyer, Cabrera had represented the big Anglo-American Tlahualilo (cotton) Company; yet he also had good revolutionary credentials, having been an early proponent of land reform in Congress.[55] In conversation with Wilson, Cabrera stressed that the revolution was no narrow political battle, still less an opportunistic squabble for power; rather, it embodied the social aspirations of the Mexican people, including their aspiration for land (in which respect Cabrera was right; hence he had the advantage of spinning a true story). He managed to convince Wilson, who came to see the Mexican Revolution in grand historical terms; no people, he asserted, had won freedom without fighting for it themselves; "liberty is always attained by the forces working below by the great movement of the people."[56] Wilson discerned parallels between the Mexican and the French revolutions,[57] and between Mexican reformism and contemporary American Progressivism, of which, of course, he was a leading protagonist.[58] These parallels were not fanciful; Mexican reformers borrowed from Progressivism, just as American Progressives— politicians, journalists, and "public intellectuals"—sympathized with the Mexican Revolution: examples would include John Kenneth Turner, Lincoln Steffens, Carleton Beals, and Ernest Gruening. Critics of Wilson believed him to be naive and deluded, incapable of distinguishing between principled reform and common banditry; the British regarded Cabrera's notions as nonsensical.[59] But Mexican lobbying, designed to present the revolution in a favorable light, was successful, and helped massage American opinion, above all the official opinion of the administration. A similar ploy was evident twenty years later, when Mexican officials strove to sell their radical and nationalist reforms: Cardenismo was no more than a Mexican "New Deal"; President Cárdenas, far from being a Bolshevik, was a grateful disciple of FDR.[60] Imitation was the sincerest form of flattery.

Beyond the narrow circle of government, American public opinion also played a part, although how big a part it is hard to say.[61] The voluminous Wilson archive suggests ample support for the president's policy: first, his refusal to recognize the usurper Huerta (a decision that could be construed as either—mildly—interventionist or noninterventionist);[62] second, his lifting of the arms embargo in February 1914 (when, Link records, "reaction in the US was generally favorable");[63] third, and most contentiously, his decision to seize Veracruz, in order to ensure Huerta's downfall;[64] and, fourth, most clearly of all, his refusal to march on Mexico City, which would have turned an intervention into a full-scale invasion. This final— negative, self-denying, hence "anti-imperialist"—decision was the clearest litmus test of American opinion toward Mexico. A minority—headed by the likes of Hearst, Roosevelt, and Lodge[65]—favored a forward policy, involving some kind of protectorate or even annexation. Such a policy would be humanitarian (it would help the poor Mexicans: here we detect echoes of Cuba and 1898; indeed, it seems that veterans of that "splendid little war" tended to be more belligerent than, for example, Civil War veterans);[66] in terms of national interest, it would protect American lives in Mexico or along the border (Governor Colquitt of Texas was strident for intervention);[67] and, since the original casus belli—soon to be lost in the fog of war—was a supposed insult to the American flag, intervention was consistent with national honor.[68] Invasion was rarely advocated as means to protect American material assets: the big oil and mining interests elicited scant sympathy; and those interests, by and large, did not favor American invasion anyway, preferring a collaborative liaison with Mexican elites and a strong-arm Mexican government, like Díaz's or Huerta's. Their critique of Wilson was not that he intervened, but that he intervened on the wrong side (that of the revolution).

For its part, the anti-interventionist, anti-imperialist chorus decried the alleged warmongering of the big trusts, proclaimed, sometimes in Christian terms, the supreme value of peace, and echoed the president's opinion that the Mexican Revolution represented a legitimate struggle for sociopolitical reform that should be allowed to proceed without—potentially costly and bloody—U.S. involvement.[69] Protestant missionaries to Mexico, along with their home churches, tended to favor the revolution: it was progressive, it opposed the Catholic Church, and it included a few Protestants in its ranks.[70] Anti-Semites also denounced a war fought in the interests of "Jewish usury."[71] The anti-imperialists welcomed Wilson's opposition to Huerta's military dictatorship (opposition that could be construed as cautious progressive interference) but opposed belligerent intervention. Civil War veterans seem to have swung in this direction; and the South (not counting, that is, the rabble-rousing governor of Texas) generally supported Wilson—he was one of their own, the South did not love northeastern big business, and southerners recoiled from the notion of U.S. troops marching south to straighten out a supposedly backward society of feudal landlords and exploited peons.[72]

Two years later a comparable scenario emerged, at least on the American side. In defeat, Pancho Villa, previously something of a favorite of the United States,[73] turned against his erstwhile partners, killing several Americans at Santa Ysabel and raiding Columbus, New Mexico. Wilson, running for reelection, could hardly sit on his hands: after Columbus, "it was clear that nothing short of the punishment of Villa and his followers would satisfy public sentiment."[74] Wilson therefore dispatched the so-called Punitive Expedition into Mexico, with the aim of capturing or killing Villa and ending his anti-American vendetta; unlike the Veracruz fiasco of 1914, the decision was, in the circumstances, rational and measured. Again, Wilson intervened in Mexico—perhaps behaved in a modestly imperialistic fashion—and, again, his critics (including Lieutenant George Patton, serving in the ranks of the expedition) blamed him for being too pusillanimous, for hedging the mission with restrictions, for being overly considerate of Mexican sensibilities: Wilson "has not the soul of a louse, nor the mind of a worm. Or the backbone of a jellyfish."[75] Again, progressive and pacifist opinion (including organized labor) aligned with, not against, Wilson, especially after the clash of American and Mexican (government) forces at Carrizal in June 1916.[76] Wilson's sternest critics stood on the Republican Right and among business interests who, irrespective of border security, saw in the Punitive Expedition a stick to beat the Democratic administration, and a lever to shift the Carranza government, then drawing up a radical new constitution. Even the hawks in the Wilson administration—which tended to veer to the right over time—hoped that the expedition could be used to nudge the Carranza government in a more moderate direction.[77] But Carranza resisted U.S. pressure, and he could not control his own radicals anyway. The Punitive Expedition came home two weeks before the constitution was completed: it had neither caught nor killed Villa, nor had it moderated the constitution; but it helped ensure Wilson's reelection, and, no less important, it stopped short of a full-scale war with Mexico, which gave the United States a free hand for its European policy.

With the entry of the United States into the Great War, Mexico slipped down the political agenda. The new U.S. ambassador, Henry P. Fletcher, had a clear brief: "during the war my job was to keep Mexico quiet, and it was done."[78] Gradually, Mexico recovered from the ravages of the revolution, and the new regime—reformist, nationalist, and populist—was consolidated, under the leadership of a coterie of hard-headed practical *políticos*, products of the revolutionary struggle. The United States now faced not uncontrollable violent upheaval, but an increasingly stable

regime, whose policies—land and labor reform, anticlericalism and economic nationalism—affected U.S. interests in Mexico, as well as American
public opinion. By expropriating land, regulating and taxing the oil industry, and favoring organized labor, the regime offended American business, provoking strenuous criticism and demands for U.S. intervention (of
various kinds); furthermore, the U.S. administrations of the "long 1920s"
(1921–33) were Republican, beholden to business, and unsympathetic—
or downright antagonistic—to Mexican nationalism and reformism. The
Progressive Era was over, and Coolidge's "return to normalcy" included
a "normalization" of U.S.-Mexican relations according to "the dominant economic philosophy and the reinforcing legal framework of the
industrial-creditor nations": thus, respect for property rights and contracts,
payment of claims for damages, and the potential resort to extraterritorial
jurisdiction (in defiance of the Calvo doctrine).[79] By way of levering the
Mexicans, the U.S. government had several tools, which now acted upon
a single regime, not a congeries of warring factions. This shift, coinciding with the shift from Democratic to Republican policy, gave the U.S.
greater capacity to bend Mexico to its will.

In the United States, extremist voices—of widely different pitch and
timbre—called for a hard-line policy toward Mexico, implying the use of
force if necessary. Faced by a so-called "confiscatory" constitution, the oil
interests, who found a strident spokesman in Senator Albert B. Fall of New
Mexico, wanted to coerce Mexico into amending its new Carta Magna.[80]
Wilson was now preoccupied with Europe—the war and then the peace
settlement—and Mexican policy fell into the hands of State Department
professionals and "dollar-a-year" businessmen, sympathetic to business and
favoring a hard line toward Mexico.[81] The AFL, meanwhile, was shackled
by its "almost total submission . . . to the foreign policy of the Wilson
administration."[82] But calls for outright intervention never looked like succeeding: Wilson was opposed; and the United States was too busy intervening elsewhere—hence, not for the last time, global circumstances played
to Mexican advantage. The incoming Harding administration was more
sympathetic ("the policy of the Harding administration was to do with
alacrity whatever business wanted to have done");[83] but Senator Fall was
disgraced by the Teapot Dome scandal (which lowered the already low
standing of the oil companies in American eyes); and, in 1927, Hearst was
similarly disgraced by his crass attempt to implicate several U.S. senators in
a spurious Mexican bribery scandal.[84] Meanwhile, the Obregón administration (1920–24), desperate for U.S. recognition, credit, trade, and investment,

sought to placate the U.S. government, without sacrificing the basic principles of the constitution. Oil remained a key issue, never fully resolved, subject to successive spats and piecemeal compromises. But neither side wanted to stop the oil flowing.

Also among the hawks were both U.S. property-owners affected by the Mexican land reform, who now enjoyed corporate organization,[85] and, especially after 1926, when a major Catholic ("Cristero") rebellion broke out in center-west Mexico, the Catholic Church, which denounced Mexico's godless state and the persecutions—the "Herodian massacres"—it inflicted on the faithful (which, in American penny-dreadfuls, were graphically described and greatly exaggerated).[86] Unlike land and oil, anticlericalism was hard to fudge; furthermore, the alleged victims were rarely Americans, but overwhelmingly Mexicans. A final grievance, especially in U.S. government circles, was Mexico's Central American policy, where support for Nicaragua's liberals—then in rebellion against a conservative regime backed by U.S. marines—could be depicted as proxies of Mexican Bolshevism.[87] Indeed, the onset of the early Cold War—evident in the red scare and Palmer raids of 1918–19—afforded the anti-Mexican lobby a conveniently Manichaean script, which, like many yet to come (e.g., Guatemala, 1954), bore a tenuous relation to reality.[88] In 1925, when these several American grievances came together, Secretary of State Kellogg read Mexico the riot act: "the government of Mexico," he blustered, "is now on trial before the world."[89] Briefly, realistic fears of armed intervention revived, for the last time in the history of U.S.-Mexican relations.

But, chiefly for reasons of realpolitik and national interest, no intervention ensued. The Mexicans made judicious compromises; the egregious U.S. ambassador was recalled (and thereby hangs a tale);[90] while the U.S. government, however vexed by Mexico, shrank from a costly armed intervention. Indeed, the incoming Hoover administration was seeking to extricate the United States from costly and counterproductive interventions in Haiti, the Dominican Republic, and Nicaragua.[91] Well before FDR took office, the vague lineaments of the Good Neighbor Policy could already be discerned: a retreat from armed intervention (ergo, from coercive imperialism) and a reliance on forms of "soft power," broadly defined.

One of the first and most successful exponents of "soft power" (then referred to as "ham-and-eggs-diplomacy") was Dwight Morrow, sent to Mexico as ambassador in 1927.[92] Facing Catholic insurrection and a stalled economy, President Calles was disposed to temper his early radicalism and seek a settlement with the United States. Morrow too was an urbane and experienced banker (and a much better diplomat than many of the career officials who had strutted their stuff in Mexico City); he showed a genuine interest in Mexican art and culture (then undergoing a renaissance); and he was adept at public relations—famously arranging for Charles Lindbergh to fly to Mexico. As a banker Morrow could talk high finance with Calles (which Calles liked: he was an unusually numerate and cerebral revolutionary); Morrow also represented a powerful economic lobby that favored détente with Mexico. A prosperous and stable Mexico could pay its debts, including the claims for damages that had accrued during the revolution. Mexico's creditors therefore supported Morrow in his efforts at rapprochement. The oil companies remained hawkish, but their leverage was declining, not least because they were fast switching their assets to Venezuela.[93] Hearst, too, was a declining force. Morrow may have engaged, creatively, in cultural diplomacy (the softest of soft power, we might say), but the chief driver of his policy was politico-economic: Mexico wanted credit, trade, and investment, and U.S. business, marshaled by the bankers, broadly agreed. Significantly, the 1920s saw a renewal of U.S. direct investment in Mexico, now directed not toward the old "enclaves" of oil and mining, but toward manufacturing, which catered to Mexico's growing domestic market.[94] Thus, the main driver toward détente was U.S. business, which saw aggressive intervention as risky and counterproductive.

In the United States, too, "soft power" played its part. Mexico was never a major item of U.S. public concern. Ernest Angell doubted that "one voter in a thousand in this country cares a straw about the independence, political or economic, of the weaker Central and South American countries."[95] Public concern mounted when war and intervention loomed—when, in other words, Mexico became a matter of life and death—but, despite the short-lived intervention scare of 1927, this was rarely the case during the long 1920s. The debate over Mexico was conducted within a narrow coterie of politicians, businessmen (with Mexican interests), and public intellectuals. There were two partial exceptions: the Catholic Church defended its persecuted confreres in Mexico, calling for sanctions against Calles's anticlerical regime; and organized labor, chiefly the AFL, countered with support for the regime, which was closely allied with Mexico's chief labor confederation, the CROM.[96] When the Catholics called for intervention, Gompers and Green, on behalf of the AFL, advocated—in so many words—"hands off Mexico." The fact that the (interventionist) Catholic Church failed and the (anti-interventionist) AFL succeeded does not mean that their lobbying determined the outcome—détente rather than intervention, "soft power" rather than coercion. That outcome stemmed from the logic of the bilateral relationship and the balance of power among the interested parties, business especially. The AFL, whose chief concern was domestic (curtailing the influx of cheap labor from Mexico),[97] was lucky to back a winner, but did not itself cause the win. After all, the Coolidge administration did not take its cues from organized labor.

As for the church, while the militants grabbed the headlines, more sober heads favored a cautious approach, as did the Vatican. Moderate priests, like Father John Burke, played an important role in brokering a truce between church and state in 1929, in which they were materially aided by Ambassador Morrow.[98] A truce was possible because Calles had concluded that outright victory was unattainable. Both the Catholic Church and American business were divided: not regarding broad *ends* (the church wanted anticlericalism halted, business wanted to trade and invest profitably), but rather regarding the *means* to be employed. Hard-line interventionists (or "imperialists"?), like the Catholic ultras and the oil companies, favored threats and coercion; anti-interventionists (anti-imperialists? "soft imperialists"?), including Father Burke and Ambassador Morrow, preferred dialogue and blandishments. The ambivalent parentheses highlight the ambivalence of "imperialism": while there was broad consensus (rejected only by a leftist minority) that the United States had the right and even the duty to tell Mexico how to behave—in respect of its domestic policy toward religion and/or American economic interests—there was no consensus regarding how that should be done: by force (which would seem to be unequivocally "imperialist") or by noncoercive methods (whose "imperialist" status would depend on one's definition of imperialism).

Furthermore, when the Catholic Church berated Mexico, it automatically produced—by a kind of Newtonian political physics—a countervailing response from anti-Catholic, chiefly Protestant, opinion. The 1920s was a period of relative economic consensus, in which "status" politics (what today might be called "cultural" politics) bulked large.[99] If the Catholic Church denounced godless Mexico, and appeared to dictate U.S. policy toward that country, anti-Catholics, more numerous and no less vocal, rallied to the Mexican cause. Hence the anomalous case of the KKK aligning itself with U.S. progressives, leftists, and bankers in advocating "hands off Mexico."[100] And, with the caveat that the dynamics of foreign policy remain murky, it seems that U.S. presidents were leery of the Catholic lobby.[101]

Lastly, we turn to those progressives and leftists (leaving aside Gompers and the AFL, whose support for Mexico was far from disinterested).

Progressive/leftist support for revolutionary Mexico was not new; it had contributed to Wilson's pro-revolutionary policy in the 1910s. By the 1920s the Left languished under a Republican administration, and its radical outpourings were probably counterproductive, in policy terms.[102] The State Department, the oilmen, and the bankers shared the belief that U.S. leftists offered nothing more than a "monolithic misperception of Mexico."[103] In fact, the pro-Mexican Left was diverse and divided among itself; but it was quite numerous, well informed, and well organized, in part thanks, yet again, to assiduous Mexican lobbying and public relations. It was certainly more numerous and well informed than, say, its British counterpart: during the 1920s and '30s the United States produced, for example, Frank Tannenbaum, Bertram Wolfe, Ernest Gruening, Carleton Beals, and Stuart Chase; while, in contrast, the contribution of British public intellectuals to Mexican matters involved D. H. Lawrence, Aldous Huxley, Graham Greene, and Evelyn Waugh.[104] Prominent American Mexico-watchers were typically leftist "social scientists," while the British were more conservative, literary, and Catholic. Indeed, the British tended to revile not just the corrupt, authoritarian, and hypocritical revolution, but also the shoddy, kitsch folkloric culture it promoted. The American Left identified with both the revolution and Mexico's indigenous culture, then undergoing an officially sanctioned revival; and they did a good deal to popularize—and market—Mexico's cultural products, ranging from indigenous artisanry to Hollywood stars.[105] Again, it is impossible to establish any clear causal link between cultural advocacy and American policy;[106] but even if strident pro-Mexican leftism (ergo "anti-imperialism") had scant impact on policy making, nevertheless the reformulation of Mexico's "image"—from one dominated by bloody bandits and backward peons, to one that included music, murals, Hollywood pinups, and indigenous handicrafts—may well have softened that image and favored U.S.-Mexican détente. After all, it was easier to whip up warlike feelings against the Mexico of Victoriano Huerta and Pancho Villa than that of Diego Rivera and Dolores del Río.

The American Left's love affair with Mexico is, therefore, an interesting theme within U.S. political and cultural history; it also provides an insight into Mexican cultivation of U.S. intellectual interlocutors, long predating the intense pre-NAFTA lobbying undertaken by President Salinas in 1988–94. But it is hard to say how consequential it was. Woodrow Wilson paid close attention to intellectual opinion—after all, he was an academic himself, and he appears to have read his correspondence carefully. Harding and Coolidge were cast in a different mold (Hoover less so; but by 1928 the diplomatic die had been cast—in favor of bilateral peace and rapprochement—and, after October 1929, the president had other things to worry about). The pro-Mexican opinions of Gruening, Tannenbaum, and Beals helped mold sympathetic leftist opinion in the United States, and so President Calles cultivated Gruening in the 1920s, as President Cárdenas did Tannenbaum in the 1930s. But leftist opinion did not govern U.S. policy, nor did it effectively rein in right-wing interventionism: "Presidents Herbert Hoover and Franklin D. Roosevelt finally restored the marines to their barracks on behalf of a 'good neighbor' policy, not because anti-imperialists had produced a public uproar but because the United States had discerned more sophisticated means to accomplish national objectives."[107]

By way of postscript, we should consider the 1930s: the last decade of the revolution, when social reform peaked, coinciding—providentially—with a progressive administration in the United States. The Cárdenas government, as it pushed the revolution to the left, was at pains to reassure the United States: its reforms were a Mexican version of the New Deal; its stance on the threat of international fascism was firmly progressive. FDR was duly reassured, and his ambassador to Mexico, Josephus Daniels, who, having arrived under a cloud, strove to appease the Cárdenas administration. Even when Cárdenas expropriated the Anglo-American oil companies in 1938, hard-headed ministers like Hans Morgenthau favored conciliation: the United States should continue purchasing Mexican silver, he told Roosevelt, or "we're just going to wake up and find inside a year that Italy, Germany, and Japan have taken over Mexico."[108]

Like Calles before him, Cárdenas benefited from a chorus of progressive acolytes in the United States: John Lewis and the CIO replicated—in more radical fashion—the labor solidarity that Gompers and the AFL had pioneered;[109] leftists like William Townsend, Nathaniel and Sylvia Weyl, and, above all, Frank Tannenbaum, gilded President Cárdenas's reputation in the United States.[110] Their task was not to defend Cárdenas from U.S. intervention in Mexico (since the Good Neighbor Policy vetoed any such intervention); rather, they offered positive endorsement of Cardenista social reform, countering critics on the right who accused the Mexican president of being a Communist or fellow-traveler. Such critics included senior journalists like Frank Kluckhohn of the *New York Times*, as well as the hired hacks of the oil companies, who reacted to expropriation by mounting a sustained propaganda drive against Mexico.[111] Both sides traded familiar notions and polemics: Mexican nationalism and social reform, their political connotations, and how the United States should interpret and react to these developments. Again, in the 1930s as in the 1920s, the outcomes were determined less by intellectual advocacy than by politico-economic logic: who was in power, how they viewed social reform (and the vociferous oil lobby), and the pressure of global circumstances. Since FDR and the New Deal administration was in power (and Daniels occupied the U.S. embassy in Mexico City); since, on balance, they favored social reform and had no love for the oil companies; and since the threat of Japan and the Axis powers made good relations with a progressive Mexico essential, détente, rather than conflict, and collaboration, rather than coercion, were the inevitable, "overdetermined" consequences for U.S.-Mexican relations, even after the oil expropriation. "Today," Hubert Herring rejoiced, "the clamor of outraged oil operators and of William Randolph Hearst is drowned in the chorus of good neighborliness."[112] The pro-Mexican polemics of Townsend or Tannenbaum may have helped, at the margin, but they were hardly crucial; just as Kluckhohn's diatribes against Cárdenas failed to budge U.S. policy. Policy makers, then and now, can usually find both intellectual justification for their policies and intellectual justifiers who will do their bidding. But we should not mistake the talking head for the policy-making brain.

I have taken a broad approach to imperialism and anti-imperialism, defining the former to include informal as well as formal relations of control and coercion across national boundaries. Several conclusions emerge. First, whatever the United States did, when confronting the Mexican Revolution, some kind of interference, intervention, or outright invasion was inevitable; the question was the degree and character of the involvement. This inevitability reflected the asymmetrical relationship (hence, to state the obvious: the United States did things to Mexico—and contemplated doing other things—that Mexico could never reciprocate). Second, during the armed revolution, Wilson twice intervened coercively, though, on both occasions, he failed. Although anti-interventionist, hence anti-imperialist, voices were raised against Wilson, especially in April 1914, the president erred on the side of nonintervention (that is, anti-imperialism), especially when his policy is compared to a counterfactual Rooseveltian alternative. Out of office, Roosevelt no longer carried a big stick, and he felt no need to speak softly. He blustered, but to no avail. Wilson refrained from outright invasion and was reelected in 1916. However, thirdly, the failure of interventionism/imperialism, as advocated by Roosevelt, Lodge, Hearst, and the oil companies, was due less to any public outcry—though that no doubt counted—than to the circumstances of the time: the threatening global geostrategic context (especially after 1914); the sobering lessons of

U.S. interventions elsewhere in the circum-Caribbean; and the awareness that Mexico was a much tougher nut to crack than Haiti, Nicaragua, or the Dominican Republic. Circumstances chiefly determined the tolerant, hence "anti-imperialist," policy of the United States toward the revolution. Again, in the 1930s, global geostrategic considerations, coupled with the Good Neighbor Policy, mandated a moderate, noninterventionist, non-imperialistic policy. The same was not true for Guatemala in 1954, Cuba after 1959, or Nicaragua after 1979.

Fourth, what of "agency?" Clearly, *official* agency—the decision-making of Wilson or FDR—was key, even if it is difficult to unravel exactly how and why decisions were made. But, again, the chief determinants of policy making seem to be circumstantial, or even structural. Organized lobbies counted: big business, in particular, had a strong interest in Mexico (to the tune of a billion dollars of investment); so did organized labor and the Catholic Church. Self-proclaimed peace activists—some also soi-disant anti-imperialists—came some way behind, at least in terms of noise and clout. However, these diverse lobbies, while contributing to the (domestic) circumstances in which decisions were taken, displayed two weaknesses. First, they were often divided among themselves (I will stress business divisions in a moment); and second, they tended to cancel each other out. The Catholic Church divided into moderate and belligerent wings; and Catholic calls for intervention elicited anti-Catholic—often forthrightly Protestant—rejoinders of "hands off Mexico." Such canceling out created a political space in which decision makers, especially foreign-policy experts, could operate with "relative autonomy." The executive led, Congress tended to follow.[113] Furthermore, the American electorate rarely expressed a coherent or explicit opinion on Mexico: only at fleeting moments of crisis, such as 1914 and 1916, was public opinion aroused by Mexican events; on those occasions, the public mood tended to be pacific—against war, against imperialism. But these sentiments were latent; they afforded a backdrop for policy, but they did not determine how policy was made or how the story would unfold.

Two more of the "usual suspects" can be exonerated. No major ethnic lobby influenced U.S. policy toward Mexico. The Mexican population in the United States grew rapidly in these decades, but it was not an enfranchised, politically vocal lobby; its chief contribution to U.S.-Mexican relations was its support for the revolution, which made border surveillance more difficult, arms smuggling easier. More important was Mexican political lobbying (and espionage), both in the United States and at home: an old and practiced art, which brought results—that is, which helped deter U.S. interventionism—during crucial moments like 1914 or 1927, while, over time, fostering cosier relations with American labor unions, intellectuals, and cultural tourists.

In addition, broad attitudes do not explain U.S. anti-imperialism (in respect of Mexico). Racism was endemic and spanned the political spectrum: some racists advocated invasion and annexation, and some racists opposed just that, on the grounds that the United States should not absorb a degenerate mongrel population.[114] Pejorative opinions about Mexicans, whether racist or not, were similarly ambivalent: if the Mexicans were incapable of democracy, was that an argument for steering well clear of Mexican involvements, or taking the country by the scruff of its dirty neck and dragging it into the democratic nursery?[115] Religion, too, was ambivalent: Catholics were divided; and many Protestants took an interest in Mexico chiefly because they disagreed with the Catholics. Since He worked in a mysterious way, God could be invoked for any number of contradictory policies: churchmen, like Samuel Guy Inman, might oppose intervention and imperialism, but Taft could invoke the "God of Israel" as a warning to the wayward Mexicans.[116] Kipling could be quoted to justify both intervention and nonintervention.[117]

It therefore serves little purpose to explain imperialism and its critics in terms of grand disembodied discursive "isms" (racism, paternalism, anti-Semitism). They are too mushy to produce definable consequences. Much more consequential, when it comes to agency, were organized collective actors. In particular, U.S. business played a key role, especially after 1920 when Mexico stabilized and the Republicans took power. Unlike the geopolitical fantasists (such as Theodore Roosevelt), businessmen were pragmatic, preoccupied by the bottom line: "the grand schemes of the power-dreamers— the wars, the colonies, the bluffs, the endless projects—alternately irritated and frightened them."[118] Big business, too, was divided, between hawks and doves, oilmen and bankers. But the doves/bankers came out on top, because, once again, circumstances favored them: the Mexican economy revived, which meant that it needed trade, investment, and credit, while it promised healthy profits. The oil lobby, along with Hearst, lost ground.

But this leaves the relationship of business to imperialism (and anti-imperialism) moot. Was Morrow an *anti*-imperialist who worked for détente, thus averting possible intervention; or was he an imperialist who promoted U.S. interests (not least business interests) in Mexico, while helping to deradicalize the revolution? He was both, and he could be both because "imperialism"—and, logically, "anti-imperialism"—assumed different forms. A narrow emphasis on formal—essentially coercive—imperialism would absolve Morrow of the anti-imperialist charge; a broader, more inclusive definition, would make him an effective proponent of imperialism, who preferred the carrot to the stick, "soft" to "hard power," the development of *doux commerce* to the dispatching of gunboats. Beisner, in his study of the 1898 anti-imperialists, suggests that "the dominant purpose of the anti-imperialist movement was to chart a cheaper and less blatant path to empire."[119] Subsequent "anti-imperialism" had a similar role, at least with regard to Mexico. The United States desisted from armed intervention and, during the 1920s, pursued détente and renewed "collaboration" not least because American capitalists favored such policies; big business, we could say, was the biggest force for anti-imperialism. Once Huerta had gone down fighting, the best bet for business was a renewed collaborative bargain, not invasion and annexation; and geopolitical imperatives strongly reinforced these conclusions. As far as coercive imperialism is concerned, therefore, circumstances and structures counted for more than attitudes or agency: in respect of Mexico, coercive imperialism failed—was abandoned or never attempted—because the major actors in the U.S. political economy and policy-making circles saw it as costly and counterproductive, and because they could effectively protect their interests (and also the "national interest"?) by other, cheaper and better, means. Both means and interests were arguably "imperialistic" (in the broad sense): they combined to create the American empire of the twentieth century. But being "softer" and subtler, these means to maintain empire were much more sustainable.

Chapter 6

# Anti-imperialism, Missionary Work, and the King-Crane Commission

USSAMA MAKDISI

It is one of the ironies of recent history that anti-Americanism finds its most intense expression in the Middle East. A century ago a quite different—and in its broad outlines essentially positive—picture of America was widely propagated in the region. It was in the Ottoman Empire, after all, that American missionaries founded the most important American overseas universities of their age; and it was there that the Wilsonian moment reached its great crucible, as Arab and Egyptian nationalists, like Korean, Indian, and Chinese nationalists, grasped a notion of American exceptionalism to forestall or bring to an end their fate as people marked for colonization.[1]

But this late nineteenth- and early twentieth-century image of America as anti-imperial was based largely on an idealization of the United States and an acceptance at face value of various American official and missionary pronouncements about America's commitment to liberty and freedom.[2] Instead of presiding over military or economic interests in the nineteenth-century Middle East, American missionaries possessed cultural ones. They founded educational institutions that dotted the Ottoman landscape. It was not difficult, therefore, for them to proffer a notion of mission work as strictly nonpolitical. For example, the missionary Edwin Munsell Bliss wrote in the introduction to his 1896 book about the massacres of

Armenians in the Ottoman Empire that American missionaries "have no political ends to serve; we want not a square foot of the Sultan's domains, but we stand, as we have always stood, for freedom for the oppressed, for the right of every man to worship his God in the light of his own conscience."[3] Missionaries, of course, had long been warned by their sending organizations to avoid overt political entanglements. One of their mantras was "disinterested benevolence."[4] The influential mid-nineteenth-century secretary of the American Board of Commissioners for Foreign Missions (ABCFM) Rufus Anderson had famously insisted that missionaries under his authority should refrain from secular attachments and from feelings of racial superiority over non-Americans.[5] In the twentieth century, as the tide of nationalism swelled and as the epoch of decolonization approached, missionaries and their supporters were even keener to disassociate missionary work from colonialism. "Through their schools, their printing press, their general interest in the largely forgotten culture of the Arab world, as well as through their deep concern with spiritual uplift," asserted the soon-to-be president of the American University of Beirut Stephen Penrose in 1941, "[the missionaries] kindled a vital flame."[6] The son and grandson of American missionaries in the Middle East, William Eddy, a U.S. intelligence operative who acted as a translator for a meeting between U.S. president Franklin Delano Roosevelt and the Saudi monarch Ibn Saud in 1945, insisted that American missionaries in the Middle East had built up among Arabs a "reservoir of good will."[7]

But these professions of benevolence and innocence are disingenuous. The notion that the United States enjoyed a "reservoir of good will" may have been true, but this should not obscure the degree to which this reservoir itself was built to accomplish specific missionary goals. Nor, of course, should the existence of such a reservoir—that is, the cultural effects and achievements of American missionary work—be confused with anti-imperialist principles or liberal convictions on the part of American missionaries themselves. From the outset of American missionary work in the Ottoman Empire in the early nineteenth century, missionaries and their sending organizations had explicitly desired the overthrow of Islam.[8] More to the point, they had also overwhelmingly supported the colonialism of Protestant nations, whether this was the expansion of the continental United States itself or the British conquest of Egypt in 1882. The American missionary Samuel Zwemer, for example, in a speech before the Empire Club in Toronto in November 1921, admitted openly that he "identified my life with the life of the British empire."[9] Indeed, far from being anti-imperialist in an obvious or ideological sense, American missionaries in the nineteenth-century Ottoman Empire were quite deeply entrenched in a language of religious and racial paternalism. They accepted and propagated a vision of racial hierarchies in which Americans and America were preeminent.

This chapter evokes the prehistory of American imperialism in the Middle East that became manifest after 1948. It does not fundamentally dispute the idea of a "reservoir of good will." It does, however, point to the evangelical and racialist foundations of this reservoir. It suggests, moreover, that missionary thought contributed to a distinctive discourse of benevolent, and allegedly anti-imperialist, American *intervention* in the Middle East that cohered during and immediately following the First World War. In particular, it examines one of the great anticolonial documents of its age, namely the report of the American Section of Inter-allied Commission of Mandates in Turkey, popularly known as the King-Crane commission of 1919. As much as it was radically anticolonial in the case of Palestine, the King-Crane commission report was also radically interventionist in the case of Armenia. The report legitimated the idea of Western mandates over the peoples of the Middle East at the same time that it sought to imbue these mandates with an anti-imperialist ethos. This ethos was plainly contradictory to the colonial ambitions of both Britain and France, and it was unacceptable to the U.S. government itself. The suppression of the King-Crane commission report set the stage for the transition of a missionary-dominated story of U.S.-Arab relations (which itself changed dramatically across the nineteenth century) into a far more bitter story of Western, and ultimately U.S., hegemony in the modern Middle East.

## American Mission to the Middle East: Race and Empire

At the heart of the American missionary story to the Middle East lay anti-liberalism and empire.[10] The ABCFM—the most prominent and influential American foreign missionary society of the nineteenth century—emerged out of a reactionary intellectual movement in New England history. Dominated by conservative Congregationalists, the American Board was deeply opposed to the so-called liberal "heresy" of Unitarianism in Boston. It was also virulently opposed to Catholicism. But this conservatism has to be measured against the fact that the American Board also deplored what it regarded as the "sinful" treatment of the Indians and worked aggressively to assimilate them into white society. Like few other contemporary American organizations, the American Board grappled with and rejected exterminationist settler colonialism. It fought publicly against the "removal" of American Indians from the Eastern Seaboard of the United States. It and the missionaries it sent forth into the world became exemplars of an assimilationist settler colonialism, with its core conviction that *defeated* Indian communities could be incorporated into an overwhelmingly white, but ideally Christian, body politic if Indians subjected themselves to utter cultural and religious transformation.[11] The Presbyterian missionary to the Indians David Brainerd was a role model for the American Board—his hagiography by Jonathan Edwards was one that its missionaries not only studied at their seminary at Andover, but also took with them and read in the Ottoman Empire.

From the outset of their mission, the relationship between empire and missions was an ambivalent one for American Protestant missionaries. Like their British counterparts of that period, they saw the emergence of the British Empire, and the access its control of lands in the East provided for proselytization, to be evidence of God's favor. They were thus not "antiimperial" in any normative sense. They were, however, steeped in a tradition that saw in Catholic empire, and its allegedly forced conversion of native populations, particularly in Latin America, damning evidence of the depravity and falsity of Catholicism. Similarly, they viewed the Ottoman Empire as indolent and as inherently illegitimate because it was "Mohammedan." This, then, is the context within which to understand the first mission to the Holy Land launched by the American Board in 1819. From the outset, there was a clear missionary spiritual belligerence aimed at defeating, pulling down, and destroying the Ottoman Empire. Moreover, although the missionaries despised Islam as a religion of the sword, and denigrated Muhammad, whom they referred to, of course, as the "false prophet," it was Eastern Christian ecclesiastics—Maronites, Greek Orthodox, and Armenians—who very quickly bore the brunt of missionary antagonism.

American Board missionaries, in any event, initially sought out Jerusalem, but ended up in 1823 settling in Beirut, then a small walled town in the Ottoman province of Sidon. Because they spoke English, were Protestant, and were protected by British diplomats, the missionaries were initially known as al-Inkiliz, or the "English." They held, like virtually all nineteenth-century Western missionaries, paternalistic attitudes concerning the natives of the empire. They categorized the Arabic-speaking inhabitants as infidels, heathens, or "nominal" Christians. American missionaries opened the first school for girls in the Ottoman Empire in 1834 as an integral part of a civilizing mission; like natives all around the world, Eastern women and men were expected to change the way they dressed, the way they ate, the way they raised families, and above all the manner in which they prayed to a monotheistic God.[12]

But unlike many Protestant missions in an age of empire, the American Board missionaries worked in an environment where they could not rely on the coercive power of a state. Crusading rhetoric did not translate into an actual crusade. Denial of the legitimacy of Eastern faith was effectively countered by an Eastern denial of the viability, legitimacy, and meaning of an unrooted evangelical faith. From the beginning of Protestant missionary work in the Ottoman Empire, there was stubborn and overwhelming resistance, led by Eastern churches, to the proselytization of American missionaries. By midcentury, some missionaries recognized that the way forward in the Ottoman Empire lay in secular cooperation and education and not religious confrontation with local society. They were driven mostly by their inability to make significant conversions. They were also influenced by the U.S. Civil War, which dramatically reduced funding for overseas mission work, by the advent of biblical higher criticism, and by the earlier deportation of American Indians from the state of Georgia and the consequent shattering of the American Board's fantasy of an interracial Christian commonwealth in the United States. Above all, they were confronted by the outbreak of a sectarian war in Ottoman Lebanon in 1860 that left the American mission in tatters. A change was needed. Some American missionaries pushed for the establishment of a new and largely secularized institution of higher education.[13]

The establishment of institutions such as the Syrian Protestant College in Beirut in 1866 coincided with the advent of Arabic newspapers and scientific journals, many of which were founded by men who had worked with or taught alongside missionaries.[14] Together, these gave widest currency to a more constructive American missionary relationship to the Ottoman Empire, centered on the idea of modern education. Like Cyrus Hamlin's Robert College in Istanbul, the Syrian college in Beirut was independent from the American Board from the outset. Like Robert College, it reflected an attempt to cater to an obvious desire for education in the empire. Unlike Robert College, however, it created a medical school and offered instruction in Arabic literature and history in addition to ethics. There was, in addition, no seminary attached to the college. Proselytizing was relegated in importance, though as the name of the institution clearly indicated, it nevertheless remained an ultimate goal.

The founding president of the Syrian Protestant College, Daniel Bliss, declared in 1871 that "this College is for all conditions and classes of men without regard to colour, nationality, race or religion. A man white, black, or yellow; Christian, Jew, Mohammedan or heathen, may enter and enjoy all the advantages of this institution for three, four or eight years; and go out believing in one God, in many Gods, or in no God. But," Bliss insisted, "it will be impossible for anyone to continue with us long without knowing what we believe to be the truth and our reasons for that belief."[15] I have pointed out elsewhere how profoundly ambiguous was Bliss's sentiment. On the one hand, he accepted the idea that conversion in the East had to work though persuasion, not brute power. Bliss's admission that his educational enterprise might not yield immediate missionary fruits, and that it might end up confirming non-Christian and non-Protestant ways of thinking about the divine, was quite instructive. On the other hand, he also spoke at a moment when the American mission in Syria had reached an evangelical dead-end and where military power was simply not an option afforded to American missionaries. The American Board in Boston, moreover, had by the time of Bliss's statement washed its hands of the Native Americans and their conversion—note the absence of "red" in Bliss's deployment of the quintessentially *American* racial categories of "yellow," "white," and "black," none of which were salient in an Ottoman context— and when American missionaries in the Middle East increasingly identified themselves (and were identified) as "American" and subscribed to racialized notions of paternalism.[16]

## The Politics of American Sympathy

It was as if there were two American missions in the late empire: one that was slowly, and with difficulty, accommodating itself to the multireligious reality of the empire, most noticeable in Beirut at the Syrian Protestant College, and that was working to protect and expand its now huge investment in buildings, printing presses, schools, and people, whether Syrians, Egyptians, Armenians, or Alevis.[17] The other was still committed and working—in different ways—to overthrow Muslim Ottoman rule at the earliest opportunity.

A fundamental irony of the missionary situation in the late Ottoman Empire was thus expressed: on the one hand, the advent of secularized institutions of higher education in the Middle East unquestionably increased the prestige, reach, and significance of American missionaries in the region even if it effectively entailed the end of uncompromising evangelical mission work. On the other hand, this major shift was accompanied by a noticeable hardening of racial and nationalist sentiment and practice among American missionaries in the late nineteenth century.[18] These sentiments were infused and shaped by the militant enthusiasm of a new generation of Protestant missionaries working in the shadow of the greatest Western imperial expansion in history. For example, the enthusiastic American missionary embrace of the British invasion of Egypt in 1882 was one clear indication of the degree to which evangelicals openly identified with what they saw as a Protestant imperial power.[19] Once and for all, American men and women were eager to topple what they saw as the false prophet's hold on millions of Turkish and Arabic-speaking people. The shift to secular education also saw missionaries parlay their extensive experience in the field for positions as modern, objective interpreters of "Arab" and "Turkish" and "Armenian" races. Several missionaries, such as Henry Harris Jessup and Samuel Zwemer, metamorphosed into modern Orientalists. Knowledge of the Arab world, while clearly more evident than in the early days of mission, remained for the most part a means to overthrow its dominant religion.[20]

This new form of modern Protestant Orientalist militancy was given additional impetus by the Ottoman state's repression of Bulgarian revolutionaries in 1876 and its persecution of the Armenians in 1895 and 1896, and then again in 1915. The British statesman William Gladstone was revered in Anglo-American evangelical circles for his stand in 1876 against the so-called "Bulgarian horrors," for which he denounced the Turks as an "anti-human specimen of humanity."[21] The subsequent Ottoman slaughter of the Armenians, in fact, galvanized an extraordinary campaign in American Sunday schools, churches, and benevolent associations on behalf of "innocent" and "primitive" Armenians ("primitive" in a sympathetic, biblical manner as opposed to being despised "nominal" Christians as they had been previously described). This humanitarian campaign united famous suffragists such as Frances Willard with missionaries such as James Barton, who became a major force in a global missionary movement; it was built squarely on an opposition between a humane and civilized Anglo-American Christianity and a barbaric, fanatical, and misogynistic Islam.[22] A politics of sympathy predicated on a deep religious hostility to Islam— but not Muslims as individuals—laid the basis for a movement that would ultimately seek to remake explicitly the political map of the Middle East in the aftermath of the First World War. This sympathy almost always overlooked the existence of tens of thousands of Muslim victims of acts of brutality across the Balkans in this period, let alone what was happening within the United States itself to the Indians and of course the terror of the Jim Crow South.

However, the unmitigated evangelical hostility to the figure of the cruel and "unspeakable" Turk was not paralleled by the emergence of a similar specifically anti-Arab discourse. If anything, the renewed hostility to the figure of the Turk overshadowed but by no means eliminated an increasingly obvious discourse that singled out the "Syrians" as a promising, eager, if impatient race. The long-serving missionary to Syria Henry Harris Jessup wrote, for instance, about the beauty of the language and literature of the "Arab race."[23] He insisted that missionary work augmented "the finer qualities of the Syrian character, their courtesy and hospitality, their sympathy with the sorrowing and the bereaved, their loyalty to the family and home," while he hoped that the promise of religious liberty in the wake of the Young Turk revolution of 1908 might well ameliorate the "defects" of the Syrian people.[24] Such paternalism was substantially different from the overt hostility to the "Turkish race" or to ubiquitous missionary references to "Moslem fanaticism."[25]

Anti-Turkish animus also overshadowed the tentative efforts of some missionaries such as Howard Bliss, who succeeded his father Daniel to the presidency of the Syrian Protestant College in 1902, Charles Watson, who founded the American University in Cairo in 1920, and Caleb Gates, who was the head of Robert College in Istanbul, to come to terms with a dawning nationalist age. Bliss, for example, became deeply aware of the enduring presence of a majority of Muslims in the Middle East and the need for a new, more tolerant and understanding approach toward them. "We have drawn inferences from isolated passages of the Koran apart from their context," he wrote in 1913, "while repudiating a like process when applied to our Bible." Bliss urged his fellow Christians to "drop the whole vocabulary of war."[26] He famously noted in 1920 that the "modern missionary" was one who "prays for all men with a new sympathy—for all mosques and temples and synagogues as well as for all churches."[27] As much as these men were wedded to their racial paternalism and to what amounted to racially segregated institutions, they did, at least, see the writing on the wall. A constructive American presence in the region could not depend on minorities; it had to reach out to the Muslim Arab majority and come to some sort of modus vivendi with them. Luminaries of the American missionary presence such as Bliss and Watson reflected a moment of deepening ecumenism *within* the global Protestant missionary movement that was showcased at the 1910 World Missionary Conference in Edinburgh.

But this ecumenism also accepted the reality of Anglo-American imperialism, embraced the idea of a hierarchy of civilizations, and, in the face of emerging nationalist movements around the world, specifically disavowed at Edinburgh "political agitation" and instead preached obedience to "settled government."[28] In the Middle East, most Protestant missionaries were not anti-imperialist in any formal sense. The head of the ABCFM James Barton, for instance, believed in 1915 that the "modern" missionary was one who abjured sectarianism within Christianity in order to focus on "world-conquest."[29] Most missionaries remained committed to "Anglo-Saxon power."[30] During the First World War, as the Ottoman Empire appeared on the verge of collapse, missionaries indulged in what historian Joseph Grabill memorably described as fantasies of "Protestant diplomacy" that sought to redraw the political map of the Middle East.[31] Barton, for instance, having urged "aggressive conquest" in 1915, turned in 1918 to contemplating how the Ottoman Empire might be colonized, and how the United States might take a leading role in the making of a new post-Ottoman Middle East, albeit as an allegedly benevolent steward of the Armenian people in the aftermath of genocide. "It is natural," emphasized Barton, "that again attention should turn to the United States as the country that has demonstrated its ability to give good, safe local government to an Asiatic people and prepare them for self-government." Barton referred to the American conquest of the Philippines and Puerto Rico to make his point that the United States possessed a unique "reputation for [disinterested] colonization."[32]

## The Contradictions of the 1919 King-Crane Commission

The evolution and contradictions of this modern missionary Orientalism and its relationship to empire can be seen most clearly in the King-Crane commission of inquiry sent to Palestine and Syria in 1919 in order to exemplify the workings and vitality of the newly established League of Nations. The commission was allegedly the brainchild of Howard Bliss, who represented Syrians at the Paris Peace Conference of 1919 in sympathetic yet deeply paternalistic terms. Appearing on the afternoon of February 13 before Woodrow Wilson, Lloyd George, Georges Clemenceau, and Italian prime minister Vittorio Orlando, Bliss stood with a missionary sympathy for the Arabs. Like almost all missionaries in the region, he did not actively champion Arab independence, nor did he embrace Zionism. But he did represent one strand of the legacy of one hundred years of mission work among the peoples of the Middle East, a century that had changed profoundly both Arabs and the Americans among them. Bliss knew that he had a precious opportunity to demonstrate the purpose of the modern American missionary. He was brief and to the point. "Mr. President, Gentlemen," Bliss began, "I shall not detain you long. My deep interest in the people of Syria, irrespective of race, creed or condition, bred from a long residence among them—in fact I was born on Mt. Lebanon—is my only excuse for detaining you at all."

Drawing on Wilsonian language and on various allied promises to the Arabs, Bliss pleaded "on behalf of the people of Syria"—they, after all, were not allowed to represent themselves formally at the conference. He criticized Turkish policies that had long oppressed the region, an outlook undoubtedly meeting with the unanimous approval of all the powerful men in the chamber. His deep paternalism regarding the Syrians, whom he claimed were a "loveable" but defective "race" and who had to be treated with "sympathy, firmness, and patience" and guided "into a capacity for self-determination," fit perfectly with Wilson's own attitude toward Mexicans, Haitians, and Filipinos. Bliss spoke also about the need for an "absolute separation between religion and the state" and about how the allies and the United States had worked together "for the establishment of freedom of the world." These sentiments too would not have caused any consternation among either the British or the French. But far more significantly, he asked for "an Inter-Allied or a Neutral Commission, or a Mixed Commission, be sent to Syria—including Lebanon—to express in a perfectly untrammeled way their [the Syrian people's] political wishes and aspirations, viz: as to what form of government they desire and as to what Power, if any, should be their Mandatory Protecting Power."[33]

Such a commission was ultimately created with the approval of President Wilson and despite the wishes of the French and the British. Its formal name was the American Section of the Inter-allied Commission on Mandates in Turkey. It was charged by Wilson "to acquaint itself as intimately as possible with the sentiments of the people of these regions with regards to the future administration of their affairs."[34] The commission was meant to reconcile the notion of self-determination with that of "mandates." According to Article 22 of the League of Nations, mandates constituted a "sacred trust of civilisation" that had to guide native peoples "not yet able to stand by themselves under the strenuous conditions of the modern world."[35] The two imperial powers of Britain and France, however, had already secretly partitioned the Ottoman Empire according to the 1916 Sykes-Picot agreement. Britain, in addition, had also issued the 1917 Balfour Declaration. The commission, in any case, has become known after its two American commissioners, Henry King, who was at the time the president of Oberlin College (with its own radical abolitionist roots), and Charles Crane, a philanthropist, closely tied to the missionary establishment, a contributor to President Woodrow Wilson's campaign, and heir to the Chicago-based Crane plumbing fortune.

The departure of the King-Crane commission for the region reflected a moment of new and intense American diplomatic involvement in Middle Eastern affairs. Wilson, after all, was a towering figure at the Paris peace conference. He blessed the disastrous Greek invasion of Izmir in May 1919. He also flirted with the idea of an American mandate over Armenia (and ultimately sent in August 1919 an American military commission, the Harbord Commission, to investigate the feasibility of an American mandate over Armenia).[36] The King-Crane commission propagated a notion of "disinterested" American benevolence in order to advocate a direct U.S. role in determining the future of the post-Ottoman Middle East. The commission, for example, insisted that the "American People had no political ambitions in Europe or the Near East; preferring, if that were possible[,] to keep clear of all European, Asian, or African entanglements, but nevertheless sincerely desiring the most permanent peace . . ., recogniz[ing] that they cannot altogether avoid responsibility for just settlements among the nations following the war, and under the League of Nations."[37] The commissioners, moreover, upheld the fiction that the mandate system was an alternative to "colonies in the old-sense," and repeatedly stressed that their task was simply to comply with Article 22 of the League of Nations, that is to ultimately recommend a Western power best suited for the arduous task of trusteeship over native peoples.

Although it worked within the confines of the incipient mandatory regime, the King-Crane commission did suggest a fundamental break with European colonialism that went far beyond anything that American diplomacy in 1919 was willing or able to countenance. The American report, in other words, had radical implications that clearly indicate it was *not* an expression of Western imperialism. Rather, it represented a secularization of an American missionary approach to the Middle East. Its religion was Wilsonianism. As a result of its travel to Palestine and Syria in June and July 1919, and the scores of interviews it held in both areas, the commission was unquestionably a watershed in international affairs: it was the first such international commission that asked indigenous populations how they envisioned their own *political* future (as opposed to the Congress of Berlin, or, more pertinently, the Sykes-Picot agreement, or the Philippine Commission that had been established as part of a U.S. pacification campaign against Filipino nationalists). The tenor of the report was distinctly anti-Turkish because of what the commissioners believed was Turkish complicity in the Armenian genocide. Its criticisms of the Turks, however, stemmed not from a discussion of the alleged fanaticism of Islam, as had earlier discussions of the Armenian question, but from an avowedly scientific, objective, and modern analysis of the despotic form of government that had ruined, the commissioners said, the Ottoman Empire. The "Government of the Turkish Empire has been for the most part a wretched failure, in spite of generally good laws," the commissioners opined. "And the treatment of the other subject races has been still worse than that of the Turks," they insisted.[38]

For them nothing has been secure—whether property, lives, wives, or children. To all this have been added the horrible massacres of the Armenians, especially since Ab-dul-Hamil's time, and somewhat similar deportations of the Greeks. Both races have proved themselves abler, more industrious, enterprising, and prosperous than the Turks, and so have made themselves feared and hated doubtless not altogether without some provocation on their part in certain cases. And these massacres have been due to deliberate and direct government action, in which the Turkish people themselves have been too willing to share. They have not been crimes of the passion of the moment. And they have involved cruelties horrible beyond description.[39]

The commissioners were influenced by the resurgent campaign on behalf of the Armenians that had coalesced at the time. They were also heavily dependent for their descriptions of the Ottoman Empire on the British work of William Mitchell Ramsey (1897, *Impressions of Turkey*) and the 1916 Bryce report, a war-era compendium of narratives, statements, and allegations of Turkish genocide against the Armenians that largely constituted British propaganda to discredit the Ottoman state. Citing these accounts specifically, as well as drawing on the reality of the mass deportations of the Armenians, the commissioners recommended a separate Armenian mandate in "historical Armenia," although the Armenians had been reduced to a small minority of the population. Undeterred, the commissioners insisted that the Armenians might become a majority within a few years. They said that the United States (whom they recommended to take the mandate for Armenia) could and should grant them a "larger share in the administration from the start" than their current demographic weight justified. They also suggested the "migration" of Turks and Kurds from the proposed Armenian mandate. To justify this creation of a mandate in a part of the empire where the Armenians were in a minority, King and Crane declared that they would give the Armenians "the benefit of their entire losses in Turkey during the war." They added one million to the population of the Armenians in their calculations to create a theoretical, counterfactual, Armenian majority in the interests of "justice" and what the commissioners hoped would become a separate and ultimately independent Armenian state in Anatolia.

The combination of paternalism, Orientalism, and humanitarianism is evident in the Armenian section of the report. The same commissioners, however, came to radically different conclusions when they turned their gaze to the Arab provinces.[40] There they advocated not partition but a unitary Arab state. They had, to be sure, toured Palestine, Lebanon, and Syria and held hundreds of interviews with the local population. They had been inundated with petitions and appeals—including one from an Arab nationalist congress in Damascus that was on the verge of proclaiming Faysal, son of the Sharif of Mecca, head of a constitutional Arab kingdom. Like Saad Zaghlul of Egypt, and like Iraqi nationalists, the Syrian nationalists embraced what historian Erez Manela has called the "Wilsonian moment."[41] The Arabs referred to the exceptionalism of the United States—its supposed lack of an imperialist tradition—as the reason why they put their faith in America to secure their self-determination.

Flattered by such self-serving but genuine appeals, King and Crane recommended first and foremost an independent unified Arab state in Syria, Palestine, and Lebanon—because, they said, people of this region spoke the same language and shared the same culture. The commissioners wrote that, if necessary, this state should be placed under American mandatory control because, they claimed, Arabs had explicitly expressed more faith in America than in any other great power because of its lack of colonial ambition, its missionary presence, its educational efforts, its democracy, and because of Arab emigration to the United States. As much as commissioners believed that they, and the country they represented, were immune from old-style colonialism, they saw self-determination not as an inherent right, but as the final stage in an inevitable tutelary period through which natives—in Haiti as in the Philippines as in Syria and Palestine—would have to be readied for the arduous task of independence.

It was on the subject of Palestine that the King-Crane commissioners were most prophetic. Like many American Protestants, the commissioners associated the Jews with the Holy Land, and so, by their own admission, began "predisposed" in Zionism's favor. They could understand why it was that Jews wanted a state of their own. Yet the commissioners departed the Arab provinces with radically different conclusions: like some of the missionaries before them, the commissioners were not oblivious to local realities and sentiments, and they adapted their views accordingly. They insisted that if the Wilsonian principle of self-determination was to be taken seriously, Zionism had to be seriously modified:

> In his address of July 4, 1918, President Wilson laid down the following principle as one of the four great "ends for which the associated peoples of the world were fighting"; "The settlement of every question, whether of territory, of sovereignty, of economic arrangement, or of political relationship upon the basis of the free acceptance of that settlement by the people immediately concerned and not upon the basis of the material interest or advantage of any other nation or people which may desire a different settlement for the sake of its own exterior influence or mastery." If that principle is to rule, and so the wishes of Palestine's population are to be decisive as to what is to be done with Palestine, then it is to be remembered that the non-Jewish population of Palestine—nearly nine tenths of the whole—are emphatically against the entire Zionist program. The tables show that there was no one thing upon which the population of Palestine were more agreed than upon this. To subject a people so minded to unlimited Jewish immigration, and to steady financial and social pressure to surrender the land, would be a gross violation of the principle just quoted, and of the people's rights, though it kept within the forms of law.

The American commissioners further warned that Zionism could only be accomplished through violence. "Decisions," they wrote in 1919, "requiring armies to carry out, are sometimes necessary, but they are surely not gratuitously to be taken in the interests of a serious injustice. For the initial claim, often submitted by Zionist representatives, that they have a 'right' to Palestine, based on an occupation of two thousand years ago, can hardly be seriously considered."[42]

The commissioners rejected Zionism because they made a vital distinction between the cases of Armenia and Palestine. On Armenia, the commissioners were willing to create a separate Armenian mandate in defiance of Turkish and Kurdish wishes. They acted in the name of humanitarian compassion; they believed in Turkish culpability and understood that the Armenians were native to the land. They encouraged, in fact, the removal of Kurds and Turks from the region because both had had a hand in the slaughter of the Armenians. On Palestine, however, the American commissioners rejected the urgency of Zionism. They saw no relationship between European anti-Semitism and the Arab inhabitants of Palestine, and they recognized, despite their Christian backgrounds, that European Jewish Zionists could in no contemporary or legal sense be considered native. They thus refused to recommend a separate Jewish state.

Some of their advisers, notably Captain William Yale, dissented on the grounds that the Jews, as he intimated, constituted a unique race; they were more civilized and modern, had a deeper historic attachment to what he regarded as their ancestral land than any other people, and could not be assimilated into the West. For Yale, then, the question of self-determination in Palestine had to be considered in light of these points, and ought to include all the Jews of the world.[43] Yale issued a dissenting opinion in which he anticipated Lord Balfour's own memorandum to his cabinet, in which Balfour dismissed the American commission and justified his government's commitment to Zionism because it was "rooted in age-long traditions, in present needs, in future hopes, of far profounder import than the desires and prejudices of the 700,000 Arabs who now inhabit that ancient land."[44]

## The Scramble for the Middle East

From a Western colonial standpoint, the King-Crane commission report was dangerously idealistic. It diverged far too much from the British and French imperial designs on the Middle East. The report was suppressed, the Arab world was colonized, and the proposed Armenian state was stillborn. The demise of the King-Crane commission report reflected, as Manela has demonstrated in his recent work on Wilsonianism, how quickly Wilson himself backed away from democratic interpretations of his own principles in the Middle East and elsewhere. The U.S. Senate refused to ratify U.S. participation in the League of Nations in November 1919, and in 1922 the U.S. Congress overwhelmingly embraced the Balfour Declaration and consistently thereafter supported Zionist colonization of Palestine.

Although missionaries had never been ideologically anticolonial or anti-imperialist, they could scarcely have imagined the contours of U.S. policies in the post-Ottoman Middle East that differed in quite dramatic ways from the nineteenth-century evangelical and educational enterprises. The U.S. government accepted the British and French partition of the Middle East. It asked, in return, for "open door" economic and commercial access in the various mandates in the region. At the same time, the U.S. government made its peace with the anti-Armenian disposition of Mustafa Kemal's Turkey, which remained deeply hostile to American missionaries because of their advocacy on behalf of the Armenians. Albert Lybyer, who had served on the King-Crane commission, conceded that "the Turks" had staged a "marvelous recovery" by 1923 but also condemned what he called the "passive selfishness" and "practical policy" followed by the U.S. government that had encouraged European imperialism and that had, as a result, produced a powerful Turkish nationalist backlash.[45] In Arabia, the descendants and supporters of missionaries, including Charles Crane and William Eddy, played a role in supporting the rise of the conservative, but pro-American, monarchy of Ibn Saud.[46] As historian Hans-Lukas Keiser has put it, American "collaboration" with both the Kemalist and Saudi regimes broke decisively with the missionary era.[47]

As the missionary age entered its twilight, it was replaced by a different kind of American presence in the Middle East. If in 1923 Albert Lybyer could plausibly echo the King-Crane commission report by contrasting "European imperialism" with "the time-honored American policy of non-intervention," in 1948 the U.S. role in the Middle East changed dramatically.[48] Palestine, ironically, was at the center of this shift. Many American missionaries and educators resident in the Middle East found themselves deeply at odds with their government's open support of Zionism at the expense of the Arab majority in Palestine. They echoed directly the prophetic anti-Zionist assessment of the King-Crane commission report. American missionaries, to be sure, remained in the interwar period more concerned with protecting their privileges and properties from growing Egyptian and Arab nationalism than with actively intervening on behalf of the Palestinian Arabs.[49] However, because of the Palestine question, several American missionaries and educators with extensive experience in the Middle East, such as Charles Watson and Bayard Dodge, emphasized the threat that American support for a Jewish state posed to American interests, and to a century of goodwill toward America that had been supposedly built up among Arabs by their forebears. For example, the head of the American University in Cairo at the time of the partition of Palestine, John Badeau, vigorously protested Truman's precipitous recognition of Israel. "The recognition of a de facto Zionist government," he said, "is unjust to Palestinian Arab rights and prejudicial to the best interests of the United States in the Middle East."[50] The heirs to the American missionary project were, however, cast adrift by the pro-Israel policy that did more to associate the United States, and by extension the American missionary legacy, with colonialism in the region than any other single issue. The subsequent Arab disillusionment with the United States tore away the mythology cultivated by many missionaries that America was a force for freedom and anti-imperialism. It also immeasurably strengthened a crude nationalist view that American missionaries and educators had always been little more than a bridgehead for Western colonialism.[51]

PART III

# THE EXTENT AND LIMITS OF ANTI-IMPERIALISM

Chapter 7

# Global Anti-imperialism in the Age of Wilson

EREZ MANELA

This chapter contends that, while anti-imperialism as a critique and a movement had been around for some time before 1914, the period of the Great War and its aftermath marked the first emergence of anti-imperialism as a principle for the restructuring of global order. But first, what do we mean by anti-imperialism? Resistance to rule by foreigners, however conceived, is as old as history itself. Even the Old Testament, when it tells us of Moses demanding of Pharaoh to let his people go, does not claim that the young rebel invented this sentiment. But anti-imperialism is not simply resistance to foreign rule, though it is that. It is, much more broadly, a critique of a territorial-expansionist state policy and of an international order built around such states and such policies. The anti-imperialist critique sees such policies as not only wrongheaded but illegitimate, and not simply contingently, in a particular set of circumstances, but rather as a universal principle, under any and all conditions.

This notion, rooted as it is in a particular understanding of what makes for a legitimate international system, took awhile to evolve. As Richard Koebner showed several decades ago, the term "imperialism" itself—born as a *critique* of empire, and so its emergence could well be considered the birth point of anti-imperialism—first came into use in 1870s Britain as a domestic critique of expansionist foreign policy. The word, and the attending critique, spread in subsequent decades and with similar connotations to other countries, for example to the United States in 1898.[1] While these anti-imperialist critics did occasionally dwell on the wrongs perpetrated by empire upon the peoples it colonized, this aspect of the critique tended to be peripheral to the main thrust, which had more to do with what imperialism was doing to "us," the colonizers—to our political institutions, to our men in uniform, to our treasury, to our morale, to our morality.[2]

The peoples living under the boot of European (and American, and Asian) imperial powers often resisted and rose up against their oppressors from the outset. But this resistance tended to be directed against specific rulers and tyrannies rather than against "imperialism" per se as a global principle of rulership and order. The articulation of anti-imperialism as such, if that is how we agree to define it, came later. Important signposts in its emergence include J. A. Hobson's turn-of-the-century synthesis of the domestic British critique of expansionism with a socialist-internationalist sensibility, and then V. I. Lenin's merger of this critique with Marxist historicism to craft the iconic formulation of imperialism as the highest stage of capitalism.[3] It is to Lenin that we owe the paradigmatic formulation of anti-imperialism as a project or world-reordering. But it is to Woodrow Wilson that we owe the operationalization of this critique in international politics with his adoption and popularization of the principle of self-determination as a pillar of international order. This is in spite of the fact that Wilson's critique of imperialism was belated, largely indirect, and, to a significant extent, unintended and misconstrued. The role of what I have elsewhere called the "Wilsonian moment" of 1919 in galvanizing anti-imperialism as a transnational movement aimed at reconfiguring world order is one of the great ironies of the Great War.[4]

What follows lays out some elements of the story of the global anticolonial contagion of 1919 by turning the spotlight of the international history of the era, usually resolutely Eurocentric, toward the colonial world, focusing on the nature and significance of the responses of colonial peoples to that Wilsonian moment. It does this by analyzing the impact of the Wilsonian imagery and rhetoric, and of the opportunities that appeared to open with Wilson's arrival in Europe, on the perceptions, expectations, representations, and actions in the international arena of Chinese, Indians, and Egyptians. In 1919, Indians and Egyptian were, of course, ruled by British overlords, while the Chinese, though nominally independent, had their sovereignty severely restricted by so-called "unequal treaties" with the major powers. For each of these groups, the spring of that year was a watershed in the development of anti-imperialist sentiments and movements, heralding the emergence of anti-imperialism as the central imperative of political life. This moment, under different names, is etched into the historiographies of these nations—the May Fourth Movement in China; the launching of Gandhi's Satyagraha movement, which culminated in the massacre at Amritsar; and the 1919 Revolution in Egypt.

The experiences and efforts of these three peoples at the time were not unique. The wake of the Great War saw similar movements among Arabs and Jews, Turks, Armenians, Kurds, Assyrians and Tunisians, Koreans and Indochinese, and many others. Although in all of these cases there were myriad forces—political, economic, social, and cultural—that converged at that moment of crisis and transformation, the upheavals that erupted in 1919 were all intimately tied to expectations and disappointments related to the new world order that was to emerge after the armistice. After the spring of 1919, the imperial world order never regained the stability and legitimacy that it had possessed before the war.

There were, to be sure, previous moments when anticolonial sentiments and imaginaries coalesced transnationally, most notably following the defeat of the forces of the Russian Empire by Japan in the Russo-Japanese War of 1904–5. The Japanese victory reverberated around the colonial world, with people across Asia and the Middle East—from Egypt to Iran to China— interpreting it as a harbinger of the end of Western, white dominance over peoples of other regions and races.[5] But while the Japanese military success excited much discussion and debate on what explained it and how it might be emulated, it did not mobilize mass movements, nor did it serve as a catalyst for direct challenges to the prevailing international order, even if it did help advance a push for institutional reforms in a number of countries then wrestling with the challenge of Western imperialism. Even more importantly, while the Russian defeat challenged the idea of Western superiority, it did so by showing that Japan, an "Eastern" nation, could play the game of empire just as well as the Western powers and pursue territorial expansion through military force, and so did nothing to challenge the centrality of imperial expansion and competition as a principle of international order. Japan's victory over Russia was many things, but anti-imperialist it was not.

Like the Napoleonic Wars a century earlier but unlike the Russo-Japanese War, the Great War demolished the old order in international affairs. In fact, 1919 was arguably more of a revolutionary moment than 1815, since the latter saw the European state system reconstituted more or less to the status quo ante, while the former saw the collapse of four major, long-standing empires—the Hohenzollern, the Habsburg, the Romanov, and the Ottoman—and the advent of the Russian Revolution, an event that would shape world affairs profoundly in the twentieth century. The peace treaties that emerged out of the negotiations of 1919 radically redrew patterns of territory and sovereignty not only across Europe but elsewhere around the world, most notably in the Middle East but also in Africa and Asia. This demolition of the old order and the expectations it created for the new one were indispensable in fashioning the dynamics of global anti-imperialism in the Age of Wilson.

While the term "Wilsonian moment" serves here as a convenient short-hand for a historical conjuncture, its use by no means implies that Wood-row Wilson single-handedly created, intended, or even imagined the full extent of the transformation it wrought. Indeed, the U.S. president was hardly the first world leader to articulate the vision of an international order based on self-determination. That notion had a long history in the liberal tradition from which Wilson came, going back at least as far as the late eighteenth century, when Immanuel Kant published his famous essay *Perpetual Peace*.[6] Even among the wartime leaders, Wilson was not the first to propose a peace based on self-determination. Rather, he was preceded in this not only by the Russian Bolsheviks but also by the British prime minister David Lloyd George.[7] Still, as the American president endorsed the principle of self-determination with increasing emphasis in the concluding phases of the war, he soon eclipsed all others in the imaginations of people across the world, not least in the colonial world, as a transcendent figure who came to symbolize the promise of the coming era.

The rise to power of the Bolsheviks in Russia paralleled the emergence of Wilson and the United States to international preeminence, and some decades ago the historian Arno Mayer conceptualized the period as a clash between these two rising global forces.[8] Mayer's focus was on the struggle within the European Left between the Wilsonian and Leninist options, and he concluded that Wilson had won, as evidenced in the general failure of the revolution to spread beyond the borders of Russia. Mayer's work, however, says nothing of the world outside Europe. Indeed, from the per-spective of colonial nationalists in 1919 there could be no equivalence be-tween Wilson and Lenin. Of the two, Wilson was generally far more widely known across these regions and was commonly depicted and imagined as the preeminent and most powerful world leader at the time, one who had arrived in Europe to forge a new, peaceful international order. At the same time, the Bolsheviks were commonly believed, at least until their consolidation of power at the very end of 1919, to be on the verge of annihilation by the White Russian forces in the Russian civil war. Only after it became clear that colonial peoples would be largely excluded from the application of Wilsonian principles did the Russian Bolsheviks begin to emerge, as they did for the young Vietnamese activist who would later be known as Ho Chi Minh, as alternative sources of ideological guidance and practical support in the struggle for self-determination.

This chapter advances three related arguments. First, that the combination of rhetorical iconoclasm and political opportunity that characterized the Wilsonian moment played an important—though by no means exclusive—role in galvanizing major movements of anticolonial nationalist resistance in Asia and the Middle East in 1919. Second, that viewed from this perspective, the Paris Peace Conference, often interpreted as heralding an unprecedented expansion of European imperialism, in fact marked the beginning of the end of the European imperial project by fatally undermining its legitimacy at home and abroad—not least among the colonized peoples themselves. Third, that the evolution of anticolonial nationalist sentiments among elites in the colonies was inseparable from the new world order that they perceived emerging around them in the immediate wake of the war; one that encouraged, indeed required, that groups who wished to rule themselves appeal to the doctrine of national self-determination and reimagine themselves as a nascent nation-state as they claimed a legitimate place within the expanding and reconfiguring structure of international society.

The notion of a right to national self-determination was introduced into the international debate over war aims by Russian revolutionaries in mid-1917. The term had long been current in internal debates among socialists, though it was controversial: Marx himself had shown only intermittent support for nationalist movements in Europe during his lifetime, depending on their perceived relationship to the interests of the proletariat. During the Great War, the Bolsheviks remained divided on the issue, with one camp viewing nationalism as a dangerous, irrational force in conflict with the goal of international proletarian solidarity. Lenin, however, felt that Bolshevik support for national self-determination, defined as a right of secession from imperial rule, was crucial in undermining the imperial regime in Russia and gaining the support of subject peoples for the revolution.[9] In March 1917, even before the Bolshevik seizure of power, Lenin declared that when the Bolsheviks ruled Russia their peace plan would include "the liberation of all colonies; the liberation of all dependent, oppressed, and non-sovereign peoples."[10] That spring the Russian Provisional Government, under pressure from the Bolshevik-controlled Petrograd Soviet, became the first among the belligerent governments to call officially for a peace settlement based on a right of "self-determination of peoples."[11]

This call for a settlement based on national self-determination, however, was aimed not at the subject peoples of Asia, who were initially of little interest to the Russian revolutionaries, but rather at the anti-imperialist Left in Europe, especially in Britain, France, and Germany.[12] It was in this context, the battle for European opinion, that the British prime minister David Lloyd George first incorporated the term "self-determination" into the war-aims rhetoric of the Western allies. President Wilson had already spoken repeatedly of the need for a postwar settlement based on "the consent of the governed"—long a favorite phrase of his, borrowed from a tradition of American political rhetoric going back to the Declaration of Independence. Lloyd George, who was growing worried that the enthusiasm for the rhetoric of both Wilson and Lenin on the domestic Left in Britain and other Allied countries would undermine the Allied war effort, moved to redefine British war aims in line with it. In an address before the British Trades Union League on January 5, 1918, he managed to merge Wilson's rhetoric with Lenin's: the peace, he said, must be based "on the right of self-determination or the consent of the governed."[13] By assimilating the Bolshevik call for self-determination to Wilson's notion of the "consent of the governed," the prime minister obfuscated the wide gap between the revolutionary anti-imperialist agenda of the former and the gradualist, liberal reformism implied in the latter.

Wilson and Lenin came from very different political contexts and had in mind two very different things when they spoke of self-determination: Wilson, seeing autocracy and militarism as the main causes of the war, envisioned a peace based on the republican principles of government by consent, while Lenin, whose immediate concern was toppling the Russian empire and gaining the support of its subject peoples, explicitly defined national self-determination as a right of secession from a multinational empire. Thus, the Bolsheviks invariably spoke of the right to *national* self-determination, a qualification reflecting the term's origin in Marxist theory as distinct from other forms of self-determination—individual, proletarian, etc. In its broader sense within the Bolshevik revolutionary strategy, it was a call for the overthrow of imperial rule through an appeal to nationalism among subject peoples, even as the final goal remained the institution of a global Communist world order in which national distinctions would be subsumed. Wilson, on the other hand, seldom described the right to self-determination as specifically national. Instead, he viewed it in the context of Enlightenment-derived notions of popular sovereignty, of government by consent; and though in his speeches he did not explicitly limit its application to Europe, he saw it as immediately relevant only to the territories of the defeated empires. Eventually, he imagined, it might apply in other colonial situations, but if so it would be through gradual processes of tutelage and reform such as he had himself initiated in the U.S. colonial administration of the Philippines, and not through the revolutionary overthrow of colonial rule.[14]

Nonetheless, Wilson himself completed this terminological conflation in the months that followed, adopting the phrase "self-determination" as his own with growing fervor and emphasis. Despite a common conception to the contrary, the term itself was nowhere to be found in the Fourteen Points, though several of the points—the resurrection of Poland, the evacuation of Belgium, and the call for the "autonomous development" of the peoples of the Ottoman and Habsburg empires—implied at least a partial application of this principle.[15] Wilson's first public, explicit use of the term "self-determination" came the following month, in February 1918, when he addressed Congress again to outline the U.S. peace plan. In the coming settlement, he said, "national aspirations must be respected; people may now be dominated and governed only by their own consent. 'Self-determination' is not a mere phrase. It is an imperative principle of action, which statesmen will henceforth ignore at their peril."[16] It is significant to note that in his draft of the address—he composed his speeches himself—Wilson had placed the phrase "self-determination" within quotation marks, suggesting that he realized he was incorporating a novel term into his lexicon. Calls for a peace based on self-determination would thereafter recur regularly, alongside references to the "consent of the governed," in Wilson's wartime rhetorical arsenal.[17] This was no accident. As with Lloyd George's earlier use of the term, it was designed to co-opt Bolshevik rhetoric to the Allied cause in an effort to neutralize its appeal within the European Left. The new terminology may not have changed the essence of Wilson's vision in his own mind, but it lent his pronouncements a more radical tone, amplifying their impact as his words reverberated worldwide.

Neither Wilson and Lloyd George nor Lenin and Trotsky saw the subject peoples of the global South as the audience for their declarations in support of self-determination, but their rhetoric nevertheless echoed far beyond the European audiences it was intended for. By the time of the armistice in November 1918, nationalists across the colonial world had adopted the language of self-determination, adapted it to their own needs and circumstances, and mobilized campaigns to bring their claims against imperialism to the peace conference and the assembled world leaders, Wilson foremost among them. By late 1918, the notion that the postwar settlement would be based on "President Wilson's principle of self-determination" had become commonplace in political discourse across the colonial world, and Wilson himself was widely lionized in print as the harbinger of a new era in international affairs. A contemporary liberal Indian intellectual, noting the rapturous reception Wilson encountered in London in December 1918, wrote: "Imagination fails to picture the wild delirium of joy with which he would have been welcomed in Asiatic capitals. It would have been as though one of the great teachers of humanity, Christ or Buddha, had come back to his home."[18]

Like the closely related ideas of nationalism, the global spread of anti-imperialist ideas depended on the rise of communications, in this case the rapid expansion in the technologies of the telegraph and of mass print media across much of the global South by the turn of the twentieth century. In 1905, India, for example, already had more than thirteen hundred newspapers in English and Indian languages, which were estimated to reach two million subscribers. In China, a political press that first appeared in coastal cities in the 1890s had burgeoned in the first decades of the twentieth century with the expansion of literacy.[19] In Egypt, too, modern newspapers had developed and spread considerably by the time of the First World War, and though censorship did exist, it was largely directed against critiques of the government, not international news. China, India, and Egypt all had numerous dailies and magazines in vernacular that published news about international affairs. Moreover, copies of European papers were often widely available to those who could read European languages.[20] By 1918 all of these places had seen the emergence of politically-aware, articulate publics who were broadly interested in and informed about national and international developments.

   In some cases, these new venues of mass communication were also the targets of direct American propaganda efforts aimed at spreading the Wilsonian message, carried out during the war by the U.S. government's Committee on Public Information (CPI). This committee, established by executive order in April 1917, was led by the Progressive journalist George Creel, who was fiercely loyal to the president and his ideals and saw in the CPI an opportunity to spread the Wilsonian gospel of progressivism and democracy on a global scale. The goal of the CPI propaganda efforts abroad, Creel wrote, was "to drive home the absolute justice of America's cause, the absolute selflessness of America's aims."[21] To that end Creel made creative use of the recent advances in communication and media technologies, such as the wireless and the moving picture, in the effort to advertise America's war aims and peace plans at home and abroad: "The printed word, the spoken word, the motion picture, the poster, the signboard—all these were used in our campaign," he boasted.[22] The CPI produced and distributed innumerable texts and images that celebrated the successes of the American war effort but also more generally the purported ideals and advantages of American society. These were then "carried to every community in the United States and to every corner of the world."[23]

Naturally, President Wilson's various pronouncements and declarations, and especially the text of the Fourteen Points, became linchpins of CPI propaganda, especially in its foreign operations. Already in mid-1917, more than a year before the CPI formally opened an office in China, American missionary volunteers translated Wilson's speeches into Chinese, and these translations were distributed, free of charge, to the vernacular press or published in pamphlet form. In the fall of 1918, at the time of the armistice, the full texts of Wilson's wartime speeches were published in Chinese translation, and the volume quickly became a best seller in China and went through several printings.[24] Carl Crow, the head of the CPI operation in China, later wrote that he received thousands of letters from Chinese citizens expressing "an air of confidence in the future, a faith in the idea that President Wilson's words would prevail and that China, as well as all other oppressed nations, would be liberated."[25] A bilingual edition of Wilson's speeches, with the original English text side by side with the Chinese translation, was also published. It circulated in Chinese schools as a textbook for English instruction, and soon Chinese students could recite the Fourteen Points by heart.[26] Crow also ordered twenty thousand large photographs of Wilson to be distributed among students at missionary schools, as well as buttons and engravings carrying the president's image.[27]

It is hard to measure with precision the impact of such CPI propaganda efforts in China or elsewhere, and of course other major belligerents, including the British, French, and Germans, had extensive international propaganda operations as well. It is clear, however, that by the time of the armistice enthusiasm for the new world order that President Wilson appeared to promise ran high among Chinese officials and intellectuals. For many Chinese at the time, who saw China's relations with the outside world in the preceding decades as a series of humiliations, the prospect of an international order predicated on the principle of self-determination held the promise of respect for the equality of nations.[28] Animated by the widespread hope that a new era was ready to dawn in international affairs and, no less importantly, by indications of U.S. support for their cause at the peace table, the Chinese delegates in Paris, as well as politically aware Chinese at home and abroad, were ready to claim their place among nations.[29]

While the role of U.S. wartime propaganda in fomenting such high expectations was important, Wilson's fame also spread in regions where the CPI was not active. In Egypt the Wilsonian message echoed widely, reportedly causing a stir "even in the remotest villages."[30] The recent spread of telegraph technology and the ubiquity of Reuters news dispatches meant that the CPI's efforts elsewhere in the world, especially its propaganda in Great Britain, were well reflected in the Egyptian press, and the texts of Wilson's wartime speeches, including his Fourteen Points, were widely available to the reading public there.[31] By mid-1918, the expectation that the emerging postwar order would reflect Wilson's wartime rhetoric was widespread. "The principles that were announced by Dr. Wilson," one Egyptian historian has written, "exerted a great influence on everyone without exception."[32]

In India, too, the vernacular and English-language press reported extensively on Wilson's utterances and his vision for a new era in world affairs.[33] In a wartime episode that raised howls of condemnation in the British Parliament, a retired Indian judge and prominent campaigner for Indian home rule wrote to Wilson after his war speech to the Senate in April 1917 to express his hope that the president would "completely convert England to your ideals of world liberation." The people of India, the judge said, had faith in Wilson and saw him as "an instrument of God in the reconstruction of the world."[34] The Indian nationalist leader Lala Lajpat Rai, living in wartime exile in the United States, also wrote the president several months later to thank him for his Fourteen Points, which, he said, were bound to "thrill the millions of the world's 'subject races.'" Wilson had introduced, Rai wrote, "a new charter of world's freedom."[35] Others in India shared the sense that the world was on the cusp of a new era. If Wilson's principles are to be the basis for the conference, opined one editorial writer, then "England has no other go but to frame her policy of governing India in accordance with them," and another exclaimed that the end of the war is "in one word, nothing but the freedom of nations, their right of self-determination." A field of opportunity, it seemed, was opening, and India, like other emerging nations, had to stake its claim.[36]

Even at the height of the Wilsonian moment there were, of course, dissenting voices among colonial intellectuals, those who did not believe that President Wilson and the United States would be of much help to colonial peoples in their struggle for self-determination.[37] But in the early days of the armistice, even many of those in the colonial world who thought Wilson's ideals insufficient or doubted his true commitment to them nevertheless adopted his rhetoric as they sought to bring their claims before the peace conference. The Russian Bolsheviks, after all, were excluded from Paris and mired in civil war, and the other major victorious powers—Britain, France, and Japan—were clamoring for the retrenchment and even expansion of the imperial order. Wilson therefore remained, at least until the spring of 1919, the leading world figure who seemed committed to a settlement that would rein in the excesses of empire and promote self-determination as a principle of international order.

The announcement of the armistice under Wilson's terms, then, launched a transnational mobilization against imperialism across much of the colonial world. In December 1918, when the Indian National Congress (INC) convened in Delhi for its annual session, one of its main resolutions demanded the "application of the Principle of Self-Determination to India." The resolution argued that, in view of the wartime pronouncements of President Wilson and other Allied leaders in favor of the principle of self-determination, the powers should recognize India as "one of the progressive nations to whom the principle of self-determination should be applied." The INC further urged that India be represented at the peace table by elected delegates, and it nominated three men for the position: the veteran home-rule advocate B. G. Tilak, the Muslim Congress leader Syed Hasan Imam, and Mohandas Gandhi, recently returned from South Africa and just beginning his rise on the Indian political scene.[38] In a coordinated campaign, dozens of local "self-rule leagues" throughout India petitioned the peace conference asking that India be granted self-determination.[39]

The British government rejected out of the hand the INC demand to allow it to choose India's delegates to the peace conference. Tilak, the fiery Marathi journalist and scholar who was already well-known for his long-standing advocacy of Indian home rule, nevertheless traveled to

London and launched a campaign for Indian home rule aimed squarely at "world opinion" and the gathering peace conference. Internationalizing India's demand for self-determination, Tilak hoped, would put pressure on the British government and force it to bend to Wilsonian principles.[40] If world order was to be transformed in Paris, India's voice would have to be counted: "I am sure the question of India will not go unnoticed in the present sitting of the Conference," he wrote to a colleague. "It is for us to see that the decision is in our favour. Government may not like the idea of our appealing to the Peace Conference. But that is no reason why we should not do so."[41] He also appealed directly to President Wilson, telling him that "the world's hope for peace and justice is centered in you as the author of the great principle of self-determination."[42]

Unlike India, China was nominally recognized as a sovereign state though its sovereignty was severely circumscribed by a battery of unequal treaties with the major powers. China had declared war on Germany in August 1917 in order to secure a seat at the peace table, and as the peace conference gathered, Chinese at home and abroad felt that the time was ripe to demand real equality for China in the international arena.[43] For them this meant the abrogation of the unequal treaties and the restoration of full Chinese sovereignty over its territory, most especially the prewar German concession in Shandong Province, which Japan had occupied during the war and was now claiming the right to keep. Chinese activists, including intellectuals, students, merchants, and other groups both in China and abroad, produced an avalanche of petitions calling for a new international order based on "the exalted ideas inspiring the immortal message of President Wilson" and demanding the application to China of his principles of self-determination and the equality of nations.[44]

The leaders of the Chinese delegation in Paris—and it was largely them rather than the weak and divided government in Beijing who spoke for China in Paris—believed that with the United States on its side China could win its case at the conference.[45] V. K. Wellington Koo (Gu Weijun), who held a PhD degree from Columbia University, and C. T. Wang (Wang Zhengting), who was a graduate of Yale, were ardent patriots who wanted to see China emerge from its state of weakness, disunity, and humiliation to take what they saw as its rightful place among nations. But they were also cosmopolitan internationalists, comfortably moving between China and the West. They hoped that in the new postwar international order China would become a full member of international society. In a coauthored pamphlet, the two compared what they described as President Wilson's vision

of international harmony to that of the Chinese sage Confucius: "Confucius saw, just as the illustrious author of the present League of Nations has
seen, the danger to civilization and humanity involved in the continued
existence of such a sad plight [of constant war]" and therefore "spared no
effort in emphasizing the need of creating and preserving a new order of
things which would ensure universal peace."[46] The Wilsonian project of
fashioning a more harmonious international order, they suggested, was the
culmination of thousands of years of Confucian teachings, and the establishment of a League of Nations would fulfill the Confucian ideal.

In Egypt, which was still under a British protectorate that had been announced early in the war, a group of prominent leaders launched into action
after the armistice, formed a delegation, and demanded permission to head
for Europe to stake their claim for Egyptian self-determination. When the
British refused, the group, headed by veteran politician Sa'd Zaghlul—later
celebrated by Egyptians as the "father of the nation"—mobilized popular
protests in the streets and launched an international propaganda campaign
for their cause. By December, the sleepy U.S. diplomatic office in Cairo
was deluged with petitions protesting the British position and demanding
that the United States support Egyptian self-determination.[47] To Wilson
himself, Zaghlul wrote that "no people more than the Egyptian people has
felt strongly the joyous emotion of the birth of a new era which, thanks to
your virile action, is soon going to impose itself upon the universe," and
asked "the eminent philosopher and statesman" to help free Egypt from
foreign domination.[48] Other petitions came from a broad cross-section of
the Egyptian upper and middle classes: legislators, government officials,
local politicians, merchants, lawyers, physicians, and army officers, all calling
for the support of the U.S. president for their bid for self-rule.[49]

By early March, the tense situation in Egypt was coming to a head. The
British authorities, increasingly anxious over nationalist agitation, decided
to move forcefully against its leadership. On March 8, Zaghlul and three of
his colleagues were arrested, and the following morning they were deported
to be interned on the island of Malta.[50] According to one biographer, one
item found on Zaghlul's person when he was arrested and searched was a
clipping from the *Daily Express* listing Wilson's Fourteen Points.[51] The ar-
rest sparked a massive wave of strikes and demonstrations across Egypt and
precipitated a period of violent clashes known to Egyptians as the "1919
Revolution." Egyptians from all walks of life took part in the uprising:
students, urban workers, professionals, and peasants. Members of religious
and ethnic minorities expressed their solidarity with the movement, and

women took to the streets with unprecedented numbers and visibility. As violent clashes proliferated and railway and telegraph lines, which were identified with British rule, were sabotaged, London countered with a strict enforcement of martial law. Over the next several months, some eight hundred Egyptians were killed in clashes, and many more were wounded; sixty British soldiers and civilians also died.[52] The 1919 Revolution was a major watershed in the development of the Egyptian struggle against empire, and according to a prominent Egyptian historian it "forms the basis for all the developments that followed" in the modern history of Egypt.[53] The violence unleashed during this period and the brutality of the British response sharply escalated Anglo-Egyptian tensions, exacerbating mutual fear and mistrust, hardening attitudes and positions on both sides, and casting a long shadow over subsequent attempts at negotiation.

Just as the Wilsonian promise began to collapse for Egyptians, Indian hopes of a hearing in Paris for their demands for self-determination were also being dashed. Though Tilak continued his campaign in London throughout the spring, by March it was already clear that the British government was determined to block any discussion of the Indian question at the peace conference. When Tilak, citing his appointment by the INC as its delegate to the peace conference, applied for a passport to travel to Paris, his application was summarily denied.[54] On the subcontinent itself, the anticipation of far-reaching change in the colonial relationship that had built up among Indians during the latter war years was replaced by bitter disillusion as the government tried to stem the tide of "sedition" with the oppressive Rowlatt Bills, which extended its wartime powers of internment without trial. Indian activists, who had expected the war to be followed by an immediate push toward self-government, were incensed. Gandhi, who had earlier campaigned to recruit Indians for the imperial war effort, now emerged as a leader of the movement to oppose these "Black Acts," calling for civil disobedience and a nationwide strike and cementing his position as a figure of national stature.[55] The colonial authorities responded violently to the mounting protests, most infamously with the killing on April 13, 1919, of nearly four hundred unarmed civilians gathered in Jallianwala Bagh, in the Punjab city of Amritsar. The Amritsar Massacre, as that event soon came to be known, came to epitomize the oppressive nature of British rule in India and augured a new stage in the evolution of Indian resistance to the empire.

Three weeks later, Chinese were shocked when it emerged that, in order to secure Japanese membership in his League of Nations, Wilson had agreed to award Japan the former German concessions in Shandong. On May 4, when students in Beijing learned of this decision, they took to the streets in violent protest. The students, who not long before had filled the streets to chant their admiration for President Wilson now saw the American president as a liar, his promise of a new world exposed as a mere illusion. Street protests and strikes spread throughout the country over the next weeks. A contemporary pamphlet summed up the prevailing sentiments: "Throughout the world like the voice of a prophet has gone the word of Woodrow Wilson strengthening the weak and giving courage to the struggling. And the Chinese people . . . looked for the dawn of this new Messiah; but no sun rose for China." One student recalled that they now "awoke to the fact that foreign nations . . . were all great liars. . . . We could no longer depend upon the principle of any so-called great leader like Woodrow Wilson . . . we couldn't help feel that we must struggle!" Like the 1919 evolution in Egypt and the Rowlett protests in India, the May Fourth Movement, as it came to be known, galvanized hitherto inchoate strands of political, social, and cultural discontent and marked a defining moment in the evolution of resistance to the imperialist world order.[56]

Though the settlement of 1919 has often been seen as a triumph of the imperialist order, this essay argues that it in fact marked the beginning of its unraveling. True, the British and French empires not only preserved but expanded their territories, and the United States failed to join the League of Nations and even retreated in the 1920s from the move toward greater Filipino self-government that was begun under Wilson. Still, after 1919, empire as a principle of international order faced a series of challenges of unprecedented scope and intensity. Egyptians, who continued to resist British rule, won partial sovereignty in 1922, and Iraq followed a decade later, even joining the League of Nations. The Shandong concessions, whose award to Japan at Versailles launched the May Fourth Movement, were in fact restored to China at the Washington Conference in 1922, and throughout the 1920s the Chinese government gradually chipped away at the unequal treaties that circumscribed its sovereignty. In India, resistance to British rule entered the Gandhian era, posing a challenge to the legitimacy of empire far more radical than any that came before the war, with the Indian National Congress in 1929 officially asserting, for the first time, the goal of *purna swaraj*, a complete independence that would sever India's connection to Britain entirely.

Anti-imperialism continued to spread and strengthen globally through depression and war, coming to fruition with the radical restructuring of international society in the massive waves of decolonization in the decades after World War II. By then, the illegitimacy of imperial formations had become an iron principle of international relations. The idea that Wilson had come to symbolize globally in 1919, that of an international order that is predicated on formally equal, self-determining nation-states, was codified in the structure of the United Nations, even as the actual distribution of power in the international arena remained, of course, anything but equal. Power—U.S. power in particular—still remains at the center of international relations. The rise of global anti-imperialism over the course of the past century, however, has transformed its patterns, territorial configurations, modes of operation, and, most notably, its discourses of legitimacy in far-reaching ways.

# Chapter 8

# Feminist Historiography, Anti-imperialism, and the Decolonial

PATRICIA A. SCHECHTER

If imperialism sits at the center of new scholarship on women and the United States, the same cannot be said for anti-imperialism.[1] Across a number of fields, anti-imperialism remains a "scholarly orphan," despite its "victorious" status in U.S. culture.[2] In 1965, Robert Beisner described anti-imperial thought in the United States as clogged by "mental sludge" and limited in its political purchase.[3] The practice of U.S. women's history reflects this landscape.[4] This chapter explores how anti-imperialism has figured—or mostly not figured—in feminist scholarship about women and the United States. In order to remedy this situation, I suggest adding the word "decolonial" to the scholarly vocabulary for capturing women's politics. Much of the intellectual currency of feminist approaches to history flows from placing women in relationship to the legal constructs of citizenship and economic relations that grew up with the modern nation-state. My survey points out some of the limits to these state-centered approaches, aware that the stakes are high for breaking what Antoinette Burton has called the "narrative contract" between modern history writing and the nation. Straying too far from nationalist concerns is a move Thomas Bender likens to "sawing off the branch upon which we [historians] are sitting."[5]

But a few things have caught my eye lately, and I will try to describe them the best I can from my own, however creaky, branch.

## Banner Moments

In 1896, Mrs. Tennie M. Fuller delivered a report called "Banner of Indian Territory W.C.T.U.—My History" at the union's tenth annual convention held in Muskogee (present-day east Oklahoma). As president of the Talequah Woman's Christian Temperance Union, Fuller recounted how she and a colleague, Mrs. Jane Stapler, were the "first Indian women to enlist under the banner 'For God and Home and Native Land.'" Yet Fuller's "History" calls up a notion of "native land" distinct from that typically evinced by the WCTU's motto, given that organization's patriotism and "allegiance to white supremacy."[6] Pointing her listeners transnationally, Fuller described how she and Stapler made sure the Indian Territory's WCTU banner would be displayed at the 1889 Exposition Universelle in Paris. They "agreed that it would never do to lose this opportunity to have our country represented across the great waters," and the banner joined that of the "other State flags," probably in the American Exposition building.[7] Fuller also attended national temperance meetings and world's fairs in the intervening years. About the World's Columbian Exposition in Chicago, Fuller noted that she "uttered a silent protest against the many wrongs my people are receiving at the hands of the American people." The "Banner of Indian Territory W.C.T.U.—My History" is a doubled story of invention and intervention, protest and silencing, and the marking and crossing of borders that left Fuller "scarred and battle-worn." The twenty-year existence of Indian Territory WCTU was subsequently ignored by the organization's official histories and has only just emerged in scholarly treatments of the otherwise well-studied WCTU.[8]

In 1934, Spanish-speaking women in Manhattan started a branch of a new transnational organization: the Unión de Mujeres Americanas (UMA). UMA's leading light was Josefina Silva de Cintrón (1884–1988), who migrated from Puerto Rico in 1927 and spent her life in New York as an arts impresario and publisher of *Artes y Letras* (1933–39), an internationally circulated magazine. UMA's early meetings featured the display of a special flag called *la bandera de la raza*, which this group adopted as its insignia. *La bandera* was designed by an Argentinian, UMA's founding group was based in Mexico City, and its New York branch was inclusive of women from many countries. The word *americanas* affirmed an encompassing, plural Americanness as the women's basis for collectivity. Under *la bandera*, UMA proclaimed "solidarity without distinction of creeds, color, races, or nationalities."[9] When Silva de Cintrón announced at UMA's founding, "*¡Adelante, hermanas de la raza!*" (Onward, sisters of the race!), she gave voice to a transnational gendered unity in opposition to racial hierarchy and exclusion, a project still awaiting a full reckoning by historians.[10]

The Indian Territory's WCTU banner and *la bandera de la raza* point to social formations and ideological terrain that historians do not know much about yet. Though I have never actually seen either one, each banner hangs over a suggestive if ambivalent set of meanings touching race, gender, and national belonging. The words "Indian Territory," "my native land, "our country," "other State flags," "my people," and "the American people" bobble and bump in Tennie Fuller's short "History." UMA's constituencies—"*las hermanas de la raza*" and "*mujeres americanas*"—could map onto a spectrum of demographies, geographies, and polities in the hemisphere. A fluttering, unstable referent, each banner—and each woman's rhetoric—evokes lively, resonant contradictions and dynamic, unresolved meanings. How should I understand Tennie Fuller to have "uttered a silent protest" at Chicago? In Silva de Cintrón's case, what do I make of the seeming contradiction of a *raza* (race) that does not discriminate by "creeds, color, races or nationalities"? As each woman moved through transnational settings like world's fairs, evangelical conferences, and the media circuits of the "Atlantic world" or the "Western Hemisphere," what other meanings attached to their work? How might their efforts inform my thinking about women and the topic "American anti-imperialism"?

Answers to these questions begin by noting how each banner, flying during the high winds of U.S. and European imperialism, unsettles and exceeds the usual categories deployed by historians to capture women's relationships to empire and state. They catch my eye—even though I can't exactly see them—out of my interest in women's critical engagement with racialization in a transnational frame for the period 1865 to 1965. A transnational perspective opens up a reading of Fuller's banner and her travels with it as more than a survivalist accommodation to colonial rule and sets *la bandera* into relief as a kind of refusal to make race at the height of scientific racism and popular eugenics in the interwar years. In the wave of transnationally focused scholarship of the last decade, I align my readings of these banners with "geneaologies of anti-imperial and decolonizing thought, ranging from anticolonial Marxism to subaltern studies to Third

World feminism and feminisms of color."[11] If, as this literature suggests, race is a primary effect of imperialism, I read Fuller and Silva de Cintrón's banners as signs of resistance to both exclusion/segregation *and* engulfment/fusion; in short, as rejections of coloniality.[12] How to name and more fully characterize their work and compare it to other domains of gendered political formations in the period, including "anti-imperialism," poses some challenges.[13]

Labeling the Indian Territory WCTU and UMA "anti-imperial" organizations implies a focus on state policy about empire that was not substantially on the agenda of either organization. The phrase "everyday resistance" as a name for oppositional practices of enslaved or subaltern women comes up short where such iconic, staged, and institutionalized activities, like the ones that produced these banners, are concerned.[14] Older words coming out of immigration studies, like "assimilation," miss the critical intent and activist spirit at the heart of each woman's work. Nor should Fuller or Silva de Cintrón be understood as a "native helper," figures who engaged with and, frequently, reinterpreted the workings of colonial institutions like schools and hospitals in their own and their community's interest.[15] Ann Stoler's framing of "the intimate" as a key domain of colonial rule puts women, sexuality, and domesticity at the center of empire, but Fuller and Silva de Cintrón made commitments to the public sphere and to naming (and making) trouble at its borders. How, then, to characterize their efforts to mark and reconfigure the boundaries between race, nation, and empire in their respective eras?

Following historian and feminist theorist Emma Pérez, I would describe the politics informing these banners as "decolonial." Pérez defines the decolonial as a politics resistant to dynamics of imperialism, especially racialization, but not exactly a conventionally independence-focused nationalist counterpoint. She labels decolonial that which disrupts the national-imperial binaries of colonizer/subaltern and citizen/alien, pairings that usually map onto a white-black racialized social imaginary in the United States. In so doing, Pérez recuperates a "third space feminism" pertinent to her writing of Chicana history.[16] Extending her paradigm, it seems to me that the decolonial can name resistance to racialized categories of state and empire for Fuller and Silva de Cintrón, women who never signed on to conventionally political anti-imperialist movements but whose ideological stance and accomplishments only become fully visible in the context of U.S. empire. Further, the idea of the decolonial invites comparisons across regimes and, within the academy, across topics usually studied separately, like "Native American history" and "Puerto Rican history." The category *decolonial* can help identify and situate stories that have remained unheard in the orchestrations of historiography whose dominant chord is feminist imperialism with a minor grace note of feminist anti-imperialism. Colonial and missionary archives tend to document white women's pro-empire activities and only sometimes their second thoughts about such projects, like indigenous child removal.[17] As a decentered, transnational category, the idea of the decolonial can respond to calls to interrogate an overly tidy elite-subaltern divide.[18]

What is the historiography of not noticing these banners and women? My survey begins in the late 1980s, with Trinh T. Min-ha's discussion of "naturalist ideology" and her schema for plotting female subject positions in the discipline of anthropology: woman, native, other.[19] Where "American anti-imperialism" is the topic, under "woman" are studies of (mostly) white female citizens, work fundamentally enabled by historian Joan Scott. Under the category "native" is a presence usually rendered as silence, unsaying, or haunted as framed by philosopher Gayatri Chakravorty Spivak. In U.S. traditions of historical writing, "other" usually signifies African Americans or "blackness." Scholarship about women sorted into this category has been deeply shaped by the work of historian Elsa Barkely Brown. In what follows, I will consider the imprint of each of these germinal thinkers as it bears on the subject of women and anti-imperialism. Reviewing the literature on anti-imperialism around the nodes woman, native, other makes visible the historiographic practices of boundary making that have kept figures like Fuller and Silva de Cintrón out of the story.

## Woman

If anti-imperialism names a concern with nation-state policy about empire, historians of U.S. women have mostly explored that topic in the terms of those closest allied, however tensely, with official state power, namely citizens. In these efforts, Joan Scott's work has been key, especially her 1986 article "Gender: A Useful Category of Analysis." Scott's supple and incisive formulations, like "gender is one of the recurrent references by which political power has been conceived, legitimated and criticized," have fueled decades of scholarship across multiple fields and topics.[20] Recent commentators credit this essay's potency in domains thought to be "most immune to the women's history enterprise," such as foreign relations and diplomacy. "Scott had specifically called for such an intervention," notes Joanne Meyerowitz, and historians of women have delivered with gusto.[21]

A leading example of such work is Kristin Hoganson's *Fighting for American Manhood: How Gender Politics Provoked the Spanish-American and Philippine-American Wars* (1998). In this compelling treatment, Hoganson elaborates on "the ways that gender worked as a motivating ideology and a political posture in debates over war and empire." In the book's last chapter, Hoganson explores anti-imperialism. Empire "lost much of [its] allure," she claims, owing to a drop in gender appeal during the Philippine insurgency. Critics identified the sexual economy of empire as a threat to marriage ties at home through prostitution, venereal disease, and the "spectre of miscegenation" abroad. Hoganson notes how peace and domesticity became more attractive than foreign exploits for working through "the problems of free men in freedom," as one worried newspaper editorial put it. Redirecting men to "homesteading"—that is, to settler colonialism in the western parts of North America—was equally fraught with imperial liabilities, though rarely named as such.[22]

Hoganson's work affirmed gender's central place in the male-dominated politics and policies of empire. Studies soon followed that described women citizens' roles in related domains. Inspired by scholarship that mapped out "imperial motherhood" and the "white woman's burden" in Britain, historians turned attention to white women U.S. citizens whose evangelicalism, temperance work, and academic and literary ambitions touched empire and racialized concepts of "civilization."[23] Louise Newman's *White Women's Rights: The Racial Origins of Feminism* (1999) stands out in this literature. Challenging the whiggish interpretation of the women's rights tradition as consonant with a larger, mythic story of expanding American democracy over time, Newman argued that feminism "developed in conjunction with—and constituted a response to—the United States' extension of its authority over so-called 'primitive' peoples." By claiming that "white women were the equals of white men," writers and activists called on the United States to "embark on a more ambitious imperialist project—to eliminate 'savagery' not just within the borders of the United States but throughout the world," a project in which women could and did take an active part.[24] Newman's historical actors were not especially focused on state power; they were mainly religious, scientific, or literary in their orientation and stressed race and civilization rather than the state as their primary source of authority. Temperance advocates best bridged the gendered domains of civilization and formal state power—the WCTU sought to "make love legislatively articulate"—but like their secular and scientific counterparts, they did so mostly in support of U.S. policy about empire.[25]

Allison Sneider's study *Suffragists in an Age of Empire: U.S. Expansion and the Woman Question, 1870–1929* (2008) refocuses the themes of women and empire around the Constitution. In a work of impressive precision, breadth, and economy, Sneider drives home a central argument: white woman suffragists used colonial and imperial moments to "[keep] alive a national discussion of the right to vote" in an age of federally sanctioned suffrage restriction at the state level. About the policy of empire itself, Sneider finds that "both imperialist and anti-imperialist visions competed for space on suffrage platforms, with neither clearly in the ascendant." And like Newman, she finds a racism "foundational and not 'expedient'" in white women's arguments for the vote, placing the racial chauvinism of Elizabeth Cady Stanton and Susan B. Anthony's political strategies in line with the civilizationist thinking of Charlotte Perkins Gilman and Alice Fletcher. In Sneider's telling, African American women suffragists "identified not as or with colonized women or as victims of 'domestic' imperialism but as representatives of American civilization on a global stage."[26]

The thinness of anti-imperialist thinking among activist women citizens of the United States should not surprise. It is consistent with Beisner's study of the Anti-Imperialist League (1898–1902). The league stressed the implications of empire for the United States as a democracy and argued against imperialism in terms of a mythic America whose "democratic people" should, ideally, be "ill-suited" to any "career as colonialists." The main exponents of the Anti-Imperialist League believed that control (without conquest) by the United States of so-called backward peoples and regions of the world was not just acceptable but expected. This standpoint allowed the league both to "ignore a long history of battles for expansion and control" on the North American continent that preceded the wars of 1898–1902 and to countenance the domination of peoples, especially nonwhite peoples, afterward—with the exception of the Philippines. According to Beisner, the anti-imperialists played the "conservator's role in protecting American innocence," a stance that fostered the "weakness" and even "impotence" of the "anti-imperialist tradition" in the United States through the end of the twentieth century.[27]

In 1996, Leila Rupp searched for opposition to imperialism in transnational women's organizations active at the time of the Anti-Imperialist League through World War II. In groups like the International Council of Women and the International Woman Suffrage Alliance, she found that "women from what would come to be called the Third World" raised criticism of empire.[28] Like Newman, Rupp described the dominant discourse in these organizations to be "feminist orientialism," a strain of civilizationist thinking that suffused Euro-American women's peace activism, suffrage work, and child welfare activities before World War II and that rarely questioned the justice or ethics of empire.[29] Hoganson then turned the question of suffrage back on the Anti-Imperialist League. In a 2001 essay, she asked why that membership took so little interest in women's suffrage, particularly when compared to the "beneficial" alliance between antislavery and women's rights before the Civil War.[30] Hoganson points to male anti-imperialists' "less-than-steadfast commitment to self-government," which undermined support for votes for women citizens. Further, following Rupp, she identifies the "racist inclinations" of white woman suffragists, which inhibited transnational alliances with, for example, Filipina nationalists.

An exception—"beyond the pale," Hoganson writes—was senior activist Mary A. Livermore's stance before the league. "Why, I am as badly off as the Filipinos!" declared Livermore in front of a Boston gathering in 1903. "I think I have got a good deal of the Filipino spirit in my veins which enables me to sympathize with the work you are doing for the Filipinos." Hoganson's gloss of Livermore as "rare" and politically "radical" looks past her stance's consistency with the overall framework of the league: anti-imperialism was about protecting democracy for white Americans, not about power imbalances across an emerging global "color line," as W. E. B. Du Bois would describe it that very same year in *The Souls of Black Folk.* Livermore endorsed moral agitation for women who lacked formal, legal rights—she was prodigiously active on the home front during the Civil War and later in the WCTU—and encouraged more of the same in the imperial era. "This power outside of ourselves that makes for righteousness has done a great work," she affirmed, "the work of bringing the whole race up to where it is today."[31] Livermore's statement of racial innocence within self-identifying U.S. anti-imperial discourses deserves further unpacking.

## Native

This stance of racial innocence—of speaking for the entire human race, or of endorsing the "natural" achievements of the "white" race, or of situating a Self by invoking and appropriating an authentic yet silent Other—is central to the construction of colonial knowledge identified by philosopher Gayatry Spivak in her groundbreaking essay "Can the Subaltern Speak?" (1988). In this essay, Spivak highlighted the habit of "render[ing] thought or the thinking subject transparent or invisible" as dependent upon "the relentless recognition of the Other" by assimilation, containment, appropriation, or other epistemic violence. Read this way, Livermore is neither "rare" nor "radical" in her invocation of Filipino "spirit" and "blood" to ground her own place and that of woman suffrage vis-à-vis the Anti-Imperialist League. Rather she extended the appropriating reflex on display within the preceding (and transnational) antislavery movement, namely, the one-sided declaration of sisterhood with enslaved women by white female abolitionists who created little more than token spaces for women like Sojourner Truth in their organizations.[32] Similarly, the appeal of Filipina nationalist Clemencia López for an alliance with the New England Woman Suffrage Association in 1902 remained a symbolic token rather than a generative moment for a new political departure, an "ignored opportunity" by white suffragists, in Hoganson's words.[33] Spivak encouraged another approach. "The question is how to keep the ethnocentric Subject from establishing itself by selectively defining the Other," she affirmed, and recommended identifying such moves in the past as well as in the present in order to get at the deeper assumptions about power at work in empire and history.[34]

One of Spivak's most serious interlocutors is Laura Briggs. Her *Reproducing Empire: Race, Sex, Science, and U.S. Imperialism in Puerto Rico* (2002) is a bracing study of reproductive politics on the island under U.S. rule. Briggs identifies the conventional framing of Puerto Rico as a "problem" for U.S. democracy to be very much in the tradition of the Anti-Imperialist League. Her story centers on the technologies of empire touching family, reproduction, and sexuality as "sites of racialization" through which the United States worked through issues of nation and empire.[35] Briggs scrupulously avoids what Spivak termed the "ventriloquist's trick" of making the subaltern speak in order to authorize her own standpoint. In an epilogue, Briggs describes her strategies to resist the pressure to (re)produce the bodies and speech of Puerto Rican women in her scholarship, domains that have been "ceaselessly appropriated" by colonizers. "I prefer them as ghosts," concludes Briggs, and "wish to afford them that privacy and dignity." "Nevertheless," she continues, "silent subalterns are troubling, and should be; they haunt texts as the victims of violence, the bad conscience of imperialism and racism." Taking Spivak's revisioning to heart, Briggs distances herself from narrative moves that, like other colonial techniques, appropriate the stories/bodies of poor women for their own ends. "Yet the desire for the knowledge of the subaltern is never innocent; neither is its absence," Briggs insists, leaving her readers to ponder this tense paradox, which she owns as the measure of an honestly engaged, inevitably political scholarship.[36]

This paradox remains a provocative tension for historians. Spivak's work offers a deep challenge to scholars who seek to unpack domains of colonial ignorance that are produced concomitantly with colonial knowledge: "There is no space from which the sexed subaltern subject can speak," she wrote, and again: "The subaltern as female cannot be heard or read."[37] Since *Reproducing Empire*, Briggs has encouraged historians of women to at least try to "do something more, like trace the processes of subalternization and ask how they have eviscerated the conditions of possibility in which certain subjectivities could be legible."[38] The anthology *Haunted by Empire: Geographies of Intimacy in North America* (2006), edited by Stoler, advanced this project. Its essays explore the techniques that produce, regulate, and deploy bodies in the far-flung yet intimate work of empire. In an echo of Briggs's earlier work, *Haunted by Empire* contains an afterword titled "Internal Colonialism and Gender," in which Linda Gordon notes the nagging "silence" in the collection around gender that needs to be "dragged out from behind screens . . . in order for us to see" it. "Gender hides itself so easily," muses Gordon, "standing so often behind racial and national and class conflicts, allowing those more assertive squabblers the spotlight."[39]

## Other

The idea of race (and class and nation) being more "assertive" than gender in historical studies of empire is a challenging formulation that leads me to consideration of the category "other" in the literature on feminist approaches to anti-imperialism. One of the stories that Briggs shares about publishing *Reproducing Empire* is a response from an acquiring editor who wanted to "see two substantive chapters on African Americans before his press considered it." If her work on Puerto Rico was to be a contribution to the scholarship on "race in the United States," it perforce had to include African Americans, the principal legitimating sign of race in U.S. historiography.[40] Gordon's epilogue in *Haunted by Empire* seems to articulate another phase of this enabling ideology for historical practice touching the United States, one that reintroduces a phase of American exceptionalism. "Internal colonialism theory in the United States was killed off," Gordon asserts, "by the centrality of the African American experience to U.S. history." "The theory could not bear the weight of having to explain the evolution, operation, appeal, dominance, and persistence of racism against blacks in the United States."[41] The reasoning here is not entirely clear, since Gordon acknowledges—and conditions facing Puerto Ricans and *mexicanos/ as* long demonstrate—that "citizen" and "subaltern" are not mutually exclusive categories, leaving "racism against blacks" to be a kind of trump card.[42] Below I discuss the work of Elsa Barkley Brown to explore how or if "black" is some sort of ultimate other in U.S. historiography and how a few scholars have reframed that kind of telling.

In "Womanist Consciousness: Maggie Lena Walker and the Independent Order of Saint Luke" (1989), Brown drew on African and African American worldviews that emphasized wholeness and unity rather than those derived from the antinomies of power, however unstable, characteristic of the European episteme. She borrowed the word "womanist" from writer Alice Walker to highlight modes of thought and action that expressed, in Anna Julia Cooper's words, the "solidarity of humanity, the oneness of life." Then she laid out how these modes became torn up and hierarchized under Western taxonomies of science, economy, and politics. In Richmond, Virginia, at the turn of the twentieth century, Brown's protagonist Maggie Lena Walker emphasized "nonexclusionary" and flexible approaches to social organization in her work as a bank president, practices that "transcended the separation of private and public spheres" normatively coded by gender and constructed by the state.[43] Brown urged a more encompassing view, a "total consciousness" approach for scholarship in order to better represent African American women in the past and to expand interpretive possibilities in the present.

Brown then extended her theorizing about democracy by taking the story of African Americans in Virginia back to the end of the Civil War. She brought her archival findings into dialogue with liberal theory via Habermas and built bridges for historians to follow on. Brown described how activities like voting, party membership, and elections among the freedpeople reflected a "radically different political world view" from the mainstream. In this worldview, family and kinship rather than individualism informed political action, mutuality rather than competitiveness animated economic decision making, and voting figured as a kind of collective property, subject to negotiations within community rather than exclusively invested in a solitary, rights-endowed body. Brown questioned whether "conceptualizations of republican representative government and liberal democracy . . .

are the most appropriate ones for understanding southern black women's search for freedom, even political freedom—following the civil war."[44] Like the banners described above, Brown's essays trace social and political terrain obscured by modern political discourses and categories. Freedpeople did not just accept the terms of citizenship conferred by the state during Reconstruction but sought to reshape those terms. Freedwomen, Brown contends, "thus invented the power that their freedom required."[45]

Elsa Barkley Brown's postwar South has a colonial-like air about it, in which Yankee missionaries, teachers, and Freedmen's Bureau agents arrive with possessive individualism, acquisitiveness, and deferred gratification to encounter a peasant, perhaps subaltern population with its own ideals, ethics, and sense of human possibility. Brown's portrait of Reconstruction strikes me as available for a "decolonial" reading. Such readings have mostly not happened, however, even though Brown cautioned her readers against the "obsession in African American women's political history with questions of legal enfranchisement" and related state-centered forms of public life.[46]

Building on Brown yet ignoring some of her more radical suggestions, subsequent work in African American women's history heeded another disciplinary admonition in the early 1990s, namely to "bring the state back in."[47] A number of books took up black women's efforts in the public sphere as wage earners, church workers, and political partisans. These studies describe the many ways in which African American women generated social, cultural, and political capital in order to make claims on power structures, including the state. Overall, these works recover a highly purposeful federalism that sought to fully nationalize U.S. citizenship and keep it free from racist limitations. They give little attention to transnational relationships or to empire, to missionaries who left the United States and returned (or not), or to black women who entered the United States or other parts of the Americas from various locations with the African diaspora. In other words, the state they brought back in was a rather exceptional, unimperial state.[48]

Questions touching African American women in empire occur less frequently under the category "nation" and much more often under the category "diaspora." Rosalyn Terborg-Penn's *Women in Africa and the African Diaspora* (1987) helped name the Atlantic and Caribbean circuitries of labor and culture involving black women and describes how scholars might theorize these domains, including the imperial dynamics of slavery and suffrage.[49] Contributors noted how words like "women" and "black" either had little significance or radically different meaning across national and transnational contexts, posing major difficulties for translation and interpretation. Nonetheless, Terborg-Penn encouraged scholars to modify their lens of analysis in order to move toward a "comparative women's history" that could prevent U.S.-based black women from being stranded (and exceptional?) within accounts of the African diaspora.[50] "Although African Americans living in the United States are not officially to be considered among the colonized," wrote Terborg-Penn, "in figurative ways we are, as literary and dramatic figures in our communities have noted for many years."[51] In the main, however, Terborg-Penn's own use of the word "colonized" to describe black women remains "figurative," and her use of the word "official" points readers to the body of U.S. law as well as conventional scholarly practices in which African Americans are either slaves or citizens of the United States, with little space in between.

## Decolonial

Though the word "decolonial" has not yet entered the English language, feminist scholars generally credit Spivak when they use it.[52] In *The Decolonial Imaginary: Writing Chicanas into History*, Pérez draws broadly on Scott, Spivak, and Chela Sandoval. She contends that the decolonial can name and organize evidence that does share the provenance of either "the colonial" or the "post-colonial." The decolonial functions similarly to "diaspora" in African American studies, as a frame for historical meaning-making that stretches beyond the hegemonic identities of slave, alien, or citizen usually derived from nation-state political formations. Part of the anti-imperial thrust of the decolonial comes from its critical stance toward nation building in general, particularly in the Americas. To decenter nationalistic habits of thought in historical writing, Pérez suggests, "perhaps our only hope is to move in many directions."[53]

This suggestion puts me in mind of Spivak's notion of aporia—a domain of suspended meaning and deferred resolution—and calls to mind something about that tree branch Bender warned about. Laura Briggs noted in her review of Pérez's book that "the 'postcolonial' is weird in the context of the Americas"; scholars might attend, instead, to what Stoler calls "compounded colonialisms," the layered social organization, threads of power, and webs of exchange that cross-cut the globe.[54] Pérez's theorizing of the decolonial offers an important category for historians of women,

as it can name resistance to empire and nation building in practices un-
evenly connected to the state. It can also foster the comparisons, however
cautious, that Terborg-Penn and Ann Stoler encourage and with which
I began this paper. While "Indian policy" often served as a precedent for
U.S. empire "abroad," Native American women's ideas about empire in
the post-Reconstruction period have yet to be given their due weight and
value.[55] Silva de Cintrón was neither a pro-independence nationalist nor
simply an assimilated figure within a colonial regime. UMA's standpoint—
"No Aceptamos Demarcaciones" (We do not accept demarcations)—raises
interesting possibilities about global or transnational feminisms.[56]

Exploring these questions will not likely yield "a" story or tidy counter-
story of the decolonial compared to the colonial (or postcolonial), but
rather stories; episodic, slow pans across a number of familiar and unfamil-
iar landscapes, less a "history" than a reading strategy. I return to Spivak's
descriptor, aporia, with which she points to a "spatial temporal indeter-
minacy" or a space "between subject and object status." Spivak uses this
word in her discussions of suttee to mark "something other than silence
and nonexistence" for the self-immolating wife, a gesture that gets at the
tenor of Fuller's "uttered silent protest" and the contradiction of *la raza* as a
race that does not discriminate; that is, a space of unresolved and unresolv-
able meaning.[57] The WCTU banner in Indian Territory and *la bandera de
la raza* suggest components of an understudied set of women's practices,
"anti-imperialism as a way of life," that haven't yet found a foothold in
academic rubrics.[58] Trinh contends that "the notion of gender is pertinent
to feminism as long as it denounces certain fundamental attitudes of imperialism and as long as it remains unsettled and unsettling."[59] In this spirit,
I read the banner of Indian Territory WCTU and *la bandera de la raza* as
evidence of a decolonial politic, pointed rejections of racialization. They
indicate women's movements, creations, ideas, organizations, newspapers,
songs, and rituals that wave us on to rethink where nations begin and end,
even when I can barely see.

Chapter 9

# Resource Use, Conservation, and the Environmental Limits of Anti-imperialism, c. 1890–1930

IAN TYRRELL

A remarkable Mark Boulos art installation, *All That Is Solid Melts into Air*, was shown at the 2008 Sydney Biennale. A dual video presentation, it focused on the commodification of oil from the Niger Delta and the social struggle over how the benefits and costs of oil production are distributed. Boulos depicts a relationship structuring both human misery and resistance in Nigeria. Globalization's impact is expressed in the film as oil prices and stock market values, and human and ecological effects of coercion are erased in these abstractions; yet, on the margins, disadvantaged people fight back and influence the metropolitan centers of financial power in Europe and the United States. As local tribesmen go out to damage pipeline facilities, the price of oil in a futures market fluctuates, and the financial well-being of the West is shown in the rising and falling dollar values on the electronic register as sabotage takes its effect.[1] A transnational corporation, Royal Dutch Shell, is the target in this Nigerian case, and the effects of oil spills there are less well known than those for the Louisiana oil spill of 2010, but the message applies to each. In our time, this joining of the human and the ecological on the one hand, with the commodification of oil on the other, has become a cogent way to analyze power relations across the globe.

The globalization of the early twenty-first century is, of course, not the same as that of the era of "high" imperialism from the 1870s to 1914. But it has connections through international struggles over resource access, struggles that have always had profound environmental effects. It should be noted that imperialism refers in what follows to the exertion of control by one nation over other peoples, whether in the political, economic, or military realm (or some combination of those), through informal or formal mechanisms (or both). The empire thus constituted is not a "thing" that can be pinned down to a simple yes or no definition. Empire requires careful historicization, with attention to the specificity of all cases. This chapter is principally concerned with U.S. formal and informal imperialism (1890s–1934), an important era for the conception of modern anti-imperialist ideas that continued to influence American thinking decades later.

Boulos's work is part of a modern concern with environmental sustainability encompassing human and nonhuman ecological systems.[2] Similar critiques centered on the exploitation of resources are found in the work of historians. Richard Tucker's *Insatiable Appetite* involves analysis of U.S. formal and (more commonly) informal imperialism, and links environmental and human impacts in a version of what environmental theorists call "social ecology."[3] That is, Tucker shows the relationship between the mass consumerism of U.S. society and what he calls the "degradation of the tropical world." As with Boulos, Tucker sees the tropical world's resources being converted into marketable commodities in ways that change ecosystems and the livelihoods of people deprived of the resources of the land.

While this work can be construed as part of a modern anti-imperialist historiography, it is unclear whether these analytical insights were present in the thought and practice of anti-imperialists in U.S. history. No history of U.S. anti-imperialism has detected an environmental, still less an ecological, discourse.[4] None, however, has asked the requisite questions. What follows explores the continuities and discontinuities between empire and environmentalist critique.

The historiography of South Asian forests suggests two ways in which such discourse might have been present. Richard Grove has shown European consciousness of damage in colonial environments long before modern ecology or environmental movements arose.[5] These proto-environmental sensibilities can be traced, Grove argues, to the work of colonial scientists and officials in tropical island colonies of the European empires. Disturbed at the negative environmental effects of colonial development through deforestation and its supposed impacts on rainfall and soil erosion, officials and scientists criticized laws and practices of private European colonists and tried to mitigate damage. Within this discourse lay the potential for critiques of imperialism when these proto-environmentalists questioned government regulations detrimental to forest protection or corrupt land practices of particular governors. Yet, *contra* Grove, practical opposition to the colonial state on forest policies was usually found among indigenous groups rather than conservationists. Indeed, colonial "conservation" as conventionally conceived developed through the imperial state and its disciplinary structures.[6]

Work on U.S. history has followed this angle only in tracing indigenous responses to environmental change *within* the expanding United States, not its external connections. Efforts to establish national parks within the United States had pronounced ecological and social effects. On occasion, these actions involved removal of American Indians from their land and prohibition of wood taking or hunting by poor whites or Indians.[7] More generally, the choice of national parks was underpinned by assumptions of their emptiness that erased the history of Indian dispossession. Arguably, the entire continental expansionism of the nineteenth century was a form of "settler colonialism" shared across the European diaspora in the Americas and elsewhere.[8] Still, no author has examined U.S. anti-imperialist discourses from a similar perspective.

These discourses do not reveal much consciousness of "settler society" issues, in part because turn-of-the-twentieth-century anti-imperialists wished to distinguish between overseas expansion and continental expansion.[9] In the latter, the areas annexed were viewed as the product of just wars and treaties, and in any case the inhabitants of these areas were accepted as citizens under territorial government, not subjects. Yet this distinction was far from clear in practice. Pro-imperialists reminded their opponents that the case of the Philippines did have precedents in the continental phase of "expansion." In particular, Alaska from 1867 was an *unincorporated* territory with its inhabitants treated as wards of the national government, not citizens. Chief Justice John Marshall's "domestic dependent nations" ruling of 1831 and subsequent court decisions on the status of Indians as wards of the nation also underpinned the imperialists' case.[10] Because pro-imperialists had the better of the argument over precedent, anti-imperialist discourse focusing on indigenous land rights, whether in the Philippines or the American West, was closed off. For anti-imperialists, the history of the republic itself could be explained as an exceptionalist story of extending liberty, but that tactic involved erasing the damage done to the indigenous population, not dwelling on it, and that is precisely how anti-imperialists dealt with the precedents. At most, some conceded uncomfortably the existence of Indians whose treatment had been poor, but argued that this problem would be magnified "a hundred fold" in the Philippines because of the size of the country and the population to be exploited.[11] The president of the New England Anti-Imperialist League, ex-senator George S. Boutwell, went further, baldly asserting that in Louisiana, California, and Alaska "there was never from any of these territories a recorded protest against the sovereignty of the United States."[12]

Strangely, this failure to consider the impact on indigenous peoples and their physical environment was not duplicated among moral reformers. Tirades against alcohol and opium foisted on "helpless" Philippine, Hawaiian, and Puerto Rican "natives" litter the speeches of moral reformers on the topic of American and European empires. But this work focused on the moral degeneration of bodies and souls, not removal from land and other material resources.[13] The failure to consider seriously the dispossession of colonized people from their connection to the land and the resources therein is a striking lacuna in anti-imperialist thought in the Progressive Era. This lacuna remains, despite the fact that environmental changes wrought by European occupation on the lands were well known at the time of westward expansion and during the formal and informal imperialism of the early twentieth century. George Perkins Marsh made the case cogently in *Man and Nature* as early as 1864, and his work had ramifications for forest policy as early as the 1870s.[14] Given this circumstance, one might expect modern studies to question whether U.S. anti-imperialism registered environmental issues, and if not, why not.

The substantial body of historiography on American empire has not raised these questions. This applies especially to New Left historians of the 1960s to 1970s who produced scholarship critical of empire. The work of William Appleman Williams and his students did not consider environmental issues regarding American "expansion" and did not focus on the history of anti-imperialism. Williams's own writing emphasized U.S. expansionism, not opposition to it. For Williams, anti-imperialism succumbed to the flaw of thinking that only the formal empire required opposition. Ironically, however, American anti-imperialists had actually won a technical victory, in Williams's view, because anti-imperialism harmonized with the informal imperialism of the Open Door policy.[15]

New Left scholarship was largely concerned with the Open Door concept and the assumption that the United States was seeking overseas markets. Environmental issues were not—and could not be—*intrinsic* to this debate, and their absence is not surprising. More promising would have been discussion of the contest for natural resources in which empires were, at times, engaged. But resource competition played little role in the New Left argument either. On the face of it, this was a sensible judgment, because the United States had such a plethora of its own resources, and took up the issues of resource use in the Philippines only *after* acquisition became a possibility.[16] Instead, New Left historians identified markets for agricultural and manufacturing products as the key contributory factors to American expansionism.[17]

The Open Door, especially in Williams's work, came to be a metaphor for an ideal in American policy. Yet the Open Door meant not only markets for U.S. manufactures but also equal access of all countries to the resources of the non-Western world, originally referring to China. American policy makers feared that European, particularly German, territorial zones of influence would restrict global access to coal and iron. Brooks Adams had argued that the world's future would be decided by the struggle over China and its mineral wealth. This approach in turn influenced Theodore Roosevelt in his assertion of the nation's global role.[18]

As historian Andrew Bacevich has noted,[19] the New Left expanded on Charles Beard's ideas of the 1930s on American empire, in which economic motives for trade and investment became allied to an aggrandizing and militarist state.[20] It is to that interwar period (1919–39) that we need to look for the modern development of a fully fledged U.S. critique of imperialism. At the practical level, anti-imperialists had to face the fundamental fact that the U.S. "empire" rested on informal control through bases and on economic penetration much more than formal colonies. (This transition did not come easily to the founding elite of the Anti-Imperialist League, which disbanded in 1921.) The political context was one of revulsion against World War I (a war commonly attributed to imperialist rivalries), the rise of international communism, and lively if minority protests against U.S. muscle-flexing in the Caribbean in the 1920s. Americans organized groups to oppose periodic U.S. intervention in Caribbean states, until 1934's Good Neighbor Policy removed the immediate spur to action. The National Citizens Committee on Relations with Latin America, for example, published in the 1920s a left-Progressive magazine, *Good Neighborship*, organized protests against "the Kellogg-Coolidge strong-arm policy for weak neighbors," and railed at U.S. Marines' occupation of Nicaragua.[21]

It was in the 1920s that a clear economic rather than moral and ideological objection to overseas imperialism congealed in the United States. This shift was closely associated with the work of the American radical Scott Nearing. After his controversial dismissal from the University of Pennsylvania in 1915, and involvement in anti–World War I activism, Nearing turned decisively from the social Gospel and Progressivism toward socialism and Marxism, though he did not become a member of the Communist (Workers) Party until 1927, and then he remained in the party only briefly.

His pamphlet *American Empire* (1921) treated the United States as a particular case within the general processes of capital accumulation. He recognized that the United States did not need great quantities of "external" resources in the nineteenth century. He did note, "There was no strategic reason that demanded the Philippines unless the United States desired to have an operating base near to the vast resources and the developing markets of China."[22] But it was not the formal empire of the late nineteenth century that interested him, because the world war had projected the United States into an economically hegemonic position within the world economy and drawn it into the solution of pressing problems of war and peace. "American imperialists are still in the making," he wrote in 1921. "Until 1900 their eyes were set almost exclusively upon empire within the United States." Though slavery's gaze had been for a time unsuccessfully fixed on the Caribbean basin, capitalists were now compelled "by virtue of the organization which their sires and grandsires established, to seek Empire outside the boundaries of North America." This shift occurred because "the resources and raw materials required by the industrial nations of Europe, the rapidly growing surplus and the newly acquired foreign markets and investments [made] the United States an integral part of the life of the world."[23]

Nearing's later work *Dollar Diplomacy* (1925) elaborated on the nature of a distinctively American phase of global capitalism.[24] Written with fellow activist Joseph Freeman, this book focused on the specifics of what the writers saw as the financial capitalism of the "new era" of the 1920s. In this context, resource availability outside the United States was becoming an important issue. The growth of the consumer economy created large demands for raw materials—most obviously rubber and oil—that could not be satisfied purely within the United States. Corporate competition and repeated scares of shortage, starting with a major oil famine just after World War I, spurred extensive exploitation of oil fields in Venezuela that ultimately drove down the real price of oil dramatically in the 1920s.[25] The intensification of commercial forestry and experimentation with rubber plantations in the Philippines also proceeded apace, and American companies acquired tropical forest acreage in Liberia and Brazil for conversion to the same use.[26]

Given the cross-national rush by the great powers to corral the world's key resources, it is not surprising that Nearing and Freeman's work on American empire should draw attention to the causes and economic functioning of imperialism, including "the search for resources and supplies of raw materials." Nearing and Freeman detailed overseas investment opportunities in manufacturing, lumbering, and mining, which depended upon such resources. Though they acknowledged also the "search for markets for surplus production,"[27] their comments indicated the growing importance of resource security, and they enumerated the list of commodities that the United States now imported. Crude raw materials for manufacture by volume rose from 6.8 percent of imports in 1850 to 36.4 percent in 1910, and the value of such materials imported rose 150 percent in the seventy years to 1920.[28] The 1920s would extend this pattern, which Nearing saw as one of greater U.S. integration in the world economy. As journalist John Franklin Carter showed in 1928, raw materials counted for more than half of all U.S. imports in the 1920s.[29] But Nearing and Freeman (and Carter, whose politics were pro-business) were interested only in the economic implications for an interdependent world of resource use, not environmental, still less ecological, impacts.

This radical anti-imperialism, focused on the economics of resource extraction, was accentuated in the Vanguard Press Series of the late 1920s and 1930s. The series was founded with American Fund for Public Service (Garland Fund) money to produce, through the Committee on Studies of American Investments Abroad, radical critiques of U.S. imperialism.[30] Nearing was on the executive of the Garland Fund dispensing the grants, and Harry Elmer Barnes of Smith College edited the series. The published studies included Leland H. Jenks, *Our Cuban Colony: A Study in Sugar* (1928); Melvin M. Knight, *The Americans in Santo Domingo* (1928); Margaret Marsh, *The Bankers in Bolivia: A Study in American Foreign Investment* (1928); Bailey W. Diffie and Justine W. Diffie, *Porto Rico: A Broken Pledge* (1931); and Charles David Kepner Jr. and Jay Henry Soothill, *The Banana Empire: A Case Study of Economic Imperialism* (1935).

Barnes made clear in his introduction to the series that no party line was expected. In place of "single track dogmas," historians must collect the facts.[31] But, reflecting the close association with left progressives, Communists, and socialists, the series' output concentrated on labor, tax, tariffs, and investments. This characteristic is confirmed by comparing Kepner and Soothill's *The Banana Empire* with Kepner's separately published PhD thesis, *Social Aspects of the Banana Industry* (1936). The latter is insightful on the environmental transformation of Central American forests in areas replaced by banana plantations. Monoculture wasted soil fertility by over-cropping and made plants vulnerable to pests and diseases that ravaged the industry. The fate of such former plantation acreage was a "reversion to the jungle" that left the local people without workable land or employment.[32] *The Banana Empire*, on the other hand, centered on the economic and political relationships of people ("the struggle for power"), not land's relations with people.[33] Possibly the best book in the Vanguard series, *Porto Rico: A Broken Pledge*, briefly discussed negative effects of crop specialization, especially sugar, and mentioned monoculture's harmful impacts on soil fertility. But the emphasis again was upon labor exploitation and the peasantry's marginalization; the Diffies argued that extractive resource-based imperialism under U.S. rule from 1898 had impoverished an already poor Puerto Rican people.[34]

This almost total absence of an environmental context in the anti-imperialist literature occurred despite the fact that Marxists have unearthed thinking about these issues from within the corpus of work laid down by Karl Marx and Friedrich Engels. Perhaps the best examples are from Engels, in comments reflecting Victorian-era debates over human-induced deforestation and desiccation. Late in life Engels wrote: "Let us not . . . flatter ourselves overmuch on account of our human conquests over nature. For each such conquest takes its revenge on us." His argument bore the marks of the contemporary discourse on forest destruction.[35] For Engels, "The people who, in Mesopotamia, Greece, Asia Minor and elsewhere destroyed the forests to obtain cultivable land, never dreamed that they were laying the basis for the present devastated condition of those countries, by removing along with the forests the collecting centres and reservoirs of moisture."[36]

Marx's contribution came earlier, and was apposite to his theory of class conflict. He emphasized that the struggle between classes occurred over resources, thus indicating a form of social environmental protest. "All progress in capitalistic agriculture is a progress in the art, not only of robbing the labourer, but of robbing the soil," he wrote in *Capital*. Here, proto-ecological ideas surfaced in similar ways to those of Engels: "all progress in increasing the fertility of the soil for a given time, is a progress towards ruining the lasting sources of that fertility. The more a country starts its development on the foundation of modern industry, like the United States . . . the more rapid is this process of destruction."[37] Marx therein equated "the soil and the laborer" as "the original sources of all wealth."[38] Marx's argument showed the influence of German soil science, as in the work of Justus von Liebig.[39] Marx, however, took up Liebig's soil science and linked it with class analysis, arguing that Liebig had capitulated to Malthusianism when he undervalued the role of labor in improving soil in "scientific" and post-capitalist conditions.[40] This link with what Marx called "political economy" was clear: "Capitalist production, by collecting the population in great centers . . . disturbs the circulation of matter between man and the soil, i.e., prevents the return to the soil of its elements consumed by man in the form of food and clothing; it therefore violates the conditions necessary to lasting fertility of the soil . . . upsetting the naturally grown conditions for the maintenance of that circulation of matter."[41] This circulation of matter demanded "restoration as a system" at a higher level through a "regulating law of social production," that is, dialectically achieved socialism.[42] As historians of the Soviet Union have pointed out, these proto-sustainability perspectives did not stand out in the thicket of Marxist theory and were overrun by Stalinist technological utopianism in the 1930s. Nevertheless, they indicated an eagerly sought pedigree and intellectual resource for green/left politics in the late twentieth century.[43]

The homegrown American Left also had an environmental pedigree from a very early time. Nearing was a pioneering environmentalist fondly remembered in the 1960s and 1970s, and his back-to-nature works won widespread appeal within the counterculture.[44] Yet Nearing was not merely an Old Leftist responding belatedly to modern environmentalism's rise. He had become an advocate of the back-to-the-land movement prior to World War I, before his major anti-imperialist and antiwar tracts were written.[45]

Given the presence of proto-environmentalist ideas in both classical Marxism and American radicalism, the question arises why anti-imperialists failed to join the dots. The most obvious reason is the focus of the radical movement in the 1920s on immediate issues of labor exploitation through the political agitation discussed above. A second and more important but equally obvious reason is the absence of an environmental movement. No such mass movement existed in the United States until the 1960s and 1970s, and before that, ecological issues were marginal in conservationist debates. Ecology did exist as a fledgling concept from the 1870s, and had begun to penetrate American academia by the early twentieth century. In 1915 the Ecological Society of America was founded, and some ecologists were politically active in the 1920s and 1930s as wilderness and national park advocates, but ecology, environment, and empire just did not come together in an obvious way. Third, U.S. anti-imperialism had, in the struggle over the annexation of the Philippines, derived from moral critiques centered on humanitarianism and evangelicalism, as well as concern for republicanism with a small r. This tradition continued to influence the conceptualization of empire in the 1920s. These objections to imperialism on grounds of republican values, constitutionalism, and/or humanitarianism were rooted in U.S. exceptionalism.[46]

Even in the case of Richard Pettigrew, where both anti-imperialism and concern over conservation were manifest, the two issues remained mostly at arm's length. Pettigrew, a two-term senator from South Dakota and a silver (cheap money) Republican (from 1896), was a sponsor of the 1897 act to create a framework for the National Forest Reserves,[47] an important landmark in the development of an administrative structure for forest conservation. Pettigrew was also an anti-imperialist who vigorously opposed in the U.S. Senate the annexation of Hawaii and the Philippines. His anti-imperialist work has been neglected because he lacked political success, but it did represent a link between turn-of-the-century anti-imperialism and that of the 1920s and beyond.[48] When dealing with imperialism, Pettigrew displayed the moral and republican traditions common in the debates over annexation of the Philippines, but his thoughts, drawn together in *Imperial Washington*, were influenced also by socialist denunciations of economic imperialism. There, Pettigrew explicitly raised the struggle over resources, and linked it to labor exploitation. "The imperialists' aim is to assimilate, not the people of these possessions" such as the Philippines, Costa Rica, and Haiti, he wrote in 1922, but "their lands and their wealth" and to "exploit their labor as well as the resources of their respective countries."[49]

But in 1899, his concern over land was chiefly to indicate how empire deprived poor American farmers or would-be settlers upon the nation's public lands of the benefits of conservation initiatives by draining revenues to futile campaigns abroad: "Instead of spending hundreds of millions in conquering the Philippines, it would have been far better economy and better business judgment to spend it in reclaiming the arid lands of the west."[50] Through irrigation, the people of the American West "would cause its revivified soil to produce abundantly of the fruits of the earth."[51]

This republic of small farmers would be white, "a kindred race" that would build the networks of commerce and prosperity within the United States.[52] In the debates over Hawaii's annexation in 1898, Pettigrew emphasized the incompatibility of American democratic and constitutional government with a "tropical" environment where "an inferior race" proliferated: "Therefore, if we adopt a policy of acquiring tropical countries, where republics can not live, and where free, self-governing people have never lived since the world had a history, we overturn the theory upon which this Government is established and we do violence to our Constitution."[53] This racial environmentalist foundation to republicanism was a common theme in anti-imperialism, though by no means uncontested by anti-imperialists in the abolitionist tradition, who saw empire's acquisitions as the true source of racist beliefs.[54]

Of Progressive anti-imperialists, Pettigrew came the closest to grasping an environmental critique of imperialism, but his attack reflected antimonopoly values and moral republicanism more than analysis of the struggle over resources and its environmental impact. He believed the desire for colonial resources was an illegitimate motive for imperialism, but he couched his opposition to empire in terms familiar to the Progressive movement. In his summation of his anti-imperialist views in *Imperial Washington*, he saw a record of resource plundering that shifted from domestic to foreign targets. As with the socialists who increasingly influenced Pettigrew's thinking (Nearing wrote the foreword in 1920 to Pettigrew's collected speeches, *The Course of Empire*),[55] his interest was with the moral wrongs of annexation and its economic impacts upon people. His rhetoric castigating the quest for resources regularly deployed terms such as "steal" and "robbery":

> After all, why talk nonsense? Why lie to others? Why seek to deceive ourselves? An imperial policy has as its object the enrichment of the imperial class. The plain man—the farmer, the miner, the factory worker—is not the gainer through imperialism. Rather the monopolist, the land owner, the manufacturer, the trader, the banker—who have *stolen* what there is to *steal* at home, devote their energies to the pursuit of empire because the pursuit of empire gives them an opportunity to *exploit* and *rob* abroad.[56]

If Marxist economism (or, for that matter, the radical critique of land use coming from the labor reformer Henry George) could bring anti-imperialism and conservation together in the same analytical frame, the puzzle deepens when we consider the strength of conservationist sentiment in the United States before World War I. To restate the obvious, there was no ecological "movement" or cause known as environmentalism at that time. But there certainly was a conservation movement. Theodore Roosevelt's highly influential form of Progressivism made vital the conservation of resources as well as national parks and the preservation of wild life.[57]

In practice, conservation sentiment in the first decade of the twentieth century was far more often pro-imperialist than anti-imperialist, as with Roosevelt and his right-hand man, Gifford Pinchot, chief forester, 1898–1910. One might expect this, since historians of the Progressive Era have noted close affinities between key sections of Progressivism and imperialism. Republican progressives overwhelmingly followed Roosevelt into "expansionism" abroad. A free-silver Republican, Pettigrew is typically seen as an exception because his economic views on cheap credit had made him persona non grata for the Republican Party.[58] But the conservationist beliefs of Progressive Republicans had an impact in creating ill ease with empire in terms of seeing in the record of wasted resources at home a cause for concern over duplication of waste abroad. Added to the anxiety was the perceived need to conserve foreign resources for the future American and world economies.

In practice, the conservation movement tended to preempt anti-imperialism at the level of formal empire but was simultaneously critical of American private interests abroad, a circumstance that mostly though not invariably coincided with cases of informal economic control rather than colonial rule. This judgment was exhibited by Gifford Pinchot and his followers in regard to U.S. economic penetration in the Americas, especially in Mexico and Canada. Thomas E. Will was a staunch Pinchot supporter and, as editor of *Forestry and Irrigation* from 1907 until 1910, acted as an outlet for the Roosevelt-Pinchot line on conservation. In October 1907, Will wrote on "Timber Lands in Mexico": "Many Americans hope for relief from lumber scarcity in the United States by importations from Canada and Mexico; but this relief can only be temporary, unless these countries also will conserve their forests in a scientific manner" rather than let in "American investors to devour them hastily."[59]

Rooseveltian progressives such as Will looked forward not to the end of the formal empire that the United States had acquired, but to a different set of relations between nation-states that would be internationalist rather than imperialist. The pro-Roosevelt magazine *Outlook* favored this cooperation.[60]

It editorialized that the North American Conservation Conference called by Roosevelt for February 1909, involving the United States, Canada, and Mexico, would produce a "public sentiment" that could spread across "the entire continent." A genuinely preservative spirit, *Outlook* argued, would emerge to husband resources for "enduring profit, replacing the present temporary profits" derived from timber and other resource exploitation across the continent. The meeting was necessary because "purely artificial lines separate our country from its neighbors," and natural resources "are, of course, not limited by such boundary lines." To conserve U.S. resources, Americans must know their neighbors and cooperate with them.[61] At the opening of the North American conference, Roosevelt stated it to be in the interests of international relations that all countries be "elevated," not "depressed." Here he modified his well-known pro-imperialist views, and looked toward cooperation between weaker and stronger states, not geo-political rivalry.[62]

For Pinchot and his allies in the conservation movement, this cooperative internationalism referred to relations with other governments exposed to the informal empire that, through business activities, involved the United States. Yet Progressive conservation could also be critical of private and government conduct in the Philippines under the ambit of the Bureau of Insular Affairs. There, *Forestry and Irrigation* editor Will favored the "conservation of the equal rights, liberties, and opportunities" of "all the people."[63] The "people" in need of protection, in Will's view, evidently included the nation's colonial subjects of the Philippines. In "Philippine Forest Resources" (1907), Will wrote that the forestry department of the "insular possessions" might one day benefit the United States. Yet a few "adventurers" had obtained concessions that would undermine the progress of sustainable forestry. Americans must remember, Will stressed, that the islands' forests were to be kept primarily for the benefit of the Philippine people. "If Americans should go in there and strip these forests, it would be robbery."[64]

In the Philippines there were American foresters willing to criticize the colonial administration, too, with arguments based on conservationist and proto-ecological grounds. Barrington Moore Sr., a forester in the islands from 1908 to 1910, helped found the American Ecological Society in 1915 and served for two terms as its president.[65] He condemned the foreign exploitation of resources and implicitly defended the rights of indigenous peasants against persistent allegations that they were the chief source of forest degradation. Moore observed that regulations governing lumber concessions on public land encouraged exploitation in order to gain for the Philippine government self-sufficiency in revenue through royalties to the Bureau of Forestry: "these concessions must be given on ruinously favorable terms: at extremely low stumpage rates . . . and for long periods of years. . . . Otherwise, nobody will embark on such a new and untried venture."[66] Because the most valuable trees were often thought to be thinly dispersed in these tropical forests, the commercial exploitation tended to be harsh when added to the lease terms.[67]

In addition to noting commercial logging's impact and the inadequacy of the colonial forest laws, Moore linked fire damage in Philippine forests to the socioeconomic condition of the peasantry. The development of planta-tion agriculture and the land claims of the caciques (prominent Filipino vil-lagers) had driven caingin (swidden, or shifting slash-and-burn) cultivators into desperate practices on the margins of the plains where "virgin" for-est could be burned without interference. The resultant cogans (regrowth weed areas) were abandoned, because if fully cultivated they were likely to encourage land claims from the powerful caciques.[68]

Richard Tucker has pursued the implication that U.S. policy was sup-portive of the landed elites against the landless in the Philippines, and against the preservation of a social and ecological balance, whereas Moore stepped back from this judgment. Probably in deference to his superiors in the colonial government, he repeated the cliché that landless Filipinos had an "aversion to the harder kinds of manual labor," and preferred "making a [new] Caingin in the forest to cultivating the Cogan by hand."[69] A scion of the Chelsea-Moore investment and real estate fortune and a graduate of the Yale Forestry School, Moore had loyalties to Pinchot.[70] He concluded that Americans should rejoice in the landmark work being done in tutelage of the Filipino people, who had to be guided toward correct conservation strategies.[71] "It should, therefore, be the proud duty of every American to give his hearty support to work . . . upon which in such a vital degree depends the whole future development and prosperity of a people whose best interests his country has pledged its honor to care for." For Moore, Americans would be modernizers. While forestry administration had tech-nical problems, and foresters made mistakes in not adapting enough to local conditions, the idea of scientifically grounded and sustainable forestry required, in Moore's view as in Pinchot's, U.S. supervision. This was hostile to anti-imperialism when applied to the case of formal empire.

Was the absence of ecology in the American case unique? Ecology did in-fluence the conservation of nature in at least one other empire, the French, but in a specific way that reinforces the argument offered here. In effect, in both the United States and France, ecologists accepted the separation between the human and the ecological and reserved the latter to scientific conservation, though conservation was in turn conceived of somewhat differently in each country. In the French African empire, efforts were made to address the damage apparent in colonial environments. But the response was to isolate special representative areas of ecosystem diversity for rehabilitation, in much the same way as ecologists in the United States advocated through the work of Victor Shelford and the Committee for the Preservation of Natural Conditions after 1917.[72] The American Ecological Society's work paralleled that of the French but occurred in the continental United States rather than its territories. In neither case were sociologically constituted ecosystems produced by centuries of peasant or tribal exploitation of environments considered.[73]

Some European ecologists did come closer to affecting a critique of imperialism than this, to be sure. The Swiss zoologist Paul Sarasin, who influenced Swiss national park ideas, sought ecosystem protection. Moreover, in his speech to the 1913 International Conservation Congress in Berne, the world's first such meeting, Sarasin viewed indigenous people as in need of protection from the land-grabbing effects of Euro-American imperialism in the same way as "nature" and its animals ought to be protected. The Swiss (and German) conservationists called these "indigenous" people the *Naturvölker*. (This has been understood as "primitive," though the term and its application by Sarasin as "natural" people retain ambiguities never resolved.) These ideas did not have practical effects at the time because World War I shattered the nascent international conservation cooperation begun at the meeting, but they did foreshadow an ecologically based critique of imperialism,[74] without amounting to a social ecology.[75] To move in this latter direction would have required developing the insights of Barrington Moore Sr., and divorcing Moore's observations from their attachment to the colonial state.

The elusive ecologically related anti-imperialism keeps vanishing before our eyes, but, viewed from the perspective of Filipinos, a different picture emerges. One form of anti-imperialist resistance came from subsistence agriculture among landless peasants. Continued use of firewood and the making of caingins that Moore deplored were contrary to colonial authority, and these plagued the revenues of the Philippine Commission that depended on forest income for the functioning of colonial government. The result was de facto anti-imperial resistance in the forests. In 1905, peasant resistance forced the government to loosen rules on indigenous firewood use, just a year after tightening them. Authorities feared that resentment over banning of firewood gathering without license might fuel anti-government sentiment.[76] In 1910, they established communal reserves for tribal timber uses, and by 1914 some reserves for the landless were introduced. These, it was hoped, would induce shifting cultivators to change their practices and farm regularly instead of continuing the slash-and-burn agriculture considered so ruinous to forests. In the hope that regulation would work better than banning, certain caingins were sanctioned.[77] However, illegal as well as legalized caingins remained a serious problem for the management of forests, still evident in the 1930s.[78] In Puerto Rico, too, U.S. Bureau of Forestry official John Gifford's 1905 account shows, parallel practices could be observed; traditional wood gathering, as well as a culturally distinctive attitude to the forests as the homes of ancestral spirits, myths, and legends, undermined the utilitarianism of the colonial conservation elite.[79]

Filipino responses to American ideas of national parks provide further examples of this struggle over resources. Not until the early 1930s did the colonial authorities, under pressure to engage in nation building and prepare for decolonization, work with Philippine nationalists to produce a law for national parks. Arthur Fischer, head of the Bureau of Forestry in Manila and a Yale Forestry School graduate, toured with Philippine senator Camilo Osias from Luzon to Mindanao on a fact-finding mission prior to the passage of the colony's national park law in 1932.[80] Once the legislation was in force, College of Agriculture professor at the University of the Philippines Hugh Curran publicized the newly designated spaces in terms similar to those applying to American parks: "for those who love nature in its untamed form."[81]

Yet the Philippine people themselves claimed these spaces and redefined them. National parks were promoted in the pro-modernizing *Philippine Magazine*—a vehicle for the Philippine *ilustrado* elite with European-style aesthetics—to satisfy "vacationists" and "nature lovers," yet were, even in the 1930s, not what they appeared to be. Close to the surface, the popular Filipino conception of nature resisted compartmentalization of the secular and the sacred into ordinary space and "national space." The national parks included leases for forestry, manufactures, caingins, and communal firewood concession zones. Some of these uses were legacies of pre-1932 acts with licenses that had several years to run, but others were "gratuitous" allowances for short-term exigencies, and still others displayed a variety of criminal activities.[82]

As in Europe in the Middle Ages, forests were places of industry, but at the same time they were sites of folklore symbolic of indigenous religious beliefs. For Filipinos, mountains and forests were traditionally sacred and possessed of spirits. Filipino forester Fidel Paz recommended that his countrymen visit Makiling National Park, because of the legends of Mariang Makiling, the bountiful but elusive goddess. She rewarded those who accepted the sovereignty of Mariang over nature and who hunted within her prescribed limits. It was she, said Paz, "who guided the fisherman on Laguna de Bay" and gave them fruitful harvests that campers could enjoy. Filipino myth translated and subverted U.S. impulses to create separate national spaces rooted in a modernist ideology of the nation-state in place of indigenous tradition.[83] These Filipino constructions of nature—both symbolic and religious on the one hand and subsistence agricultural on the other—profoundly affected the national parks that American officials and Filipino collaborators belatedly assembled in the 1930s, as the survival of illegal wood taking and indigenous occupation in the parks demonstrated.[84]

Conservationist sentiments often underlay criticism of the waste of resources by U.S. companies abroad and illustrated the potential for, but not the realization of, an environmentally based critique of empire. That this did not develop in the period of high American formal and informal imperialism (1890s–1930s) was not due to the absence of an environmental movement or ecological insights but the presence of a conservationist movement deployed in favor of imperial regulation of nature and its rationalized exploitation. A close association between anti-imperialism and conservation was rare because pro-imperial forces preempted the ground of conservation and put it to use in justifying colonial rule. Only in relation to unregulated American business activity abroad could this outlook fuel anti-imperialism, and in the Roosevelt-Pinchot formulation, it was an imperialist form of anti-imperialism devoted to the extension of state power against the "robbery" of resources by entrepreneurial capitalists.

Meanwhile, the core of more conventional anti-imperialist thought developed outside conservation discourses. Turn-of-the-twentieth-century anti-imperialism consisted initially in moralistic, antistatist, and antimonopoly opinion hostile to erosion of republican freedoms and to the "sins" that colonialism might bring. These continued to be key sources of anti-imperialist opinion, but after World War I, economic criteria began to dominate understandings of U.S. actions that seemed imperialistic. The growth of the far more important informal empire and the first serious steps toward Philippine self-rule (in the 1916 Jones Act) marginalized the critique of formal empire, as Charles Beard noted in the 1930s.[85] Interwar anti-imperialism looked beyond sovereignty to economic coercion and control. In that context, it acknowledged the increased role of resource procurement in shaping the U.S. empire. Through the Garland Series and Scott Nearing's books, anti-imperialism offered a critique of resource misallocation that European and American imperialism produced. That approach was shared with staunch objectors to the annexation of the Philippines such as Richard Pettigrew. It later provided evidence to develop more ecologically based critiques, but the economic bias at the core of the original analysis, together with the conception of conservation as efficient resource management, kept this potential unrealized until recent years. Conservation understood as economic efficiency conceptually dominated the relationship of nature and humans, while the developing science of ecology dealt separately with the nonhuman realm. Only among colonial subjects did an environmentally oriented resistance to colonialism rooted in social ecology exist, and then in practical action rather than a consciously developed theory of anti-imperialism.

PART IV

# ANTI-IMPERIALISM IN THE AGE OF AMERICAN POWER

Chapter 10

# Promoting American Anti-imperialism in the Early Cold War

LAURA A. BELMONTE

Throughout the Cold War, U.S. and communist propagandists repeatedly accused each other of exploiting the developing world and promoting imperialism. With much of the globe in flux following World War II and the rise of decolonization, each side worked to persuade foreign audiences to align with its particular political and economic system.[1] In this chapter, I explore how and why U.S. officials used anti-imperialist propaganda as a means of refuting communist attacks on democratic capitalism and of celebrating Americans as a people who escaped colonialism.

As they prepared to launch America's first peacetime propaganda offensives in the aftermath of World War II, U.S. information experts expressed dismay at international distortions of American democracy. On February 26, 1946, Assistant Secretary of State for Public Affairs William B. Benton told the House Appropriations Committee:

The nature of the American democratic system, with its disagreements and its individual liberty, is bewildering to a world emerging from the throes of authoritarianism. It is easy for foreigners, without knowing the real situation, to get the impression that this is a land of strife and discord, with race set against race, class set against class, religion set against religion, the rich oppressing the poor, the poor revolting against the rich, gangsters roaming the streets of our cities, cowboys shooting up wild west saloons, and Congress weltering in a whirl of filibusters and cocktail parties.[2]

Alarmed by these stereotypes and competing with foreign images of the United States shaped by Hollywood films, private citizens, and multinational corporations, U.S. propagandists embraced soft power as a means of conveying the advantages of the American democratic system to a world reeling from war and economic dislocation.[3]

U.S. officials quickly realized that the successful promotion of democratic capitalism required persuading foreign audiences of the anti-imperialist nature of the United States and its foreign policy. This would prove no easy task. In February 1947, intelligence analysts at the Department of State completed an exhaustive study of communist propaganda. It revealed that Soviet radio broadcasts and printed materials disseminated throughout the world alleged that U.S. policy makers were "supporting and encouraging reactionary forces in all parts of the world" in order to achieve economic and political hegemony.[4] Communist propagandists told Europeans that the "imperialistic and expansionistic" United States was using "dollar, atomic, and cruiser diplomacy" to conquer foreign peoples. In the Middle East, a successful Soviet initiative described the United States "as an imperialist power which seeks to make Iran a pawn in its conflict with the USSR." In the Far East, communist propagandists claimed that America was "a reactionary, undemocratic, imperialistic, and militaristic country" aiming "to keep Korea in a colonial status indefinitely." In the absence of a concerted U.S. effort to refute these claims, the State Department analysts concluded, it would be almost impossible to convince foreign audiences of America's anti-imperialist intentions.[5]

Accordingly, the Truman administration adopted a tougher posture toward Soviet expansionism and subjugation of foreign peoples. On February 21, 1947, after British leaders informed American officials that financial difficulties necessitated the termination of British military assistance to Greece and Turkey, U.S. policy makers decided that the United States must defend the eastern Mediterranean from possible communist aggression. Rather than retreat into political isolationism and economic nationalism, America would champion democratic capitalism abroad.[6]

On March 12, the so-called Truman Doctrine speech heralded this change. In a special joint session of Congress, the president appealed for $400 million in aid to Greece and Turkey and enunciated an implicit contrast between democracy and communism. "Nearly every nation," Truman proclaimed, "must choose between alternative ways of life." He continued, "One way of life is based upon the will of the majority and is distinguished by free institutions, representative government, free elections, guarantees of individual liberty, freedom of speech and religion, and freedom from political oppression. The second way of life is based upon the minority forcibly imposed upon the majority. It relies upon terror and oppression, a controlled press and radio, fixed elections, and the suppression of personal freedoms."[7] Without mentioning the Soviet Union, Truman eloquently articulated the benefits of classical liberalism. His juxtaposition of democracy and communism would infuse American propaganda throughout the Cold War.

Throughout 1947, the ideological conflict between the United States and the USSR continued to sharpen. In June, Secretary of State George Marshall publicly offered U.S. economic aid to Europe. The European Recovery Plan (ERP, or "Marshall Plan") challenged Joseph Stalin's tightening grip on Eastern Europe and served American economic and political interests.[8] In July, unwilling to permit Western intrusion into his sphere of influence, Stalin ensured that the Czech, Polish, and Yugoslav governments did not pursue aid under the ERP.[9]

Deflecting attention from these actions, the Soviets quickly characterized the Marshall Plan as thinly veiled colonialism. On October 5, the Soviet Union announced the creation of the Cominform (the Information Bureau of Communist Parties) to combat American "dollar imperialism." The Soviets painted a stark global contrast between the "Soviet Union and other democratic countries" and "the camp of imperialism and anti-democratic forces whose chief aim is the establishment of a worldwide American imperialist hegemony." Seeking to align foreign communists firmly with the Soviet Union, the Cominform declaration signaled the consolidation of Soviet power in Eastern Europe.[10]

U.S. officials in the USSR found these developments ominous. On November 15, Ambassador to Moscow Walter Bedell Smith warned Marshall that the totalitarian Soviet propaganda machine could destroy American plans for the economic rehabilitation of the postwar world. Unless the United States disproved communist claims of political and economic superiority, Smith asserted, Europeans would continue to misunderstand democratic capitalism.[11]

Smith therefore recommended that the State Department's Office of Information and Educational Exchange (OIE) begin stressing the inconsistencies between Soviet words and deeds. He suggested that the United States publicize Soviet subjugation of Eastern Europe, the impotence of Soviet labor unions, and the drudgery inflicted on women and children in the USSR. Smith urged U.S. propaganda strategists, in addition to exposing Soviet lies, to demonstrate the advantages American capitalism accorded the average worker. "Above everything else, and by all possible means," Smith pleaded, "counteract the terrible and developing fear of imminent war which is overpowering Europe and which the Soviet Union is fostering by 'warmonger' propaganda in order to retard economic recovery." This fear, he concluded, loomed as the biggest obstacle to the implementation of the Marshall Plan.[12]

Already considering more stringent measures to combat Soviet propaganda, State Department leaders welcomed Smith's remarks. On December 1, 1947, no longer willing to ignore "the unscrupulous measures and techniques currently employed against us by elements seeking to discredit the U.S.," the OIE released new guidelines to counter anti-Americanism. Calling for a continuation of "factual, truthful and forceful presentation of U.S. foreign policy and American ways of living," the OIE focused the American information campaign on "impressing the peoples of the world with the reliability, consistency and seriousness of the U.S. and its policies." OIE strategists sought to counter Soviet accusations by affirming American policies, rather than denouncing communist ones. "The U.S.," it declared, "should not give the impression that it is on the defensive, or vulnerable to hostile charges, but rather that Soviet policy, where it conflicts with ours, works to the detriment of the particular country, while U.S. policy consistently supports the principles of freedom, prosperity, and independence implicit in the Charter of the United Nations."[13]

U.S. information officials considered freedom the most appealing element of democracy. Echoing rhetoric found in the Truman Doctrine speech, they distinguished the national and individual liberties of the free world from the "slavery" of communist countries. On April 7, 1948, William B. Benton, while serving as a U.S. delegate to a "Freedom of Information" conference at Geneva, asserted:

> I find it not at all ludicrous that all around the clock and in several languages Soviet propagandists appropriate, degrade, and bastardize the words which are the hard-earned and world-accepted currency of free men. Liberty, equality, fraternity, independence, justice, freedom, democracy. For these, brave men have died at the hands of tyrants for thousands of years.

Now the USSR insists with a thousand amplified voices that repression is freedom, and that true freedom elsewhere in the world is slavery; they insist that the police state is democracy, and that democracy in other countries is dictatorship by monopoly capitalists.[14]

By equating democracy with freedom, American propagandists imbued their proclamations with implied moral superiority.

But privately, U.S. officials acknowledged the enormous difficulties they faced in challenging international perceptions of the United States as an imperialist nation. In a July 20, 1948 memorandum, Marshall stressed the continued importance of reporting only "the truth about United States life, policies, and actions." "We should bear in mind," Marshall declared, "that the people of third countries do not react with shock, anger, or indignation to the charges made in anti-American propaganda as do some Americans." Marshall added that foreign peoples cared about "the righteousness of United States aims or the sincerity of the United States motives" only when doing so served their direct interests.[15]

This ambivalence, Marshall argued, made it necessary to correct "the false or distorted stereotypes concerning the United States." Marshall explained that Soviet propaganda had instilled perverse notions that Americans possessed unlimited wealth and that "monopoly capitalists" dominated the imperialistic U.S. government. Foreigners believed "Americans are wholly materialistic, have no culture worthy of mention, and judge everything by its value in dollars." They perceived U.S. citizens as libertines with little regard for family life. Many assumed that "American democratic principles are loudly proclaimed as a cloak for undemocratic practices and for the purpose of concealing widespread racial and economic discriminations and extensive concentration of political and economic power in the hands of the few." Unwilling to allow the Soviets to continue denigrating the United States, Marshall directed U.S. information officials "to demonstrate the difference between Soviet pretensions in support of the sovereignty and independence of smaller nations and Soviet actions resulting in the domination and exploitation of smaller nations."[16]

U.S. propaganda materials defining the United States as an anticolonial power with genuine interest in the principle of national liberation soon appeared. In addition to advocating independence for all nations, they attacked Soviet claims that Wall Street financiers dominated American politics.[17] U.S. information strategists also assailed the Soviet Union for exploiting weaker nations.

*Russia the Reactionary*, a 1949 booklet denouncing Soviet attacks on national and individual liberties, exemplifies these themes. A chapter titled "Russia Destroys National Independence" condemned the Soviets' seizure of land and personal property for collective farms. After recounting the communist annexation of Eastern Europe, the text asserted:

> Throughout the USSR and the satellite countries the entire educational, informational, and legal structure has been used to wipe out every culture, every belief, every person that stood in the way of complete conformity to the Moscow party line. Experiences of all nations under the domination of the Kremlin prove that only one way of life is tolerated among those nations—the Soviet way of life. National independence and love of country must be subordinated to allegiance to the Communist Party. There can only be one kind of patriotism—Soviet patriotism.[18]

The Soviets, U.S. officials argued, completely disregarded legitimate aspirations for national independence among Eastern Europeans. Instead, communist authorities created police states that consigned people to lives of poverty, desperation, and subjugation.

Eager to refute Soviet allegations of U.S. imperialism and warmongering, the United States Information and Educational Exchange Program (USIE) immediately adopted a more stridently anticommunist tone.[19] While professing American support for the Soviet populace, USIE harshly condemned Stalinism. Cognizant of mass discontent in the USSR, U.S. propagandists used Voice of America broadcasts and printed materials to reach the Soviet citizens most likely to abhor communism such as intellectuals, industrial workers, demobilized soldiers, and agricultural laborers. USIE materials directed at Soviet youth capitalized on their interest in American consumer products and culture.[20]

At the same time, Soviet officials proclaimed the virtues of communism and the evils of democratic capitalism. Like their U.S. counterparts, they defined the Cold War as a struggle between slavery and freedom. Communist propagandists accused "Wall Street capitalists" and "American imperialists," of "enslaving" U.S. workers. They denied that the United States protected freedom and individual rights. For example, on February 14, 1950, Radio Bucharest announced: "Wall Street tolerates and encourages the Ku Klux Klan, lynchings, and the indescribable misery of the Negroes. [Abraham] Lincoln opposed exploitation of slaves but Wall Street daily intensifies the bloody exploitation of U.S. people and other peoples kneeling under Yankee imperialism."[21] The United States, communist officials contended, was an oligarchic, racist, imperialist, and immoral nation unconcerned with the lives of "the people." In a direct attack on U.S. political discourse, they adopted the phrase "people's democracy" when advocating communism.[22]

In April 1950, a U.S. National Security Council memo, NSC-68, indicated U.S. willingness to use propaganda as part of a global effort to stop communist misinformation and expansionism. Prepared by Paul Nitze, the head of the State Department's Policy Planning Staff, NSC-68 juxtaposed the slavery imbued in the Soviet system and the freedom inherent in democracy. Nitze described "a basic conflict between the idea of freedom under a government of laws, and the idea of slavery under the grim oligarchy of the Kremlin." In an impassioned defense of democracy, he praised "the marvelous diversity, the deep tolerance, [and] the lawfulness of the free society." Unless the United States protected these values, Nitze warned, communists would destroy freedom throughout the world. He recommended exponential increases in defense spending and the American nuclear arsenal.[23]

Although Truman feared that the enormous defense budget Nitze advocated would jeopardize social programs, the president immediately adopted the rhetoric of NSC-68.[24] On April 20, in an address before the American Society of Newspaper Editors, Truman called for the United States to mount a "Campaign of Truth" designed to expose "deceit, distortion, and lies" used by the Soviets. "All too often," he continued, "the people who are subject to Communist propaganda do not know Americans, or citizens of the other free nations, as we really are. They do not know us as farmers or as workers. They do not know us as people having hopes and problems like their own. Our way of life is something strange to them. They do not even know what we mean when we say democracy." Echoing calls for an improved information program, Truman proclaimed that America must "promote the cause of freedom against the propaganda of slavery."[25]

But U.S. information strategists faced enormous challenges in disseminating Truman's inspiring message. On April 15, the communist Chinese had outlawed listening to "reactionary" Voice of America broadcasts. On April 19, the Foreign Ministry of Czechoslovakia had publicly accused U.S. Information Service (USIS) officials of espionage and other antistate activities. The Czech authorities then demanded the immediate closure of the USIS libraries in Prague and Bratislava and the removal of Joseph C. Kolarek, the American press attaché for USIS affairs in Czechoslovakia.

The following day, after USIS published an announcement offering free American books, magazines, and phonograph records, five thousand Czechs packed the USIS library in Prague. Although State Department leaders denied that Kolarek and other USIS officials had engaged in improper activities, they agreed to close the libraries and remove Kolarek, but they also demanded that the Czech government shut its consulate office in Chicago. In late April, U.S. diplomats in the Soviet Union complained of continuing Soviet restrictions on the distribution of *Amerika*, a monthly magazine published by USIS.[26]

On June 25, 1950, the invasion of South Korea by North Korea raised the stakes in the propaganda war. Two days later, the United Nations Security Council voted to "repel the armed attack and to restore international peace and security to the area." Throughout the summer, as an American-led UN force struggled to hold on to the Korean peninsula, the Soviet media released a torrent of vicious anti-American propaganda.[27]

In August 1950, U.S. information leaders strategized about how to challenge Soviet attacks on "Yankee imperialism." Although they acknowledged that "fears of American imperialism are more emotional than logical and are therefore difficult to allay with facts," they remained convinced that "the facts, properly marshaled and presented, cannot help but have an impact upon intelligent persons, however biased." To disprove Soviet accusations of U.S. political and economic imperialism, they directed U.S. officials to point to concrete examples of when the United States "not only . . . voluntarily abandoned . . . control over many areas but also . . . encouraged other Western powers to do likewise."[28]

State Department information leaders offered detailed examples of anti-imperialism to be promoted in U.S. propaganda materials and broadcasts. They pointed to America's granting of independence to the Philippines, leadership in "eliminating extra-territoriality in China," the Good Neighbor Policy in Latin America, and abstention from "interference in the internal affairs of all countries." They stressed the role of the United States in the preservation of the independence of Thailand and expediting "the independence of India, Pakistan, Burma, Ceylon, Indochina, the Associated States of Indochina, and other countries." "This is a creditable record by any standards," U.S. information experts argued. "It becomes all the more creditable when compared with the undeniably aggressive imperialism of the USSR."[29] Convinced of the righteousness of these claims and determined to refute Soviet misinformation, Congress approved a $79.1 million appropriation for USIE, a sum more than twice the previous year's amount.[30]

This augmented budget had an immediate impact on U.S. information activities. By 1951, USIE targeted ninety-three countries, distributed over sixty million pamphlets, and orchestrated VOA broadcasts in forty-five languages.[31] Extolling film's unique ability to inform, USIE's International Motion Picture Division (IMP) selected, acquired, produced, and distributed films shown in eighty-five nations. Often collaborating with foreign governments and private organizations, IMP tailored films for specific countries and translated them into local languages. IMP also supplied projection equipment, mobile units, and informational materials. By 1951, USIE claimed that four hundred million people annually watched its films. These motion pictures featured "Americans at home, at work, and at play" and demonstrated "the story of democracy in action, the perils of communism, and the genuine concern of the citizens of the United States for the freedom and welfare of others." Through highlighting American standards of living and U.S. achievements in science, technology, and industry, IMP aimed to convince foreigners of their "own potentialities as individuals and nations."[32] Such claims of the universality of the American experience and the malleability of other countries became key themes in U.S. propaganda during the 1950s.[33]

Cognizant that communist attacks on American foreign policy were appealing to much of the global audience, U.S. propagandists attempted to deflect communist accusations of U.S. territorial and economic imperialism. Whenever possible, they stressed the "reckless nature of Soviet policy and its consequences." They pointed to Stalinist excesses and the isolation of Eastern Europe as evidence of Soviet political oppression and territorial ambitions.[34] USIS distributed hundreds of thousands of copies of *Who Is the Imperialist?* The booklet listed population and square mileage figures for all the territories and nations annexed by the USSR beginning in 1939. It also described communist "imperialism" in North Korea, Poland, Vietnam, and Tibet.[35]

To counteract communist distortions of democracy, U.S. information strategists employed a variety of propaganda tactics. Most materials were simple. In 1950–51, USIS officers distributed over half a million copies of *Herblock Looks at Communism* in English, Chinese, German, Indonesian, Malay, Telugu, Spanish, Tamil, Thai, and Vietnamese. In the preface, editorial cartoonist Herbert Block wrote, "If liberty existed in communist lands there probably would have been no occasion to draw the cartoons in this pamphlet—and we would all be living in a happier world." In several drawings, Block mocked the communist "peace offensive." In another section titled "Life in a Communist State," Block derided Soviet efforts to censor musicians, scientists, art, literature, and architecture. Throughout his cartoons, Block flatly denied that the Soviet government valued individual freedom, world peace, or political debate.[36]

U.S. propagandists also created cartoons that bitterly satirized the communist system. In 1951–52, the USIS released half a million copies of *Glossary of Soviet Terms*, a booklet of sardonic pictures. "Classless society" depicted the "people's commissariat" riding in a limousine past two Soviet beggars. "People's democracy" showed two Soviet policemen forcing a couple to enter a detention camp. "Democratic elections" featured an armed soldier guarding a single ballot box labeled "yes." All the cartoons in the *Glossary* attacked communist attempts to usurp democratic rhetoric.[37]

The USIS comic book *The Free World Speaks* hammered similar themes and offered a ringing defense of U.S. foreign policy. U.S. officials distributed over 1.3 million copies in fourteen different languages. It celebrated the Truman Doctrine, the Marshall Plan, the Berlin airlift, and UN military actions targeting "red aggression in Korea." *The Free World Speaks* contrasted the U.S. decision to demobilize millions of U.S. troops in the immediate aftermath of World War II to the Soviets' maintenance of "the largest ground army in world." It blamed the Soviets for the failure of UN efforts to halt an international arms race and to control atomic energy. Recounting the recent independence of the Philippines, India, Pakistan, Burma, Indonesia, and Israel, the text declared, "The Free World stood for independence; the USSR reduced its neighbors to vassals." Rather than opposing colonialism, the Soviets "used subversive puppet parties and the threat of military force to gain control of country after country."[38]

U.S. information leaders excoriated communist police states. In May 1951, VOA blasted the communist regimes of China and Poland for issuing decrees mandating the death penalty for a long list of "political crimes" including "cooperating with imperialism," corruption, insurrection, and espionage.[39] Two years later, the U.S. Information Agency (USIA) released *You Can't Win!* and *This Is the Story of Sergei*. The former was a list sarcastically defining the thirty-seven ideological "crimes" punished under East German law. "Pacifism" indicated a "failure to see that the USSR maintains the world's largest army in order to 'liberate' nations like Czechoslovakia." "Imperialism" encompassed "any opposition to the policies of the Soviet Union." The sarcastic tone of the pamphlet illustrated U.S. disdain for the communist legal system.[40] *This Is the Story of Sergei* featured a man with "one terrible misfortune"—living under communism. The cartoon showed Sergei protesting Soviet housing conditions, censorship, and "re-educational methods." Soviet authorities are depicted as murdering Sergei for these offenses.[41]

In addition to highlighting Soviet violations of civil liberties, U.S. propagandists eviscerated communist claims of support for the world's poor. In May 1952, the USIS broadside *By Their Fruits Ye Shall Know Them* asserted: "For too long has the Kremlin talked of its concern for the unfortunates of the world. For too long has the Soviet Union orated about its self-proclaimed benevolence. For too long have Communist claims of championing the underdog gone unchallenged." The pamphlet then pointed out that the USSR had contributed nothing to the U.N. International Children's Emergency Fund, the International Refugee Organization, or the World Health Organization. The United States, of course, had provided generous assistance to all these organizations.[42] Special USIA packets directed at women abroad frequently included stories about American charities and government programs for the needy. At the same time, the agency printed articles like "Aid to Blind Denied by Communists," claiming that Czech authorities refused to supply "seeing eye" dogs for "non-communist blind, or those who have not sufficiently proved their loyalty to the communist regime."[43] Not only did American democracy offer greater individual freedom, the USIA argued, but the U.S. government cared deeply about others' welfare.

As the war in Korea raged and the Truman administration increased its support for the French war against the Vietminh, U.S. information experts often used narratives written in the first person to convey America's anticolonialist, democratic aims abroad. In *An American Speaks to His Asian Friends*, a pamphlet distributed in Vietnam and Indonesia in 1952, an unnamed author declares, "In many ways, very important ways, I am just like you. I wish only to live quietly with my family, to be able to feed and clothe them, and to forget the threat of war and the fear and misery that come with war." The narrator identifies himself as "an ordinary American citizen" who desires to explain why the United States "wants to work with you free peoples of Asia in finding the road to peace." He accuses the Russians of thwarting world peace.[44]

The narrator then assures his readers that the United States does not support imperialism. He describes communist aggression in Eastern Europe, China, Burma, the Philippines, Malaya, and Vietnam. "The pattern has become clear," he asserts; "Russia seeks to control all of Europe. Nor would that be the end. *Russia wants the world.*" He then proclaims America's commitment to defend freedom and to combat poverty. "That is why we are sending supplies and equipment and technical experts to your countries." Americans, he avows, "ask nothing in return. Our motive . . . is an ardent desire to live in peace."[45]

USIA placed major emphasis on American anti-imperialism throughout the decade. In August 1954, a summary of agency operations stressed that the unification of the "Free World" remained the key theme of the U.S. ideological offensive. Achieving this goal necessitated continuous exposure of "Red Colonialism—the communist conspiracy as a foreign force directed from Moscow or Peiping [Beijing] for expansionist purposes." To promote these themes of anti-imperialism and communist aggression, the agency disseminated two book series to its foreign libraries: one comprising thirty-three volumes on democracy, the other a collection of fifty-four works analyzing communism.[46]

Other USIA publications extolled U.S. democracy. In *A Picture Story of the United States*, the agency quoted famous U.S. historical figures describing freedom in the United States. Roger Williams declares, "I'll start a settlement where ALL can worship as they please, government must never interfere with a man's belief!" John Peter Zenger asserts: "The press must be free to print the truth, no matter whom it offends!" Other cartoons portrayed abolitionism, women's rights, and the rise of organized labor. After illustrating the growth of American industrial and economic power, the booklet defended the capitalist system, stating, "But with all this material progress and prosperity, Americans did not lose sight of the foundations on which their blessings rested; free education for all, the free spread of knowledge and ideas, the right to worship as they chose." Overall, the pamphlet presented the United States as a nation of diversity, equality, and morality.[47]

This emphasis on America's revolutionary heritage proved a useful tool in countering Soviet efforts to portray the United States as "another Western colonial power."[48] USIA continuously stressed America's desire to "assist subject peoples to attain independence by peaceful methods" and to support newly independent states. In order to demonstrate this mutuality of interests, USIA publications publicized the colonial origins of the United States in order "to establish a basis of America's understanding and sympathy with subject peoples."[49]

Not surprisingly, American policy makers rushed to exploit Soviet repression of the 1956 Hungarian Revolution. USIA officials showed the film *Hungary's Fight for Freedom* to audiences all over the world. The agency printed a special edition of its subtly named journal, *Problems of Communism*, exposing the Soviet attack on democratic reforms in the East Bloc.[50] USIS centers circulated the pamphlet *Bitter Harvest: The October Revolution in Hungary and Its Aftermath.* The booklet described the Hungarians' quest for free elections and multiparty government. By crushing legitimate demands for representative government, *Bitter Harvest* concluded, the Soviets had exposed the fraudulent nature of their support for national liberation movements.[51]

But Soviet despotism in Hungary gave the United States only a fleeting advantage in the global battle to win the loyalties of colonized and formerly colonized peoples. In March 1957, when Vice President Richard Nixon traveled to Ghana to attend official ceremonies marking the nation's independence from Great Britain, USIA celebrated U.S. support for "the legitimate aspirations of colonial people for independence" and determination "to aid those who have gained independence in their progress toward economic and social betterment." Communist Chinese and Soviet propagandists retaliated by questioning the sincerity of such proclamations in view of America's close alliances with "colonialist partners" in the North Atlantic Treaty Organization. With three NATO nations battling over the status of Cyprus and a burgeoning independence movement in Algeria, the National Security Council warned that USIA would continue to face "the perennial information problem of colonialism and the aggressive posture of the Soviets and Red Chinese as the only sincere friends of people seeking independence."[52]

The USIA post in India reported similar trends. While a majority of Indians viewed the initial U.S. response to the Suez Canal crisis as evidence of America's genuine opposition to colonialism, this praise gave way to criticism after President Eisenhower issued a doctrine pledging to block the spread of communism in the Middle East, and violent mobs opposed the integration of Central High School in Little Rock, Arkansas.[53] By September 1958, during a U.S. invasion of Lebanon, USIA reported that a majority of Indians described the United States as "a somewhat warlike country, allied with colonial, imperialistic, and reactionary powers, while the image of the Soviet Union is of a somewhat more peaceful and progressive nation." Determined to counter these perceptions, U.S. policy makers emphasized India and America's common colonial heritage. They sought to convince Indians that the United States assisted subject peoples in securing independence peacefully and becoming economically and politically stable.[54]

In presenting such messages to specific countries, USIA often linked famous Americans and figures revered by local audiences. A host of events and publications commemorating the 150th anniversary of Abraham Lincoln's birth provide good illustrations. In February 1958, USIA officer Manning H. Williams expressed concern that if the agency did not make "a major effort on Lincoln" the following year, "we may well find that the Soviets have stolen our own show." Manning warned that the Soviets "outdid us on the recent 250th anniversary of Benjamin Franklin." In order to rebut Soviet propaganda suggesting that the "America of Washington and Lincoln" differed from the current "American reality," Manning urged his superiors "to demonstrate that the democratic and humanitarian ideals of Lincoln are revered in the America of today, but overlooked in the Soviet Union."[55]

Acting on Manning's suggestion, the USIA organized global celebrations of Lincoln throughout 1959. USIS motion picture units screened *In Search of Lincoln*, a short biographical sketch of the sixteenth president superimposed over images of fawning crowds at the Lincoln Memorial and somber shots of books and artifacts connected to Lincoln.[56] In the spring, the USIS office in Madras hosted an exhibit titled *Lincoln-Gandhi, They Belong to the Ages*. Large photographs of Lincoln and Mahatma Gandhi were placed on a simple yellow wall. A sculpture of Lincoln sat in the center of the hall. Attendants distributed pamphlets and posters. A majority of visitors responded positively to the exhibit. The statement of a salesman was typical: "May Mr. Lincoln's and M. Gandhi's teachings help us preserve our national solidarity and freedom."[57]

Nonetheless, USIA surveys indicated a general erosion of America's international prestige that greatly alarmed U.S. policy makers. On September 30, 1958, USIA director George V. Allen offered a bleak assessment of "the Image of America" to the National Security Council. He began by describing a Canadian audience cheering at film footage showing the failure of a Vanguard rocket, America's technological response to the Soviet launch of *Sputnik* in October 1957. Many foreigners, Allen explained, want "to see the giant stub his toe. Unfortunately, we aggravate this desire by our bragging and boasting."[58]

In Allen's opinion, international perceptions of the United States as an imperialist power remained deeply entrenched despite more than a decade of U.S. information activities designed to challenge such views. He warned that the use of U.S. economic aid "to compensate for not taking a country's position politically" probably hurt America's reputation more than it improved it. He stressed that foreign audiences continued to believe that the United States defended other nations' imperialism and pursued its own imperialistic aims. In attempting to explain why these claims persisted,

Allen asserted: "Certainly our wealth, our overseas investments, our loans, our cultural penetration, and our military bases and deployment of forces all have something to do with it. But more important than all of these factors, I believe, is the idea that we are *political* imperialists, growing out of our complete control of such 'independent' states as Taiwan, South Korea, and South Vietnam, and lesser control of other states."[59] With the United States continuing to back the autocratic regimes of Jiang Jieshi and Syngman Rhee and escalating its support for Ngo Dinh Diem, U.S. propagandists could not credibly dispute such claims.

Allen was, however, careful to highlight regional differences in the foreign image of America. The French (unable to persuade the United States to intervene militarily in their failed imperialist war against the Vietminh) and the Dutch (pressured by U.S. policy makers to grant independence to Indonesia) not surprisingly described the United States as anticolonial. By contrast, respondents in the Near East claimed that the U.S. government supported "oil sheiks and Israel" and wanted "to keep the Arab world divided and weak" in order to control it.[60] To improve its international image, Allen concluded, the United States should avoid entanglement in foreign situations that defied easy solution, should become more selective in choosing recipients of U.S. economic and military aid, and should more rigorously use multilateral institutions like the United Nations.[61] U.S. policy makers disregarded Allen's caveats, and the contradictions between professed U.S. anti-imperialist aims and actual U.S. actions continued. By late 1967, with the United States deeply entrenched in the Vietnam War, USIA leaders conceded their ongoing failure in combating the "colonialism syndrome" among peoples in the developing world.[62]

While many aspects of the U.S. campaign to promote democratic capitalism internationally succeeded, the message of American anti-imperialism fell flat. When the United States quickly veered from anti-imperialist initiatives to antidemocratic actions at home or abroad, foreign audiences justifiably remained skeptical about U.S. criticisms of colonialism. Although many foreigners praised the United States for creating a society that allowed multiparty elections, representative government, and open political debate to flourish, they remained wary of U.S. declarations of benign intentions toward developing nations. However effectively U.S. propagandists attacked police surveillance, detention camps, and violations of civil liberties in the communist world, their efforts to convince colonized and formerly colonized peoples that the United States shared their antipathy toward colonialism proved less compelling.

Chapter 11

# Ruling-Class Anti-imperialism in the Era of the Vietnam War

ROBERT BUZZANCO

Meeting in Port Huron, Michigan, in June 1962, students and young activists offered a striking assessment of America's global role in the Cold War era, one quite different from the then dominant view of the "American Century." The organizers of the Students for a Democratic Society (SDS) found "tarnish" on the nation's image and "disillusion" because of the "hypocrisy" of America's actions compared to its rhetorical ideals. "The worldwide outbreak of revolution against colonialism and imperialism," the Port Huron Statement observed, "the entrenchment of totalitarian states, the menace of war, overpopulation, international disorder, supertechnology—these trends were testing the tenacity of our own commitment to democracy and freedom and our abilities to visualize their application to a world in upheaval."[1]

Five years later, speaking to the American Bar Association, Senate leader J. William Fulbright, the most eloquent of the "establishment" critics of the Vietnam War, used rhetoric not dissimilar to that of the student radicals. "We are well on our way to becoming a traditional great power," Fulbright warned, "an imperial nation if you will—engaged in the exercise of power for its own sake, exercising it to the limit of our capacity and beyond, filling every vacuum and extending the American 'presence' to the farthest reaches of the earth. And, as with the great empires of the past, as the power grows, it is becoming an end in itself . . . governed, it would seem, by its own mystique, power without philosophy or purpose."[2]

The juxtaposition of SDS and Fulbright—the "kids" and a wise elder statesman—both excoriating the American "empire" generally frames the narrative about anti-imperialism in the Vietnam War era. On one hand, student radicals, often in the streets, attacked the U.S. military role in Indochina and, in a larger sense, Washington's post–World War II hegemonic mission. On the other, establishment liberals saw the war as a betrayal of America's republican ideals and saw the country losing its soul in search of, as John Quincy Adams might have said, "monsters to destroy."

"Anti-imperialism," however, meant more than students and activists and even senators might have understood. Surely, it was both a visceral and analytical response to America's destruction of Vietnam, as well as its invasive policies in Greece, Iran, Guatemala, Cuba, and many other places in the Cold War era. The critique of the American empire, however, could be applied quite differently, as an enlightened call for a change of course in order to extend American power and influence. Much the same way that Woodrow Wilson was an "anti-imperialist" in order to expand the Open Door and commerce, significant segments of the ruling class in the 1960s, particularly the Pentagon and Wall Street, argued against escalation in Vietnam on the grounds of national and class self-interest.

The "ruling class" in the 1960s held effective power to determine American economic and foreign policies. In the main, they represented the leaders of corporate America, bankers and industrialists with global business concerns, and the politicians they helped put into office and supported. Not unlike C. Wright Mills's notion of a "power elite," such capitalists acted in their own interests—as an oligarchy, if you will—often pursuing programs that diminished the democratic rights of the people.[3] The ruling class, however, was not homogeneous. Construction companies like Brown and Root and other heavy-industry firms that were engaged in war matériel production were not opposed to the U.S. intervention and escalation into Southeast Asia, because it brought contracts and profits, while media outlets initially supported the war but turned on it when it became clear that there would not be a successful outcome and continued fighting was bringing economic ruin.[4]

In the Vietnam era the most influential members of this ruling class were the financial interests, the bankers and other corporate elites who had global visions for American investment and commerce and came to believe that the war in Vietnam damaged their interests because it focused resources on Indochina and undermined their larger goals by running up huge deficits and provoking resistance from traditional European allies. Military leaders, a vital component in executing and enforcing ruling-class policies and programs, also had a negative view of fighting in Indochina, which they considered a peripheral area outside the arc of American interests and a diversion from their larger Cold War missions. And so significant elements in the ruling class opposed the war in Vietnam. They did so not because they believed the war was wrong, but because they believed it undermined the imperial interests of the United States. This was a limited and episodic "anti-imperialism," one based not on an ideology of self-determination or a policy system of nonintervention, but rather upon realpolitik and cost-benefit analysis. It belongs in the history of U.S. anti-imperialism because of the traction it had in elite policy-making circles.

## "Occupying an Essentially Hostile Foreign Country"

U.S. military officials offered candid and usually negative appraisals of intervention in Vietnam. In the main, they opposed making a military commitment to Indochina and especially sending in American troops. To some extent, they understood that the civilian leaders were convinced of the need to fight in Vietnam, and so various generals hoped to end things quickly with a limited involvement. General Curtis LeMay, for instance, infamously called for bombing Vietnam into oblivion. But this recommendation came from his desire to avoid a protracted ground war.

Military opposition and pessimism about war in Vietnam began at the outset of the Cold War. American officers attached to the Office of Strategic Services during the war had good relations with Ho Chi Minh, with General Philip Gallagher, the U.S. adviser to Chinese occupation forces in northern Vietnam, wishing that the Vietminh "could be given their independence."[5] In July 1949 the Joint Chiefs of Staff (JCS) policy paper JCS 1992/4 offered a prescient warning of the perils of Indochina. The "widening political consciousness and the rise of militant nationalism among the subject people," they understood, "cannot be reversed." To attempt to do so would be "an antihistorical act likely in the long run to create more problems than it solves and cause more damage than benefit." The army's Plans and Operations Division added, likewise pessimistically, that the Vietminh would drive the French out of Indochina on the basis of popular support alone, not Chinese or Soviet assistance. Ho enjoyed the support of 80 percent of the Vietnamese people, yet 80 percent of his followers were not communists. Such indigenous appeal, as well as limited PRC support, virtually assured Vietminh success.[6]

Despite such warnings, President Harry Truman increased support to the French suppression of Vietnamese nationalism, especially after 1950. But still the military balked, with the Joint Strategic Plans Committee (JSPC) opposed to using U.S. troops in a "series of inconclusive peripheral actions which would drain our military strength and weaken . . . our global position." Army Chief of Staff J. Lawton Collins was more blunt. "France will be driven out of Indochina," he prophesied, and was "wasting men and equipment trying to remain there," and even rejected the "domino theory" in Southeast Asia. When JCS chair Omar Bradley expressed doubt that "we could get our public to go along with the idea of our going into Indochina in a military way," Collins agreed and concluded that "we must face the probability that Indochina will be lost." In the meantime the JSPC warned that even limited involvement in Vietnam "could only lead to a dilemma similar to that in Korea, which is insoluble by military action."[7] Already in the 1950s one could observe the dialectic of military reluctance and civilian enthusiasm for war in Indochina. Collins and others, taking into account "a military point of view," understood that Vietnam was not vital to American interests, was not an area conducive to military success, was engaged in a revolution-cum-civil-war brought on by centuries of outside aggression and colonialism, and was likely to be hostile to a U.S. presence. The Vietminh, as the JCS recognized, held the military initiative and had successfully identified itself with the struggle for "freedom from the colonial yoke and with the improvement of the general welfare of the people."[8] Civilian policy makers, however, had larger visions, seeing Vietnam as an important piece in containing communism and, even more, the larger reconstruction of capitalism and Japanese economic health in Asia.[9]

Such criticism grew alongside the expansion of the American war in Vietnam. Over a decade later, in a perceptive analysis of U.S. policy, Commander William Westmoreland and his staff in Saigon opposed sending combat forces to Vietnam, and recommended continuing on the limited, and flawed, path of providing operational support and advisers. As the staff saw it, the United States had already spent a great deal of time trying to develop the southern military, and "if that effort has not succeeded, there is even less reason to think that U.S. combat forces would have the desired effect." The Vietnamese, Westmoreland assumed, would either let Americans carry the burden of war or actively turn against the U.S. presence in their country. Given such circumstances, U.S. officers concluded that the involvement of American ground forces in the south "would at best buy time and would lead to ever increasing commitments until, like the French, we would be occupying an essentially hostile foreign country." Even Maxwell Taylor, past chair of the JCS and later the U.S. ambassador to Saigon, opposed such steps. In memorandums to the president and others in 1965, he detailed the risks of intervention and bleak prospects facing American soldiers in southern Vietnam. Taylor insisted that political turmoil in Saigon was the major obstacle to success, and that the series of coups d'état after the overthrow of Ngo Dinh Diem put Washington in a position where it might have to accept consequences "which might entail ultimate withdrawal."[10]

Even the commencement of the massive Rolling Thunder bombing campaign did not appreciably change conditions inside southern Vietnam, so, in March 1965, Johnson deployed the first ground troops, a marine brigade, to guard a U.S. base at Da Nang. Westmoreland cautioned that it was "most important . . . to avoid the impression by friends and enemies that [the] U.S. has taken over responsibility for war from the Vietnamese." American officers like Westmoreland had firmly rejected such proposals earlier, but with civilian authorities in Washington rushing in that direction, JCS chairman General Earle Wheeler, Westmoreland, and others fell in line, as concerned with the political impact of decision making as with the war in Vietnam itself. The deployment to Da Nang resulted from civilian pressure, not military factors, and was in the cards even prior to the events of early 1965. As General William DePuy, Westmoreland's deputy, later observed, the commitment of combat forces was *not* the "product of a Westmoreland concept for fighting the war." The MACV staff, he explained, still expected U.S. troops to advise and assist the ARVN, not fight the war themselves.[11]

The civilians, however, saw it otherwise, and beginning in July 1965, American troops began to pour into Vietnam, with over five hundred thousand in-country by 1968, when the war came to a boil in January as the enemy launched the Tet Offensive. In the aftermath of Tet, which had undermined Westmoreland's claims that there was "light at the end of the tunnel," Wheeler traveled to Saigon, where he offered a gloomy appraisal of conditions in Vietnam—his famous "it was a very near thing" report. But the real issue became not the war, but the political question of who would be blamed for defeat, and the military wanted to avoid such accusations. Wheeler and Westmoreland requested 206,000 more troops and the activation of about 200,000 reservists. It was clear, however, that major reinforcement was not forthcoming in early 1968. Wheeler recognized the pervading gloom in the White House, admitting that "Tet had a tremendous effect on the American public . . . on leaders of Congress . . . on President Johnson. As a result, while Wheeler was in Vietnam, Bruce Palmer, a MACV officer, informed Westmoreland that General Dwight Beach, the army's Pacific commander, had been aware of the new reinforcement request and "had commented that it would shock them [Washington officials]."[12] But Wheeler and Westmoreland were fighting a political battle in the United States more than a war in Vietnam with the request for more troops and reservists. They understood the war had reached its nadir and that success was less likely than ever, but also knew that the White House could not meet such an immense request and thus would have to bear the burden for failure in Vietnam. Though committed to Vietnam for almost two decades by that point, American leaders realized Tet had shown them that the costs of continued war were now too large and onerous to meet, both from a domestic standpoint—as media and antiwar movement criticism peaked—and because of the disastrous effects on the world economy, as we shall see below.

Westmoreland himself admitted that he and Wheeler "both knew the grave political and economic implications of a major call-up of reserves." Westmoreland tried to be upbeat but saw that Wheeler was "imbued with the aura of crisis" in Washington and thus had dismissed any optimistic briefings. "In any event," he added, the JCS chair "saw no possibility at the moment of selling reinforcements" unless he adopted an alarmist tone to exploit the sense of crisis. "Having read the newspapers," Westmoreland wondered, "who among them [civilian leaders] would even believe there had been success?" Wheeler's approach to the issue notwithstanding, Westmoreland suspected that "the request may have been doomed from the first in any event" because of long-standing political pressure to de-escalate.[13] Army chief of staff Harold K. Johnson suspected as much. In their initial meetings after the Tet attacks began, the chiefs decided to wait for the dust to settle before making recommendations for future strategy. Within days, however, it was clear that they did not have that luxury and would have to make a prompt policy statement. Instead of deliberating over the proper course for the future, Johnson observed, the brass just endorsed a program for major reinforcements. "I think this was wrong," the army chief later asserted. "There should have been better assessment" of the situation before forwarding military plans to the White House. The chiefs, despite their

misconceptions, approved the reinforcement request anyway, essentially because they did not want to reject the chair's suggestion. "If you want it bad,"
General Johnson sardonically remarked, "you get it bad."[14]

And they did get it bad. Political leaders had made it clear that substantive reinforcement would not be forthcoming. President Johnson, meeting
with his advisers, charged that "all of you have counseled, advised, consulted
and then—as usual—placed the monkey on my back again. . . . I do not
like what I am smelling from those cables from Vietnam."[15] In his first
post-Tet press conference, the president asserted that he had already added
the men that Westmoreland thought were necessary. "We have something
under 500,000," Johnson told reporters. "Our objective is 525,000. Most
of the combat battalions already have been supplied. There is not anything
in any of the developments that would justify the press in leaving the impression that any great new overall moves are going to be made that would
involve substantial movements in that direction." By the following week,
with more advisers expressing their concern about Tet and the war in
general, it was clear to the president that the military could exploit White
House division over Vietnam. "I don't want them [military leaders] to ask
for something," Johnson worried aloud, "not get it, and have all the blame
placed on me."[16]

That, to a large degree, was precisely what happened. In the aftermath
of Tet and the reinforcement request, Johnson found himself in an untenable position, unable to send more troops to Vietnam given the shocking
nature of the enemy offensive, and unwilling to admit defeat and move on.
Subsequently, conservatives and military officials began to attack Johnson
for his tentative approach to Vietnam, for not activating reserves, for not
conducting operations north of the seventeenth parallel, for not giving the
military the resources it needed to win, for making American soldiers fight
"with one hand tied behind their back."

## Wall Street Laments the Empire

The early months of 1968 are among the most important in the history
of the American empire, yet not well known. While Tet showed that the
Americans would not militarily defeat the communists in Vietnam, but
that the military would successfully navigate the politics of civil-military
relations to make the "stabbed in the back" explanation of the war popular,
the global economy was in dire straits, and the ruling class was in a panic

over its potential consequences. The reinforcement request triggered a fundamental reexamination of the war, and in the end the Americans realized that disengagement from Indochina was their only option if they were to retain global economic power. The war had simply become too costly. While Vietnam is seen, rightly, as a military defeat for the United States, the economic consequences of the war were more important and long-lived.

Vietnam exposed and exacerbated two major flaws in the postwar U.S. economy: a persistent deficit in balance of payments (BOP) and a worrisome outflow of gold. Balance of payments referred to monetary transactions between the United States and the rest of the world, the cumulative ledger of payments for exports and imports, investments, and foreign and military spending abroad. Gold was particularly vital to the global economy because it was the hard currency that backed the convertibility of the dollar, in accordance with the international agreements made at Bretton Woods in 1944; since currencies were fixed, any central bank could trade in their money, convertible to dollars, and receive gold. As the Vietnam War grew, these problems became increasingly severe. In the earliest stages of American involvement, prior to 1965, the projected solution for the BOP and gold deficits was a program of military spending cuts. After the 1965 decisions to "Americanize" the war, however, such reductions were off the table, so the war wreaked havoc on the U.S. economy, something that Wall Street and government financial and monetary advisers saw coming much earlier. Indeed, in November 1960, just after the election, President Dwight Eisenhower and his successor met, and, as Eisenhower's diary noted, he mentioned to John F. Kennedy "the grave situation with regard to the outflow of gold" and feared that "no one really understands what to do about it." The next month, Eisenhower and Kennedy met again to discuss the possibility of redeploying troops from Europe to help ease the BOP deficit burden. Perhaps surprisingly, they did not see growing tensions in Berlin and the possibility of a troop call-up as a deterrent to cutting defense spending.[17]

Kennedy, thus informed and warned, would make the BOP problem a top priority. Meeting with Eisenhower's treasury secretary, Robert Anderson, just before the inauguration, the incoming president learned that the BOP deficit between 1958 and 1960 had exceeded $10 billion, and officials in both administrations agreed it was "more important" to fix the American financial structure than to spend money on military assistance and foreign development (agreeing, in a sense, with Eisenhower's "military-industrial complex" analysis). Because currencies were fixed, foreign central banks were withdrawing gold—$1.7 billion in 1960 alone—to stem the inflation the deficits were causing (deficits were weakening the dollar, thus "exporting inflation" as the European bankers saw it; so taking out gold instead of dollars made good monetary sense). Indeed, all of America's key allies, except Japan, had surpluses in dollar reserves by 1961. The so-called postwar dollar gap—the shortage of U.S. currency in foreign hands that could be used to purchase American-made goods, which had led to the creation of the Bretton Woods institutions, the Marshall Plan, and NSC-68—was now a "dollar glut," and U.S. money men would have to devise a way to create equilibrium, and defense cuts seemed to be the agreed-upon strategy.[18]

Economic vitality, not military power, was a key to imperium. To Kennedy, BOP and gold were a pressing problem, so he delivered a special message to Congress on the issue in early February 1961, explaining that expenditures on the military overseas, as well as private capital investments and foreign aid, had caused the deficits to soar. Dollar holdings in foreign countries had nearly doubled between 1950 and 1957. While earlier deficits had subsidized the dollar gap, the deficits now caused exports to lag and imports to rise. Growing BOP deficits led Kennedy to announce a program to reduce the outflow of dollars, including real cuts in the Pentagon's budget; in fact, Defense Secretary Robert McNamara pledged to save at least $1 billion in his first year alone.[19]

Kennedy's early efforts did little to help the deficits, however. Two years later, in National Security Action Memorandum 225, the administration admitted that prospects "are not bright" and therefore "we must be sure that any financial transactions and arrangements we make with other countries tie in with our foreign policy objectives," which would presumably include the escalation in Vietnam. Still, the president saw military reductions as a key way to reduce the BOP deficit, and hoped that other countries would follow the lead of the Federal Republic of Germany, which pledged to spend aid money from America on military equipment and facilities. Meanwhile, McNamara again promised cuts, $500 million over the next two years. By summer, the problem grew, and Kennedy again delivered a special message on BOP. Americans had invested over $60 billion abroad, while government loans exceeded $11 billion. Given such outlays overseas, small wonder that Pentagon cuts, less than a billion dollars in 1962, did little to help the deficits. By September of that year, as the Buddhist Crisis in Vietnam exploded and the Ngo Dinh Diem regime was in its last days, leading to an expanded U.S. role there, Kennedy still made the BOP issue a priority, telling the International Monetary Fund that the wealthier nations would need to make a concerted effort to get dollars into less-affluent countries for rebuilding and development as a way to restore U.S. industry and make American capital available. Kennedy himself would be assassinated in November, but the dilemma of a growing war in Vietnam and a growing crisis in deficits in the BOP would not go away.[20] It was clear, however, that the U.S. government could not reconcile these two huge goals, preserving a client state in southern Vietnam *and* reducing the BOP deficits.

By 1965, Vietnam had grown into a major war that exacerbated the BOP deficit. The weakening dollar prompted foreign governments to cash in their American currency for gold, which in turn undermined the international monetary structure. Although BOP reductions occurred in 1965 and 1966, "the emergence of war in Southeast Asia," as Secretary of the Treasury Henry Fowler explained, "prevented the United States from approaching equilibrium in those years."[21] Such imbalances grew in concert with the intensified commitments to Vietnam, a war costing in the vicinity of $20–25 billion per annum by 1967–68, and thereby made it impossible to improve upon the shortfall or, because of the inflationary impact of the war, stem the outflow of gold from the United States. U.S. gold reserves, $23 billion in 1957, dropped to $16 billion in 1962 and decreased progressively thereafter. In 1965 alone, foreign central banks had redeemed dollars for $1.7 billion in gold.[22] At the same time, European governments began to openly criticize the U.S. war in Vietnam. French officials especially complained that Vietnam-induced BOP deficits and inflation, which averaged about 5 percent during the Vietnam era, were undermining their own economy. The British government felt likewise, prompting Johnson's national security adviser, McGeorge Bundy, to charge that the British were "constantly trying to make narrow bargains on money while they cut back on their wider political and military responsibilities. . . . [T]here is no British flag in Vietnam."[23]

Throughout 1966 and 1967, BOP deficits grew larger, gold continued to leave the United States, and foreign flags were still absent from Vietnam. Inflation was rising as well, with import demand up and export growth down. America's share of world trade, which approached 50 percent after World War II, was down to 25 percent in 1964 and fell to just 10 percent by 1968. The annual, publicly stated, "official" cost of Vietnam between 1964 and 1967 was about $3.5–4 billion, of which over half was probably attributable to inflation. Treasury officials estimated that the BOP deficit would continue to soar, due "entirely to our intensified effort in Southeast Asia," while "a further $200 million increase in [military] expenditures may occur next year [fiscal year 1967] and worsen the projected deficit by that amount."[24] Then, in 1967, a full-blown monetary crisis emerged. Speculators, rather than member nations of a multinational "gold pool," were absorbing virtually all the world's new gold production, leading to a run on American gold reserves—$1.2 billion in 1967 alone.[25] President Johnson, like his predecessors, vowed to maintain full convertibility at the par value of $35 per ounce, despite the new shortfalls. The French, more alarmed than ever about Vietnam-induced inflation, advocated a higher gold price and began cashing in their dollars. More critically, Britain devalued its pound sterling in November 1967.[26]

The British devaluation—lowering the price of the pound from $2.80 to $2.40—created a monetary crisis. Speculators anticipated an increase in the official price of gold, so withdrew $641 million—60 percent from U.S. reserves—from the gold pool in the week of November 20–27. National Security Adviser Walt Rostow warned the president to "expect further heavy losses this week."[27] De Gaulle then weighed in with a strident public attack on U.S. monetary policy. The French continued to push for a hike in the Bretton Woods price of gold to stem the "*American takeover* of our businesses" that had resulted from the "exportation of inflated dollars." The deficit had to be addressed, de Gaulle insisted, so that it would not continue "to be a means of taking over European industry." In the last quarter of 1967, however, the BOP deficit soared to an annual rate of $7 billion, tripling the previous rate for the year.[28]

Facing economic pressure abroad and at home, President Johnson announced a program on January 1, 1968, to reduce the BOP deficit by $3 billion in the coming year by tightening regulations on the export of capital, asking Americans to travel abroad less, and cutting back on foreign and military assistance. He also put pressure on Congress to pass a 10 percent surtax on individual and corporate incomes, a move he previously had opposed. Johnson did not mention Vietnam, perhaps because, as Treasury officials earlier understood, the "European monetary authorities do not accept the Vietnam War as a justification" for American economic distress.[29] The French nonetheless responded with "shock and surprise, sour grapes, and fear of the consequences for France and Europe," while de Gaulle personally "ran through the usual routine about the overriding power of the U.S. and the necessity of opposing the U.S. in order to help restore equilibrium in the world."[30]

At home, private-sector economic experts warned of worse to come. Edward Bernstein, who had been a Treasury Department and IMF official and was a high-powered financial consultant, told a Wall Street gathering that "no international monetary system can be devised under which foreign central banks can be induced to acquire unlimited amounts of dollars." The well-known economist Barbara Ward Jackson, in a memo widely circulated by Rostow, warned of "dangerous overtones of the 1929–31 disaster" in the current situation and feared that "depression and massive unemployment could occur in Europe if world trade did not stabilize."[31] Gardner Ackley and Rostow both thought Jackson's scenario was too pessimistic, but, as Rostow put it, "the overall problem Barbara has raised is real and, in one way or another, we shall have to meet it in the weeks and months ahead."[32]

Economic crisis, however, was then put on the political back burner as Tet began, and in February and early March the White House had to confront the breakdown of its policies in Indochina. But money and war were colliding too. The military's request for massive reinforcement, McNamara warned, would require additional appropriations of $25 billion for 1969 and 1970 alone, without the likelihood, let alone promise, of turning the corner in Vietnam.[33] At the same time the Europeans, fearing the economic effects of another escalation in Vietnam, began cashing in their dollars for gold. During the last week of February, the gold pool sold $119 million in hard currency; on March 3 and 4, losses totaled $141 million; and by early March new Council of Economic Advisers chair Arthur Okun, describing *"a bad case of the shakes"* in world financial markets, reported that the BOP deficit for the first week of March had risen to $321 million, while gold losses soared to $395 million, including $179 million on March 8 alone.[34] Had such withdrawals continued to mount, the depletion of gold reserves could have caused a devaluation of the dollar, which in turn could have ignited a series of currency devaluations not unlike those of the 1930s.[35]

With the crisis intensifying, the administration scrambled for a response. An Advisory Committee established by Henry Fowler, headed by Douglas Dillon and including various leaders of the Washington and Wall Street establishments, again insisted that Johnson impose that 10 percent surtax, retain the $35 price of gold despite European calls for an increase, and, if the problems deepened, consider closing the gold pool. "My own feeling," Rostow admitted, "is that the moment of truth is close upon us."[36] He was right. On March 14 the gold pool lost $372 million—bringing the March losses to date to $1.26 billion—and American officials anticipated that the next day's withdrawals could top $1 billion. The administration, as Rostow lamented, "can't go on as is, hoping that something will turn up."[37]

The Europeans also pressured the United States to act, so Johnson, on the fifteenth, persuaded London to close its gold market for the day, a Friday—typically the heaviest trading day of the week—and called an emergency meeting of central bankers.[38] That weekend, governors of the central banks of the United States, the UK, Germany, Italy, Belgium, the Netherlands, and Switzerland—but not France—met in Washington to deliberate world monetary conditions. The governors, not for the first time, called on the Americans, and British, to improve their balance-of-payments positions, urged the president to retain the official price of gold, and called for a "two-tiered" system for gold in which private markets could float their rates.[39] Perhaps the major reform emerging from the crisis was the establishment of "special drawing rights." Created by the International Monetary Fund, these international reserve units—"paper" gold—provided the world monetary system with internationally managed liquid assets to avoid future massive hard-currency withdrawals. The U.S. Congress, prompted by the crisis, finally gave in on the surtax as well, and LBJ signed it into law in June, turning an estimated deficit of $25 billion for fiscal year 1968 into a $3 billion surplus for fiscal 1969, but not slowing down the economy or stemming inflation.[40]

While the governors had stemmed the crisis with such action, LBJ was feeling more political heat than ever. The CIA warned the White House to expect more criticism from France and continued attacks on the dollar. Rostow and economic adviser Ernest Goldstein told the president to anticipate additional costs for Vietnam in the $6–8 billion range in 1969. And, in a biting analysis, presidential aide Harry McPherson berated Johnson for asking Americans to keep supporting a war that was already excessively costly and had no end in sight. Perhaps most important, new defense secretary Clark Clifford, a paragon of the financial establishment, reevaluated the war and concluded that a gradual disengagement was in order.[41] Johnson, however, did not have to be told how bad the situation had turned. At a March 26 meeting he lamented the "abominable" financial situation, with rising deficits and interest rates and growing danger to the pound and dollar. Worse, Westmoreland's request for 206,000 troops would cost $15 billion, which "would hurt the dollar and gold." The United States, he went on, is "demoralized." The president thus anticipated "overwhelming disapproval in the polls and elections. I will go down the drain. I don't want the whole alliance and military pulled in with it."[42] Although the war in

Vietnam would continue for five more years, Johnson had to admit failure in early 1968. The United States could no longer afford the war, no longer use its military and economic power in the same, often unrestrained, fashion that it had in the generation after World War II. Critically, as Okun emphasized, unless the world financial community regained confidence in the dollar, the *"consequences for prosperity at home are incalculable."*[43]

The American financial community likewise understood just how seriously the war was affecting the economy. Walter Wriston, the president of Citibank, told a group of European financial leaders in January that it would be possible to overcome the monetary crisis without changing the gold standard, but "the chances would be greater if the Vietnamese war ended." Roy Reierson, senior vice president and chief economist at the Bankers Trust Company on Wall Street, complained in March that Vietnam had caused domestic inflation and had unduly burdened the BOP position. In an address amid the Tet and gold crises, a partner at Salomon Brothers, Sidney Homer, observed that "military setbacks in Southeast Asia will surely intensify attacks on the dollar." Vietnam had not alone caused the economic crises of the 1960s, Homer went on, but it had "aggravated our problems and in a sense frozen them." In a report to investors, Goldman, Sachs economists simply explained that reduced spending in Vietnam "could contribute significantly to the solution of many of the problems currently plaguing the U.S. economy."[44]

Most strikingly, the venerable chair of the Federal Reserve System, William McChesney Martin, offered an alarming public analysis of America's economic future. Speaking to financial leaders amid the March crisis, he admonished that "it's time that we stopped talking about 'guns and butter,' it's time that we stopped assuming that we are in a 'little war' in Vietnam, and face up to the fact that we are in a wartime economy." Because of "an intolerable budget deficit and an intolerable deficit in our balance of payments," Martin predicted "either an uncontrollable recession or an uncontrollable inflation." The combination of Vietnam and BOP deficits had put the United States, Martin feared, "in the midst . . . of the worst financial crisis since 1931." The Fed chair, by spring 1968, had become increasingly frustrated with Johnson's attempts to pay for Vietnam and the Great Society without a tax increase. Writing to a relative shortly after the uproar over his public pronouncements, he complained that "I have been trying for the past two years to make the point on 'guns and butter' and the cost of the Vietnam war, economically, without too much success but I think in due course the chickens will come home to roost." By late 1968,

Martin could only lament that the surtax was "18 months late . . . guns and butter [are] not attainable in wartime."[45] The Bretton Woods system and military Keynesianism—which had driven economic growth in the Cold War—had been dealt a serious blow by the Vietnam War, and the United States would henceforth have to negotiate its hegemony and economic influence with Western Europe and Japan.[46] With the established system of hegemony undermined by the war and the economic crises it spawned, the government and corporate elite would have to find new strategies to expand commerce, increase wealth, and assert power.

## From Old Empire to New

The confluence of military dissent and Wall Street alarm over the Vietnam War has to be addressed in any conversation about post-1945 American empire and anti-imperialism. The anti-imperialism of the military and financial elite was different from that of the better known antiwar protesters, who presented themselves as the inheritors of the principles of 1776. This anti-imperialism, in contrast, was a critique of specific policies of imperial overstretch, rather than an overarching condemnation of the U.S. imperial system itself. Furthermore, it aimed to preserve and enhance U.S. global power, as well as the interests of those, such as high financiers, who benefited most from it. As the well-known diplomat George F. Kennan candidly explained, "We have about 50% of the world's wealth but only 6.3% of its population. Our real task in the coming period is to devise a pattern of relationships which will permit us to maintain this position of disparity without positive detriment to our national security." To do so, Kennan continued, the American elite would have to be realistic about pursuing this position: "We will have to dispense with all sentimentality and day dreaming; and our attention will have to be concentrated everywhere on our immediate national objectives. We need not deceive ourselves that we can afford today the luxury of altruism and world benefaction."[47]

By the mid-1960s, however, that unsentimental hegemony seemed to be in tatters as the communist-nationalist forces in Vietnam were defeating the mighty U.S. military, while the costs of the war were creating an untenable monetary and diplomatic situation. Amid the crisis, Americans dissented at levels unmatched since the U.S. Civil War, but, despite the allure and even political power of critics like SDS or J. William Fulbright, it was the active opposition from Wall Street bankers and military officers that really brought the crisis home and forced the Johnson administration to begin

to wind down the war. With a few exceptions (such as ex-marine com-
mandant David Shoup, whose mentor was the famed military critic General
Smedley Butler, and who urged the United States to "keep its dirty, bloody,
dollar-crooked fingers" out of Vietnam),[48] military and monetary officials
criticized the Vietnam War not out of moral opprobrium or a political
analysis of security threats, but because the war undermined the objectives
of this imperialist "ruling class."

In Indochina, U.S. troops would continue fighting until 1973, but the
oligarchy understood that the United States would never have been able to
conclude the war successfully prior to that time. Economically, the dollar
gap, so essential to European recovery after the war, had become the dollar
glut, with Vietnam causing unbearable BOP deficits. Europeans, feeling the
effects of American inflation and handcuffed by fixed exchange rates and
the gold standard, led the attack on the old system, and just three years later,
Richard Nixon officially ended Bretton Woods by taking the United States
off the gold standard and devaluing the dollar. The American economy, as
business writer Hobart Rowan put it, "continued to show the effects of
the deep distortions of the Vietnam War, which had drained the nation's
wealth, triggered the inflation, and exacerbated the balance of payments and
trade deficits. The dollar's devaluation . . . was a confession of the failure
of economic policy."[49] General Michael Davison, who had served as the
chief of staff and deputy commander in chief of the army's Pacific Command during the Vietnam War, likewise scored the cost of intervention.
National leaders, he contended, "should have had their nose pressed to the
fiscal wall. . . . And we could have saved billions of dollars, and those billions that we wasted out there were contributory to the later *inflation* and
*recession* in my view, and they were contributory to the political ferment
when the American people saw the billions of dollars flowing out there and
for what purpose?"[50]

By the time the war came to a close, the world looked much different
than it had when Kennedy made his first commitments in Vietnam. The
American military, and the American empire, had suffered grievous blows.
The postwar economic system was transformed, and American economic
clout was on the wane. American capital went abroad, and foreign capital
arrived in the United States at an increased pace. The number of U.S. banks
with branches overseas rose tenfold between 1965 and 1974, and their assets
increased by 1,400 percent. At the same time the number of foreign banks
with Wall Street branches doubled, with their assets increasing by 600 percent. The so-called eurodollar market—the acquisition by foreign banks of
dollar deposits on American banks from, for instance, imports sold in the

United States, and then loaned out to other parties at interest—which was unregulated and not restrained by domestic currency markets, flourished, rising from $36 billion to $80 billion between 1967 and 1969 alone. Other nations could also deposit dollars in foreign banks where they could be lent out, again shifting economic power away from Wall Street. The Soviet Union, in fact, held its dollar accounts in Europe, outside U.S. jurisdiction. At the same time, multinational financial institutions sensed that a domestically based manufacturing economy was losing steam and emphasized global capital investment in areas where lower, nonunion, labor costs and hospitable climates for foreign investment offered a better return than the home market. Whereas Johnson relied on traditional strategies of military power and economic growth to sustain American imperium, financial elites recognized that governments and national economies were giving way to a truly global financial and monetary system, and adapted accordingly.

When the dust finally settled, with the war and Bretton Woods ending nearly at the same time, economic equilibrium was restored, but at a cost. Economic progress and rising standards of living stalled in much of the world, and transnational corporations expanded their dominion over national economies in the less-developed world, eventually leading to the "Walmart model" of global business. American wages declined rapidly as businesses moved abroad, and the liberal compact of the New Deal order came under intense scrutiny. And the war created major deficits; by intervening in and then escalating the war in Vietnam, Kennedy and Johnson prevented American capital, labor, and energy from being used at home. Money that would have been spent on production, research and development, perhaps even social services, went to Vietnam instead. While millions of Americans protested in the streets, ultimately the government could ignore them. But it was harder to dismiss the warnings and fears of businessmen and generals. Treasury and Federal Reserve officials, bankers, and military officers, ultimately, made it necessary for Johnson to start getting out of the war. The "ruling class," more than the kids or Fulbright, had seen the harm Vietnam was causing, but from its own perspective, one of power and wealth, not democracy or idealism. The world, it seemed in 1973, had changed; the Americans would no longer be able to coerce other countries. But that was not to be. The "old" empire may have taken blows, but it survived, and the ruling class, more transnational than ever, in the subsequent decades became more powerful than ever. Vietnam thus marked the end of one strategy of empire and the launching of another.

Chapter 12

# Whither American Anti-imperialism in a Postcolonial World?

IAN TYRRELL AND JAY SEXTON

In logical terms, without imperialism there would be no anti-imperialism. From the 1870s to the 1950s the ideology of anti-imperialism was closely tied to the existence of European empires and to leftist critiques of that imperialism. Liberal critiques had also been made, based on ideas of empire as a vestige of premodern state structures and authoritarianism. An American variation on the latter idea linked imperialism to denial of U.S. constitutional traditions. What made the United States exceptional, critics insisted, came from its anti-monarchical and republican origins. To have an "empire" that ruled over foreign peoples who were not to be citizens flew in the face of those republican values. Portents of this anti-imperial critique can be seen among opponents of continental expansion in the nineteenth century, but it was not until 1898, when the United States acquired "insular" possessions in the Caribbean and Pacific, that the idea gained widespread traction. Most of the chapters in this book have dealt with those phases of imperialism and its opponents. But what of the years since 1945 in which U.S. global power was at its height?

Here, two themes stand out, both of which relate to the changing forms of imperialism in an era in which it became decoupled from full-blown, permanent colonial rule. First is the generally decreasing susceptibility of

American actions abroad to be categorized as imperial on conventional "republican" grounds, as decolonization of the old empires took place across the globe from 1945 to 1970. The second involves grappling with U.S. military, political, and economic coercion beyond the nation's borders as globalization intensified since the 1970s. Extension of U.S. power abroad from that time could not easily fit into ideas of a territorially based imperialism, and social movements, political critics of American actions, and theorists of empire have struggled with how to define the power that modern means of communications and technologies of war allow. While national borders have appeared in some respects to have weakened in this phase of "new" globalization—sociologists and geographers of globalization write of a "de-territorialization" process—the exertion of U.S. power, especially since 9/11, has recalled both older forms of territorial aggression and occupation that have traditionally provoked anti-imperialist critiques, and new forms of power that can be explained not as de-territorialization but a remaking of the spaces of sovereignty to enable a de facto empire to conduct its business.

In each of these stages, the evolving nature of imperialism has had its counterpart in the changing face of anti-imperialism. This chapter examines the different manifestations of anti-imperialism in an era in which imperialism took new and often less visible forms. Anti-imperialism's most prominent form can be found in movements against foreign war (most notably those in Vietnam and Iraq), but more wide-ranging critiques of empire—indeed, new definitions of what constitutes empire—also have been advanced. The story of recent anti-imperialism is one of both continuity and departure from the themes examined in previous chapters. The symbols and languages used by the opponents of empire in previous eras have remained in currency. Yet the origins of recent anti-imperialism can be traced not only to nineteenth-century traditions, but also to contemporary social movements and, as increasingly has become the case, foreign and transnational currents of opposition to empire and U.S. foreign policy.

## The Age of Decolonization

The global ascendancy of the United States in the second half of the twentieth century occurred against the backdrop of the decolonization of European empires. A crude conclusion to draw would be that the rise of U.S. power in some way propagated anti-imperialism. Yet the U.S. position on

imperialism was uneven and mixed, a fact revealed in the limited decolonization of its own empire. The United States granted political independence
to its largest colonial possession, the Philippines, on July 4, 1946. But the
United States did not give up its military bases there. Nor did it relinquish
its other island territories—Guam, Samoa, and Puerto Rico, not to mention Guantánamo Bay in Cuba, the Panama Canal Zone (until 1999),[1] and
the Virgin Islands. Despite radical nationalists in Puerto Rico attempting
to assassinate President Truman in 1950, the U.S. grip on the island intensified economically and politically. Puerto Rico was given "commonwealth status" in 1952, with control over foreign affairs, defense, and other
important areas of government reserved in U.S. hands. U.S. decolonization presented, therefore, a mixed record, rendered comfortable only by
the small size and obscurity of this remaining and still existing bunch of
quasi-colonial possessions.

The U.S. position on the decolonization of European empires was also
uneven, and dependent largely on the geopolitics of the Cold War. The
classic example of U.S. anti-imperial foreign policy in this period was the
Suez Crisis in 1956. When the French and British invaded Suez to preserve
their control of the canal in the wake of its nationalization by Egypt, the
United States stood in opposition. Under American pressure, Britain and
France were forced to withdraw in humiliation, and U.S. relations with
Britain's former colonial protectorate improved temporarily. But this episode should not be seen simply as revealing the power of anti-imperialism
in the United States. The overriding factor in the diplomacy was the fear of
Soviet influence expanding in the Middle East. By opposing the Suez invasion, Secretary of State John Foster Dulles sought to make the United States
appear evenhanded in the region, to compensate for the pro-Israeli slant
in foreign policy that Arab nations detected in former president Truman's
policies. The events coincided also with the Soviet invasion of Hungary,
and calculations over this major source of Cold War tension in Europe
influenced American responses to Egypt, turning Washington in an anticolonial direction in the Suez Crisis.

In the case of Southeast Asian decolonization, Cold War strategies also
profoundly influenced the outcome. Vietnamese opponents of French rule
initially hoped that the United States might support their cause. Ho Chi
Minh's declaration of independence famously opened with quotations from
the U.S. document of 1776.[2] Yet the United States gave financial support
to the French. U.S. motivations concerned the potential "loss" of the wider
Southeast Asian region to communist control and represented geopolitical

support for the imperialism of a European ally, irrespective of whether the United States intervened directly or owned colonies itself. The U.S. supply of $400 million in aid to the beleaguered French forces in 1953 was undertaken, President Eisenhower explained, because "if Indochina goes, several things happen right away. The Malayan peninsula would be scarcely defensible—and tin and tungsten we so greatly value from that area would cease coming." Such an outcome would be "very ominous" for the United States because "if we lost all that, how would the free world hold the rich empire of Indonesia?" This was a time when the United States became acutely concerned over the reservation of such supplies of raw materials, which were needed for the nation's worldwide military commitments gained as a result of the Cold War. A Presidential Commission on Strategic Raw Materials had in 1952 identified the nation's dependence on the import of many of these items.[3]

If imperialism is defined as physical intervention in foreign countries *and* the aspiration to rule over them directly and permanently, then U.S. policy in this period does not qualify. There was little in this period akin to the open embrace of full-blown imperialism that marked the 1898 era. But this does not mean that U.S. policy was purely anti-imperial. Not only did support of European allies at times necessitate backing their imperial holdings, but U.S. policy toward newly independent countries also could entail intervention in them to prevent communist takeovers and to obtain, by indirect control, access to the resources necessary to stop what was perceived in Washington as the enslavement of the world by communism. The line between opposing other empires and promoting an informal U.S. empire remained as blurred in the Cold War as it had in earlier periods. Paul Kramer's concept of "nation-based empire"—a "limited liability empire" that sought to avoid the high military, political, and ideological costs of full-blown colonialism by fostering nation-states sympathetic to American objectives—is informative of U.S. grand strategy in the age of decolonization and rising American power.[4]

Though the United States eschewed imperialism as traditionally defined, its "nation-based empire" nonetheless could lead toward intervention, occupation, and assertion of political control. After 1965, direct U.S. involvement in Southeast Asia became so massive an undertaking—eventually there would be 540,000 American soldiers in Vietnam, as well as saturation bombing of North Vietnam and other communist-controlled regions in Cambodia and Laos—that the label of "imperialism" seemed to critics an appropriate one. "Imperialism" seemed a plausible judgment on the streets, but the argument went further than that, indeed to the highest echelons of the U.S. Congress.[5] Senator Wayne Morse of Oregon made this same call. He denounced the "stark, ugly imperialism" of the administration.[6] Yet Morse was one of only two U.S. senators who opposed the 1964 Gulf of Tonkin Resolution that sanctioned military intervention. Most Americans did not agree that the United States was imperialist. In fact Morse lost his bid for reelection in 1968, though only narrowly, and not only because of his opposition to the Vietnam War.

The Vietnam War led to a revival of American anti-imperialism. Its rallying point was not a broad and coherent critique of empire, but rather a narrower, reactive anti-imperialism that focused on ending the war in Southeast Asia. Campus demonstrations and Students for a Democratic Society (SDS) activism included denunciation of U.S. imperialism, but this was only one of several motives. Protest centered more commonly on the concrete issue of the war. As Barbara Tischler has put it, the objectives of protesters included "to end the war, to struggle against American imperialism, to stop the killing of American men and women, or simply to keep one's self from the harm of war."[7] Within SDS, the focus of the majority was on the war itself, though left-wing groups such as the small Marxist organization, the Progressive Labor Party, took a more explicit anti-imperialist line and infiltrated SDS.[8]

In general, the origins of the antiwar movement could be traced to civil rights and campus protest as much as it could to the intellectual and social traditions of anti-imperialism. The SDS's Port Huron Statement (1962), for example, fused a critique of U.S. militarism with condemnations of domestic segregation and the bureaucracy of higher education.[9] The civil rights movement emerged as a powerful source of opposition to the war as the decade progressed. Martin Luther King Jr. came to see an antiwar stance as an extension of the campaign against racism and poverty at home. "Our only hope today lies in our ability to recapture the revolutionary spirit and go out into a sometimes hostile world declaring eternal hostility to poverty, racism, and militarism," he declared in 1967. King went further, presenting the war in Vietnam as "but a symptom of a far deeper malady within the American spirit." He criticized not only the Vietnam War, but also U.S. policy toward Guatemala, Peru, Venezuela, Thailand, and Cambodia, which he saw as stemming from America's refusal "to give up the privileges and the pleasures that come from the immense profits of overseas investment." King also explicitly introduced the concept of colonialism. Unless the United States withdrew from Vietnam, he warned, the world would conclude "that our minimal expectation is to occupy it as an American colony."[10] King provides a revealing example of how opposition to the Vietnam War could lead to the formulation of a broader, anti-imperial critique of U.S. foreign policy.[11]

While advocates of a more explicit anti-imperialism could plausibly attach their own broader analysis of the forces bringing the United States into the Vietnam conflict, it became harder to maintain this anti-imperialist critique once American troops were withdrawn in 1973. Anti-imperialist sentiment declined in the United States after 1975, when the South Vietnamese government fell and national "liberation," the stated goal of the Vietnamese communists, was achieved. The fate of America's erstwhile South Vietnamese allies under Hanoi's totalitarian regime undermined portrayals of the new regime as promotive of justice and self-determination. A retreat from seeing the larger meaning of the Vietnam War in anti-imperialist terms was reflected in the legacy of the veterans' movement. The sectarian controversies within SDS over an explicitly anti-imperialist analysis were reproduced. The Vietnam Veterans against the War perpetuated opposition to U.S. involvement in foreign wars, applying the Vietnam lesson to Iraq and Afghanistan after 2003. Yet they rejected the more strident left-wing critique of the United States from dissenters who joined that movement to take it over. The organization split between the Vietnam Veterans against the War (VVAW) and the Vietnam Veterans against the War Anti-Imperialist (VVAW-AI), a far smaller group.[12] The VVAW did not engage in an explicitly anti-imperialist critique. It continued, however, to oppose American engagement in foreign wars that have, reputedly, been undertaken to secure political dominance over another people or resources such as oil. This constituted a de facto anti-imperialism. The VVAW also criticized the poor treatment of veterans and hence the internal costs of imperial overreach and pursued justice for veterans in such issues as homelessness and veterans' benefits. These efforts may be interpreted as a campaign against an imperial state, but the connection is rarely made explicit.[13]

Though a small and generally leftish minority continued to promote anti-imperialism in the years after 1975, the acute public debates about American empire that characterized the Vietnam era faded from view. This decline in anti-imperial discourse reflected a changed historical context. If we understand the Vietnam War controversies over empire as a product of *decolonization*, and of consequent large-scale military action abroad (*boots on the ground*), or support for other imperial powers that resisted nationalist movements, the waning of the decolonizing phase in European history

removed circumstances favorable to seeing the United States as an imperial power. The Vietnam War demonstrated the folly of direct intervention, and high political and military strategists had learned the lesson, at
least temporarily. The so-called "Vietnam syndrome," however, derived
less from anti-imperialism than it did from realpolitik. U.S. policy makers
sought to avoid full-blown intervention in Africa and Central America in
the subsequent decade, preferring instead to extend indirect support to
pro-free-market proxies. CIA complicity in the overthrow of the Salvador
Allende government in 1973 in Chile was perhaps a prototype. This episode generated anti-imperialist sentiment in Latin America, and among a
vocal minority at home. But it did not have much traction with the broader
U.S. public.

## Anti-imperialism after Vietnam

Though anti-imperialism as a social movement waned in the years after the
Vietnam War, two legacies flourished. The first was in academia. Vietnam
and other U.S. actions in the Cold War provided a powerful impetus to
a new historiographical critique of American imperialism. In some ways
this built upon the 1930s anti-imperialism and its opposition to American
involvement in foreign wars as sources of militarism and corporate profit.
But it went beyond economics to a cultural and political analysis of U.S.
foreign policy. Historian William Appleman Williams had revived the older
anti-imperial tradition and applied it within a broader theory of American
empire. Williams's work was not so much economic determinism as it was
a study of the central role of economic ideas in the search for markets to
preserve American capitalism. He posited the idea of the Open Door as
a worldview to explain U.S. foreign policy and its interventionism in a
decolonizing world. At the University of Wisconsin his interpretation influenced a number of New Left historians writing on not only the Vietnam
War, but also the early Cold War and the roots of American imperialism
in the 1890s.[14] Though not drawn directly from the Williams school, the
extensive study of the anti-imperialists of 1898–1902 also showed how the
public debates over American intervention in Southeast Asia stimulated
academic scholarship on anti-imperialism.[15] But just as the Vietnam War
agitation died, so too the scholarly study of empire lost steam in the 1980s
as post-revisionist scholarship set in. The publication of Williams's *Empire as
a Way of Life* (1980), a work that both summed up New Left thinking and

anticipated the cultural focus of future scholars, proved to be a temporary intellectual terminus for the critique.[16]

Congress was the other arena in which anti-imperialism was most visible in the years after 1973. The impetus here was the combination of Vietnam and the Watergate crisis, which triggered a set of congressional prohibitions on presidential war powers. The Watergate crisis exposed the links between presidential politics and the antiwar movement, since Nixon had peaceful protesters investigated using unconstitutional tactics such as unauthorized break-ins and phone taps. In a ringing critique of executive government, Arthur Schlesinger Jr. had already pointed to an "imperial presidency" pursuing "Messianic globalism." This critique centered American imperialism in the abuse of "the American spirit" through unrestrained executive power to conduct foreign military interventions. Through Watergate, the problem of imperialism was thereby partly translated onto the level of an internal struggle over "the constitutional balance."[17]

With Cold War competition continuing in the formerly colonial world, congressional critics of the "imperial presidency" sought to limit executive power. Concern that U.S. support of anticommunist groups in Angola might lead to further embroilment in the conflict led congressional critics to counter with a ban, under the Clark Amendment to the 1976 Arms Export Control Act, against arming Angolan anticommunists. Congressional prohibitions such as the Arms Export Control Act benefited from the attacks on presidential power in the Watergate crisis. Revelations concerning these matters contributed to a congressional form of anti-imperialism within which the terms of the Vietnam War and its aftermath were understood—that is, through bans on executive action abroad without congressional authorization. It is in this light that historian Greg Grandin has labeled the Ninety-Third Congress (1973–75) as "perhaps the most anti-imperial legislature in United States history" for beginning this process, but the same spirit continued into the following Congress.[18] From 1976 to 1987, conflicts over U.S. political and military intervention centered on concrete violation of such self-denying bans in the Cold War at a time when presidents argued that the Soviet Union and its allies were fueling Third World instability.

President Ronald Reagan worked to circumvent these restrictions in the 1980s, at home by surveillance of anti-imperialist groups seeking to expose U.S. actions in Central America, and outside the United States through aid to right-wing governments and paramilitary forces. Reagan called the latter "freedom fighters" in a clear reference to the imagined anti-imperialism of the American Revolution.[19] The Central American policies of the Reagan administration did not involve U.S. occupation of a foreign country. With "boots on the ground" being defined, courtesy of the Vietnam legacy, as imperialism, the administration sought to sidestep domestic criticism by instead extending aid to the "moral equivalents of our founding fathers," who were in fact authoritarians such as Efraín Ríos Montt in Guatemala.[20] The administration's Central American policy did produce embarrassment and criticism, but the most successful critiques within the United States were centered on the same issue of executive power that distinguished Watergate. Critics transformed the Central American issue into a scandal. The Iran-Contra Affair (fought out over what Reagan knew about the channeling of funds to the Nicaraguan Contras through arms sales to Iran) shaped the anti-imperialist discourse. This "bolt of lightning" undermined Reagan's Central American policy more effectively than any overt critique of the United States as an imperialist power.[21]

Resistance to American intervention in Central America took two overlapping forms. Catholic and other church-led pacifist and human rights advocates protested against the massacres of civilian populations that occurred under Ríos Montt and other right-wing dictators that the United States backed. Itself a demonstrably transnational force, the Catholic Church became a leading source of passive resistance to dictatorial regimes in El Salvador and Guatemala, and an aid to refugees from them. Its clergy and nuns became sometimes victims of the internecine struggles in the Central American states.[22] Meanwhile, left-wing groups explicitly argued that U.S. meddling in Central America was imperialistic. Such attacks came from the nationwide Committee in Solidarity with the People of El Salvador (CISPES), which the FBI labeled a Soviet front.[23] But mostly the left-of-center organizations remained focused on concrete goals of human rights and an end to military aid for right-wing governments.[24] Though Witness for Peace's long-term goal, for example, was to "stop imperialism, change U.S. policy, and withdraw U.S. dominance" in Central Americas, this objective was rarely articulated.[25]

The antinuclear protest movement of this era was another case of transnational action against U.S. power, with loosely connected protests in Europe and North America. Here too, protesters did not invoke anti-imperialism as an explicit critique so much as assert the need for international peace, condemning both sides in the Cold War for exacerbating the dangers of a nuclear Armageddon in Europe. The United States was not the sole target, nor was the agitation strongest there, but rather in Europe.

Nonetheless, the antinuclear agitation presented major challenges to the Reagan administration, not least when Congress debated a nuclear arms freeze in 1983 that would have prevented new deployment of cruise and Pershing II missiles in Europe.

Reagan countered the antinuclear movement by presenting U.S. policy as the anti-imperial safeguard against the "evil empire" of the Soviet Union. This time-honored political tactic resembled the efforts of nineteenth-century statesmen to present their expansionist policies as necessary to counter British and European imperialism. And just as early American statesmen depicted their anti-imperialism as ideological in nature (in opposition to foreign monarchy), Reagan presented his policies as necessary to oppose communism. Reagan belatedly inserted the "evil empire" theme into a speech given in Orlando, Florida, to the National Association of Evangelicals, a constituency he hoped to mobilize on behalf of his effort to block the nuclear freeze campaign. "So in your discussions of the nuclear freeze proposals I urge you to beware the temptation of pride—the temptation to blithely declare yourselves above it all and label both sides equally at fault, to ignore the facts of history and the aggressive impulses of an evil empire, to simply call the arms race a giant misunderstanding and thereby remove yourself from the struggle between right and wrong and good and evil." Reagan referred to communism as "the focus of evil in the modern world."[26] This invocation of anti-imperialism ironically duplicated the Soviets' use of "imperialism" as part of their own propaganda war against the United States and the former European colonial powers. While Reagan's action did not win the approval of protesters and appalled parts of the U.S. foreign policy establishment as likely to be counterproductive in Europe, it galvanized Republican support for the president's position within the United States by deflecting the epithet of imperialism onto the Soviets. The prominent evangelical Jerry Falwell duly complied by lobbying against the nuclear freeze.

Reagan's actions also affected antiwar protests, reinforcing Cold War polarities over the debate about a nuclear arms reduction. The National Nuclear Weapons Freeze Campaign was forced to remain rhetorically hostile to the Soviet Union, fearing being labeled communist-inspired (as Reagan himself implied).[27] Reagan did not stop the passage of a nuclear freeze resolution in the House of Representatives but defeated it in the Senate, where the Republicans had a majority. The nuclear deployments in Europe went ahead. Nevertheless, the antinuclear movement put pressure on the Reagan administration in the year leading up to the 1984 presidential election, and he eventually changed course to work in his second term with the Soviet Union to begin arms reduction.[28]


## The Post–Cold War World

Even though the peace movement had successfully pressured the president to modify arms policy, Reagan's "evil empire" speech has more resonance in contemporary historical memory than do the actions of the activists and peace protesters. This outcome no doubt owes much to the anticommunist revolutions in Eastern Europe that led to the tearing down of the Berlin Wall in 1989 and the reuniting of Germany. The pro-democracy revolutions in Eastern Europe represented a vindication for conservatives of the evils of the evil empire and put the United States more firmly into the putatively anti-imperialist camp. In 1991, the Soviet Union itself collapsed, and the Cold War was over. The postcolonial phase of the 1970s and 1980s had seen both the United States and the Soviets claiming to be anti-imperialist, while both used coercion, through support of proxy forces, to influence political change in the developing world. The events of 1989–91, however, ushered in a new era in which even such indirect intervention seemed slated to disappear.

According to the interpretation first articulated by the deputy director of the State Department's policy planning staff, Francis Fukuyama, the Soviet demise ushered in the global triumph of liberalism. Since a liberal regime could not be an empire, the era of anti-imperialism had arrived in fulfillment of Hegelian dialectics. Fukuyama saw anti-imperialism as a part of this liberal hegemony over the vestiges of the old, premodern, pre-liberal order. The new era was "a world dominated by economic concerns, in which there are no ideological grounds for major conflict between nations, and in which, consequently, the use of military force becomes less legitimate." Thus free markets were "in" and imperialism was permanently "out." The "legitimacy of any kind of territorial aggrandizement" had been "thoroughly discredited."[29]

The political and economic history of the 1990s did not bear out Fukuyama's interpretation of a movement toward a liberal, postimperial world, signaling the "end of history." Nor was the decade one focused exclusively on trade and commerce that would bring peace and homogeneity. But the 1990s did witness accelerated globalization, with the appearance of many nongovernmental organizations and the founding of international agreements and supranational institutions promoting this new world order. The extension of trade agreements, particularly the North American Free Trade Agreement and the World Trade Organization, established the architecture of a postcolonial world in which all were subject to a market.

These globalizing pressures forced a further rethinking among opponents of imperialism and military intervention abroad. The rapid acceleration of global integration provided the basis for one of the era's most widely read critiques of empire. In their coauthored *Empire* (2000), Michael Hardt and Antonio Negri argued that territorially based imperialism had been transcended, and that only a nonnational and de-territorialized "Empire" remained as a transnational system of networked power. Hardt and Negri wrote from a tradition of leftist anti-imperialism. But their work differed from its predecessors in arguing that the sources of empire could no longer be found within the confines of the nation-state, even one with unmatched power: "The United States does not, and indeed no nation-state can today, form the center of an imperialist project. Imperialism is over." But if imperialism was finished, "Empire" was not. It was everywhere, producing not one single crisis but an indefinite series of minor crises that amounted to an "omni-crisis." Hardt and Negri reconceptualized anti-imperialism in terms of globalization's dissolution of sovereign space. The challenge confronting present-day anti-imperialists, they asserted, "is not simply to resist these processes but to reorganize them and redirect them toward new ends."[30]

A popular parallel to this new conception of empire might be found in the globalization protests that emerged in the late 1990s, most notably during the WTO meeting in Seattle in 1999. Those opposed to liberal globalization and the international institutions that fostered it, such as the WTO, the IMF, and the World Bank, were not anti-imperialists in the traditional sense. Yet the culture of antiglobalization activism can be traced to the antiwar demonstrations of the 1960s. Furthermore, protesters deployed the language of anti-imperialism on behalf of their critique of globalization. In the crosshairs of Naomi Klein's popular manifesto *No Logo* was not the overseas extension of U.S. military power, but rather the era's emerging "corporate empires," "media empires," "cultural empire builders," and, not to be forgotten, the "Nike empire."[31] In this formulation, anti-imperialism constituted opposition to the free-market forces that empowered, as Klein put it, a "select group of corporate Goliaths that have gathered to form our de facto global government."[32]

Critiques of empire that emerged at this time from the fields of cultural and literary studies similarly eschewed traditional conceptions of imperialism as territorial aggrandizement or even the overseas extension of the power of the nation-state. The seminal work here was a 1994 volume of essays edited by Amy Kaplan and Donald Pease. Inspired by postcolonial theory and the work of cultural critic Edward Said, *Cultures of United States Imperialism* collapsed the distinction between the foreign and domestic. Kaplan asserted that "foregrounding imperialism in the study of American cultures shows how putatively domestic conflicts are not simply contained at home but how they both emerge in response to international struggles and spill over national boundaries to be re-enacted, challenged, or transformed."[33] The cultural and literary imperialism examined in Kaplan and Pease's volume was not neatly derivative of the nation-state. Indeed, one of the volume's achievements was to show how the American historical experience of empire could be viewed alongside the production of imperial and anti-imperial discourses that scholars of non-U.S. colonial and postcolonial settings had long identified.

These and other works laid the groundwork for new explorations and critiques of de-territorialized empire. Yet what most gave new life to post–Cold War anti-imperialism was the reemergence of boots-on-the-ground interventions and occupations in the aftermath of 9/11. The two wars against Iraq—one preceding and one after 9/11—illustrate how different U.S. policies triggered differing anti-imperial responses. There was relatively little anti-imperial agitation during the 1991 Gulf War. The explanation lies in the multilateral work of the United States with the UN to provide aid to the independent state of Kuwait against Saddam Hussein's aggression. By not pursuing Saddam's forces into Iraq, the first Bush presidency avoided the possibility of being pinned down in a protracted war that might have triggered the opposition seen in the Vietnam era. In contrast, the preemptive 2003 Iraq War quickly revived fears of an expansionist U.S. state intent on forcibly exporting a version of democracy conducive to its geopolitical and economic interests.

## The New Debate over Empire

Not since the aftermath of 1898 had empire been as explicitly and prominently debated in the United States as it was in the years immediately following September 11, 2001. The policies of the second Bush administration— the invasion of Afghanistan, the "Patriot Act" that gave the central state new powers of surveillance and detention, and, above all, the Iraq War of

2003—produced sustained criticisms at home and abroad. Yet most of the officials and supporters of the Bush administration, such as those in the Project for the New American Century (PNAC), denied being advocates of empire. The Iraq War, the PNAC argued along with Secretary of Defense Donald Rumsfeld and President George W. Bush, was merely a temporary invasion of a foreign country that presented a threat to the United States itself, not an act of empire building. "America has never been an empire," Bush declared. "There is a vital distinction between being powerful—even most powerful in the world—and being an empire," Robert Kagan, then of PNAC, asserted. "Economic expansion does not equal imperialism."[34] For neoconservatives, anti-imperialism encompassed only a prohibition on *permanent* occupation of a country against its will. How long an occupation had to be in order to be considered "permanent" was not stated. Once again, the U.S. state and its influential architects of foreign policy interpreted the world through a classical liberal lens and saw U.S. actions as anti-imperial.

Whatever the technical merits of these denials under the territorial principle, the so-called Bush doctrine of unilateral and interventionist foreign policies led to a sudden reassertion of the importance of the empire idea. As in earlier periods, this was perhaps most visible within the academy. Historian after historian came forward to produce works on imperialism and empire over the next few years. Many of these situated the Bush administration's actions in historical context. Soon, all that remained of the old view that the United States had not been an empire was smoldering rubble. One prominent history of the nineteenth century began its introduction with a ten-reason list why the United States should be considered an empire.[35] Works of this nature spanned the political spectrum. Left-leaning scholars, whose roots could be traced either to Williams's Wisconsin school or more recent cultural studies circles, had little difficulty picking up where their forebears had left off. But examinations of the history of American empire now also came from the Right, which hitherto had tended to deny or understate the importance of empire in U.S. history. John Lewis Gaddis and British émigré Niall Ferguson, for example, wrote books that presented historical parallels and justifications for the actions of the Bush administration.[36] There was less certainty, however, when it came to interpreting the history of anti-imperialism, which, though referenced in many of these works, was rarely the focus of sustained discussion. Some authors identified a persistent and heroic strain of anti-imperialism in American history that extended legitimacy to contemporary opponents of the Iraq War.[37] But others dismissed the opponents of empire as internally divided, politically impotent, and easily steamrolled by a hegemonic imperialist culture. A "Myth of America cultural hegemony marginalized anti-imperialists as elite, feminine, and subversive of national destiny," wrote Walter Hixson in his cultural history of American imperialism.[38]

If most of these debates took place within academia, the scholarly discussion of empire should not be dismissed as irrelevant. The scholarship that established America's imperial past informed public debate on the foreign policies of the second Bush administration. This was true of works from across the political spectrum. "America broke away from the British empire, and now it's building its own British-style empire," wrote popular *New York Times* columnist Maureen Dowd in 2003. "We are, as Niall Ferguson, the author of 'Empire,' put it, 'an empire in denial.'"[39] Furthermore, rather than passively observing public discussion of empire, scholars and historians sought broader public connections. The Historians against the War, a network of scholars and teachers formed in 2003, organized against the "imperial efforts by the United States and other powerful nations to dominate the internal life of other countries." On the worldwide web, historians have adopted the term "empire" through many blogs such as the American Empire Project, where Andrew Bacevich and the late Howard Zinn have been involved.[40]

Yet irrespective of this scholarly impact, anti-imperialism once again took popular as well as academic forms. The left-wing ANSWER Coalition (Act Now to Stop War and End Racism) linked its opposition to the war to an explicit anti-imperialism, but the biggest umbrella group was the more moderate United for Peace and Justice (UFPJ), to which the Historians against the War affiliated. Both these groups remained active in 2013, and both in their own way critiqued American imperialism.[41] A coalition of many international and U.S.-based organizations, UFPJ claimed at one time to be opposed to "our government's policy of permanent warfare and empire-building."[42] Yet UFPJ's "Unity Statement" later modulated this direct critique. In 2013 UFPJ no longer used the terms "empire" or "imperialism" on its website, though its web content continued to critique wars of aggression and proclaimed that "sovereign nations" have the right to determine their own future, free from the threat of "pre-emptive attacks" and "regime change," military occupation, "and outside control of their economic resources."[43] This version of anti-imperialism avoided the name but located the issue not in whether the American actions might be militarily temporary but in the undeniable fact that the United States practiced coercion and regime change.

As in the case of Vietnam, opposition to a foreign war became a cause around which the otherwise inchoate sentiments of anti-imperialism could be organized. Though much of the agitation was directly against war, the common call of "blood for oil," coupled as it often was with reference to international law and the lack of an explicit U.N. mandate for preemptive and unilateral military action in Iraq, indicated more than an opposition to going to battle and loss of lives. Especially given that in contrast to the Vietnam War, the U.S. Army was now an all-volunteer force, opposing war to stop American coercion of a foreign country and the expected corralling of the resources of that country by American corporations constituted a reasonable and common-sense understanding of anti-imperialism.

The demonstrations against the trend toward war in 2003, in which protest groups tried to dissuade Congress, were not successful, but it is not adequate to portray this opposition as a minor matter because it failed in its immediate objective. The campaign mobilized the largest public antiwar demonstrations since the Vietnam War era. This practical anti-imperialism at the grassroots level was also transnational in scope, with marches in some sixty countries worldwide on February 15, 2003.[44] The London event, estimated to be the largest demonstration in the city's history, with one million participants, appeared to have more than doubled its largest American counterpart in New York.[45] To the extent that the global demonstrations did not stop the war, this failure reflected in large part the obstinacy, determination, and even deceit with which the Bush administration campaign for war was waged both with Congress and at the United Nations, since the documentation presented to both has subsequently been found faulty and misleading. The evidence of weapons of mass destruction in Iraq did not exist, and the CIA was, in effect, pressured into preparing briefs claiming that they did.[46]

To dismiss the antiwar movement as thereby inconsequential would overestimate the extent to which the will of a nation's people to avoid a foreign war could be denied in the long run. Even in the short run, these demonstrations did have their effect. Though anti-imperialism in 2003 did not stop the American invasion, policy responses were sensitive to, and affected by, domestic and international opposition. The Bush administration was not only forced to deny that the United States was an empire, but it acted with obvious haste to hand over formal sovereignty to Iraq after the removal of Saddam Hussein, despite the unpreparedness of Iraqi institutions to fill the vacuum in mid-2004. This urgency to transfer *formal* sovereignty stemmed precisely from touchiness over the assumption of an overtly imperial position. Without granting Iraqi sovereignty, the administration's professions of anti-imperial intent could not be sustained.

The significance of the antiwar anti-imperialism of this period is perhaps most evident in how politicians, particularly of the Democratic Party, came to embrace bottom-up opposition to the Iraq venture. Some 40 percent of Democrats in the House and 58 percent of those in the Senate voted for the October 2002 joint resolution that authorized the use of force in Iraq. Those Democrats who supported intervention, such as New York senator Hillary Clinton, would later pay a political price, whereas those who opposed it, such as Barack Obama (who in 2003 did not yet hold federal office), reaped political benefit. During the hotly contested presidential primaries of 2008, the major Democratic candidates vied to be the most vocal critic of the Bush team's foreign policy. Once elected, President Obama promoted the view of the United States as anti-imperial provided it withdrew from the (mistaken) military occupation of Iraq. This rhetoric was intended for both domestic and international consumption. In his Cairo speech of 2009, the new president linked U.S. national exceptionalism to anti-imperialist values: "America is not the crude stereotype of a self-interested empire. The United States has been one of the greatest sources of progress that the world has ever known. We were born out of revolution against an empire. We were founded upon the ideal that all are created equal, and we have shed blood and struggled for centuries to give meaning to those words—within our borders, and around the world."[47]

Those on the libertarian right of American politics were also fulsome on the fundamentally anti-imperial nature of the United States, and the need to extricate the country from the embarrassment of Iraq. Ron Paul, the doyen of this political persuasion, was one of only six House Republicans (out of 223) to vote against the 2002 resolution. Paul's opposition derived from his reading of the Constitution and his fear of unchecked executive power: "This is exactly what our Founding Fathers cautioned against when crafting our form of government: most had just left behind a monarchy where the power to declare war rested in one individual. It is this they most wished to avoid."[48] Paul's views came to be embraced in the coming decade by radical Republicans who formed "Tea Party" groups to protest governmental activism. The Tea Party nostalgically looked back to an imagined past in which America opposed monarchical imperialism and promoted a limited foreign policy of non-entanglement. Yet what gave their foreign-policy vision clout were the links they made between a big-spending state apparatus and the tendency of U.S. governments to send troops to—and maintain extensive bases in—many foreign countries. The U.S. invasion of Iraq was mounted from a constellation of military bases in foreign lands, including in two newly independent Central Asian states of the former Soviet Union; in Kuwait; in Ramstein in Germany as well as other sites in Europe; and elsewhere. The continuation of the wars in both Iraq and Afghanistan made Obama himself seem apostate from anti-imperialism once president in 2009. In fact the Obama administration wished to retain bases in Iraq even after American "withdrawal," but the Iraqi government would not accede to these terms. The long-running war there and the struggle in Afghanistan opened the way for the new American Right to capitalize on antiwar feeling across the country. This attack was backed up by the Tea Party rank-and-file that surged in opposition to Obama's domestic policies in 2010.

Tea party anti-imperialism was deeply rooted in American antistatist ideology, a point its champions lost no opportunity to make. In *Ain't My America: The Long, Noble History of Antiwar Conservatism and Middle-American Anti-imperialism*, Bill Kauffman constructed a linear history of conservative anti-imperialism, one whose roots could be traced back to conservative critics of the wars overseen by Democratic administrations in the twentieth century, the Anti-Imperialist League of 1898, and even to George Washington's Farewell Address of 1796. "There is nothing freakish, cowardly, or even anomalous about these Middle Americans who are turning against foreign war," Kauffman wrote. "They are acting in the best traditions of their forebears."[49] Like others of his political persuasion, Kauffman linked U.S. imperialism to the growth of a tyrannical state at home. This historical case was made most vigorously by Andrew Napolitano, a New Jersey judge and media personality who in his 2012 book, *Theodore and Woodrow: How Two American Presidents Destroyed Constitutional Freedoms*, denounced both Woodrow Wilson and Theodore Roosevelt as responsible for the modern American state and its expansionist imperialism. Thanks to Roosevelt's foreign meddling, the nation had become in Napolitano's estimate the "most imperialistic country in the history of the world."[50] It would be easy to dismiss Napolitano as an intellectual fringe dweller. But he was also a Fox News commentator, and his book was published by a subsidiary of News Corporation. Anti-imperialists from the Ludwig Von Mises Institute, a radical free-market group and think tank devoted to Austrian economics, also came to the fore in this debate. Thomas E. Woods Jr., a Von Mises Institute fellow, provides an outspoken example. He revived the reputation of the old Anti-Imperialist League of 1898–1920 and opposed the Bush-era policies, wondering how anyone could support a president whose Iraq war resulted in "hundreds of thousands of casualties, a Shiite-dominated regime, and regional chaos." This stance was not simply a pragmatic opposition to the blowback of war but an indication of "how important it is to oppose empire with every ideological tool at our disposal."[51]

Right-wing anti-imperialism also penetrated the presidential contest in 2012. Among radical Republicans, George W. Bush was very unpopular. In the election primaries of that year, Ron Paul gained noticeable support from young voters precisely because of his attacks on U.S. strategic policy. Some have argued that Paul's anti-imperialism is mere show, that his "supposed 'anti-imperialism' is just a distraction from his material support for imperialism and terror by his efforts to divide and confuse people."[52] On the other hand, certain left-liberals have recognized how seductive the anti-imperialist and antistatist strain contained in Paul's candidacy might be. Andrew Levine, a political philosopher and senior scholar at the Institute for Policy Studies in Washington, DC, noted that Paul was the "only anti-war candidate running for president." More importantly, he wanted "to do away with overseas bases and reduce the military to the strictly defensive force envisioned in the Constitution." Paul reportedly wished "to dismantle the apparatus of empire and to halt American meddling in the affairs of foreign countries." Among other things, this meant "the end of all Bush-Obama wars, the demise of the military-industrial complex, and the termination of America's virtually unconditional military, economic and diplomatic support for Israel." Paul's candidacy drew support from only a small minority, a fact that reflected the limits to his anti-imperialist and small government appeal. These limits, however, arguably involved his positions on many other issues. It was more telling that Paul did not "claim to be anti-imperialist" but rather an "anti-interventionist."[53] As in so many other cases, American anti-imperialism was not articulated as an unqualified and coherent ideology but woven deeply into traditional American ideas of liberalism and republicanism.

In the light of widespread repugnance concerning empire, it might seem that Americans could modify the famous Jeffersonian quip and state "We are all anti-imperialists now." But many outside the United States would disagree. Foreign critiques of U.S. imperialism continue to proliferate, particularly in Latin America and the Middle East, where anti-imperialism continues to be closely tied to anti-Americanism and resistance to U.S. foreign policy. To be sure, such foreign anti-imperialist concerns are not directed exclusively toward the United States. As geographer Richard Phillips has pointed out, Robert Mugabe tended to blame British imperialism "past and present" for the crisis in Zimbabwe, and the late Hugo Chávez of Venezuela did more than equate George W. Bush with the sulfurous odor (*azufre*) of the devil (*Ayer estuvo el diablo aquí*); Chávez could equally accuse the king of Spain of possessing an "enduring colonial superiority complex." Evo Morales has "optimistically" heralded that his election as Bolivia's "first indigenous president" marked "the end" of a generic "colonial and neoliberal era" for his country.[54] But in most cases this anti-imperialism has been strongest when directed against the United States. The left-wing leaders of Venezuela, Bolivia, Argentina, and Ecuador have all, along with Cuba, continued to raise the question of a specifically U.S. imperialism, though Argentina has also denounced British imperialism in the Malvinas Islands (the Falklands).

This international anti-imperialism is of concern to U.S. policy makers. Obama's anti-imperialist speech of 2009 was delivered in Cairo for good reason; it was part of an attempt to improve relations with the Muslim world. But the effects of this global sentiment have also been felt on the domestic scene. This is particularly the case with the use of unmanned drones, an increasingly automated and impersonal manifestation of empire. Used by the George W. Bush administration but employed to a much greater extent by Obama, drones have been favored by U.S. policy makers to avoid putting boots on the ground. As one critic notes, "With manpower tied up" in Afghanistan, and anti-base movements growing abroad, Washington bureaucrats "desperately looking for places to cut the U.S. budget" found drones "an attractive alternative."[55] The government thus moved toward "an ever greater outsourcing of war to things that cannot protest, cannot vote with their feet (or wings), and for whom there is no 'home front' or even a home at all," stated journalist Tom Engelhardt.[56] This policy has spurred "enormous" anti-American sentiment abroad.[57]

Though the nature of this form of imperialism is novel (and, indeed, unacknowledged by the U.S. government), the critical American argument against drones is one of constitutionality, an old theme in anti-imperial discourse. Engelhardt writes sarcastically: "the U.S. is performing its age-old 'inalienable' right to act as judge, jury, and executioner on a planetary scale, attracting a storm of legal challenge and international condemnation."[58] The reproof harks back to the Constitution since it concerns the rights of expatriate Americans, judged by the U.S. government to be terrorists, who are arbitrarily subject to assassination without trial. But the use of drones also concerns state violence against peoples outside the normal American legal jurisdiction and international law. Thereby the practice renders the boundaries of nations almost irrelevant. Power is exerted in a way that de-territorializes; yet this is not the purely de-territorialized "Empire," with a capital *E*, of Hardt and Negri's theory. At the same time that it dis-solves borders, the use of drones creates new territorialized spaces. Outside the formal boundaries of the United States are other spaces in which the United States has arrogated the sovereign right to terminate lives and de-stroy property, using rules laid down in secret, based on a highly contestable reading of the Constitution. This is a process of re-territorialized empire because it asserts American authority and sanctions coercion within these new spaces, viewed not as sovereign political territory but spaces of assas-sination. A parallel case is the spying upon foreigners via the Internet, and the attempt to apprehend individuals who have violated American law on cyber crime (especially espionage or copyright) while never actually setting foot in the United States or contravening the laws of their home country. These, too, are re-territorialized spaces, and they make the notion of a U.S. empire beyond official national borders explicit.[59]

Respondents to websites dealing with the issue make clear that drone warfare constitutes an empire of the drones. This categorization may be humorous at times, as in reviews posted on Amazon.com for the Predator Drone toy advertised as suitable for children three years and up:

> My son is very interested in joining the Imperial forces when he grows up. He says he's not sure if he wants to help police the homeland or if he wants to invade foreign countries. So I thought a new Predator drone toy would be a nice gift for him. These drones are used both domestically and internationally, to spy on people and assassinate them at the Emperor's discretion. He just loves flying his drone around our house, dropping Hell-fire missiles on Scruffy, our dog. He kept saying that Scruffy was a terror suspect and needed to be taken out. I asked him if Scruffy should get a trial first, and he quoted Lindsay Graham, Imperial Senator: "Shut up Scruffy, you don't get a trial!" I was so proud.[60]

Humorous as it is, the post articulates a serious anti-imperialist sentiment that reaches into vernacular culture, based on widespread concern about the moral and legal status of drone strikes. Yet despite articulate critics in

America, drone policy faces its strongest opponents outside U.S. borders: only 28 percent of foreign respondents to a 2012 Pew Survey supported drone strikes, while 62 percent of Americans did. More than 85 percent of people in some Arab countries opposed the use. Even among American allies, opinion has been against such strikes, and concern is growing that drones heighten anti-American feeling abroad.[61]

By 2013, some Americans harbored a new form of anti-imperialism fashioned in large measure from their government's concrete exercise of force in other countries—all done without ground troops and beyond the rule of law. As the deployment of military, economic, and political power changes across national boundaries, conceptions of empire are continually contested and reshaped. Opposition to this power waxes and wanes, but can only be properly understood within a tradition of anti-imperialist thought and practice.

What then to conclude about anti-imperialism in a postcolonial era of global integration and U.S. superpowerdom? First, the traditions of anti-imperialism that emerged in the experience of the American Revolution and during the nineteenth century remain alive. The old symbols (the Declaration, the Constitution) and languages (republicanism, liberalism) have lingered and are invoked across the political spectrum. Even Hardt and Negri saw the U.S. Constitution as an inclusive political framework for an enlightened world future.[62] Yet these traditional symbols have been fused with practices of more recent vintage, as well as vested with new meanings. The protest culture born in the civil rights era has informed popular anti-imperialism more than have the institutions and practices of the nineteenth century. When those opposed to the invasion of Iraq took to the streets in 2003, they drew upon the protest culture forged during the 1950s and '60s, and honed during the globalization protests of the 1990s, more than they looked to the practices of the patrician Anti-Imperialist League of 1898. Even Tea Party groups, whose political agenda derives from classical liberalism, have protested in a manner more reminiscent of the second half of the twentieth century than of the late-eighteenth that they hold so dear.

Second, American anti-imperialism has become increasingly transnational. This is not altogether new, as preceding chapters in this volume, particularly those of Go and Manela, have made clear, but it has become an ever more salient feature of the relationship between the United States and anti-imperialism in an age of accelerating globalization and the ascendancy of U.S. power. Those abroad who oppose U.S. power, or who seek to harness opposition to it for their own ends, draw upon American national anti-imperial traditions. Furthermore, many of the era's signature anti-imperial treatises and actions have come from outside the United States, perhaps not surprisingly, given the reach of U.S. power. The transnational traffic in anti-imperialism has reshaped its American iterations. American anti-imperialists on the left are now as likely to point to U.N. charters, international law, and global opinion as they are to their hoary national symbols and precedents. In terms of intellectual and academic anti-imperialism, transnational networks and theories, such as postcolonialism, have shaped the views of the American intelligentsia. Given all this, it is becoming increasingly difficult to identify a particularly national brand of anti-imperialism, even if its symbols and languages can be found across the world.

Third, the new forms that empire has assumed in a postcolonial and increasingly interconnected world have changed anti-imperialism. Recent anti-imperial critiques have targeted de-territorialized forms of empire. Ironically, the retro, boots-on-the-ground approach of the George W. Bush era might have stunted the development of this kind of anti-imperial thought, fueling instead a resurgent antiwar anti-imperialism characteristic of the Vietnam era. The fact that empire has been a moving target in this period—and that few openly advocate imperialism as traditionally defined—helps to explain why anti-imperialism has been varied and episodic in nature.

Fourth, anti-imperialism as a political force has met with mixed results. Popular protest movements did not prevent U.S. interventions abroad, most notably in Iraq in 2003. But they did demonstrate public disapproval of foreign wars and hastened U.S. withdrawals in Vietnam and Iraq. Though anti-imperial critiques emerged from these protest movements, they were most potent when framed in narrower antiwar terms or when linking policy makers to domestic scandals. The effect of all this is that U.S. policy makers, in general terms, have become disinclined to engage in full-blown foreign interventions and occupations, preferring instead covert action, indirect support of proxies, and, in recent times, the use of unmanned drones. In this regard, the politics of anti-imperialism have shaped the practice of American empire.

As in the past, the future of anti-imperialism will depend on the forms taken by its alter ego. It is easy to imagine that tomorrow's anti-imperialists will pick up from where the theorists of de-territorialized empire left off, though now taking into account the new technologies of state military power such as drones. But it is just as possible to imagine other contingencies. Might ongoing instability in the Middle East suck the United States, perhaps even against its better judgment, into further occupations such as the one that triggered global opposition during the Iraq War? Or, alternatively, might an increasingly nationalist and expansionist China once again place the United States in the role of opposing a foreign empire, as it did Britain in the nineteenth century and the Soviet Union in the twentieth? The answer to such questions is anyone's guess. But one thing remains certain: as imperialism continues to evolve, so too will anti-imperialism.

# Notes

## Introduction

1. "William Jennings Bryan: The Paralyzing Influence of Imperialism," in *Official Proceedings of the Democratic National Convention Held in Kansas City, Mo., July 4, 5 and 6, 1900* (Chicago: McLellan Printing Co., 1900), 205–27, http://www.mtholyoke.edu/acad/intrel/bryan.htm.

2. Democratic Party Platform of 1900, July 4, 1900, http://www.presidency.ucsb.edu/ws/index.php?pid=29587#axzz1lx1KYDmS.

3. "William Jennings Bryan: The Paralyzing Influence of Imperialism."

4. Samuel Flagg Bemis, *A Diplomatic History of the United States*, 5th ed. (New York: Holt, Reinhart, and Winston, 1963), 463.

5. Quoted in Patricia Nelson Limerick, "Empire and Amnesia," *Historian* 66, no. 3 (2004): 532–38, at 532; Niall Ferguson, *Colossus: The Rise and Fall of the American Empire* (London: Penguin, 2005), 1.

6. For a recent examination of this literature see Paul Kramer, "Power and Connection: Imperial Histories of the United States in the World," *American Historical Review* 116, no. 5 (December 2011): 1348–91.

7. Max Boot, "American Imperialism? No Need to Run Away from Label," http://www.usatoday.com/news/opinion/editorials/2003-05-05-boot_x.htm; Ferguson, *Colossus*; Max Boot, *The Savage Wars of Peace: Small Wars and the Rise of American Power* (New York: Basic Books, 2002).

8. Fred H. Harrington, "The Anti-imperialist Movement in the United States, 1898–1900," *Mississippi Valley Historical Review* 22, no. 2 (September 1935): 211–30. For the Vanguard Press Series see Ian Tyrrell's essay in this volume.

9. See Daniel Schirmer, *Republic or Empire: American Resistance to the Philippine War* (Cambridge, MA: Schenkman Publishing Co., 1972); Robert L. Beisner, *Twelve against Empire: The Anti-Imperialists, 1898–1900* (New York: McGraw-Hill, 1968); E. Berkeley Tompkins, *Anti-Imperialism in the United States: The Great Debate, 1890–1920* (Philadelphia: University of Pennsylvania Press, 1970); Christopher Lasch, "The Anti-Imperialists, the Philippines, and the Inequality of Man," *Journal of Southern History* 24, no. 3 (August 1958): 319–31; James A. Zimmerman, "Who Were the Anti-imperialists and the Expansionists of 1898 and 1899? A Chicago Perspective," *Pacific Historical Review* 46, no. 4 (November 1977): 589–601; Richard E. Welch Jr., *Response to Imperialism: The United States and the Philippine-American War, 1899–1902* (Chapel Hill: University of North Carolina Press, 1978).

10. An exception is M. Patrick Cullinane, *Liberty and American Anti-imperialism, 1898–1909* (New York: Palgrave Macmillan, 2012).

11. Erin Leigh Murphy, "Women's Anti-imperialism, 'The White Man's Burden,' and the Philippine-American War: Theorizing Masculinist Ambivalence in Protest," *Gender & Society* 23 (2009): 244–70; Allison L. Schneider, *Suffragists in an Imperial Age: U.S. Expansion and the Woman Question, 1870–1929* (New York: Oxford University Press, 2008); Erin Leigh Murphy, "Anti-imperialism during the Philippine-American War: Protesting 'Criminal Aggression' and 'Benevolent Assimilation'" (PhD diss., University of Illinois at Urbana-Champaign, 2009).

12. Gerald Horne, *Black and Red: W. E. B. Du Bois and the Afro-American Response to the Cold War, 1944–1963*, SUNY Series in Afro-American Society (Albany: SUNY Press, 1986), 19; Judith Stein, *The World of Marcus Garvey: Race and Class in Modern Society* (Baton Rouge: Louisiana State University Press, 1986); W. E. B. Du Bois, "The Souls of White Folk," in *Writings* (New York: Library of America, 1986), 926; Penny M. Von Eschen, *Race against Empire: Black Americans and Anticolonialism, 1937–1957* (Ithaca, NY: Cornell University Press, 1997); Kevin Gaines, *American Africans in Ghana: Black Expatriates and the Civil Rights Era* (Chapel Hill: University of North Carolina Press, 2006); "M. W. Saddler: Letter from a Black U.S. Soldier in the Philippines (1899)," in *World at War: Understanding Conflict and Society*, ABC-CLIO, 2012; Willard B. Gatewood Jr., *"Smoked Yankees" and the Struggle for Empire: Letters from Negro Soldiers, 1898–1902* (Urbana: University of Illinois Press, 1971) argues that African Americans were split over the issue of imperialism during the period 1898–1902.

13. Richard Seymour, *American Insurgents: A Brief History of American Anti-Imperialism* (San Francisco: Haymarket Books, 2012).

14. John Nichols, *Against the Beast: A Documentary History of American Opposition to Empire* (New York: Thunder's Mouth Press / Nation Books, 2003); Philip Foner and Richard Winchester, eds., *The Anti-Imperialist Reader: A Documentary History of Anti-imperialism in the United States*, 2 vols. (New York: Holmes and Meier, 1984); Philip Foner, *Inside the Monster: Writings on the United States and American Imperialism* (New York: Monthly Review Press, 1975).

15. Hence David Mayers focuses on "establishment dissenters." Mayers, *Dissenting Voices in America's Rise to Power* (Cambridge: Cambridge University Press, 2007).

16. A point explored in Frank Ninkovich, *The United States and Imperialism* (Oxford: Blackwell, 2001).

17. Gregory Claeys, *Imperial Sceptics: British Critics of Empire, 1850–1920* (New York: Cambridge University Press, 2010); Mira Matikkala, *Empire and Imperial Ambition: Liberty, Englishness and Anti-imperialism in Late Victorian Britain* (London: Tauris Academic Studies, 2011); David Paul Bargueño, "Imperial Discontents: A Review Essay," *South African Historical Journal* 63, no. 4 (December 2011): 594–615; Nicholas Owen, *The British Left and India: Metropolitan Anti-imperialism, 1885–1947* (Oxford: Oxford University Press, 2008); P. J. Cain, "Capitalism, Aristocracy and Empire: Some 'Classical' Theories of Imperialism Revisited," *Journal of Imperial and Commonwealth History* 35, no. 1 (March 2007): 25–47; Bernard Porter, *Critics of Empire: British*

*Radicals and the Imperial Challenge* (London: I. B. Tauris, 2008) and *The Absent-Minded Imperialists: Empire, Society, and Culture in Britain* (Oxford: Oxford University Press, 2006); Stephen Howe, *Anticolonialism in British Politics: The Left and the End of Empire, 1918–1964* (Oxford: Clarendon Press, 1993).

18. William Appleman Williams, *The Tragedy of American Diplomacy* (New York: Dell Publishing Co., 1972), 18–58.

19. R. Koebner and H. D. Schmidt, *Imperialism: The Story and Significance of a Political Word, 1840–1960* (Cambridge: Cambridge University Press, 1964); Mark F. Proudman, "Words for Scholars: The Semantics of 'Imperialism,'" *Journal of the Historical Society* 8, no. 3 (September 2008): 395–433.

20. Charles Sumner, *Are We a Nation?* (New York: Young Men's Republican Union, 1867).

21. See, for example, Bill Kauffman, *Ain't My America: The Long, Noble History of Antiwar Conservatism and Middle-American Anti-Imperialism* (New York: Metropolitan Books, 2008); Pat Buchanan, *A Republic, Not an Empire: Reclaiming America's Destiny* (Washington, DC: Regnery Publishing, 1999).

22. Christopher McKnight Nichols, *Promise and Peril: America at the Dawn of a Global Age* (Cambridge, MA: Harvard University Press, 2011).

23. Alan Dawley, *Changing the World: American Progressives in War and Revolution* (Princeton, NJ: Princeton University Press, 2003). Allison Schneider shows that suffragists compromised their anti-imperialist stance by using the legal debates over the nation's new overseas possessions as a forum to push for pro-suffragist policies in both the new possessions and at home (*Suffragists in an Imperial Age*, 8, 100–101).

24. David Armitage, *The Declaration of Independence: A Global History* (Cambridge, MA: Harvard University Press, 2007).

25. See, for example, Emily Rosenberg, *Financial Missionaries to the World: The Politics and Culture of Dollar Diplomacy, 1900–1930*, American Encounters / Global Interactions (Durham, NC: Duke University Press, 2003), esp. 232–37; Ian Tyrrell, *Reforming the World: The Creation of America's Moral Empire* (Princeton, NJ: Princeton University Press, 2010), 179.

26. Roger Baldwin to Theodore Debs, May 25, 1928, in "Wabash Valley Visions & Voices: A Digital Memory Project," January 14, 2011, http://visions.indstate.edu/cdm4/item_viewer. php?CISOROOT=/evdc&CISOPTR=980&CISOBOX=1&REC=3 (quote); FBI Records, "All American Anti-Imperialist League," http://vault.fbi.gov/All%20American%20Anti%20 Imperialist%20League.

27. Cf. Williams, *Tragedy of American Diplomacy.*

28. Geir Lundestad, "Empire by Invitation? The United States and Western Europe, 1945–1952," *Journal of Peace Research* 23, no. 3 (September 1986): 263–77.

29. A residue of this was the Vietnam Veterans against the War Anti-Imperialist, at http://www.vvawai.org/index.php?option=com_content&view=category&layout=blog&id=1&Ite mid=10.

30. Randall B. Woods, ed., *Vietnam and the American Political Tradition: The Politics of Dissent* (Cambridge: Cambridge University Press, 2003).

31. Tyrrell, *Reforming the World*, chap 7.

32. Farah Reza, ed., *Anti-Imperialism: A Guide for the Movement* (London: Bookmarks Publications, 2003).

33. Daniel Rodgers, *Atlantic Crossings: Social Politics in a Progressive Age* (Cambridge, MA: Harvard University Press, 1998).

34. M. Patrick Cullinane, "Transatlantic Dimensions of the Anti-imperialist Movement, 1899–1909," *Journal of Transatlantic Studies* 8, no. 4 (December 2010): 301–14; and Cullinane, *Liberty and American Anti-imperialism.*

35. Vladimir Ilyich Lenin, *Imperialism, the Highest Stage of Capitalism: A Popular Outline* (New York: International Publishers, 1977).

36. See Michael Schneider, *J. A. Hobson* (New York: St. Martin's Press, 1996), 129–30.

37. Thorstein Veblen, "Review of J. A. Hobson's *Imperialism: A Study*," *Journal of Political Economy* 11, no. 2 (March 1903): 311–14.

38. W. E. Minchinton, "Hobson, Veblen and America," *Bulletin of the British Association for American Studies* 8 (1959): 29–34, at 29; Timo Särkkä, *Hobson's Imperialism: A Study in Late-Victorian Political Thought*, Jyväskylä Studies in Humanities, no. 118 (Jyväskylä: University of Jyväskylä, 2009), 52–53.

39. Tyrrell, *Reforming the World*, chap. 7.

40. For the latter see Francis Shor, *Dying Empire: US Imperialism and Global Resistance* (New York: Routledge, 2010), 109–24.

41. Bernard Porter, *Empire and Superempire: Britain, America and the World* (New Haven, CT: Yale University Press, 2006), esp. 91. A rare instance that emphasizes by its very nature the need for further work is Steven C. Call, "Voices Crying in the Wilderness: A Comparison of Pro-Boers and Anti-Imperialists, 1899–1902" (unpublished MA thesis, University of Nebraska, 1991).

42. "Philadelphia November 5 Protest Unites Emerging Movement against Wall Street with Historic Black Rights Struggle," *Uhuru News*, November 2, 2011, http://uhurunews.com/story?resource_name=philadelphia-november-5-protest-unites-emerging-movement-against-wall-street-with-historic-black-rights-struggle (quote).

43. Barack Obama, "Remarks by the President on a New Beginning," Cairo, Egypt, June 4, 2009, http://www.whitehouse.gov/the-press-office/remarks-president-cairo-university-6-04-09.

# 1. Imperialism and Nationalism in the Early American Republic

1. Seymour Martin Lipset, *The First New Nation: The United States in Historical and Comparative Perspective* (New York: Basic Books, 1963); Richard B. Morris, *The Emerging Nations and the American Revolution* (New York: Harper & Row, 1970). On the importance of the "metageographical" conception of an American "continent" for American nationhood see James D. Drake, *The Nation's Nature: How Continental Presumptions Gave Rise to the United States of America* (Charlottesville: University of Virginia Press, 2011).

2. T. H. Breen, "An Empire of Goods: The Anglicization of Colonial America, 1660–1776," *Journal of British Studies* 25 (1986): 467–99; Breen, "Ideology and Nationalism on the Eve of the American Revolution: Revisions Once More in Need of Revising," *Journal of American History* 84, no. 1 (1997): 13–39.

3. Declaration, in Merrill Peterson, ed., *Thomas Jefferson: Writings* (New York: Viking, 1984), 23.

4. For a fuller elaboration of this theme see Peter S. Onuf, *Jefferson's Empire: The Language of American Nationhood* (Charlottesville: University of Virginia Press, 2000).

5. Gettysburg Address (final draft), November 19, 1863, in *The Collected Works of Abraham Lincoln*, 8 vols., ed. Roy P. Basler (New Brunswick, NJ: Rutgers University Press, 1953–55), 7:23, http://quod.lib.umich.edu/l/lincoln/.

6. Jefferson to Roger C. Weightman, June 24, 1826, in Peterson, *Jefferson: Writings*, 1517.

7. *Summary View*, ibid., 119.

8. Jefferson to Henry Lee, May 8, 1825, ibid., 1501.

9. Lincoln to Henry L. Pierce and Others, Springfield, April 6, 1859, in Basler, *Works of Abraham Lincoln*, 3:375.

10. Lincoln, Speech at Carlindale, Illinois, August 31, 1858, ibid., 3:80. On natural-rights thinking in American history see Mark Hulliung, *The Social Contract in America: From the Revolution to the Present Age* (Lawrence: University Press of Kansas, 2007).

11. Lincoln to Henry L. Pierce and Others, Springfield, April 6, 1859, in Basler, *Works of Abraham Lincoln*, 3:375.

12. Francis Fukuyama, *The End of History and the Last Man* (New York: Free Press, 1992).

13. Louis Hartz, *The Liberal Tradition in America: An Interpretation of American Political Thought since the Revolution* (New York: Harcourt, Brace, 1955).

14. Gordon S. Wood, *The Radicalism of the American Revolution* (New York: Knopf, 1992). The quotation is from John Adams, as cited in the epigraph of Bernard Bailyn's influential *Ideological Origins of the American Revolution* (Cambridge, MA: Belknap Press of Harvard University Press, 1967), 1.

15. Gary B. Nash, *The Unknown American Revolution: The Unruly Birth of Democracy and the Struggle to Create America* (New York: Viking, 2005).

16. Christopher Tomlins, *Freedom Bound: Law, Labor, and Civic Identity in Colonizing English America, 1580–1865* (Cambridge: Cambridge University Press, 2010), 398.

17. *Federalist* no. 14 (James Madison), in *The Federalist*, ed. Jacob E. Cooke (Middletown, CT: Wesleyan University Press, 1961), 88.

18. David Armitage, *The Ideological Origins of the British Empire* (Cambridge: Cambridge University Press, 2000).

19. Kathleen Wilson, *The Sense of the People: Politics, Culture and Imperialism in England, 1715–1785* (Cambridge: Cambridge University Press, 1995).

20. Jack P. Greene, *Evaluating Empire and Confronting Colonialism in Eighteenth-Century Britain* (Cambridge: Cambridge University Press, 2013).

21. See the essays collected in Jack P. Greene, *Imperatives, Behaviors, and Identities: Essays in Early American Cultural History* (Charlottesville: University of Virginia Press, 1992).

22. Greene, *Evaluating Empire*, 85–86.

23. *The Letters of Governor Hutchinson and Lieutenant Governor Oliver, &c. Printed at Boston, and Remarks Thereon. . . .* (Dublin, 1774), 13.

24. Adam Smith, *An Inquiry into the Nature and Causes of the Wealth of Nations*, ed. R. H. Campbell and A. S. Skinner, 2 vols. (Indianapolis: Liberty Classics, 1981), 2:946–47.

25. Jefferson, *Summary View of the Rights of British America* (1774), in Peterson, *Jefferson: Writings*, 119, 106, 110.

26. On "the language of alterity" see Greene, *Evaluating Empire*, 50–83 (quotation at 64).

27. Thomas Jefferson, *Notes on the State of Virginia*, ed. William Peden (Chapel Hill: University of North Carolina Press, 1954), Query 18 ("Manners"), 162.

28. Samuel Johnson, *Taxation No Tyranny* (1775), quoted in Eliga H. Gould, "A Slaveholding Republic: The American Revolution, the Law of Nations, and the U.S. Response to the Rise of Antislavery in the Western Atlantic," in *State and Citizen: British America and the Early United States*, ed. Peter Thompson and Peter Onuf (Charlottesville: University of Virginia Press, forthcoming). See Gould's essay for compelling elaboration of this point.

29. Smith, *Wealth of Nations*, 448. See Thomas L. Haskell, "Capitalism and the Origins of the Humanitarian Sensibility, Part I," *American Historical Review* 90, no. 2 (1985): 339–61.

30. Eliga H. Gould, "Zones of Law, Zones of Violence: The Legal Geography of the British Atlantic, circa 1772," *William and Mary Quarterly* 60, no. 3 (2003): 472–510. See also Gould, *The Persistence of Empire: British Political Culture in the Age of the American Revolution* (Chapel Hill: University of North Carolina Press, 2000) on the changing character of the empire in the American Revolutionary period.

31. Julie Flavell, "Decadents Abroad: Reconstructing the Typical Colonial American in London in the Late Colonial Period," in *Old World, New World: America and Europe in the Age of Jefferson*, ed. Leonard J. Sadosky et al. (Charlottesville: University of Virginia Press, 2010), 32–60.

32. Linda Colley, *Britons: Forging the Nation, 1707–1837* (New Haven, CT: Yale University Press, 1992), 350–60; Christopher Brown, *Moral Capital: Foundations of British Abolitionism* (Chapel Hill: University of North Carolina Press, 2006).

33. Jack P. Greene, *The Constitutional Origins of the American Revolution* (New York: Cambridge University Press, 2011).

34. *Common Sense*, February 14, 1776, in *Thomas Paine: Collected Writings*, ed. Eric Foner (New York: Library of America, 1995), 28.

35. Andrew McLaughlin, "The Background of American Federalism," *American Political Science Review* 12 (1918): 215–40; Jack P. Greene, *Peripheries and Center: Constitutional Development in the Extended Polities of the British Empire and the United States, 1607–1788* (Athens: University of Georgia Press, 1986); and the essays collected in Greene, *Negotiated Authorities: Essays in Colonial Political and Constitutional History* (Charlottesville: University of Virginia Press, 1994).

36. Peter Onuf, "Anarchy and the Crisis of the Union," in *"To Form a More Perfect Union": The Critical Ideas of the Constitution*, ed. Herman Belz, Ronald Hoffman, and Peter J. Albert (Charlottesville: University Press of Virginia, 1992), 272–302.

37. David C. Hendrickson, *Peace Pact: The Lost World of the American Founding* (Lawrence: University Press of Kansas, 2003).

38. Minutes of the Board of Visitors, March 4, 1825, in Peterson, *Jefferson: Writings*, 479. For fuller discussion see my "A Declaration of Independence for Diplomatic Historians," *Diplomatic History* 22, no. 1 (Winter 1998): 71–83; and *Jefferson's Empire: The Language of American Nationhood* (Charlottesville: University of Virginia Press, 2000).

39. Montesquieu, *The Spirit of the Laws*, trans. and ed. Anne M. Cohler et al. (Cambridge: Cambridge University Press, 1989), bk. 11, chap. 5, p. 156; bk. 19, chap. 27, p. 329; bk. 9, chap. 1, p. 131. See also *Federalist* no. 9 (Alexander Hamilton), in Cooke, *Federalist*, p. 53; and *The Substance of a Speech Delivered by James Wilson, Esq . . . in the Convention of the State of Pennsylvania; On Saturday the 24th of November, 1787* (Philadelphia, 1787), in *The Documentary History of the Ratification of the Constitution Digital Edition*, ed. John P. Kaminski et al. (Charlottesville: University of Virginia Press, 2009), 2:341–42: "a federal republic naturally presented itself to our observation as a species of government which secured all the internal advantages of a republic, at the same time that it maintained the external dignity and force of a monarchy. The definition of this form of government may be found in Montesquieu, who says, I believe, that it consists in assembling distinct societies, which are consolidated into a new body capable of being increased by the addition of other members; an expanding quality peculiarly fitted to the circumstances of America."

40. Alison L. LaCroix, *The Ideological Origins of American Federalism* (Cambridge, MA: Harvard University Press, 2010).

41. Tomlins, *Freedom Bound*, 5.

42. Ibid., 165.

43. Ibid., 184.

44. On late imperial threats to slaveholders' vital interests see George Van Cleve, *A Slaveholders' Union: Slavery, Politics, and the Constitution in the Early American Republic* (Chicago: University of Chicago Press, 2010).

45. Tomlins, *Freedom Bound*, 128.

46. Greene, *Constitutional Origins*. For a full and authoritative study of the "constitutional forensics" leading to independence see John Phillip Reid, *The Constitutional History of the American Revolution*, 4 vols. (Madison: University of Wisconsin Press, 1986–93).

47. Patrick Griffin, *American Leviathan: Empire, Nation, and Revolutionary Frontier* (New York: Hill & Wang, 2007).

48. See Patrick Henry, "those nations who have gone in search of grandeur, power and splendor, have also fallen a sacrifice, and been the victims of their own folly: While they acquired those visionary blessings, they lost their freedom," in Kaminski et al., *Documentary History of the Ratification*, 9:954.

49. Jefferson, first inaugural address, March 4, 1801, in Peterson, *Jefferson: Writings*, 494. On the parallels between metropolitan corruption in Britain and America—and between the regimes of Robert Walpole and Alexander Hamilton—see Lance Banning, *The Jeffersonian Persuasion: Evolution of a Party Ideology* (Ithaca, NY: Cornell University Press, 1978).

50. Peter S. Onuf, *Statehood and Union: A History of the Northwest Ordinance* (Bloomington: Indiana University Press, 1987).

51. Tomlins, *Freedom Bound*, 1–190.

52. Sam W. Haynes, *Unfinished Revolution: The Early American Republic in a British World* (Charlottesville: University of Virginia Press, 2010).

53. Bernard Semmel, *The Rise of Free Trade Imperialism: Classical Political Economy; The Empire of Free Trade and Imperialism, 1750–1850* (Cambridge: Cambridge University Press, 1970).

54. My understanding of Anglo-American relations in the nineteenth century is indebted to Jay Sexton's superb new synthesis, *The Monroe Doctrine: Empire and Nation in Nineteenth-Century America* (New York: Hill & Wang, 2011). For specific examples, including the United States, see the essays collected in Jack P. Greene, ed., *Exclusionary Empire: English Liberty Overseas, 1600–1900* (New York: Cambridge University Press, 2010), and Lisa Ford, *Settler Sovereignty: Jurisdiction and Indigenous People in America and Australia, 1788–1836* (Cambridge, MA: Harvard University Press, 2010).

55. Maya Jassanoff, *Liberty's Exiles: American Loyalists in the Revolutionary World* (New York: Knopf, 2011).

56. Peter S. Onuf and Nicholas Onuf, *Nations, Markets, and War: Modern History and the American Civil War* (Charlottesville: University of Virginia Press, 2006); Haynes, *Unfinished Revolution*.

57. Haynes, *Unfinished Revolution*.

# 2. Native Americans against Empire and Colonial Rule

1. Peter S. Onuf, "Imperialism and Nationalism in the Early American Republic," this volume.

2. Shari M. Hundorf, *Mapping the Americas: The Transnational Politics of Contemporary Native Culture* (Ithaca, NY: Cornell University Press, 2009), 15–19.

3. Lorenzo Veracini, *Settler Colonialism: A Theoretical Overview* (New York: Palgrave Macmillan, 2010).

4. Colin G. Calloway, *The American Revolution in Indian Country: Crisis and Diversity in Native American Communities* (Cambridge: Cambridge University Press, 1995), 28–31; Gregory Evans Dowd, *War under Heaven: Pontiac, the Indian Nations, and the British Empire* (Baltimore: Johns Hopkins University Press, 2002), 54–113.

5. Calloway, *American Revolution in Indian Country*, 122, 191, 194–95; Gregory Evans Dowd, *A Spirited Resistance: The North American Struggle for Unity, 1745–1815* (Baltimore: Johns Hopkins University Press, 1992), 47–48, 123; William L. Saunders, ed., *The Colonial Records of North Carolina*, vol. 10 (Raleigh, NC: Josephus Daniels, 1890), 778.

6. John Heckewelder, *A Narrative of the Mission of the United Brethren among the Delaware and Mohegan Indians from Its Commencement in the Year 1740 to the Close of the Year 1808* (Philadelphia: McCarty & Davis, 1820), 379–84.

7. Dowd, *Spirited Resistance*, 99–109; Helen Hornbeck Tanner, "Coocoochee: Mohawk Medicine Woman," *American Indian Culture and Research Journal* 3, no. 3 (1979): 23–41; Milo Milton Quaife, ed., *The Indian Captivity of O. M. Spencer* (Chicago: R. R. Donnelley & Sons, 1917), 127.

8. John Sugden, *Blue Jacket: Warrior of the Shawnees* (Lincoln: University of Nebraska Press, 2000), 99–127, 172–207.

9. R. David Edmunds, *The Shawnee Prophet* (Lincoln: University of Nebraska Press, 1983), 29–38.

10. Ibid., 42–47, 50–54.

11. Robert M. Owens, *Mr. Jefferson's Hammer: William Henry Harrison and the Origins of American Indian Policy* (Norman: University of Oklahoma Press, 2007), 200–206; R. David Edmunds, *Tecumseh and the Quest for Indian Leadership* (Glenview, IL: Scott Foresman and Co., 1984), 124–32; Logan Esarey, ed., *Messages and Letters of William Henry Harrison*, 2 vols. (Indianapolis: Indiana Historical Commission, 1922), 1:460, 464–67.

12. Edmunds, *Shawnee Prophet*, 97–116, 128–42; Dowd, *Spirited Resistance*, 167–73, 185–87.

13. Michael Adas, *Prophets of Rebellion: Millenarian Movements against the European Colonial Order* (Cambridge: Cambridge University Press, 1987); Anthony F. C. Wallace, "Revitalization Movements," *American Anthropologist* 58 (April 1956): 264–81.

14. Joel W. Martin, *Sacred Revolt: The Muskogees' Struggle for a New World* (Boston: Beacon Press, 1991), 183–84.

15. David J. Silverman, *Red Brethren: The Brothertown and Stockbridge Indians and the Problem of Race in Early America* (Ithaca, NY: Cornell University Press, 2010), 33–53, 112, 117–18; Calloway, *American Revolution in Indian Country*, 85–107.

16. Silverman, *Red Brethren*, 138–43.

17. Arnold Krupat, *All That Remains: Varieties of Indigenous Expression* (Lincoln: University of Nebraska Press, 2009), 75–76; William Apess, "An Indian's Looking-Glass for the White Man," in *On Our Own Ground: The Complete Writing of William Apess, a Pequot*, ed., Barry O'Connell (Amherst: University of Massachusetts Press, 1992), 157.

18. Lisa Brooks, *The Common Pot: The Recovery of Native Space in the Northeast* (Minneapolis: University of Minnesota Press, 2008), 198; William Apess, "Eulogy on King Philip," in O'Connell, *On Our Own Ground*, 280–81, 290, 295, 306, 308, 310; Jill Lepore, *The Name of War: King Philip's War and the Origins of American Identity* (New York: Vintage Books, 1999), 197–218; Jean M. O'Brien, *Firsting and Lasting: Writing Indians out of Existence in New England* (Minneapolis: University of Minnesota Press, 2010), 186–87.

19. Elias Boudinot, "An Address to the Whites," in *Cherokee Editor: The Writings of Elias Boudinot*, ed. Theda Perdue (Athens: University of Georgia Press, 1996), 170–71, 179; Andrew Denson, *Demanding the Cherokee Nation: Indian Autonomy and American Culture, 1830–1900* (Lincoln: University of Nebraska Press, 2004), 28, 40–41; Maureen Konkle, *Writing Indian Nations: Native Intellectuals and the Politics of Historiography, 1827–1863* (Chapel Hill: University of North Carolina Press, 2004), 51.

20. Gary E. Moulton, ed., *The Papers of Chief John Ross*, 2 vols. (Norman: University of Oklahoma Press, 1985), 1:459.

21. Kevin Bruyneel, *The Third Space of Sovereignty: The Postcolonial Politics of U.S.-Indigenous Relations* (Minneapolis: University of Minnesota Press, 2007), 6; Stephen Hay, ed., *Sources of*

*Indian Tradition*, vol. 2, *Modern India and Pakistan*, 2nd ed. (New York: Columbia University Press, 1988), 97–101.

22. Ben Kiernan, *Blood and Soil: A World History of Genocide and Extermination from Sparta to Darfur* (New Haven, CT: Yale University Press, 2007), 330.

23. David Thompson, *Columbia Journals*, ed., Barbara Belyea (Montreal: McGill–Queen's University Press, 1994), 160; *David Thompson's Narrative, 1784–1812*, ed., Richard Glover (Toronto: Champlain Society, 1962), 367; Gray H. Whaley, *Oregon and the Collapse of Illahee: U.S. Empire and the Transformation of an Indigenous World* (Chapel Hill: University of North Carolina Press, 2010), 51–53, 214; Alexandra Harmon, *Indians in the Making: Ethnic Relations and Indian Identities around Puget Sound* (Berkeley: University of California Press, 1998), 85–87.

24. Julie Roy Jeffrey, *Converting the West: A Biography of Narcissa Whitman* (Norman: University of Oklahoma Press, 1991), 213; Isaac Ingalls Stevens, *A True Copy of the Record of the Official Proceedings at the Council in the Walla Walla Valley 1855*, ed., Darrell Scott (Fairfield, WA: Ye Galleon Press, 1985), 80, 82.

25. J. W. MacMurray, "The Dreamers of the Columbia River Valley," *Transactions of the Albany Institute* 11 (1887): 248; Andrew H. Fisher, *Shadow Tribe: The Making of Columbia River Identity* (Seattle: University of Washington Press, 2010), 84–85; E. L. Huggins, "Smohalla, the Prophet of Priest Rapids," *Overland Monthly*, 2nd ser., 17 (February 1891): 214.

26. Fisher, *Shadow Tribe*, 85; Robert H. Ruby and John A. Brown, *Dreamer-Prophets of the Columbia Plateau: Smohalla and Skolaskin* (Norman: University of Oklahoma Press, 1989), 30.

27. Elliott West, *The Last Indian War: The Nez Perce Story* (New York: Oxford University Press, 2009), 118, 293.

28. James O. Gump, *The Dust Rose Like Smoke: The Subjugation of the Zulu and the Sioux* (Lincoln: University of Nebraska Press, 1994), 75–76, 87–88.

29. Robert M. Utley, *The Lance and the Shield: The Life and Times of Sitting Bull* (New York: Henry Holt, 1993), 73; E. Adamson Hoebel, "The Comanche Sun Dance and Messianic Outbreak of 1873," *American Anthropologist* 43 (April–June 1941): 302; Loretta Fowler, *Arapahoe Politics, 1851–1978: Symbols in Crises of Authority* (Lincoln: University of Nebraska Press, 1982), 38; Peter Cozzens, *Eyewitnesses to the Indian Wars, 1865–1890*, vol. 3, *Conquering the Southern Plains* (Mechanicsburg, PA: Stackpole Books, 2003), 111–12; Henry M. Stanley, *My Early Travels and Adventures in America* (1895; Lincoln: University of Nebraska Press, 1982), 248.

30. Patrick Wolfe, "Settler Colonialism and the Elimination of the Native," *Journal of Genocide Research* 8 (December 2006): 387–409; Frederick E. Hoxie, *A Final Promise: The Campaign to Assimilate the Indians, 1880–1920* (Lincoln: University of Nebraska Press, 1984); Isabel C. Barrows, ed., *Proceedings of the National Conference of Charities and Correction at the Nineteenth Annual Session Held in Denver, Col., June 23–29, 1892* (Boston: George H. Ellis, 1892), 46.

31. Frederick E. Hoxie, *Parading through History: The Making of the Crow Nation in America, 1805–1935* (Cambridge: Cambridge University Press, 1995), 154–64; Rebecca Kugel, *To Be the Main Leaders of Our People: A History of Minnesota Ojibwe Politics, 1825–1898* (East Lansing: Michigan State University Press, 1998), 186.

32. Denson, *Demanding the Cherokee Nation*, 227–28, 239–42; Janey B. Hendrix, "Redbird Smith and the Nighthawk Keetoowahs," *Journal of Cherokee Studies* 8 (Fall 1983): 80.

33. Jeffrey Ostler, *The Plains Sioux and U.S. Colonialism from Lewis and Clark to Wounded Knee* (Cambridge: Cambridge University Press, 2004), 243–55; J. B. Peires, *The Dead Will Arise: Nongqawuse and the Great Xhosa Cattle-Killing Movement of 1856–7* (Johannesburg: Ravan Press, 1989), 133; Jean E. Rosenfeld, "Pai Marire: Peace and Violence in a New Zealand Millenarian Tradition," in *Millennialism and Violence*, ed. Michael Barkun (London: Frank Cass, 1996), 87–88.

34. Ostler, *Plains Sioux*, 260–61, 278–79, 301–5, 332–34, 338–45.

35. Charles A. Eastman (Ohiyesa), *From the Deep Woods to Civilization: Chapters in the Autobiography of an Indian* (1916; Lincoln: University of Nebraska Press, 1977), 92; Sally Zanjani, *Sarah Winnemucca* (Lincoln: University of Nebraska Press, 2001), 284.

36. Siobhan Senier, *Voices of American Indian Assimilation and Resistance: Helen Hunt Jackson, Sarah Winnemucca, and Victoria Howard* (Norman: University of Oklahoma Press, 2001), 116; Sarah Winnemucca Hopkins, *Life among the Piutes: Their Wrongs and Claims*, ed., Mrs. Horace Mann (1883; Reno: University of Nevada Press, 1994), 207, 70, 77, 86; Ned Blackhawk, *Violence over the Land: Indians and Empires in the Early American West* (Cambridge, MA: Harvard University Press, 2006), 272; Frederick E. Hoxie, *This Indian Country: American Indian Political Activists and the Place They Made* (New York: Penguin, 2012), 143–80.

37. Eastman, *From the Deep Woods*, 114; Heather Cox Richardson, *Wounded Knee: Party Politics and the Road to an American Massacre* (New York: Basic Books, 2010), 313; Charles Alexander Eastman (Ohiyesa), *The Soul of An Indian: An Interpretation* (1911; Lincoln: University of Nebraska Press, 1980), 24.

38. Bruyneel, *Third Space of Sovereignty*, 103–9; David Martínez, *Dakota Philosopher: Charles Eastman and American Indian Thought* (St. Paul: Minnesota Historical Society Press, 2010), 6.

39. Gump, *Dust Rose Like Smoke*, 135; Jeff Guy, *The Maphumulo Uprising: War, Law, and Ritual in the Zulu Rebellion* (Scottsville, South Africa: University of KwaZulu-Natal Press, 2005), 1–27.

40. Thomas E. Mails, *The Cherokee People: The Story of the Cherokees from Earliest Origins to Contemporary Times* (Tulsa, OK: Council Oaks Books, 1992), 341.

## 3. "The Imperialism of the Declaration of Independence" in the Civil War Era

1. David Meyers, *Dissenting Voices in America's Rise to Power* (Cambridge: Cambridge University Press, 2007).

2. Seward in *Congressional Globe*, 32nd Cong., 2nd sess., App., 127; Lincoln quote from *The Collected Works of Abraham Lincoln*, ed. Roy P. Basler (hereafter cited as *CW*), 9 vols. (New Brunswick, NJ: Rutgers University Press, 1953–55), 2:364.

3. Frederick Douglass, "Reconstruction," *Atlantic Monthly*, December 1866, 761–65.

4. Charles Sumner, *Are We a Nation?* (New York: Young Men's Republican Union, 1867).

5. *CW*, 4:240.

6. John Quincy Adams, *Niles' Weekly Register*, July 21, 1821.

7. *CW*, 2:116.

8. Richard Carwardine, "Lincoln's Horizons," in *The Global Lincoln*, ed. Carwardine and Jay Sexton (New York: Oxford University Press, 2011), 28–43.

9. *CW*, 2:255, 275–76.

10. *CW*, 2:361.

11. *CW*, 3:522–50.

12. *CW*, 4:270.

13. *CW*, 3:534, 541.

14. *CW*, 2:324.

15. Don E. Fehrenbacher, *The Dred Scott Case: Its Significance in American Law and Politics* (New York: Oxford University Press, 1978), 494–96.

16. *Journal of the Convention of the People of South Carolina* (Charleston, SC: Evans & Cogswell, 1861), 334.

17. William Freehling, *The Road to Disunion: Secessionists Triumphant, 1854–1861* (New York: Oxford University Press, 2007), 345–51.

18. John Majewski, *Modernizing a Slave Economy: The Economic Vision of the Confederate Nation* (Chapel Hill: University of North Carolina Press, 2009).

19. David Waldstreicher, *In the Midst of Perpetual Fetes: The Making of American Nationalism, 1776–1820* (Chapel Hill: University of North Carolina Press, 1997).

20. Henry Cabot Lodge, "Colonialism in the United States," *Atlantic Monthly*, May 1883, 612–27.

21. Sam Haynes, *Unfinished Revolution: The Early American Republic in a British World* (Charlottesville: University of Virginia Press, 2010).

22. Jay Sexton, *The Monroe Doctrine: Empire and Nation in Nineteenth-Century America* (New York: Macmillan, 2011).

23. Jefferson Davis, Farewell Address to U.S. Senate, January 21, 1861.

24. *CW*, 4:271.

25. *CW*, 4:426, 432.

26. David Hendrickson, *Union, Nation, or Empire: The American Debate over International Relations, 1789–1941* (Lawrence: University Press of Kansas, 2008), 225.

27. D. P. Crook, *The North, the South and the Powers, 1861–1865* (London: John Wiley & Sons, 1974 ), 262.

28. Joshua Leavitt, *The Monroe Doctrine* (New York: Sinclair Tousey, 1863).

29. *CW*, 4:438.

30. Joel Silby, *A Respectable Minority: The Democratic Party in the Civil War Era, 1860–1868* (New York: Norton, 1977), 74.

31. Adam I. P. Smith, *No Party Now: Politics in the Civil War North* (New York: Oxford University Press, 2006); Brian Balogh, *A Government out of Sight: The Mystery of National Authority in Nineteenth-Century America* (Cambridge: Cambridge University Press, 2009), 290; J. Matthew Gallman, *The North Fights the Civil War: The Home Front* (Chicago: Ivan R. Dee, 1994), 109–15.

32. Richard Carwardine, *Lincoln: A Life of Purpose and Power* (New York: Knopf, 2006).

33. Richard Bensel, *Yankee Leviathan: The Origins of Central State Authority in America, 1859–1877* (Cambridge: Cambridge University Press, 1990); Gallman, *North Fights the Civil War*, 111; Balogh, *Government out of Sight*, 285–86.

34. Melinda Lawson, *Patriot Fires: Forging a New American Nationalism in the Civil War North* (Lawrence: University Press of Kansas, 2002), 40–64.

35. *CW*, 5:504.

36. William Gienapp, *The Origins of the Republican Party, 1852–1856* (New York: Oxford University Press, 1988).

37. Eric Foner, *The Fiery Trial: Abraham Lincoln and American Slavery* (New York: Norton, 2010), 272.

38. Hans Trefousse, *Thaddeus Stevens: Nineteenth-Century Egalitarian* (Chapel Hill: University of North Carolina Press, 1997), 133.

39. Michael Les Benedict, *The Fruits of Victory: Alternatives in Restoring the Union, 1865–1877* (Lanham, MD: University Press of America, 1986), 116.

40. Eugenio Biagini, "Lincoln in Germany and Italy," in Carwardine and Sexton, *Global Lincoln*, 76–94.

41. Eric Foner, *Reconstruction: America's Unfinished Revolution, 1863–1877* (New York: Harper & Row, 1988), 533.

42. Morton Keller, *Affairs of State: Public Life in Late Nineteenth Century America* (Cambridge, MA: Belknap Press of Harvard University Press, 1977).

43. Michael Les Benedict, *Preserving the Constitution: Essays on Politics and the Constitution in the Reconstruction Era* (New York: Fordham University Press, 2006), 13.

44. James McPherson, *Battle Cry of Freedom: The Civil War Era* (New York: Oxford University Press, 1988), 859.

45. Rogan Kersh, *Dreams of a More Perfect Union* (Ithaca, NY: Cornell University Press, 2001), 228–29.

46. Bensel, *Yankee Leviathan*, 303–65; Heather Cox Richardson, *The Death of Reconstruction: Race, Labor, and Politics in the Post–Civil War North, 1865–1901* (Cambridge, MA: Harvard University Press, 2001).

47. Henry Cabot Lodge, "Our Blundering Foreign Policy," *Forum* 19 (March 1895): 12–15.

48. *CW*, 3:312 (October 15, 1858).

49. Julian Go, *Patterns of Empire: The British and American Empires, 1688 to the Present* (Cambridge: Cambridge University Press, 2011), 49.

50. Lydia Maria Child, "An Appeal for the Indians," 1868, in *A Lydia Maria Child Reader*, ed. Carolyn L. Karcher (Durham, NC: Duke University Press, 1997), 79–94.

51. The classic work remains Walter LaFeber, *The New Empire: An Interpretation of American Expansion, 1860–1898* (Ithaca, NY: Cornell University Press, 1963).

52. Nicholas Guyatt, "America's Conservatory: Race, Reconstruction, and the Santo Domingo Debate," *Journal of American History* 97, no. 4 (March 2011): 974–1000.

53. Robert Beisner, *Twelve against Empire: The Anti-Imperialists, 1898–1900* (New York: McGraw-Hill, 1968), 228.

54. John Kasson, "The Monroe Declaration" and "The Monroe Doctrine in 1881," in *North American Review*, September–October 1881.

55. Leavitt, *Monroe Doctrine*.

56. Edward Crapol, *James G. Blaine: Architect of Empire* (Wilmington, DE: Scholarly Resources, 2000).

57. William A. Williams, *The Tragedy of American Diplomacy* (New York: Norton, 1972), 18–58.

58. Banerjee to Seward, April 5, 1871, Seward Papers [microfilm], reel 109, Vere Harmsworth Library, University of Oxford.

59. Nicola Miller, "Images of Lincoln in Latin America," in Carwardine and Sexton, *Global Lincoln*, 206–22.

60. Alfred E. Eckes, *Opening America's Market: U.S. Foreign Trade Policy since 1776* (Chapel Hill: University of North Carolina Press, 1990), 28.

# 4. Anti-imperialism in the U.S. Territories after 1898

For the invitation to write this chapter, the author thanks Jay Sexton and Ian Tyrrell. For comments and suggestions, the author also thanks the participants of the "American Anti-imperialism since 1776" conference, an anonymous reader for Cornell University Press, as well as Erez Manela, David Armitage, and the participants of the Harvard International and Global History Seminar. Sole responsibility for this chapter lies with the author.

1. W. E. B. Du Bois, *The Souls of Black Folk*, Everyman's Library (New York: Knopf; distributed by Random House, 1993).

2. W. E. B. Du Bois, "The Present Outlook for the Dark Races of Mankind," in *The Oxford W. E. B. Du Bois Reader*, ed. Eric J. Sundquist (New York: Oxford University Press, 1996).

3. Marika Sherwood, "'There Is No New Deal for the Blackman in San Francisco': African Attempts to Influence the Founding Conference of the United Nations," *International Journal of African Historical Studies* 29, no. 1 (1996): 77–78.

4. The colonial empire, even excluding Alaska and Hawaii, also included the U.S. Virgin Islands, Samoa, the Panama Canal Zone, and Micronesia. I focus on Puerto Rico, the Philippines, and Guam in this chapter because I know them best and because those three share a prior history of Spanish rule, which makes a comparison across them particularly informative.

5. See Stephen Hunter and John Bainbridge Jr., *American Gunfight: The Plot to Kill Harry Truman—and the Shoot-Out That Stopped It* (New York: Simon & Schuster, 2005).

6. The Insular Police was America's colonial police force in Puerto Rico. As distinct from the municipal police force, it was under the charge of the Insular Government headed by the U.S.-appointed governor.

7. A. D. Hall, *Porto Rico: Its History, Products and Possibilities* (New York: Street & Smith Publishers, 1898), 112.

8. José Augustín Aponte, *Vida política y literaria: Campaña unionista de 1906* (Mayaguez, Puerto Rico, 1908), 77.

9. Ángel Rivero Méndez, *Crónica de la guerra hispano-americana en Puerto Rico* (Madrid: Sucesores de Rivadenyera Artes Gráficas, 1922), 210–11.

10. "Discurso de Muñoz Rivera al regresar de los Estados Unidos," in Reece B. Bothwell González, *Puerto Rico: Cien años de lucha política*, 2 vols. (Río Piedras: Editorial Universitaria, Universidad de Puerto Rico, 1979), 2:118.

11. "Programa del Partido Federal," ibid., 1:271.

12. *La Democracia*, March 29, 1899, p. 2, orig. cap. For more on these visions see Julian Go, *American Empire and the Politics of Meaning: Elite Political Cultures in the Philippines and Puerto Rico during US Colonialism* (Durham, NC: Duke University Press), 80–90.

13. Christina Duffy Burnett and Burke Marshall, *Foreign in a Domestic Sense: Puerto Rico, American Expansion, and the Constitution* (Durham, NC: Duke University Press, 2001).

14. Cayetano Coll Cuchí, *La ley Foraker. Estudio histórico-político comparado* (San Juan: Tipografía del Boletin Mercantil, 1904), 71, 106, 108, 151–52.

15. House of Delegates to President Roosevelt, August 13, 1907, Bureau of Insular Affairs, United States National Archives, Record Group 126 (file 9–9–18).

16. Go, *American Empire*, 211–39.

17. *La correspondencia de Puerto Rico*, San Juan, Puerto Rico, March, 12, 1909, p. 1; see also Truman R. Clark, "President Taft and the Puerto Rican Appropriation Crisis of 1909," *Americas* 26, no. 2 (1969/70): 156–58.

18. Cayetano Coll Cuchí, *Por Patria* (San Juan: Tip. M. Burillo, 1909), 64.

19. "Porto Ricans Unfit to Rule, Says Taft," *New York Times*, May 11, 1909, p. 4.

20. Cayetano Coll Cuchí, *Historias que parecen cuentos* (Río Piedras: Colección Uprex, Editorial Universitaria, Universidad de Puerto Rico, 1972), 150.

21. Luis Muñoz Rivera, *Obras completas de Luis Muñoz Rivera, seleccionadas y recopiladas por Luis Muñoz Marin*, 4 vols. (Madrid: Editorial Puerto Rico, 1925), 3:154–56.

22. Rosendo Matienzo Cintrón, "Colonia inglesa," in Luis M. Díaz Soler and Matienzo Cintrón, *Rosendo Matienzo Cintrón* ([Río Piedras]: Instituto de Literatura Puertorriqueña Universidad de Puerto Rico, 1960), 2:154. Also see César J. Ayala and Rafael Bernabe, *Puerto Rico in the American Century: A History since 1898* (Chapel Hill: University of North Carolina Press, 2007), 70.

23. Coll Cuchí, *La ley Foraker*.

24. Arturo Morales Carrión, *Puerto Rico: A Political and Cultural History* (New York: Norton, 1983), 221.

25. Hunter and Bainbridge, *American Gunfight*, 27.

26. Federico Ribes Tovar, *Albizu Campos: Puerto Rican Revolutionary*, Puerto Rican Heritage Series (New York: Plus Ultra Educational Publishers, 1971), 35–38.

27. Anthony M. Stevens-Arroyo, "The Catholic Worldview in the Political Philosophy of Pedro Albizu Campos: The Death Knell of Puerto Rican Insularity," *U.S. Catholic Historian* 20, no. 4 (2002): 67.

28. Ribes Tovar, *Albizu Campos*, 49.

29. Stevens-Arroyo, "Catholic Worldview," 67.

30. Quote from Richard F. Pettigrew, *The Course of Empire, an Offical Record* (New York: Boni & Liveright, 1920), 285.

31. On the war see, among others, Brian Linn, *The Philippine War, 1899–1902* (Lawrence: University Press of Kansas, 2000) and Angel Velasco Shaw and Luis Francia, *Vestiges of War: The Philippine-American War and the Aftermath of an Imperial Dream, 1899–1999* (New York: NYU Press, 2002).

32. See Richard E. Welch, *Response to Imperialism: The United States and the Philippine-American War, 1899–1902* (Chapel Hill: University of North Carolina Press, 1979), 133–49.

33. Stanley Karnow, *In Our Image: America's Empire in the Philippines* (New York: Ballantine Books, 1989), 196–98.

34. Leon Wolff, *Little Brown Brother: How the United States Purchased and Pacified the Philippines* (Oxford: Oxford University Press, 1991); Thomas Bender, *A Nation among Nations: America's Place in World History* (New York: Hill & Wang, 2006), 223.

35. W. Cameron Forbes, *The Philippine Islands*, rev. ed. (Cambridge, MA: Harvard University Press, 1945), 374.

36. Roosevelt quoted in Foster Rhea Dulles and Gerald E. Ridinger, "The Anti-Colonial Policies of Franklin D. Roosevelt," *Political Science Quarterly* 70, no. 1 (1955): 3.

37. See Julian Go, *Patterns of Empire: The British and American Empires, 1688–present* (New York: Cambridge University Press, 2011), 65.

38. Federal Party of the Philippine Islands, *Manifesto of the Federal Party* (Manila: Tip. "La Democracia," 1905).

39. T. H. Pardo de Tavera, "A History of the Federal Party, by Dr. T. H. Pardo de Tavera," in *Report of the U.S. Philippine Commission to the Secretary of War, Part I* (Washington, DC: Government Printing Office, 1901), 164.

40. "El partido federal . . . en Filipinas," *La Democracia*, April 17, 1902, p. 3.

41. On the St. Louis Exposition see Paul Kramer, "Making Concessions: Race and Empire Revisited at the Philippine Exposition, St. Louis, 1901–1905," *Radical History Review* 73, nos. 74–114 (1999).

42. Michael Cullinane, *Ilustrado Politics: Filipino Elite Reponses to American Rule, 1898–1908* (Manila: Ateneo de Manila University Press, 2003); Go, *American Empire*; Norman G. Owen, ed., *Compadre Colonialism: Studies in the Philippines under American Rule* (Ann Arbor: Michigan Papers on South and Southeast Asia, no. 3, 1971), among others.

43. Bernardita Reyes Churchill, *The Philippine Independence Missions to the United States, 1919–1934* (Manila: National Historical Institute, 1983).

44. Vicente Rafael, "White Love: Surveillance and Nationalist Resistance in the U.S. Colonization of the Philippines," in *Cultures of United States Imperialism*, ed. Amy Kaplan and Donald Pease (Durham, NC: Duke University Press, 1993), 206.

45. Reynaldo C. Ileto, "Orators and the Crowd: Philippine Independence Politics, 1910–1914," in *Reappraising an Empire: New Perspectives on Philippine-American History*, ed. Peter Stanley (Cambridge, MA: Harvard University Press, 1984), 95–96.

46. Ibid.

47. Reynaldo C. Ileto, *Payson and Revolution: Popular Movements in the Philippines* (Quezon City: Ateneo de Manila University Press, 1979).

48. Ileto, *Payson and Revolution*, 209–51.

49. Keith Thor Carlson, "Born Again of the People: Luis Taruc and Peasant Ideology in Philippine Revolutionary Politics," *Historie sociale / Social History* 4, no. 82 (2008).

50. Floro C. Quibuyen, "Japan and America in the Filipino Nationalist Imagination: From Rizal to Ricarte," in *The Philippines and Japan in America's Shadow*, ed. Kiichi Fujiwara and Yoshiko Nagano (Singapore: National University of Singapore Press, 2011), 116. Not all Filipinos shared this view of Japan. See Paul A. Rodell, "Southeast Asian Nationalism and the Russo-Japanese War: Reexamining Assumptions," *Southeast Review of Asian Studies* 29 (2007): 20–40.

51. Quibuyen, "Japan and America," 112–18.

52. Ileto, *Payson and Revolution*, 239.

53. Ileto, "Orators and the Crowd," 101.

54. *Philippine Review*, May 1, 1901, 42–45, 64.

55. For more see Julian Go, "Modes of Rule in America's Overseas Empire," in *The Louisiana Purchase and American Expansion*, ed. Sanford Levinson and Bartholomew H. Sparrow (Lanham, MD: Rowman & Littlefield, 2005), 209–29.

56. UN report quoted in Timothy Maga, *Defending Paradise: The United States and Guam* (New York: Garland, 1988), 196.

57. Quoted in Henry P. Beers, *Administrative Reference Service Report No. 6: American Naval Occupation and Government of Guam, 1898–1902* (Washington, DC: Office of Records Administration, Administrative Office, Navy Department, 1944), 18.

58. For a comparative analysis of the colonial governments see Julian Go, "The Provinciality of American Empire: 'Liberal Exceptionalism' and U.S. Colonial Rule," *Comparative Studies in Society and History* 49, no. 1 (2007): 74–108; Lanny Thompson, *Imperial Archipelago: Representation and Rule in the Insular Territories under U.S. Domination after 1898* (Honolulu: University of Hawai'i Press, 2010).

59. U.S. Congress, House, Petition Relating to Permanent Government for the Island of Guam, House Doc. 419, 57th Congr., 1st sess., Feb. 27, 1902, 1–2.

60. Governor of Guam, *Annual Reports of the Governor of Guam*, 1902, p. 3.

61. "First Session Guam Congress," *Guam News Letter* 8, no. 8 (February 1917), quoted in Hofschneider, *A Campaign for Political Rights in the Island of Guam, 1899–1950* (Saipan: CNMI Division of Historic Preservation), 57–59.

62. Quoted in Hofschneider, *Campaign for Political Rights*, 63.

63. "Chamorros Make Plea for United States Citizenship," *Guam Recorder*, July 1925, p. 113. The Virgin Islands continued to be a reference for Guam congressmen making their case. See for example "Guam Delegate Admits Defeat on Citizenship," *Washington Post*, July 2, 1937, p. 6.

64. "Chamorros Make Plea," *Guam Recorder*, pp. 113, 132.

# 5. U.S. Anti-imperialism and the Mexican Revolution

1. This is a shortened—hence, at times, terse—version of a longer paper.

2. Archibald Cary Coolidge, *The United States as a World Power* (New York: Macmillan, 1908), 283.

3. Robert L. Beisner, *Twelve against Empire: The Anti-Imperialists, 1898–1900*, 2nd ed. (Chicago: University of Chicago Press, 1985), 31.

4. Friedrich Katz, *The Secret War in Mexico: Europe, the United States, and the Mexican Revolution* (Chicago: University of Chicago Press, 1981).

5. Robert Freeman Smith, *The United States and Revolutionary Nationalism in Mexico, 1916–1932* (Chicago: University of Chicago Press, 1972), x.

6. On the notion of the "collaborating elite" see Ronald Robinson, "Non-European Foundations of European Imperialism: Sketch for a Theory of Collaboration," in *Studies in the Theories of Imperialism*, ed. Roger Owen and Bob Sutcliffe (London: Longmans, 1972), 124.

7. *Malinchismo*, from Malinche, the Indian princess who allied with Cortés, denotes a perverse preference for the foreign over the national.

8. Daniela Spenser, *The Impossible Triangle: Mexico, Soviet Russia, and the United States in the 1920s* (Durham, NC: Duke University Press, 1999), 14–15, 18–19, 26–28; Robert Dallek, *Franklin D. Roosevelt and American Foreign Policy, 1932–1945* (Oxford: Oxford University Press, 1979), 176.

9. Jürgen Buchenau, *In the Shadow of the Giant: The Making of Mexico's Central American Policy, 1876–1930* (Tuscaloosa: University of Alabama Press, 1996).

10. John A. Britton, *Revolution and Ideology: Images of the Mexican Revolution in the United States* (Lexington: University of Kentucky Press, 1995); Helen Delpar, *The Enormous Vogue of Things Mexican: Cultural Relations between the United States and Mexico, 1920–1935* (Tuscaloosa: University of Alabama Press, 1992).

11. Hubert Herring, *Good Neighbors: Argentina, Brazil, Chile, and Seventeen Other Countries* (New Haven, CT: Yale University Press, 1941), 306.

12. Britton, *Revolution and Ideology*, 13.

13. E. Berkeley Tompkins, *Anti-Imperialism in the United States: The Great Debate, 1890–1920* (Philadelphia: University of Pennsylvania Press, 1970), 264.

14. This, of course, is an old historiographical dichotomy: historians are forever—and necessarily—applying "anachronistic," ex post facto labels to both people and phenomena: the middle class, patriarchy, Native Americans, the industrial revolution, the industrious revolution, the First (*sic*) World War.

15. Tompkins, *Anti-Imperialism*, 272–73, 277, 284, 288.

16. Richard H. Immerman, *Empire for Liberty: A History of American Imperialism from Benjamin Franklin to Paul Wolfowitz* (Princeton, NJ: Princeton University Press, 2010), 2. Beisner, *Twelve against Empire*, xiv, affirms that this "aberrational" view is shared by "most Americans."

17. A view shared by many, including Immerman, *Empire for Liberty* (note the subtitle: "from . . . Franklin to . . . Wolfowitz") and Beisner, *Twelve against Empire*, xi. Louis A. Pérez Jr., "Dependency," in *Explaining the History of American Foreign Relations*, ed. Michael J. Hogan and Thomas G. Paterson (Cambridge: Cambridge University Press, 1991), 100–101, locates "imperialism" within a broader framework of "dependency," although the competing concepts are ill-defined.

18. Examples, taken from the Woodrow Wilson Papers, Library of Congress (hereafter cited as WWP), would include the American Anti-Intervention Society, the American Peace Arbitration League, and the World Peace Foundation. The residual Anti-Imperialist League also experienced a modest revival in the 1920s: see Robert David Johnson, *Ernest Gruening and the American Dissenting Tradition* (Cambridge, MA: Harvard University Press, 1999), 52–53, which recounts how Gruening favored a new label—the "Pan-American Freedom League"—but was overruled by those who stressed the "traditional American ideals" inherent in the old anti-imperialist moniker. Irrespective of name, the league does not appear to have played a major role in U.S.-Mexican relations.

19. Smith, *United States and Revolutionary Nationalism*, 238.

20. Alan Knight, "Rethinking British Informal Empire in Latin America (Especially Argentina)," in *Informal Empire in Latin America*, ed. Matthew Brown (Oxford: Blackwell, 2008),

24; Frank Ninkovich, *The United States and Imperialism* (Oxford: Blackwell, 2001), 5–6; Thomas G. Paterson, *American Imperialism and Anti-imperialism* (New York: Thomas Y. Crowell Co., 1973), 2.

21. David Montejano, *Anglos and Texans in the Making of Texas, 1836–1980* (Austin, University of Texas Press, 1987), chap. 8; William D. Carrigan and Clive Webb, "The Lynching of Persons of Mexican Origin or Descent in the U.S., 1848–1928," *Journal of Social History* 37, no. 2 (Winter 2003): 411–38.

22. Arthur S. Link, *Wilson: Confusions and Crises, 1915–1916* (Princeton, NJ: Princeton University Press, 1964), 282.

23. In an Athenian/American nutshell: "the strong do what they have the power to do and the weak accept what they have to accept": Thucydides, *The Peloponnesian War* (Harmondsworth, UK: Penguin Books, 1984), 402.

24. Indeed, the United States, as it adjusted the Monroe Doctrine to new conditions, concluded that, rather than outright land-grabbing, "foreign financial control now posed the main threat to national independence" in the Americas: see Lansing's memo of June 1914, cited in Mark T. Gilderhus, *Pan American Visions: Woodrow Wilson in the Western Hemisphere, 1913–1921* (Tucson: University of Arizona Press, 1986), 35.

25. Jonathan Brown, *Oil and Revolution in Mexico* (Berkeley: University of California Press, 1993), chap. 4.

26. The quixotic Plan of San Diego of 1915 involved armed Mexican subversion—sporadic raids and rebellions—in Texas. It lacked official Mexican backing; and, consonant with the asymmetry of the bilateral relationship, it had scant impact, although it provoked a violent reaction against resident Mexicans. See Linda B. Hall and Don M. Coerver, *Revolution on the Border: The United States and Mexico, 1910–1920* (Albuquerque: University of New Mexico Press, 1988), 23–25.

27. N. Gordon Levin Jr., *Woodrow Wilson and World Politics: America's Response to War and Revolution* (New York: Oxford University Press, 1968), 25–26, argues that "Wilson opposed traditional exploitative imperialism, involving territorial annexations, armed force, protectionism and war. The President did not, however, question either the structural inequitability of the commercial and financial relationships between the agrarian and industrialized areas of the world or the correlative economic and political world predominance of the West."

28. Geir Lundestad, "Empire by Invitation? The United States and Western Europe, 1945–1952," *Journal of Peace Research* 23, no. 3 (September 1986): 263–77.

29. Jorge I. Domínguez, *Order and Revolution in Cuba* (Cambridge, MA: Harvard University Press, 1979). Compare Robert O. Keohane, *After Hegemony: Cooperation and Discord in the World Economy* (Princeton, NJ: Princeton University Press, 1984), 32, 45.

30. On "soft" or "cooptive" power see Joseph S. Nye Jr., *Bound to Lead: The Changing Nature of American Power* (New York: Basic Books, 1990), 31–32. Nye contrasts "cooptive" power—diffuse, cultural, and indirect—with "directive or commanding power"; however, the latter embodies two very different forms: "inducements ('carrots')" and "threats ('sticks')." As Nye's diagram, p. 267, makes clear, we have at least *three* categories: (i) "coercion"; (ii) "inducements"; and (iii) "attraction"; (ii) and (iii) are both noncoercive, but only (iii) corresponds to Nye's much-vaunted "soft power."

31. Spenser, *Impossible Triangle*, 139. Cf. Bryce Wood, *The Making of the Good Neighbor Policy* (New York: Norton, 1967).

32. Thus, the liberal journalist Ernest Gruening considered Thomas Lamont—Morrow's business partner and co-architect of U.S. financial policy toward Mexico—as representative of "the most active imperialist force in the world today: the power of American money": Johnson, *Ernest Gruening*, 50.

33. The seizure of the Philippines—a clear-cut case of coercive imperialism—provoked strenuous anti-imperialist protest; by 1909–12, however, as U.S. investment flowed into the islands, protest—now more muted—focused on the resulting "economic exploitation" of the colony, undertaken, in the words of Moorfield Storey, by "the very trusts we are seeking to break up in the United States." However, "economic exploitation" proved a much less effective grievance: Tompkins, *Anti-imperialism*, 278–79.

34. In a previous attempt to gauge public reactions to U.S. policy toward Mexico, I used *New York Times* coverage of Mexico (1909–39) as a crude proxy. The results showed major spikes in 1911, 1914, and 1916–17—the first coinciding with the original Madero revolution, the second and third marking moments when U.S. forces were involved on Mexican soil. No post-1917 crisis achieved anything like the same salience. See Alan Knight, *U.S.-Mexican Relations, 1910–1940: An Interpretation* (San Diego: University of California–San Diego, Center for U.S.-Mexican Studies, 1987), 16.

35. Melvin Small, "Public Opinion," in Hogan and Paterson, *Explaining the History of American Foreign Relations*, 166–67, compares 1917—"when almost all Americans held opinions about their country's posture towards Germany"—and the 1933 intervention in Cuba, about which "only a few cared or even knew." The Mexican crises of 1914 and 1916–17 would fit somewhere in between. Small also posits a tripartite division of opinion: a "very small coterie" of politicians, officials, and writers; the "attentive public," who are "well-educated and well-read" and may constitute up to 25 percent "on some issues"; and the "more than 75% of the population [that] makes up the mass public that usually does not care much about foreign affairs until the US is in a crisis." I have no idea how Small arrives at these figures, and I have doubts about the supposed correlation between interest and formal education, but the implication—that a great deal of policy is made within an official bubble, which bursts only at moments of crisis—seems to be valid for the Mexican case.

36. This should be stressed, since many historians, some reputable, persist in implying, even if they do not explicitly state, that Wilson intervened in Mexico "counter-revolutionarily," in order to halt, not to advance, the revolution: for example, William Appleman Williams, *American Confronts a Revolutionary World: 1776–1976* (New York: William Morrow, 1976), 140.

37. Arthur S. Link, *Wilson: The New Freedom* (Princeton, NJ: Princeton University Press, 1956), 350, 379.

38. Ibid., 349, 351. There is abundant evidence of business favoring Huerta; furthermore—given that I later argue for major divisions within business opinion—I would stress that in 1913 pro-Huerta opinion was solid, spanning both Wall Street in general and businesses engaged in Mexico.

39. P. A. R. Calvert, *The Mexican Revolution, 1910–1914: The Diplomacy of Anglo-American Conflict* (Cambridge: Cambridge University Press, 1968), is the fullest study.

40. Wilson looked "parchmenty" when he received news of the Veracruz casualties: Link, *Wilson: The New Freedom*, 402.

41. Robert E. Quirk, *An Affair of Honor: Woodrow Wilson and the Occupation of Veracruz* (New York: Norton, 1967).

42. The army and navy—who were at odds with each other—also found Wilson's decision to stay put in Veracruz (when existing war plans called for an advance on Mexico City) to be both perplexing and frustrating: Richard D. Challenger, *Admirals, Generals, and American Foreign Policy, 1898–1914* (Princeton, NJ: Princeton University Press, 1973), 393–97.

43. Since it enabled Huerta to appeal to nationalist sentiment: a particular example of a broad phenomenon—a kind of interventionist "blowback"—which I discuss later. In fact, being both deeply unpopular and on the brink of defeat, Huerta benefited relatively little from

Wilson's clumsy intervention: compare Link, *Wilson: The New Freedom*, 400, which exaggerates the nationalist reaction, and Alan Knight, *The Mexican Revolution* (Cambridge: Cambridge University Press, 1986), 2:158–59.

44. Link, *Wilson: The New Freedom*, 404; Knight, *Mexican Revolution*, 2:155–56. Wilson said that he felt "shame as an American over the first Mexican War" and thus had no intention of starting a second: Link, *Confusions and Crises*, 292.

45. Link, *Wilson: The New Freedom*, 404, notes that "there was no material demand for war from the financial leaders who had a large material stake in Mexico" (even though they opposed Wilson's repudiation of Huerta and support for the revolution: ibid., 349, 351). Thus, Wall Street behaved toward Mexico in 1914 much as it had toward Cuba in 1898, according to Julius W. Pratt, *Expansionists of 1898* (Baltimore: Johns Hopkins University Press, 1936).

46. Larry Hill, *Emissaries to a Revolution: Woodrow Wilson's Executive Agents in Mexico* (Baton Rouge: Louisiana State University Press, 1973).

47. Carlos Pascual, the U.S. ambassador to Mexico, was recalled in April 2011, because he too freely expressed his low opinion of President Calderón and the Mexican security services.

48. Dallek, *Roosevelt and American Foreign Policy*, 8–9.

49. Graham H. Stuart, *Latin America and the United States*, 4th ed. (New York, Appleton-Century Co., 1943), 183.

50. Chalmers Johnson, *Blowback: The Costs and Consequences of American Empire* (New York: Henry Holt, 2000), 8–10.

51. Isaiah Berlin, *The Hedgehog and the Fox: An Essay on Tolstoy's View of History* (New York: Simon & Schuster, 1966).

52. John Dwyer, "Diplomatic Weapons of the Weak: Mexican Policy-Making during the U.S.-Mexican Agrarian Dispute, 1934–1941," *Diplomatic History* 26, no. 3 (2002): 375–95, adapts James Scott's "weapons of the weak" perspective to explore U.S.-Mexican relations in the 1930s, with reference to Cardenista land reform.

53. On Sheffield see Smith, *United States and Revolutionary Nationalism*, 232–34, and Britton, *Revolution and Ideology*, 82–83. The spoils system cannot necessarily be blamed for these failures: Wilson was a career diplomat, Daniels—a political appointee in the 1930s—was a successful ambassador.

54. Link, *Wilson: The New Freedom*, 389, Kendrick A. Clements, "Emissary from a Revolution: Luis Cabrera and Woodrow Wilson," *Americas* 35 (1979): 353–71.

55. Eugenia Meyer, *Luis Cabrera: Pensamiento y acción* (Mexico, UNAM, 2002).

56. Link, *Wilson: The New Freedom*, 393.

57. Fred C. Howe to Wilson, October 29, 1915, and Wilson's reply, November 1, 1915, WWP.

58. The parallels with Progressivism are suggested in Knight, *U.S.-Mexican Relations*, 4–5. President Wilson's capacious academic mind ranged further: to one journalist he suggested that Mexico's land problem might be addressed by means of reforms inspired by New Zealand: Britton, *Revolution and Ideology*, 32.

59. Knight, *Mexican Revolution*, 2:140, 558; Link, *Wilson: The New Freedom*, 391, cites negative British press comment, which mirrored conservative (and often racist) American critiques of Wilson's pro-revolutionary policy.

60. E. David Cronon, *Josephus Daniels in Mexico* (Madison: University of Wisconsin Press, 1960), 27–28; 135.

61. When it comes to American foreign policy and public opinion, polling data do not become available until the 1930s (Small, "Public Opinion," 171). Regarding revolutionary Mexico, I have encountered only one relevant poll, right at the end of the period, regarding the 1938 oil expropriation: Irwin F. Gellman, *Good Neighbor Diplomacy: United States Policies in Latin America, 1933–1945* (Baltimore: Johns Hopkins University Press, 1979), 53.

62. Stuart, *Latin America and the United States*, 157.

63. Link, *Wilson: The New Freedom*, 139.

64. The occupation of Veracruz, Wilson's most unilateral intervention, was probably his least popular, since it offended both pacifists and leftists who opposed coercive measures and jingoes and conservatives who favored Huerta and reviled the revolution. However, Link's description of a "tidal wave of denunciation" (*Wilson: The New Freedom*, 403) seems rather strong; Quirk, *Affair of Honor*, 113–14, suggests that "the public gave its approval to the use of force at Veracruz" and "most citizens" supported Wilson's action. Furthermore, since it soon became clear that no full-scale invasion would follow, the (pacifist/leftist) fuss soon blew over.

65. Link, *Wilson: The New Freedom*, 399; 404. William C. Gebhart, Clinton, NJ, to Tumulty ("dear Joe"), April 27, 1914, WWP, claims that "I talk over the situation with almost everyone I meet" and reports that "at least three fourths of the people do not want war with Mexico." Walter Lippman, who would later play a big part in U.S.-Mexican relations, concurred that there was a "general sentiment that war should be avoided": *Public Opinion* (1921; New York: Free Press, 1997), 129.

66. Milland J. Bloomer (New York) to Wilson, April 27, 1914, WWP, reports a lack of belligerence: whereas in 1898 "the hall leading to my former office which became a recruiting station for volunteers was constantly filled with men anxious to serve their country . . . in the present difficulty no such sentiment prevails, despite the inflaming articles on the front pages of our newspapers."

67. Hall and Coerver, *Revolution on the Border*, 54; H. F. Montgomery, Houston, to Wilson, April 22, 1914, WWP, asserts that "the great mass of the people of Texas" disagreed with their governor's belligerent stance.

68. Charles F. Champion (Chicago mining entrepreneur, with Mexican experience) to Wilson, n.d. (April 1914), WWP, claims that Americans had been butchered and tortured in Mexico; that Wilson and Bryan (for whom he voted) had been pusillanimous; that, in consequence, "contempt" for Americans would spread "from (Ciudad) Juárez to Sandy Point in the Straits of Magellan"; and that the United States "should take possession of Mexico at once and give their country civilized government."

69. H. L. Bowlby (Lord's Day Alliance of the U.S., New York) to Wilson, April 28, 1914, WWP, reports that, after a two-thousand-mile trip across country, "I find the pulpits almost unanimously commending your course of action . . . and doing all within your power to avert war."

70. Deborah J. Baldwin, *Protestants and the Mexican Revolution* (Urbana: University of Illinois Press, 1990), offers a good overview, chiefly of the Mexican side.

71. Laleine Carley (Hood River, OR) to Wilson, August 17, 1913, WWP.

72. M. J. Lawrence (Civil War veteran, Washington, DC) to Wilson, November 10, 1913, opposes war against Mexico (given the "low pedigree and grosely [*sic*] immoral character of the great mass of the Mexican people"); W. M. Polland (Civil War veteran and judge, Nashville, TN) to Wilson, November 7, 1913, WWP, calls for peace in a "spirit of conservatism," mindful of the horrors of war. Wilson, of course, was a southern president, who played on southern sentiments: Arthur S. Link, "Woodrow Wilson: The American as Southerner," *Journal of Southern History* 36 (February 1970): 3–17.

73. Link, *Wilson: The New Freedom*, 403; and Arthur S. Link, *Wilson: The Struggle for Neutrality, 1914–1915* (Princeton, NJ: Princeton University Press, 1960), 235–36, 239.

74. Link, *Wilson: Confusions and Crises*, 207.

75. Patton to Papa, September 28, 1916, Patton Papers, Library of Congress, box 8.

76. Link, *Confusions and Crises*, 315. Gompers claimed to his Mexican labor counterparts—with whom he was busy forging closer relations—that he had been instrumental in averting

further intervention; in fact, "Gompers had never publicly or privately opposed the expedition": Harvey Levenstein, *Labor Organizations in the United States and Mexico* (Westport, CT, Greenwood, 1971), 37–39.

77. Secretary of the Interior Franklin K. Lane served as a U.S. member of the Joint Commission, which sought to negotiate an end to the crisis while extracting concessions from Mexico regarding foreign interests, claims, and religious toleration: Smith, *United States and Revolutionary Nationalism*, 55–57.

78. Ibid., 93.

79. Ibid., 4; and, on the Calvo doctrine, which the new Mexican government espoused, 27–29.

80. Linda B. Hall, *Oil, Banks, and Politics: The United States and Postrevolutionary Mexico, 1917–1924* (Austin: University of Texas Press, 1995), chap. 3.

81. Smith, *United States and Revolutionary Nationalism*, 95–98; 150–74.

82. Levenstein, *Labor Organizations*, 56.

83. John D. Hicks, *Republican Ascendancy, 1921–1933* (New York: Harper & Row, 1960), 50.

84. W. A. Swanberg, *Citizen Hearst* (New York: Bantam Books, 1961), 467–78.

85. The National Association for the Protection of Property Rights in Mexico (NAPARM), founded in 1919 and committed to a "hardline policy against Mexico": Smith, *United States and Revolutionary Nationalism*, 151.

86. Matthew A. Redinger, *American Catholics and the Mexican Revolution, 1924–1936* (Notre Dame, IN: University of Notre Dame Press, 2005), 45, 75. Catholic diatribes included Francis McCullagh, *Red Mexico: A Reign of Terror in the Americas* (London: Brentano's, 1928) and Francis C. Kelly, *Blood-Drenched Altars* (Milwaukee: Bruce Publishing Co., 1935).

87. Hence Secretary of State Kellogg's memorandum to the U.S. Senate in 1926, "Bolshevik Aims and Policies in Mexico and Latin America": Smith, *United States and Revolutionary Nationalism*, 238. On the Nicaraguan imbroglio see Buchenau, *Shadow of the Giant*.

88. I follow N. Gordon Levin in seeing an early ideological polarization between the "mutually exclusive visions" of Leninist revolution and Wilsonian "anti-imperialism" (even if the full institutional bipolarity of the Cold War had to wait another thirty years): *Woodrow Wilson and World Politics*, 6–7, 13–14. The U.S. propensity to equate nationalism with communism was presciently perceived by Walter Lippmann: Britton, *Revolution and Ideology*, 91–92.

89. Smith, *United States and Revolutionary Nationalism*, 234.

90. Sheffield was withdrawn in part because the major Mexican labor confederation—the CROM—had compromised the embassy's security and, taking advantage of a hard-drinking, womanizing, and indebted military attaché, had filched secret documents outlining U.S. policy and war plans toward Mexico. This successful espionage contributed not only to the withdrawal of Sheffield but also to the softening of the U.S. stance, thus favoring a peaceful resolution of the 1927 crisis. There is abundant documentation in the Archivo Calles-Torreblanca, Mexico City.

91. Gellman, *Good Neighbor Diplomacy*, chap. 1; Wood, *Making of the Good Neighbor Policy*, part 1.

92. Spenser, *Impossible Triangle*, 134–47; Stanley R. Ross, "Dwight Morrow and the Mexican Revolution," *Hispanic American Historical Review* 38 (November 1958): 506–28.

93. Jonathan Brown, "Why Foreign Oil Companies Shifted Their Production from Mexico to Venezuela during the 1920s," *American Historical Review* 90 (April 1985): 362–85. The relative positions of the hawkish oilmen and the dovish bankers is described in Hall, *Oil, Banks, and Politics*.

94. These included Ford, GM, Colgate, and ITT. In 1930, twenty-five hundred American businessmen and political leaders attended President Ortiz Rubio's inauguration; in the same year, Mexico harbored more U.S. subsidiaries than any other Latin American country: Delpar, *Enormous Vogue*, 57; Spenser, *Impossible Triangle*, 149–50; Thomas F. O'Brien, *The Revolutionary*

*Mission: American Enterprise in Latin America, 1900–1945* (Cambridge: Cambridge University Press, 1996), chap. 11.

95. Angell to Gruening, 1924, in Johnson, *Ernest Gruening*, 53.

96. Levenstein, *Labor Organizations*, chap. 9.

97. Ibid., 98–99; 119–20; 142.

98. On Burke, and his dealings with Morrow, see Redinger, *American Catholics and the Mexican Revolution*, chap. 4, esp. 75–88.

99. Knight, *U.S.-Mexican Relations*, 8–9.

100. Smith, *United States and Revolutionary Nationalism*, 238.

101. Wilson professed concern for the plight of Mexico's Catholics but pleaded impotence: Redinger, *American Catholics and the Mexican Revolution*, 36–37. Twenty years later, FDR regarded Catholic scare stories as "fishy" and "refused to budge" in the face of Catholic lobbying: Dallek, *Roosevelt and American Foreign Policy*, 123.

102. Certainly the U.S. embassy in Mexico was often scathing—and inaccurate—in its reports on the activities of local American leftists: Carleton Beals was "an alleged slacker and Bolshevik leader" (which he wasn't), while Ernest Gruening was a "Harvard Jew" (which he also wasn't): see John A. Britton, *Carleton Beals: A Radical Journalist in Latin America* (Albuquerque: University of New Mexico Press, 1987), 20, 55.

103. Britton, *Revolution and Ideology*, 78.

104. Britton, *Revolution and Ideology*, and Delpar, *Enormous Vogue*, offer a collective portrait of American intellectuals and cultural tourists in Mexico; on their contrasting British counterparts see Alan Knight, "Anglo-Mexican Relations and Perceptions in the 19th and 20th Centuries," in *Europe and Latin America—Looking at Each Other?* ed. Ryszard Stemplowski (Warsaw: Polish Institute of International Affairs, 2010), 133–35.

105. On the indigenous aspect of the revolution and American perceptions see Delpar, *Enormous Vogue*, chap. 3.

106. Delpar, *Enormous Vogue*, 203, reaches a somewhat cryptic conclusion: "that diplomatic rapprochement was required for the flowering of cultural relations is as likely as the reverse."

107. Beisner, *Twelve against Empire*, ix.

108. John Morton Blum, *From the Morgenthau Diaries: Years of Crisis, 1928–1938* (Boston: Houghton Mifflin, 1959), 494; see also Dallek, *Roosevelt and American Foreign Policy*, 175.

109. Levenstein, *Labor Organizations*, chap. 10.

110. Britton, *Revolution and Ideology*, chap. 9.

111. Ibid., 135–39.

112. Herring, *Good Neighbors*, 325.

113. In fact, Congress rarely expressed vigorous dissent in respect to Wilson's Mexican policy: at the time of Veracruz, no opposition was expressed (while the Lodge/Root group in the Senate spoke out: for more intervention, not less): Quirk, *Affair of Honor*, 76.

114. This, of course, was an old argument, going back at least to 1848.

115. For illustrative cartoons, showing Uncle Sam confronting a wayward Mexican child, see John J. Johnson, *Latin America in Caricature* (Austin: University of Texas Press, 1980), 137, 145, 147, 149.

116. Baldwin, *Protestants and the Mexican Revolution*, 140–42; David H. Burton, *Taft, Wilson, and World Order* (Madison, NJ: Farleigh Dickinson University Press, 2002), 45.

117. For Kipling ("Lest we forget") quoted in opposition to intervention: *Washington Herald*, June 28, 1914 (taken from WWP).

118. Robert H. Wiebe, *The Search for Order, 1877–1920* (New York: Hill & Wang, 1967), 235–36.

119. Beisner, *Twelve against Empire*, viii.

# 6. Anti-imperialism, Missionary Work, and the King-Crane Commission

1. For a discussion of the "Wilsonian moment" see Erez Manela, *The Wilsonian Moment* (Oxford: Oxford University Press, 2006).

2. Ussama Makdisi, *Faith Misplaced: The Broken Promise of U.S.-Arab Relations, 1820–2001* (New York: Public Affairs, 2010), 55–102.

3. Edwin Munsell Bliss, *Turkey and the Armenian Atrocities: A Reign of Terror* (Philadelphia: Hubbard Publishing Co., 1896), vii.

4. William R. Hutchison, *Errand to the World: American Protestant Thought and Foreign Missions* (Chicago: University of Chicago Press, 1987), 49.

5. Paul William Harris, *Nothing but Christ: Rufus Anderson and the Ideology of Protestant Foreign Missions* (New York: Oxford University Press, 2000), 99.

6. Stephen B. L. Penrose Jr., *That They May Have Life: The Story of the American University of Beirut, 1866–1941* (1941; Beirut: American University of Beirut Press, 1970), 5.

7. Cited in Makdisi, *Faith Misplaced*, 332.

8. Ussama Makdisi, *Artillery of Heaven: American Missionaries and the Failed Conversion of the Middle East* (Ithaca, NY: Cornell University Press, 2008).

9. "The Egyptian and Arabian Problems: An Address by Samuel M. Zwemer, D.D., LL.D, F.R.G.S. before the Empire Club of Canada, Toronto, Nov. 3, 1921," http://speeches.empireclub.org/62693/data?n=4.

10. This section draws on Makdisi, *Artillery of Heaven*, 51–71.

11. The most revealing book is this regard remains John A. Andrew III's biography of the American Board leader Jeremiah Evarts, *From Revivals to Removal: Jeremiah Evarts, the Cherokee Nation, and the Search for the Soul of America* (Athens: University of Georgia Press, 1992).

12. Makdisi, *Artillery of Heaven*, 72–102; A. L. Tibawi, *American Interests in Syria, 1800–1901* (Oxford: Oxford University Press, 1966), 31–90. Ellen Fleischmann, "The Impact of American Protestant Missions in Lebanon on the Construction of Female Identity, c. 1860–1950)," *Islam and Christian-Muslim Relations* 13 (2002): 411–25.

13. For more details on these processes of transformation see Marwa Elshakry, "The Gospel of Science and American Evangelism in Late Ottoman Beirut," *Past and Present*, 2007, 173–214; Makdisi, *Artillery of Heaven*, 180–213; Tibawi, *American Interests*, 191–274; Shafik Jeha, *Darwin and the Crisis of 1882 in the Medical Department*, trans. Sally Kaya, ed. Helen Khal (Beirut: American University of Beirut Press, 2004); and Ussama Makdisi, "Reclaiming the Land of the Bible: Missionaries, Secularism, and Evangelical Modernity," *American Historical Review* 102, no. 3 (June 1997): 680–713.

14. On American institutions see Jens Hanssen, *Fin de Siècle Beirut: The Making of an Ottoman Provincial Capital* (Oxford: Oxford University Press, 2005), and on their impact on late Ottoman education see Benjamin Fortna, *Imperial Classroom: Islam, the State and Education in the Late Ottoman Empire* (Oxford: Oxford University Press, 2002).

15. Daniel Bliss, *The Reminiscences of Daniel Bliss* (New York: Fleming H. Revell Co., 1920), 198.

16. Makdisi, *Artillery of Heaven*, 141–79.

17. Hans-Lukas Kieser, *Nearest East: American Millennialism and Mission to the Middle East* (Philadelphia: Temple University Press, 2010), 63–98.

18. Well documented by scholars such as Edward Blum, *Reforging the White Republic: Race, Religion, and American Nationalism, 1865–1898* (Baton Rouge: LSU Press, 2005), Kidd, *American Christians and Islam*, 58–74, and Makdisi, *Artillery of Heaven*, 141–79.

19. Heather J. Sharkey, *American Evangelicals in Egypt: Missionary Encounters in an Age of Empire* (Princeton: Princeton University Press, 2009), 49.

20. Perhaps the clearest example of this is the holding of the 1906 Cairo conference on the "Mohemmedan" missionary problem. See S. M. Zwemer, E. M. Wherry, and James L. Barton, eds., *The Mohammedan World of Today* (New York: Fleming H. Revell Co., 1906). For a criticism of the missionary perspective see Jeremy Salt, *Imperialism, Evangelism and the Ottoman Armenians, 1878–1896* (London: Frank Cass, 1993).

21. William Gladstone, *Bulgarian Horrors and the Question of the East* (New York: Lovell, Adam, Wesson & Co., 1876), 10.

22. For the Armenian situation see Barbara J. Merguerian, "Missions in Eden: Shaping an Educational and Social Program for the Armenians in Eastern Turkey, 1855–1895," in *New Faith in Ancient Lands: Western Missions in the Middle East in the Nineteenth and Early Twentieth Centuries*, ed. Heleen Murre-van den Berg (Leiden: Brill, 2006), 241–63; see also Hans Lukas Keiser, "Removal of American Indians, Destruction of Ottoman Armenians: American Missionaries and Demographic Engineering," *European Journal of Turkish Studies* (2008), http://ejts.revues. org/index2873.html.

23. Henry Harris Jessup, *Fifty Three Years in Syria*, 2 vols. (New York: Fleming H. Revell Co., 1910), 2:689.

24. Jessup, *Fifty Three Years in Syria*.

25. See Cyrus Hamlin's letter to the *New York Herald* reproduced in Frederick Davis Greene, *The Armenian Crisis in Turkey* (New York: G. P. Putnam's Sons, 1895), 167.

26. Howard Bliss, "The Balkan War and Work among Moslems," in *The International Review of Missions*, vol. 2, ed. J. H. Oldham (Edinburgh: International Review of Missions, 1913), 653, 655.

27. Cited in Makdisi, *Artillery of Heaven*, 214.

28. Brian Stanley, *The World Missionary Conference, Edinburgh 1910* (Grand Rapids, MI: William B. Eerdmans Publishing Co., 2009), 260.

29. James L. Barton, "The Modern Missionary," *Harvard Theological Review* 8 (1915): 6.

30. Jessup, *Fifty Three Years in Syria*, 2:766.

31. Joseph L. Grabill, *Protestant Diplomacy and the Near East: Missionary Influence on American Policy, 1810–1927* (Minneapolis: University of Minnesota Press, 1971).

32. James L. Barton, "The Ottoman Empire and the War," *Journal of Race Development* 9 (1918): 14.

33. *Papers Relating to the Foreign Relations of the United States: The Paris Peace Conference, 1919*, vol. 3 (Washington, DC: Government Printing Office, 1943), 1016–21.

34. See the newly established King Crane Commission Digital Collection of the Oberlin College Archives, "Introduction," note 4, report, "Future Administration of Certain Portions of the Turkish Empire under the Mandatory System," March 25, 1919, 3. Henry Churchill King Presidential Papers, RG 2/6, box 128, folder 1, Oberlin College Archives, http://dcollections. oberlin.edu/u?/kingcrane,230.

35. Article 22, Covenant of the League of Nations, http://avalon.law.yale.edu/20th_century/ leagcov.asp#art22.

36. See *Conditions in the Near East: Report of the American Military Mission to Armenia by Maj. Gen. James G. Harbord, April 13, 1920* (Washington, DC: Government Printing Office, 1920).

37. The King-Crane report is available online at http://wwi.lib.byu.edu/index.php/The_ Commission_Report. All others citations in my essay are from this version. The only major scholarly book of the King-Crane commission remains Harry N. Howard, *The King-Crane Commission: An American Inquiry in the Middle East* (Beirut: Khayats, 1963). A recent review of the King-Crane commission is Michael Reimer, "The King-Crane Commission at the Juncture of Politics and Historiography," *Critique: Critical Middle Eastern Studies* 15 (2006): 129–50; see also James L. Gelvin, "The Ironic Legacy of the King-Crane Commission," in *The Middle East and the United States*, 4th ed., ed. David W. Lesch (Boulder, CO: Westview Press, 2007), 13–29, and

Leonard V. Smith, "Wilsonian Sovereignty in the Middle East: The King-Crane Commission Report of 1919," in *The State of Sovereignty: Territories, Law, Populations*, ed. Douglas Howland and Luise White (Bloomington: Indiana University Press, 2009).

38. The King-Crane report at http://wwi.lib.byu.edu/index.php/The_Commission_Report.

39. Ibid.

40. Smith, "Wilsonian Sovereignty in the Middle East," 69, also juxtaposes a reading of the Syrian and Palestinian sections of the report with that of the Armenian section but, rather oddly, it seems to me, he takes the commissioners to task for not showing the same sympathy or passion for the Jews as they did for the Armenians. Smith does not explain why he expects to find such sympathy, given that it was the Armenians who had been the victims of genocide.

41. Manela, *The Wilsonian Moment*. For a critical interpretation of the King-Crane commission undertaking in Syria see James L. Gelvin, *Divided Loyalties: Nationalism and Mass Politics in Syria at the Close of the Empire* (Berkeley: University of California Press, 1998), 35, 150–60. For further analysis and criticism also relating to the data complied in Syrian section of the report see Reimer, "King-Crane Commission," 136–38.

42. "Recommendations of the King-Crane Commission," in http://wwi.lib.byu.edu/index.php/The_Commission_Report.

43. For the Yale report see Howard, *King-Crane Commission*, 205–6.

44. "Memorandum by Mr. Balfour Respecting Syria, Palestine, and Mesopotamia, 1919," in *From Haven to Conquest: Readings in Zionism and the Palestine Problem until 1948*, ed. Walid Khalidi (Washington, DC: Institute for Palestine Studies, 1987), 208.

45. Albert Howe Lybyer, "The Return of the Turk," *Forum*, May 1923, pp. 1544, 1550, and *Forum*, June 1923, p. 1628.

46. Toby Craig Jones, *Desert Kingdom: How Oil and Water Forged Modern Saudi Arabia* (Cambridge, MA: Harvard University Press, 2010), 36; William A. Eddy, *F.D.R. Meets Ibn Saud* (American Friends of the Middle East, 1954).

47. Hans-Lukas Kieser, *The Nearest East: American Millennialism and Mission to the Middle East* (Philadelphia: Temple University Press, 2010), 113.

48. Lybyer, "Return of the Turk," 1635. For more on Arab views of America in this period see Makdisi, *Faith Misplaced*, 147–204.

49. Sharkey, *American Evangelicals*, 165.

50. Cited in Lawrence R. Murphy, *The American University in Cairo: 1919–1987* (Cairo: American University in Cairo Press, 1987), 110.

51. Hence the title and thesis of the first and by far the best-known nationalist account in Arabic, published in 1953 by 'Umar Farukh and Mustafa Khalidi, *Al-tabshir wa al-isti'mar fi al-bilad al-'arabiyya* [Mission and colonialism in the Arab lands] (Beirut: al-maktaba al-'ilmiyya, 1953).

# 7. Global Anti-imperialism in the Age of Wilson

1. Richard Koebner and Helmut Dan Schmidt, *Imperialism: The Story and Significance of a Political Word, 1840–1960* (Cambridge: Cambridge University Press, 1964).

2. A *locus classicus* for this sentiment in the British case is George Orwell's famous essay, *Shooting an Elephant*, first published in 1936. For a pioneering discussion of British anti-imperialists see Bernard Porter, *Critics of Empire: British Radicals and the Imperial Challenge*, 2nd ed. (London: I. B. Tauris, 2008); for the U.S. case, Robert L. Beisner, *Twelve against Empire: The Anti-imperialists, 1898–1900* (New York: McGraw Hill, 1968).

3. J. A. Hobson, *Imperialism: A Study* (London: J. Nisbet, 1902); V. I. Lenin, *Imperialism: The Highest Stage of Capitalism* (Moscow: Foreign Languages Press, 1920).

4. See Erez Manela, *The Wilsonian Moment: Self-Determination and the International Origins of Anticolonial Nationalism* (New York: Oxford University Press, 2007). The discussion that follows draws substantially on that volume.

5. Cemil Aydin, *The Politics of Anti-Westernism in Asia: Visions of World Order in Pan-Islamic and Pan-Asian Thought* (New York: Columbia University Press, 2007), 71–93.

6. Immanuel Kant, *To Perpetual Peace: A Philosophical Sketch*, translated, with introduction, by Ted Humphrey (Indianapolis: Hackett, 2003). The essay was originally published in 1795.

7. See Max Beloff, *Britain's Liberal Empire, 1897–1921*, vol. 1, *Imperial Sunset* (New York: Knopf, 1970), 265–66; Arno J. Mayer, *Political Origins of the New Diplomacy, 1917–1918* (New Haven: Yale University Press, 1959), 245–66.

8. Mayer, *Political Origins*. This book was republished in 1964 under the title *Wilson vs. Lenin*.

9. V. I. Lenin, "The Socialist Revolution and the Right of Nations to Self-Determination," in his *Collected Works*, 45 vols. (Moscow: Progress Publishers, 1960–72), 22:143–56 (first published in October 1916). See also Jeremy Smith, *The Bolsheviks and the National Question, 1917–1923* (London: Macmillan, 1999), 8–20.

10. Mayer, *Political Origins*, 248, 298–303.

11. Ibid., 74–76.

12. Ibid., 385–87.

13. Thomas J. Knock, *To End All Wars: Woodrow Wilson and the Quest for a New World Order* (New York: Oxford University Press, 1992), 143. See also George W. Egerton, *Great Britain and the Creation of the League of Nations: Strategy, Politics, and International Organization, 1914–1919* (Chapel Hill: University of North Carolina Press, 1978), 57–59. The full text of the prime minister's address was published as David Lloyd George, *British War Aims: Statement by the Prime Minister, the Right Honourable David Lloyd George, on January 5, 1918* (London: Hazell, Watson, & Viney, 1918).

14. Lloyd E. Ambrosius, *Wilsonianism: Woodrow Wilson and His Legacy in American Foreign Relations* (New York: Palgrave Macmillan, 2002), 125–43; William R. Keylor, "Versailles and International Diplomacy," in *The Treaty of Versailles: A Reassessment after 75 Years*, ed. Manfred F. Boemeke et al. (Cambridge: Cambridge University Press, 1998), 475 and n. 12 there; N. Gordon Levin, *Woodrow Wilson and World Politics: America's Response to War and Revolution* (New York: Oxford University Press, 1968), 247–51.

15. Address to a joint session of Congress, January 8, 1918, *The Papers of Woodrow Wilson* (hereafter cited as *PWW*), ed. Arthur S. Link et al., 69 vols. (Princeton, NJ: Princeton University Press, 1966–94), 45:534–39.

16. Address to Congress, February 11, 1918, *PWW*, 46:321.

17. For more on Wilson's thinking on the concept of self-determination see Michla Pomerance, "The United States and Self-Determination: Perspectives on the Wilsonian Conception," *American Journal of International Law* 70 (1976): 1–27.

18. D. V. Gundappa, "Liberalism in India," *Confluence* 5, no. 3 (1956): 217, quoting V. S. Srinivasa Sastri's introduction to an Indian edition of Wilson's selected speeches.

19. Leo Lee and Andrew J. Nathan, "The Beginnings of Mass Culture," in *Popular Culture in Late Imperial China*, ed. David Johnson et al. (Berkeley: University of California Press, 1985), 368–78; Joan Judge, *Print and Politics: "Shibao" and the Culture of Reform in Late Qing China* (Stanford, CA: Stanford University Press, 1996).

20. P. J. Vatikiotis, *The History of Modern Egypt: From Muhammad Ali to Mubarak*, 4th ed. (Baltimore: Johns Hopkins University Press, 1991), 179–88.

21. George Creel, *Complete Report of the Chairman of the Committee on Public Information* (Washington, DC: Government Printing Office, 1920), 1.

22. Ibid., 2.

23. Ibid., 4.

24. George Creel, *How We Advertised America: The First Telling of the Amazing Story of the Committee on Public Information That Carried the Gospel of Americanism to Every Corner of the Globe* (New York: Harper, 1920), 362; Hans Schmidt, "Democracy for China: American Propaganda and the May Fourth Movement," *Diplomatic History* 22, no. 1 (Winter 1998): 3.

25. Carl Crow, *China Takes Her Place* (New York: Harper, 1944), 113–15; also Crow, *I Speak for the Chinese* (New York: Harper, 1937), 27–29.

26. Creel, *How We Advertised America*, 362.

27. Schmidt, "Democracy for China," 11–12.

28. See, e.g., Tang Zhenchang, *Cai Yuanpei zhuan* (Shanghai: Shanghai People's Press, 1985), 159. Cai was the president of Peking University at the time.

29. Koo to Lansing, November 25, 1918, in Record Group (RG) 03–12 (Archives of Chinese Embassy in Washington), box 8, fol. 2, 477, at the Waijiaobu (Foreign Ministry) Archives, Academia Sinica, Taipei, Taiwan.

30. Ronald Wingate, *Wingate of the Sudan* (London: Murray, 1955), 228, 232.

31. James D. Startt, "American Propaganda in Britain during World War I," *Prologue* 28, no. 1 (Spring 1996): 17–33; Peter Buitenhuis, "Selling the Great War," *Canadian Review of American Studies* 7, no. 2 (Fall 1976): 139–50.

32. 'Abd al-Rahman Rafi'i, *Thawrat sanat 1919: Tarikh misr al-qawmi min sanat 1914 ila sanat 1921* (Cairo: Mu'assasat Dar al-Sha'b, 1968), 57; 'Abd al-Khaliq Lashin, *Sa'd Zaghlul wa-dawruhu fi al-siyasah al-Misriyyah* (Beirut: Dar al-'Awdah, 1975), 126–27.

33. S. Natarajan, *A History of the Press in India* (Bombay: Asia Publishing House, 1962), 183.

34. Subramanya Aiyar to Woodrow Wilson, June 24, 1917, in the National Archives of India, New Delhi (hereafter cited as NAI), Home Department / Political Branch, Deposit File, February 1918, file no. 36, "Action taken in regard to a letter sent by Sir Subramanya Aiyar to the President of the United States of America invoking his aid in obtaining Home Rule for India," 3–6. Also see India Office Library, London (IOL), V/26/262/9 (Hunter Committee Report), 7:3.

35. "Editorials," *Young India* 1, no. 3 (March 1918): 1–3.

36. *Mahrátta*, October 6, 1918, "Bombay Press Abstract, 1918," IOL, L/R/5/174, 19; *Tribune* (Lahore), December 20, 1918, "Punjab Press Abstract, 1919," IOL, L/R/5/201, 3; *Hindi Brahmin Samachar*, November 25, 1918; *Kesari* (Poona), n.d., IOL, L/R/5/200, 596.

37. Skeptics included M. N. Roy and Li Dazhao, who would soon thereafter be among the founders of communist parties in India and China, respectively. See, e.g., *Selected Works of M. N. Roy*, ed. Sibnarayan Ray, 4 vols. (Delhi: Oxford University Press, 1987), 1:67–83; Li Dazhao, "*Wei-er-xun yu pinghe*," February 11, 1917, in *Li Dazhao wenji*, 1:271; and Li Dazhao, "Bolshevism de shengli," *Xin Qingnian* 5, no. 5, November 1918.

38. Thirty-third INC session, Delhi, December 1918, Nehru Memorial Museum and Library, New Delhi (hereafter NMML), All-India Congress Committee, file 1, part 2, 347.

39. UK National Archives, Kew (hereafter UKNA), FO 608/211, fol. 126–36.

40. Memorandum, dated London, December 11, 1918, enc. in Tilak's letter to Khaparde, December 18, 1918, NAI, G. S. Khaparde Papers, file 1, 1–2.

41. Tilak to D. W. Gokhale, London, January 23, 1919, NAI, Khaparde Papers, file 1, 4–7.

42. Close to Tilak, January 14, 1919, quoted in T. V. Parvate, *Bal Gangadhar Tilak* (Ahmedabad: Navajivan, 1958), 463.

43. On China's wartime policy and experience, see Xu Guoqi, *China and the Great War: China's Pursuit of a New National Identity and Internationalization* (Cambridge: Cambridge University Press, 2005).

44. Reinsch to Lansing, November 8, 1918, U.S. National Archives and Records Administration (hereafter NARA), RG 256, 893.01/1. Also see excerpts from the *Peking Leader*, November 3–5, 1919, enclosed in RG 256, 893.00/5; and Foreign Minister of Canton Government to Lansing, January 23, 1919, RG 256, 893.00/18.

45. Wunsz King, *China at the Peace Conference in 1919* (Jamaica, NY: St. John's University Press, 1961), 3.

46. V. K. Wellington Koo and Cheng-ting T. Wang, *China and the League of Nations* (London: Allen & Unwin, 1919).

47. A few examples among many include a petition from Leon S. Farhj, an official at the Egyptian Ministry of Agriculture, December 11, 1918, and a petition from members of the "Egyptian National Delegation," December 12, 1918, enc. in Gary to secretary of state, December 30, 1918, NARA, RG 256, 883.00/4 and FW 883.00/30.

48. E.g., Zaghlul to Wilson, December 14, 1918, December 27, 1918, and January 3, 1919. For telegrams from Zaghlul to Wilson see George E. Noble, "The Voice of Egypt," *Nation*, January 3, 1920, 861–64.

49. See examples enclosed in Gary to secretary of state, December 30, 1918, NARA, RG 256, 883.00/4; Gary to DOS, December 19, 1918, RG 256, 883.00/3.

50. Isma'il Ṣidqi, *Mudhakkirati* (Cairo: Maktabat Madbuli, 1991), 46–49; Gary to the secretary of state, March 10, 1919, NARA, RG 256, 883.00/37.

51. Lashin, *Sa'd Zaghlul*, 128.

52. See PID reports in UKNA, FO 371/4373, 35, 51. Also Gary to the secretary of state, and March 10, 11, and 16, 1919, NARA, RG 256, 883.00/37, 41 and 53.

53. Rafi'i, *Thawrat sanat 1919*, 5. Tahrir (or Liberation) Square in Cairo, which stood at the heart of the "Arab Spring" protests of 2011, first acquired its name as a result of the upheaval of 1919, when it also served as a center for protests.

54. Tilak to D. W. Gokhale, February 6, 1919, NAI, Khaparde Papers, file 1, 8–10; Tilak to D. W. Gokhale, London, January 23, 1919, NAI, Khaparde Papers, file 1, 4–7; Unsigned memorandum titled "How We Get On II," enc. in Tilak's letter from London, March 20, 1919, NAI, Khaparde Papers, file 1, 13–14.

55. Gandhi to Chelmsford, February 24, 1919, and March 11, 1919, NMML, Chelmsford Papers, roll 10.

56. Schmidt, "Democracy for China," 16; Chow Tse-tsung, *The May Fourth Movement: Intellectual Revolution in Modern China* (Cambridge, MA: Harvard University Press, 1960), 92–93.

# 8. Feminist Historiography, Anti-imperialism, and the Decolonial

Thanks to Ian Tyrrell for the conference invitation and to participants for feedback. At Portland State University, Jennifer Tappan, the history graduate colloquium, and my seminar students provided excellent comments on this essay, as did the anonymous readers at Cornell University Press.

1. Laura Briggs, "Gender and U.S. Imperialism in U.S. Women's History," in *The Practice of Women's History: Narratives, Intersections, Dialogues*, ed. Jay Kleinberg, Eileen Boris, and Vicki L. Ruiz (New Brunswick, NJ: Rutgers University Press, 2007), 146.

2. Frank Ninkovich, "Culture and Anti-Imperialism" (paper presented at the American Anti-Imperialism since 1776 conference, Oxford University, April 2011).

3. Robert L. Beisner, *Twelve against Empire: The Anti-Imperialists, 1898–1900*, 2nd ed. (Chicago: University of Chicago Press, 1985), xvii.

4. Julie Des Jardins, *Women and the Historical Enterprise in America: Gender, Race, and the Politics of Memory, 1880–1945* (Chapel Hill: University of North Carolina Press, 2003).

5. Antoinette Burton, "Introduction: On the Inadequacy and Indispensability of the Nation," in *After the Imperial Turn: Thinking with and Through the Nation*, ed. Burton (Durham, NC: Duke University Press), 7; Thomas Bender, "Introduction: Historians, the Nation, and the Plentitude of Narratives," in *Rethinking American History in a Global Age*, ed. Bender (Berkeley: University of California Press, 2002), 10.

6. Edward J. Blum, *Reforging the White Republic: Race, Religion, and American Nationalism* (Baton Rouge: LSU Press, 2005), 178.

7. Tennie M. Fuller, "Banner of Indian Territory W.C.T.U.—My History," *Tenth Annual Convention of the Woman's Christian Temperance Union of the Indian Territory Held at Muskogee, Ind. Terr., May 5, 6, and 8, 1896* (Muskogee, Indian Territory: Phoenix Printing Co., 1896), 38; Sam Maddra, "American Indians in Buffalo Bill's Wild West," in *Human Zoos: Science and Spectacle in the Age of Colonial Empires*, ed. Blancard Pascal (Liverpool: Liverpool University Press, 2008), 134–41.

8. Elizabeth Putnam Gordon, *Women Torch-Bearers: The Story of the Woman's Christian Temperance Union* (Evanston, IL: National WCTU Publishing House, 1924), 97–98; Abbie B. Hillerman, *History of the Woman's Christian Temperance Union of Indian Territory, Oklahoma Territory, State of Oklahoma, 1888–1925* (Sapulpa, OK. Jennings Co., 1925), 26–29; Ruth Bordin, *Woman and Temperance: The Quest for Power and Liberty, 1873–1900* (New Brunswick, NJ: Rutgers University Press, 1981); Izumi Ishii, *Bad Fruits of the Civilized Tree: Alcohol and the Sovereignty of the Cherokee Nation* (Lincoln: University of Nebraska Press, 2008).

9. "'UMA,' Unión de Mujeres Americanas," *Artes y Letras*, September 1934, p. 7.

10. "Unión de Mujeres Americanas, 'UMA,'" *Artes y Letras*, October 1934, p. 4; Virginia Sánchez Korrol, *From Colonia to Community: The History of Puerto Ricans in New York City* (Berkeley: University of California Press, 1994), 113.

11. Laura Briggs, Gladys McCormick, and J. T. Way, "Transnationalism: A Category of Analysis," *American Quarterly* 60, no. 3 (September 2008): 625–48; Inderpal Grewal, *Transnational America: Feminisms, Diasporas, Neoliberalisms* (Durham, NC: Duke University Press, 2005); Caren Kaplan, Norma Alarcón, and Minoo Moallem, eds., *Between Woman and Nation: Nationalisms, Transnational Feminisms, and the State* (Durham, NC: Duke University Press, 1999); Kimberly Jensen and Erika Kuhlman, eds., *Women and Transnational Activism in Historical Perspective* (St. Louis: Republic of Letters, 2010); Debra A. Castillo, Mary Jo Dudley, and Breny Mendoza, eds., *Rethinking Feminisms in the Americas* (Ithaca, NY: Cornell University Press, 2000); Elisa Camiscioli, "Women, Gender, Intimacy, and Empire," *Journal of Women's History* 25, no. 4 (2013): 138–48.

12. Ann Stoler, *Carnal Knowledge and Imperial Power: Race and the Intimate in Colonial Rule* (Berkeley: University of California Press, 2002), 24.

13. Mrinalini Sinha, "Mapping the Imperial Social Formation: A Modest Proposal for Feminist History," *Signs* 25, no. 4 (2000): 1077–82.

14. Stephanie M. Camp, *Closer to Freedom: Enslaved Women and Everyday Resistance in the Plantation South* (Chapel Hill: University of North Carolina Press, 2004).

15. Peggy Pascoe, *Relations of Rescue: The Search for Female Moral Authority in the American West, 1874–1939* (New York: Oxford University Press, 1990); Catherine Ceniza Choy, *Empire*

*of Care: Nursing and Migration in Filipino American History* (Durham, NC: Duke University Press, 2003).

16. Emma Pérez, *The Decolonial Imaginary: Writing Chicanas into History* (Bloomington: Indiana University Press, 1999), xiii–xix; Irene Lara, "Goddess of the Americas in the Decolonial Imaginary: Beyond the Virtuous Virgin/Pagan Puta Dichotomy," *Feminist Studies* 34, no. 1 (2008): 99–127; Walter Mignolo, "Epistemic Disobedience, Independent Thought and Decolonial Freedom," *Theory, Culture and Society* 26, nos. 7–8 (2009): 159–81.

17. Margaret D. Jacobs, *White Mother to a Dark Race: Settler Colonialism, Maternalism, and the Removal of Indigenous Children in the American West and Australia, 1880–1940* (Lincoln: University of Nebraska Press, 2009); Barbara Reeves-Ellington, Kathryn Kish Sklar, and Connie Anne Shemo, *Competing Kingdoms: Women, Mission, Nation, and the American Protestant Empire, 1812–1960* (Durham, NC: Duke University Press, 2010).

18. Chris Bayly, "AHR Conversation: On Transnational History," *American Historical Review* 11, no. 5 (December 2006): 1452; Françoise Lionett and Shumei Shi, eds., *Minor Transnationalism* (Durham, NC: Duke University Press, 2005).

19. Trinh T. Minh-ha, *Woman, Native, Other: Writing Postcoloniality and Feminism* (Bloomington: Indiana University Press, 1989).

20. Joan Scott, "Gender: A Useful Category of Analysis," *American Historical Review* 91, no. 5 (1986): 1067 and 1073.

21. Joanne Meyerowitz, "A History of 'Gender,'" *American Historical Review* 113, no. 5 (2008): 1350.

22. Kristin L. Hoganson, *Fighting for American Manhood: How Gender Politics Provoked the Spanish-American and Philippine-American Wars* (New Haven, CT: Yale University Press, 1998), 9, 180–99.

23. Anna Davin, "Imperialism and Motherhood," *History Workshop* 5 (1978): 9–65; Antoinette M. Burton, *Burdens of History: British Feminists, Indian Women, and Imperial Culture, 1865–1915* (Chapel Hill: University of North Carolina Press, 1994); Gail Bederman, *Manliness and Civilization: A Cultural History of Gender and Race in the United States, 1880–1917* (Chicago: University of Chicago Press, 1995).

24. Louise Newman, *White Women's Rights: The Racial Origins of Feminism in the United States* (New York: Oxford University Press, 1999), 181–83.

25. Gordon, *Women Torch-Bearers*, 86; Ian Tyrrell, *Transnational Nation: United States History in Global Perspective since 1789* (Basingstoke, UK: Palgrave Macmillan, 2007), 144.

26. Allison Sneider, *Suffragists in an Imperial Age: U.S. Expansion and the Woman Question, 1870–1929* (New York: Oxford University Press, 2008), 7–8, 116.

27. Beisner, *Twelve against Empire*, 238, xvii–xviii.

28. Leila J. Rupp, "Challenging Imperialism in International Women's Organizations, 1888–1945," *NWSA Journal* 8, no. 1 (1996): 8–27.

29. Leila Rupp, "Constructing Internationalism: The Case of Transnational Women's Organizations, 1888–1945," *American Historical Review* 99, no. 5 (1994): 1571–1600.

30. Kristin L. Hoganson, "'As Badly Off as the Filipinos': U.S. Women's Suffragists and the Imperial Issue at the Turn of the Twentieth Century," *Journal of Women's History* 13, no. 2 (2001): 9–10.

31. "Remarks by Mrs. Mary A. Livermore," *Report of the Fifth Annual Meeting of the New England Anti-Imperialist League* (Boston: New England Anti-Imperialist League, 1903), 34.

32. Nell Irvin Painter, "Representing Truth: Sojourner Truth's Knowing and Becoming Known," *Journal of American History* 81, no. 2 (1994): 461–92.

33. Hoganson, "'Badly Off as the Filipinos,'" 25.

34. Gayatri Chakravorty Spivak, "Can the Subaltern Speak?" in *Can the Subaltern Speak? Reflections on the History of an Idea*, ed. Spivak and Rosalind C. Morris (New York: Columbia University Press, 2010), 262.

35. Laura Briggs, *Reproducing Empire: Race, Sex, Science, and U.S. Imperialism in Puerto Rico* (Berkeley: University of California Press, 2002), 9.

36. Ibid., 202–9.

37. Spivak, "Can the Subaltern Speak?" 281, 282.

38. Briggs, "Gender and U.S. Imperialism," 156.

39. Linda Gordon, "Internal Colonialism and Gender," in *Haunted by Empire: Geographies of Intimacy in North American History*, ed. Ann Stoler (Durham, NC: Duke University Press, 2006), 444, 450.

40. Briggs, "Gender and U.S. Imperialism," 146.

41. Gordon, "Internal Colonialism and Gender," 433.

42. Ibid., 433, 435; Mae M. Ngai, *Impossible Subjects: Illegal Aliens and the Making of Modern America* (Princeton, NJ: Princeton University Press, 2004); Jorge Duany, *The Puerto Rican Nation on the Move: Identities on the Island and in the United States* (Chapel Hill: University of North Carolina Press, 2002).

43. Elsa Barkley Brown, "Womanist Consciousness: Maggie Lena Walker and the Independent Order of Saint Luke," *Signs* 14, no. 3 (1989): 610–33.

44. Elsa Barkley Brown, "Negotiating and Transforming the Public Sphere: African American Political Life in the Transition from Slavery to Freedom," *Public Culture* 7 (1994): 107–46, and Brown "To Catch the Vision of Freedom: Reconstructing Black Women's Political History," in *Unequal Sisters: An Inclusive Reader in U.S. Women's History*, ed. Vicki L. Ruiz with Ellen C. Du Bois (New York: Routledge, 2008), 156.

45. Brown, "To Catch the Vision of Freedom," 169.

46. Ibid., 160.

47. Peter B. Evans, Dietrich Rueschemeyer, and Theda Skocpol, *Bringing the State Back In* (Cambridge: Cambridge University Press, 1985); Linda Gordon, ed., *Women, the State, and Welfare* (Madison: University of Wisconsin Press, 1990), and Linda K. Kerber, Alice Kessler-Harris, and Kathryn Kish Sklar, eds., *U.S. History as Women's History: New Feminist Essays* (Chapel Hill: University of North Carolina Press, 1995).

48. Evelyn Brooks Higginbotham, "In Politics to Stay: Black Women Leaders and Party Politics in the 1920s," in *Women, Politics, and Change*, ed. Louise A. Tilly and Patricia Gurin (New York: Russell Sage, 1990), 199–220; Glenda Elizabeth Gilmore, *Gender and Jim Crow: Women and the Politics of White Supremacy in North Carolina, 1896–1920* (Chapel Hill: University of North Carolina Press, 1996); Tera W. Hunter, *To 'Joy My Freedom: Southern Black Women's Lives and Labors after the Civil War* (Cambridge, MA: Harvard University Press, 1997); Patricia A. Schechter, *Ida B. Wells-Barnett and American Reform, 1880–1930* (Chapel Hill: University of North Carolina Press, 2001); Lisa G. Materson, *For the Freedom of Her Race: Black Women and Electoral Politics in Illinois, 1877–1932* (Chapel Hill: University of North Carolina Press, 2009); Crystal Nicole Feimster, *Southern Horrors: Women and the Politics of Rape and Lynching* (Cambridge, MA: Harvard University Press, 2010).

49. Rosalyn Terborg-Penn, Sharon Harley, and Andrea Benton Rushing, eds., *Women in Africa and the African Diaspora* (Washington, DC: Howard University Press, 1987/1996).

50. Paul Gilroy, *The Black Atlantic: Modernity and Double Consciousness* (Cambridge, MA: Harvard University Press, 1993); Deborah Gray White, "'YES,' There Is a Black Atlantic," *Itinerario* 23, no. 2 (1999): 127–40; Nikhil Pal Singh, *Black Is a Country: Race and the Unfinished Struggle for Democracy* (Cambridge, MA: Harvard University Press, 2004); Kevin Kelly Gaines, *American Africans in Ghana: Black Expatriates and the Civil Rights Era* (Chapel Hill: University of North Carolina Press, 2006); Elizabeth Anne Pryor, "'Jim Crow' Cars, Passport Denials and Atlantic Crossings: African-American Travel, Protest, and Citizenship at Home and Abroad, 1827–1865" (PhD diss., University of California, Santa Barbara, 2008).

51. Rosalyn Terborg-Penn, "Enfranchising Women of Color: Woman Suffragists as Agents of Empire," in *Nation, Empire, Colony: Historicizing Gender and Race*, ed. Ruth Roach Pierson and Nupur Chaudhuri (Bloomington: Indiana University Press, 1998), 42, 54.

52. Laura E. Donaldson, *Decolonizing Feminisms: Race, Gender, and Empire Building* (Chapel Hill: University of North Carolina Press, 1992); Linda Tuhiwai Smith, *Decolonizing Methodologies: Research and Indigenous Peoples* (Dunedin, New Zealand: University of Otago Press, 1999).

53. Pérez, *Decolonial Imaginary*, 20.

54. Laura Briggs, "In Contested Territory," *Women's Review of Books*, March 2000, p. 21; Ann Stoler, "Tense and Tender Ties: The Politics of Comparison in North American History," in *Haunted by Empire*, 55.

55. Duane Champagne, "In Search of Theory and Method in American Indian Studies," *American Indian Quarterly* 31, no. 3 (2007): 353–73; Frederick E. Hoxie, "Retrieving the Red Continent: Settler Colonialism and the History of American Indians in the U.S.," *Ethnic and Racial Studies* 31, no. 6 (2008): 1153–67.

56. "No Aceptamos Demarcaciones," *Artes y Letras*, August 1938, 1.

57. Spivak, "Can the Subaltern Speak?" 254.

58. Paraphrasing W. A. Williams, Julian Go used the phrase "anti-imperialism as a way of life" in response to my presentation at the conference.

59. Trinh, *Woman, Native, Other*, 113.

# 9. Resource Use, Conservation, and the Environmental Limits of Anti-imperialism

1. A film clip can be viewed at http://www.youtube.com/watch?v=y22ajVB4OzU; Mark Boulos, "All That Is Solid Melts Into Air," is discussed by Boulos at http://www.youtube.com/watch?v=BX6rYfNzTJ8.

2. "Sustainability" is closely associated with the *Report of the World Commission on Environment and Development: Our Common Future* (the "Bruntland Report"), 1987, at http://www.un-documents.net/wced-ocf.htm.

3. For analyses depending on a social ecology linking humans and nonhuman ecological systems in interdependency see Richard Tucker, *Insatiable Appetite: The United States and the Ecological Degradation of the Tropical World* (Berkeley: University of California Press, 2000); John Soluri, *Banana Cultures: Agriculture, Consumption, and Environmental Change in Honduras and the United States* (Austin: University of Texas Press, 2005), 41–42; Carolyn Merchant, *Radical Ecology: The Search for a Livable World* (London: Routledge, 1992), 132–54.

4. An "ecological" approach refers to analysis that deals with the impacts of change in ecological systems; the "environmental" includes ecological systems, but also the broader political and cultural terrain of environmental movements, ideas, and institutions.

5. Richard Grove, *Green Imperialism: Colonial Expansion, Tropical Island Edens and the Origins of Environmentalism, 1600–1860* (Cambridge: Cambridge University Press, 1995), esp. 11–12, 481.

6. Ramachandra Guha, *The Unquiet Woods: Ecological Change and Peasant Resistance in the Himalaya* (Berkeley: University of California Press, 1989).

7. Mark David Spence, *Dispossessing the Wilderness: Indian Removal and the Making of the National Parks* (New York: Oxford University Press, 1999); Karl Jacoby, *Crimes against Nature: Poachers, Squatters, Thieves, and the Hidden History of American Conservation* (Berkeley: University of California Press, 2001), 85, 88–92; Louis Warren, *The Hunter's Game: Poachers and Conservationists in Twentieth-Century America* (New Haven, CT: Yale University Press, 1997), 87–105.

8. John Weaver, *The Great Land Rush and the Making of the Modern World, 1650–1900* (Montreal: McGill–Queen's University Press, 2006); Nira Yuval-Davis and Daiva Stasiulis, eds., *Unsettling Settler Societies: Articulations of Gender, Race, Ethnicity and Class* (London: Sage, 1995).

9. Settler colonialism is conceptually distinct from other colonialisms in its erasure or attempted erasure of the conquered. Lorenzo Veracini, *Settler Colonialism: A Theoretical Overview* (Basingstoke, UK: Palgrave Macmillan, 2011), 25.

10. Walter L. Williams, "United States Indian Policy and the Debate over Philippine Annexation: Implications for the Origins of American Imperialism," *Journal of American History* 66 (March 1980) 810–31.

11. John Henry Crooker, *The Menace to America* (Chicago: American Anti-Imperialist League, 1900), noted: "We have done poorly by our Indian tribes," "mainly" because "a republic is not suitable for servile peoples" (23), but the problem should not be "intensified a hundred fold" by new subject peoples (24). Anti-imperialists knew that the bison's removal from the Great Plains had ecological effects for Native Americans but regarded the latter as complicit. For William T. Hornaday, *The Extermination of the American Bison* (1887; Washington, DC: Government Printing Office, 1889), 478, only federal coercion against both Indian and white hunters could have stemmed the damage. This position paralleled not conventional anti-imperialism but Progressive imperialism's later critique of entrepreneurial capitalism abroad.

12. "Address by the Hon. George S. Boutwell," in *Report of the Fourth Annual Meeting of the New England Anti-Imperialist League; November 29, 1902* (Boston, 1902), 6.

13. No author, *The Crowning Infamy of Imperialism: A Record of National Dishonor* (Philadelphia: American League of Philadelphia, 1900); Ian Tyrrell, *Reforming the World: The Creation of America's Moral Empire* (Princeton, NJ: Princeton University Press, 2010), chaps. 6–7; Mary Livermore, "Remarks at the Annual Meeting of the New England Anti-Imperialist League," *Report of the Fifth Annual Meeting of the New England Anti-Imperialist League* (Boston, 1903), 34.

14. George Perkins Marsh, *Man and Nature* (New York: Charles Scribner, 1864).

15. William Appleman Williams, *The Tragedy of American Diplomacy*, rev. ed. (1972; New York: Norton, 1988), 50–51.

16. *Washington Post*, June 4, 1898, p. 7.

17. William Appleman Williams, *The Roots of the Modern American Empire: A Study of the Growth and Shaping of Social Consciousness in a Marketplace Society* (New York: Random House, 1969); Williams, *Tragedy of American Diplomacy*, 30–32; Walter LaFeber, *The New Empire: An Interpretation of American Expansion, 1860–1898* (Ithaca, NY: Cornell University Press, 1963); Thomas J. McCormick, *China Market: America's Quest for Informal Empire, 1893–1901* (Chicago: Quadrangle Books, 1967).

18. Arthur F. Beringause, *Brooks Adams: A Biography* (New York: Alfred A. Knopf, 1955), 235; Brooks Adams, *America's Economic Supremacy* (New York: Macmillan, 1900); and Adams, *The New Empire* (New York: Macmillan, 1902).

19. Andrew J. Bacevich, *American Empire: The Realities and Consequences of U.S. Diplomacy* (Cambridge, MA: Harvard University Press, 2002), 24, 30–31.

20. Ibid., 18; Charles Beard, *The Open Door at Home: A True Philosophy of National Interest* (New York: Macmillan, 1934), 241–44.

21. See boxes 53–55, Mercer Green Johnston Papers, Library of Congress.

22. Scott Nearing, *The American Empire* (New York: Rand School of Social Science, 1921), 73.

23. Ibid., 220, 221.

24. Scott Nearing and Joseph Freeman, *Dollar Diplomacy: A Study in American Imperialism* (London: George Allen and Unwin, 1926).

25. John Mason Hart, *Empire and Revolution: The Americans in Mexico since the Civil War* (Berkeley: University of California Press, 2002); Jeffry A. Frieden "The Economics of Intervention: American

Overseas Investments and Relations with Underdeveloped Areas, 1890–1950," *Comparative Studies in Society and History* 31 (January 1989): 65; Diana Davids Olien and Roger M. Olien, "Running Out of Oil: Discourse and Public Policy, 1909–1929," *Business and Economic History* 22, no. 2 (Winter 1999): 36–66.

26. *Conditions in the Philippine Islands. Message from the President of the United States Transmitting a Report by Colonel Carmi A. Thompson on the Conditions in the Philippine Islands together with Suggestions with Reference to the Administration and Economic Development of the Islands* (1926), in the *New York Times*, December 23, 1926, p. 7; Greg Grandin, *Fordlandia: The Rise and Fall of Henry Ford's Forgotten Jungle City* (New York: Metropolitan Books, 2009); Tucker, *Insatiable Appetite*, chap. 5.

27. Nearing and Freeman, *Dollar Diplomacy*, 6.

28. Ibid., 7–8.

29. John F. Carter, *Conquest: America's Painless Imperialism* (New York: Harcourt, Brace, 1928), 215. On Carter see "Carter, John Franklin, 1897–1967, Journalist," *New York Times*, November 29, 1967, p. 47.

30. Stephen J. Whitfield, *Scott Nearing: Apostle of American Radicalism* (New York: Columbia University Press, 1974), 149–50; see also Elizabeth Kirkpatrick Dilling, *The Red Network: A Who's Who and Handbook of Radicalism for Patriots* (1935; Chicago: Ayer Co., 1977), 163. The American Fund for Public Service was established in 1922 with Wall Street stockbroker Charles Garland's inheritance. Gloria Garrett Samson, *The American Fund for Public Service* (Westport, CT: Praeger, 1996), 128, 142, 219–20.

31. Barnes, introduction to *Porto Rico: A Broken Pledge*, by Bailey W. and Justine W. Diffie (New York: Vanguard Press, 1931), xvi.

32. Charles David Kepner, *Social Aspects of the Banana Industry* (New York: Columbia University Press, 1936), 18, 89. Kepner noted that large forest tracts had not been ravaged, but kept in reserve for future use (214).

33. Charles David Kepner Jr. and Jay Henry Soothill, *The Banana Empire: A Case Study of Economic Imperialism* (New York: Vanguard Press, 1935), vii.

34. Diffie and Diffie, *Porto Rico*, 84, 142. On Bailey Diffie (1902–83) see Stuart B. Schwartz in *Hispanic American Historical Review* 63 (August 1983): 593–95.

35. This statement was reminiscent of the analysis of Marsh, *Man and Nature*. Yet according to Howard L. Parsons, ed., *Marx and Engels on Ecology* (Westport, CT: Greenwood Press, 1977), Marx and Engels were "humanistic naturalists" who did not know Marsh's work (22). They were merely influenced by Marsh's milieu.

36. Karl Marx, quoted in Parsons, *Marx and Engels on Ecology*, 180.

37. Quoted in Parsons, ibid., 174.

38. Ibid., 175.

39. Parsons, ibid., 19; Margaret W. Rossiter, *The Emergence of Agricultural Science: Justus Liebig and the Americans, 1840–1880* (New Haven, CT: Yale University Press, 1975).

40. Parsons, *Marx and Engels on Ecology*, 175.

41. Quoted ibid., 174.

42. Ibid.

43. Douglas R. Weiner, *Models of Nature: Ecology, Conservation, and Cultural Revolution in Soviet Russia* (Bloomington: Indiana University Press, 1988); for green Left appropriation of Marxism see Martin O'Connor, ed., *Is Capitalism Sustainable? Political Economy and the Politics of Ecology* (New York: Guilford Press, 1994); John Bellamy Foster, *Marx's Ecology: Materialism and Nature* (New York: Monthly Review Press, 2009).

44. *New York Times*, August 25, 1983, section D, p. 21.

45. John A. Saltmarsh, *Scott Nearing: The Making of a Homesteader* (White River Junction, VT: Chelsea Green Publishing, 1998), 50–58; Scott Nearing, *Anthracite: An Instance of Natural Resource Monopoly* (Philadelphia: John C. Winston Co., 1915), 20.

46. Paul T. McCartney, *Power and Progress: American National Identity, the War of 1898, and the Rise of American Imperialism* (Baton Rouge: LSU Press, 2006).

47. The Organic Act of 1897 (30 Stat. 34–36); Gifford Pinchot, *Breaking New Ground* (New York: Harcourt, Brace, 1947), 117–19; Harold K. Steen, *The U.S. Forest Service: A History* (Seattle: University of Washington Press, 1977), 34–36.

48. Richard Pettigrew, *The Course of Empire* (New York: Boni & Liveright, 1920); Pettigrew, *Imperial Washington: The Story of American Public Life from 1870 to 1920* (Chicago: C. H. Kerr & Company, 1922).

49. Pettigrew, *Imperial Washington*, 347.

50. Pettigrew, *Course of Empire*, 389.

51. Ibid.

52. Ibid.

53. *Annexation of the Hawaiian Islands. Speech of Hon. Richard F. Pettigrew, of South Dakota, in the Senate of the United States, June 22 and 23, 1898* (Washington, DC: n.p., 1898), 4, 11. See also Pettigrew, *Imperial Washington*, 366.

54. For antiracism in the anti-imperialists see James M. McPherson, *The Abolitionist Legacy: From Reconstruction to the NAACP* (Princeton, NJ: Princeton University Press, 1975), 326–31.

55. Scott Nearing, introduction to Pettigrew, *Course of Empire*, v–x.

56 "Benevolent Assimilation" [1920], in Pettigrew, *Imperial Washington*, 358 (italics added). For the origins of this comment see "The Failure of Imperialism," a speech in the Senate, January 15, 1900, in Pettigrew, *Course of Empire*, 338–39; "Let Us Be Honest," *Washington Post*, January 14, 1900.

57. Douglas Brinkley, *The Wilderness Warrior: Theodore Roosevelt and the Crusade for America* (New York: HarperCollins, 2009). For Henry George and environmentalism, see Ian Tyrrell, *True Gardens of the Gods: Californian-Australian Environmental Reform, 1860–1930* (Berkeley: University of California Press, 1999), chap. 2, esp. 37–39; Nearing, *Anthracite*, 20.

58. William E. Leuchtenburg, "Progressivism and Imperialism: The Progressive Movement and American Foreign Policy, 1898–1916," *Mississippi Valley Historical Review* 39 (December 1952): 483–504.

59. Thomas E. Will, "Timber Lands in Mexico," *Forestry and Irrigation* 13 (October 1907): 511; J. E. Dovell, "Thomas Elmer Will, Twentieth Century Pioneer," *Tequesta* 8 (1948): 21–55.

60. "Cherry Trees and Conservation," *Outlook* 9 (January 1909): 50–51.

61. Ibid.

62. Pinchot, *Breaking New Ground*, 363.

63. Thomas Will, "A Personal Word," *American Forestry* 16 (February 1910): 111.

64. Editorial, *Forestry and Irrigation* 13 (December 1907): 618.

65. *New York Times*, December 21, 1910.

66. Barrington Moore, "Forest Problems in the Philippines," *American Forestry* 16 (February 1910): 80.

67. Barbara Goldoftas, *The Green Tiger: The Costs of Ecological Decline in the Philippines* (New York: Oxford University Press, 2006), 51–52; M. Patricia Marchak, *Logging the Globe* (Montreal: McGill–Queen's University Press, 1995), 184–85; Moore, "Forest Problems in the Philippines" (pt. 2), *American Forestry* 16 (March 1910): 151 (quote).

68. Moore, "Forest Problems," 78–80; William M. Maule, "Parang and Cogonales in the Philippines," *Forest and Irrigation* 12 (July 1906): 312–17.

69. Tucker, *Insatiable Appetite*, 378; Moore, "Forest Problems," 80 (quotes); Marchak, *Logging the Globe*, 184–85; *Report of the Philippine Commission to the Secretary of War, July 1, 1913 to June 30, 1914* (Washington, DC: Government Printing Office, 1915), 114; Antonio Racelis, "Forestry Education in the Philippines," *Journal of Forestry* 31 (April 1933): 455. The swidden agriculture practices known to the American colonial officials as "caingins" is now rendered as "Kaingin" in the Philippines.

70. Though active in U.S. ecology and forest preservation circles in the 1920s (*New York Times*, March 30, 1923, p. 16), Moore faded into obscurity in the 1930s. *Journal of Ecology* 49 (June 1961): 453.

71. Moore, "Forest Problems" (pt. 2), 154.

72. Mark V. Barrow Jr., *Nature's Ghosts: Confronting Extinction from the Age of Jefferson to the Age of Ecology* (Chicago: University of Chicago Press, 2009), 209–13.

73. Caroline Ford, "Nature, Culture and Conservation in France and Her Colonies, 1840–1940," *Past and Present* 183 (May 2004): 196–98.

74. Paul Sarasin, "Ueber die Aufgaben des Weltnaturschutzes" [About the Tasks of International World Conservation], exposé read at the conference of all delegates of international conservation, Berne, November 18, 1913, trans. Nadine Kavangah (Basel: Emil Berkhauser, 1913), 16; Fiona Paisley, "Mock Justice: World Conservation and Australian Aborigines in Interwar Switzerland?" *Transforming Cultures eJournal* 3, no. 1 (2008): 1–31.

75. Cf. Murray Bookchin, *The Ecology of Freedom: The Emergence and Dissolution of Hierarchy* (Palo Alto, CA: Cheshire, 1982).

76. Carl A. Schenck, *Forest Policy*, 2nd rev. ed (Darmstadt: C. F. Winter, 1911), 112.

77. Moore, "Forest Problems" (pt. 2), 149; *Report of the Philippine Commission to the Secretary of War, July 1, 1913, to June 30, 1914* (Washington, DC: Government Printing Office, 1915), 115.

78. *Annual Report of the Director of Forestry for the Periods January 1 to November 14, 1935 and November 15 to December 31, 1935* (Manila: Bureau of Printing, 1936), 60, 62.

79. John Gifford, "The Luquillo Forest Reserve, Porto Rico," *Forestry and Irrigation* 9 (November 1903): 537–41, at 539.

80. Sonata Dulce F. Restificar, Michael J. Day, and Peter B. Urich, "Protection of Karst in the Philippines," *Acta Carsologica* 35, no. 1 (2006): 122.

81. Hugh McCallum Curran, "Makiling National Park," *Philippine Magazine* 34 (February 1937): 69, 91, 94.

82. *Annual Report of the Director of Forestry of the Philippine Islands for the Fiscal Year Ended December 31, 1933* (Manila: Bureau of Printing, 1934), 63, 64; *Annual Report of the Director of Forestry . . . 1935*, 61–62.

83. Fidel Paz, "Our Philippine National Parks," *Philippine Magazine* 33 (February 1936): 67, 97.

84. *Annual Report of the Director of Forestry . . . 1935*, 60, 62.

85. Beard, *Open Door at Home*, 54.

## 10. Promoting American Anti-imperialism in the Early Cold War

1. For examples of the robust literature on the Cold War's impact on the developing world see Odd Arne Westad, *The Global Cold War: Third World Interventions and the Making of Our Times* (Cambridge: Cambridge University Press, 2005) and Robert J. McMahon, ed., *The Cold War in the Third World* (New York: Oxford University Press, 2013).

2. William B. Benton testifying before House Appropriations Committee, February 26, 1946, RG 59, lots 587 and 52–48, Records of the Assistant Secretary of Public Affairs, Memoranda, 1945–47, box 14, National Archives II, College Park, MD (hereafter cited as NA2).

3. On soft power see Joseph Nye, *Soft Power: The Means to Success in World Politics* (Washington, DC: PublicAffairs, 2004). While this chapter is confined to the U.S. government's use of cultural diplomacy, there is also a rich literature on the transnational projection and reception of American culture and products by a host of other actors; see, for example, Mary Nolan, *The Transatlantic Century: Europe and the United States, 1890–2010* (Cambridge: Cambridge University Press, 2012); Robert Rydell and Rob Kroes, *Buffalo Bill in Bologna: The Americanization of the World, 1869–1922* (Chicago: University of Chicago Press, 2005); Richard Pells, *Not Like Us: How Europeans Have Loved, Hated, and Transformed American Culture since World War II* (New York: Basic Books, 1998).

4. "Stereotyped Concepts about the United States Presented in Selected Foreign Countries," February 5, 1947, Department of State Information Programs, Papers of Charles Hulten, folder 1947, box 9, Harry S. Truman Presidential Library, Independence, MO (hereafter HSTL).

5. Ibid., ii–viii.

6. Joseph Jones, *The Fifteen Weeks: An Inside Account of the Genesis of the Marshall Plan* (New York: Harcourt Brace Jovanovich, 1955).

7. For the text of Truman's speech see *New York Times*, March 13, 1947.

8. On the Marshall Plan and its origins see Michael J. Hogan, *The Marshall Plan: America, Britain, and the Reconstruction of Western Europe, 1947–1952* (New York: Cambridge University Press, 1987).

9. On Soviet reaction to the Truman Doctrine and the European Recovery Plan see Vojtech Mastny, *The Cold War and Soviet Insecurity. The Stalin Years* (New York: Oxford University Press, 1996), 27–29.

10. Sydney Gruson, "New Information Bureau Will Seek to Unify Strategy of Reds," *New York Times*, October 6, 1947; "Comintern Stirs U.N. Worry, Helps Marshall's Program," *New York Times*, October 7, 1947. On Cominform and its relationship to Soviet foreign policy see Vladislav Zubok and Constantine Pleshakov, *Inside the Kremlin's Cold War: From Stalin to Khrushchev* (Cambridge, MA: Harvard University Press, 1996), 110–37.

11. Smith to Marshall, November 15, 1947, *Foreign Relations of the United States, 1947*, 4:619–22 (Hereafter *FRUS*, year, volume: pages).

12. Ibid.

13. U.S. Information with Regard to Anti-American Propaganda, December 1, 1947, RG 59, lot 53D47, Records Relating to International Information Activities, 1938–1953, box 3, William T. Stone files, NA2. The State Department sent these guidelines to American embassies worldwide. See dispatch by Acting Secretary of State Robert Lovett, December 8, 1947, *FRUS, 1947*, 4:630–33. The National Security Council also called for a stronger, more coordinated response to Soviet propaganda. See Report by the National Security Council, December 9, 1947, RG 59, lot 53D47, Records Relating to International Information Activities, 1938–53, box 7, William T. Stone files, NA2.

14. Department of State, *Bulletin* 18 (April 18, 1948): 518.

15. United States Information Policy with Regard to Anti-American Propaganda, July 20, 1948, RG 59, lot 53D47, Records Relating to International Information Activities, 1938–53, box 3; William T. Stone files, NA2.

16. Ibid.

17. See, for example, "Voice of America Is Not the Voice of the American People," August 2, 1949, Iron Curtain Radio Comment on VOA, RG 306, Reports and Related Studies, 1948–53, box 8, NA2.

18. *Russia the Reactionary*, 1949, RG 59, lot 53D47, Records Relating to International Information Activities, 1938–53, William T. Stone files, box 1, NA2.

19. Country Paper for USSR, October 1950, RG59, lot 53D47, William T. Stone files, 1938–53, box 19, NA2.

20. Ibid. In late 1950, Truman also appointed a group of diplomatic, military, communications, and intelligence officials to consider ways to compel or induce the Soviets to stop jamming VOA broadcasts. See Soviet Jamming of Voice of America, December 4, 1950, *FRUS, 1950*, 4:333–36.

21. Iron Curtain Radio and Press Comment, February 1950, RG 306, Reports and Related Studies, 1948–53, box 10, NA2.

22. See, for example, U.S. Ambassador in the Soviet Union (Smith) to Secretary of State, January 17, 1947, *FRUS, 1947*, 4:521–22; Annual USIS Assessment Report, November 5, 1957, RG 306, Office of Research, Country Project Correspondence, 1952–63, India, box 10, NA2.

23. In response to the Korean War, Truman approved NSC-68 on September 30, 1950. See NSC-68, April 14, 1950, *FRUS, 1950*, 1:234–92; Ernest R. May, ed., *American Cold War Strategy: Interpreting NSC-68* (New York: Bedford Books, 1993).

24. For an analysis on the language of NSC-68 and its relation to the U.S. propaganda offensive see Emily S. Rosenberg's comments in *American Cold War Strategy*, 160–64.

25. "Truman Proclaims World-Wide Fight to Crush Red Lies," *New York Times*, April 21, 1950.

26. "Red China Bans 'Voice,'" *New York Times*, April 16, 1950; "5,000 in Prague Jam U.S. Library," *New York Times*, April 21, 1950; Editorial Note, *FRUS, 1950*, 4:550–51. On *Amerika* see Kirk to Acheson, April 25, 1950, *FRUS, 1950*, 4:1163–64.

27. On the U.S. decision to commit troops to Korea see "Resolution Adopted by the United Nations Security Council," June 27, 1950, *FRUS, 1950*, 7:211; James F. Schnabel and Robert J. Watson, *The History of the Joint Chiefs of Staff*, vol. 3, pt. 1, *The Korean War* (Wilmington, DE: Office of Joint History, 1979), 131–42. For examples of Soviet propaganda see *New York Times*, July 2 and 16, 1950.

28. Weekly Information Policy Guide, August 9, 1950, RG 59, lot 53D47, Records Relating to International Information Activities, 1938–53, William T. Stone files, box 4, NA2.

29. Ibid.

30. See *Hearings on the Supplemental Appropriation Bill for 1951: Hearings before the Subcommittee of the House Committee on Appropriations*, 81st Cong., 2nd sess., on Supplemental Appropriation Bill for 1951, Department of State (Washington, DC: Government Printing Office, 1950); Editorial Note, *FRUS, 1950*, 4:316–17; *Cong. Rec.*, 81st Cong., 2nd sess., August 26, 1950: 13532–49.

31. Kenneth Osgood, *Total Cold War: Eisenhower's Secret Propaganda Battle at Home and Abroad* (Lawrence: University Press of Kansas, 2006), 43.

32. IMP's Part in the Campaign of Truth, USIA Subject Files, Motion Pictures folder no. 1, RG 306, USIA Historical Collection, NA2.

33. These assumptions also informed the U.S. development and modernization theory of the era. See Michael Latham et al., *Staging Growth: Modernization, Development, and the Global Cold War* (Amherst: University of Massachusetts Press, 2003).

34. Emergency Plan for Psychological Offensive, March 9, 1951, *FRUS, 1951*, 4:1232–36.

35. *Who Is the Imperialist?*, 1952–58, USIA Pamphlet Files, RG 306, USIA Historical Collection, NA2. At the time that I conducted research in these materials, they were housed in a set of file cabinets at the U.S. Information Agency archives. That entire collection has now been catalogued and folded into a section of RG 306 identified as the "USIA Historical Collection."

36. *Herblock Looks at Communism*, USIA Pamphlet Files, RG 306, USIA Historical Collection, NA2.

37. *Glossary of Soviet Terms*, 1951–52, USIA Pamphlet Files, RG 306, USIA Historical Collection, NA2.

38. *The Free World Speaks*, USIA Pamphlet Files, RG 306, USIA Historical Collection, NA2.

39. VOA Poland transcript, May 9, 1951, RG 306, VOA Daily Content Reports and Script Translations, 1950–55, box 18, NA2.

40. *You Can't Win!*, 1953, USIA Pamphlets, RG 306, USIA Historical Collection, NA2.

41. *This Is the Story of Sergei*, 1953, USIA Pamphlets, USIA Historical Collection, NA2.

42. "By Their Fruits Ye Shall Know Them," May 1952, USIA Pamphlet Files, RG 306, USIA Historical Collection, NA2.

43. World in Brief, November 1954, Women's Packet no. 20, RG 306, Feature Packets, Recurring Themes, box 19, NA2.

44. *An American Speaks to His Asian Friends*, 1951–52, USIA Pamphlet Files, RG 306, USIA Historical Collection, NA2.

45. Ibid.

46. Report of the National Security Council, August 18, 1954, *FRUS, 1952–1954*, 2:1778.

47. *A Picture Story of the United States*, rev. ed., 1961, USIA Pamphlet Files, RG 306, USIA Historical Collection, NA2.

48. Report Prepared by the National Security Council, March 2, 1955, *FRUS, 1955–1957*, 9:504–7.

49. Annual USIS Assessment Report, November 5, 1957, RG 306, Office of Research, Country Project Correspondence, 1952–63, India, box 10, NA2; and Country Plan for India, September 9, 1958, RG 306, Dispatches, 1954–66, box 1, NA2.

50. Annual USIS Assessment Report, November 5, 1957, RG 306, Office of Research, Country Project Correspondence, 1952–63, box 10, NA2.

51. *Bitter Harvest: The October Revolution in Hungary and Its Aftermath*, USIA Pamphlets, RG 306, USIA Historical Collection, NA2.

52. Report Prepared by the National Security Council, September 11, 1957, *FRUS, 1955–1957*, 9:598.

53. Annual USIS Assessment Report, November 5, 1957, RG 306, Office of Research, Country Project Correspondence, 1952–63, India, box 10, NA2.

54. Proposed Country Plan for India Fiscal Year 1959, September 29, 1958, RG 306, Dispatches, 1954–56, box 1, NA2.

55. Manning H. Williams to Oren M. Stephens, February 5, 1958, White House Office files, Office of the Special Assistant for National Security Affairs, 1952–61, Operations Coordinating Board series, box 5, folder on Special OCB Committees, Dwight D. Eisenhower Presidential Library, Abilene, KS (Hereafter DDEL).

56. *In Search of Lincoln*, USIA Film Collection, RG 306, Motion Picture, Sound, and Video Records, Special Media Archives Services Division, NA2.

57. USIS Madras to USIA Washington, DC, June 1, 1959, RG 306, Records Concerning Exhibits in Foreign Countries, 1955–67, box 14, file on India, NA2.

58. Notes on "The Image of America," September 30, 1958, White House Office, NSC Staff, 1948–61, OCB Central Files, box 18, DDEL.

59. Ibid.

60. Ibid.

61. Ibid.

62. Current Psychological Climate, September 1967, Area Plan for the Near East and South Asia, Papers of Leonard Marks, folder—Program Planning Budgeting Memorandum [1 of 3], Lyndon Baines Johnson Presidential Library, Austin, TX.

## 11. Ruling-Class Anti-imperialism in the Era of the Vietnam War

1. The Port Huron Statement of 1962, http://www.hnet.org/~hst306/documents/huron.html.

2. J. William Fulbright, "The Price of Empire," delivered at meeting of American Bar Association, Honolulu, August 8, 1967, in Haynes Johnson and Bernard M. Gwertzman, *Fulbright the Dissenter* (Garden City, NY: Doubleday, 1968), 304–11.

3. C. Wright Mills, *The Power Elite* (New York: Oxford University Press, 1956).

4. James Carter, *Inventing Vietnam: The United States and State Building, 1954–1968* (New York: Cambridge University Press, 2008).

5. Commanding General (hereafter CG), U.S. Forces, India-Burma Theater, memorandum to War Department, CG, U.S. Forces, China Theater, and CG, U.S. Army Liaison Section in Kandy, Ceylon, September 11, 1945, CRAX 27516, Records of the Joint Chiefs of Staff, Record Group 218, Chairman's File, Admiral Leahy, 1942–48, National Archives, Washington, DC (hereafter RG 218, with appropriate filing information); Gallagher, Hanoi, to General R. B. McClure, Kunming, September 20, 1945, in *Vietnam: The Definitive Documentation of Human Decisions*, ed. Gareth Porter (Stanfordville, NY: E. M. Coleman Enterprises, 1979), 1:77–78, document 41 (hereafter cited as Porter, *Vietnam*, with appropriate volume, page, and document designations). See also Report on Office of Strategic Services' "Deer Mission" by Major Allison Thomas, September 17, 1945, Porter, *Vietnam*, 1:74–77, doc. 40; memorandum for the record: General Gallagher's meeting with Ho Chi Minh, September 29, 1945, ibid., 1:80–81, doc. 44; and U.S. Congress, House Committee on Armed Services, *United States–Vietnam Relations, 1945–1967: Study Prepared by the Department of Defense*, 12 vols. (Washington, DC: Government Printing Office, 1971), bk. 1, I.C.3., C-66–104.

6. JCS 1992/4, "U.S. Policy toward Southeast Asia," July 9, 1949, 092 Asia to Europe, case 40, Records of the U.S. Army Staff, RG 319 (hereafter RG 319, with appropriate filing information); Plans and Operations position paper, "U.S. Position with Respect to Indochina, 25 February 1950," RG 319, G-3 091 Indochina, TS.

7. JSPC 958/5, "U.S. Military Measures in Southeast Asia," RG 218, CCS 092 Asia (6–25–48), section 9; U.S. minutes of U.S.-UK Political-Military Conversations, October 26, 1950, U.S. Department of State, *Foreign Relations of the United States, 1950* (Washington DC, 1976), 3:1696 (hereafter cited as *FRUS* with appropriate year, volume, and page designations); substance of Discussion of State-JCS Meeting at the Pentagon Building, December 21, 1951, *FRUS, 1951* (Washington, DC, 1977), 6:568–70; and JSPC memorandum to JCS, "Conference with France and Britain on Southeast Asia," JSPC 958/58, December 22, 1951, RG 218, CCS 092 Asia (6–25–48), section 20.

8. JCS Paper, "The Situation in Indochina," February 7, 1954, RG 218, CCS 092 Asia (6–25–48), section 57.

9. Andrew Rotter, *The Path to Vietnam: Origins of the American Commitment to Southeast Asia* (Ithaca, NY: Cornell University Press, 1987); Lloyd Gardner, *Approaching Vietnam: From World War II to Dienbienphu* (New York: Norton, 1988); William Borden, *The Pacific Alliance: United States Foreign Economic Policy and Japanese Trade Recovery, 1947–1955* (Madison: University of Wisconsin Press, 1984).

10. Vincent Demma, "Suggestions for the Use of Ground Forces, June 1964–March 1965," unpublished manuscript, Center of Military History (CMH), 49; William Westmoreland, *A Soldier Reports* (Garden City, NY: Doubleday, 1976), 115.

11. Westmoreland to Sharp, February 27, 1965, "Use of U.S. Air Power," Westmoreland Papers, box 5, folder 13 History Backup, Lyndon B. Johnson Library, Austin, TX (hereafter LBJL);

see also Westmoreland, *Soldier Reports*, 123; Demma, "Suggestions"; DePuy, in William Gibbons, *The U.S. Government and the Vietnam War: Executive and Legislative Roles and Relationships, part 3, January–July 1965* (Princeton, NJ: Princeton University Press, 1989), 125.

12. Wheeler, in Merle Miller, *Lyndon: An Oral Biography* (New York: Putnam, 1980), 611; see Dave Richard Palmer, *Summons of the Trumpet: U.S.-Vietnam in Perspective* (San Rafael, CA: Presidio Press, 1978), 261; Record of COMUSMACV Fonecon with General Palmer, 0850, February 25, 1968, Westmoreland Papers, folder 450: Fonecons, February 1968, Washington National Records Center, Suitland, MD (WNRC).

13. Westmoreland paper, "The Origins of the Post-Tet 1968 Plans for Additional Forces in the Republic of Vietnam," April 1970, Westmoreland Papers, folder 493 (1 of 2): no. 37 History Files, January 1–June 31, 1970, WNRC; Westmoreland, *Soldier Reports*, 469.

14. Harold K. Johnson interview, MHI Senior Officer Debriefing Project, section 11, 14–15, used at CMH.

15. Notes of the President's Meeting with Senior Foreign Policy Advisers, February 9, 1968, Tom Johnson's Meeting Notes, box 2, folder February 9, 1968—10:15 p.m., LBJL.

16. Johnson in *New York Times*, February 2, 1968; Notes of the President's Meeting with Senior Foreign Affairs Advisory Council, February 10, 1968, Tom Johnson's Meeting Notes, box 2, folder February 10, 1968—3:17 p.m., LBJL.

17. Eisenhower Diary, November 10, 1960, and December 6, 1960, Ann Whitman file, Presidential Transition Series, Eisenhower Library, Abilene, KS (hereafter EL). I would like to acknowledge and thank Nancy Young of the University of Houston for providing me with this document.

18. Anderson Memorandum for the Record, January 16, 1961, Ann Whitman file, Presidential Transition Series, EL; Wilton Persons Memorandum for the Record, January 19, 1961, Ann Whitman File, Eisenhower Post-Presidential Papers, EL, again thanks to Nancy Young. On the importance of the "dollar gap" in postwar formulations of American power see Curt Cardwell, *NSC 68 and the Political Economy of the Early Cold War* (New York: Cambridge University Press, 2011), and more generally Thomas McCormick, *America's Half-Century: United States Foreign Policy in the Cold War and After*, 2nd ed. (Baltimore: Johns Hopkins University Press, 1995).

19. Kennedy, Special Message to the Congress on Gold and the Balance of Payments Deficit, February 6, 1961, American Presidency Project, http://www.presidency.ucsb.edu/ws/print.php?pid=8178.

20. National Security Action Memorandum 225, February 27, 1963, Digital National Security Archive, Balance of Payments, PD 00975; Cabinet Committee on the Balance of Payments to the President, April 1, 1963, Papers of William McChesney Martin, LBJL, box 75, folder Correspondence, etc., with Presidents Eisenhower and Kennedy; President John F. Kennedy, Special Message on Balance of Payments, Papers of William McChesney Martin, LBJL, box 247, folder Balance of Payments and Gold, folder 1 (of 2); John F. Kennedy Address at the International Monetary Fund, September 30, 1963, American Presidency Project, http://www.presidency.ucsb.edu/ws/print.php?pid=9444.

21. NSC History, "The Gold Crisis: November 1967–March 1968," Declassified Documents Reference System, 79, 277A.

22. Robert Buzzanco, *Masters of War: Military Dissent and Politics in the Vietnam Era* (New York: Cambridge University Press, 1996), 237–39.

23. Bundy to the President, July 28, 1965, subj: Your Meeting with Joe Fowler, National Security File (hereafter NSF), Memos to the President, McGeorge Bundy, vol. 12, LBJL.

24. Fowler to the President, November 26, 1965; Bator to the President, November 29, 1965; both in White House Confidential File, FO4, LBJL.

25. On the cost of the war see Thomas Campagna, *The Economic Consequences of the Vietnam War* (New York: Praegar, 1991); Gabriel Kolko, *Anatomy of a War: Vietnam, the United States, and the Modern Historical Experience* (New York: Pantheon Books, 1985), 283–90.

26. NSC synopsis, NSC History, "Gold Crisis," tabs 19–49; Personal Message to Mr. Secretary Fowler from the Chancellor of the Exchequer, October 14, 1967, White House Central Files (hereafter WHCF), Confidential Files, FO4, Financial Relations.

27. Rostow to LBJ, November 22, 1967, NSC History, "Gold Crisis," tabs 1–18; Ackley to LBJ, November 27, 1967, ibid., tabs 1–18; Lyndon B. Johnson, *The Vantage Point: Perspectives of the Presidency* (New York: Holt, Rinehart and Winston, 1971), 317.

28. Rostow to LBJ, November 27, 1967, subj: De Gaulle's Press Conference and Your Meeting with Ambassador Bohlen, NSF, Country File, France, folder Memos, vol. 12, de Gaulle's quotes, Rostow's emphasis; for information on the deficit see Gardner Ackley's weekly balance-of-payments reports in WHCF, Confidential Files, FO4–1, Balance of Payments (1967).

29. Treasury paper, "The Balance of Payments Program of New Year's Day, 1968," National Security File, NSC History, "Balance of Payments," tabs 1–3 (hereafter cited as NSC History, "Balance of Payments," with appropriate filing designation); Treasury paper on international monetary situation, fall 1967, WHCF, Confidential Files, FO4, Financial Relations.

30. Special Analysis by Lionel D. Edie and Co., "The Reactions in Paris to the American Balance of Payments Program," January 16, 1968, WHCF, Confidential Files, FO4–1, Balance of Payments (1968–69); Bohlen to Rusk, January 23, 1968, subj: Report of the Meeting between de Gaulle and Sulzberger, NSF, Country File, France, folder Cables, vol. 13.

31. Edward Bernstein, "Gold and the International Monetary System," January 23, 1968, WHCF, Confidential Files, FI9, Monetary Systems; Barbara Ward Jackson Memo to President, January 23, 1968, NSC History, "Gold Crisis," tabs 19–49.

32. Ackley to LBJ, January 24 and February 8, 1968, subj: Comments on the Attached Memoranda, WHCF, Confidential Files, FI9, Monetary Systems; Rostow to LBJ, January 23, 1968, subj: Prospects for Another Sterling Crisis and What It Could Mean, NSC History, "Gold Crisis," tabs 19–49.

33. McNamara in Notes of Meeting, February 27, 1968, V.N. CF, NSF, box 127, folder March 19, 1970, I.

34. Okun to LBJ, March 2 and 9, 1968, subj: Weekly Balance of Payment Report, WHCF, Confidential Files, FO4–1, Balance of Payments (1968–69); Fowler to LBJ, March 4, 1968, subj: Gold Problems, WHCF, Confidential Files, F19, Monetary Systems; Rostow to LBJ, March 8, 1968, NSC History, "Gold Crisis," bk. 1, tabs 19–49.

35. McCormick, *America's Half-Century*, 162.

36. Rostow to LBJ, March 9, 1968, subj: The Gold Issue, NSC History, "Gold Crisis," bk. 1, tabs 19–49; Rostow in Robert Collins, "The Economic Crisis of 1968 and the Waning of the 'American Century,'" *American Historical Review* 101, no. 2 (April 1996): 408.

37. Rostow to LBJ, March 14, 1968, subj: Gold, National Security File, NSC History, "The Gold Crisis, November 1967–March 1968"; WHCF, Confidential Files, F19, Monetary Systems.

38. American Consul, Frankfurt, to Secretary of State, no. 6686, and Embassy Paris to Secretary of State, no. 11520, March 15, 1968, and Embassy Paris to Secretary of State, no. 11574, National Security File, NSC History, "The Gold Crisis, November 1967–March 1968"; Rusk to European embassies, no. 130741, NSC History, "Gold Crisis," bk. 1, tabs 50–53.

39. Communique of Meeting of Central Bankers, March 17, 1968, National Security File, NSC History, "The Gold Crisis, November 1967–March 1968."

40. See Allen J. Matusow, *Nixon's Economy: Booms, Busts, Dollars, and Votes* (Lawrence: University Press of Kansas, 1998), 39–45.

41. DCI, Intelligence Memorandum, "French Actions in the Recent Gold Crisis," March 20, 1968, and Rostow to LBJ, March 20, 1968, National Security Files, Memos to the President, Walt Whitman Rostow, vol. 67; Goldstein to LBJ, March 22, 1968, WHCF, Confidential Files, folder FI11, Taxation; McPherson to LBJ, March 18, 1968, Reference File, box 1, folder Harry McPherson Memos on Vietnam.

42. Note of President's Meeting with Wheeler and Abrams, March 26, 1968, Tom Johnson's Notes, folder March 26, 1968—10:30 a.m.

43. Okun to LBJ, April 27, 1968, subj: Weekly Balance of Payments report, WHCF, Confidential Files, FO4–1, Balance of Payments (1968–69); Okun to LBJ, May 23, 1968, subj: What Fiscal Failure Means, WHCF, Confidential Files, LE/FI 11–4, emphasis in original.

44. Address by Walter B. Wriston, January 17, 1968, and Paper by Roy L. Reierson, March 4, 1968, Fowler Papers, box 82, folder Domestic Economy: Gold, 1968 (1 of 2); address by Sidney Homer, March 20, 1968, Fowler Papers, box 88, folder Domestic Economy: Gold Crisis, Meeting with Central Bank Governors (1 of 2); "Hope and Trouble," Report by Goldman, Sachs and Co., May 8, 1968, Fowler Papers, box 78, folder Domestic Economy: Economic Data, 1968 (2 of 2).

45. Summary of Martin's Remarks before the Economic Club of Detroit, March 18, 1968, Papers of William McChesney Martin, box 80, folder Miscellaneous Appearances, Federal Reserve Board (hereafter FRB), March 1968; Martin's Extemporaneous Remarks before the American Society of Newspaper Editors, April 19, 1968, Martin Papers, box 81, folder Miscellaneous Appearances, FRB, April–May 1968; Martin to Pamela Graham, May 2, 1968, ibid.; Martin in Notes of Business Council Meeting, October 17–20, 1968, Henry Fowler Papers, box 178, folder Government—Committees/Councils, all at LBJL.

46. "The economic consequences of the escalating Vietnam War so exacerbated the dollar drain, the trade imbalance, and the maladies of the civilian sector," according to Thomas McCormick, "that significant tariff cuts [as in the Kennedy Round] ironically did less to help American exports than it did to open the American market to ever-more-competitive capitalists from Germany and Japan." *America's Half-Century*, 128.

47. Policy Planning Study 23, February 24, 1948, "Review of Current Trends in U.S. Foreign Policy," February 24, 1948, *FRUS, 1948*, 1:509–29.

48. On Shoup and other military critics see Buzzanco, *Masters of War*.

49. Hobart Rowan, *Self-Inflicted Wounds: From LBJ's Guns and Butter to Reagan's Voodoo Economics* (New York: Times Books, 1994), 78.

50. Davison in Senior Officer Debriefing Program interview, MHI, 3:21–22.


# 12. Whither American Anti-imperialism in a Postcolonial World?

1. In 1979, Panama regained partial control of the zone taken by the United States in 1903, and in 1999, total control reverted to Panamanian sovereignty.

2. Fredrik Logevall, *Embers of War: The Fall of an Empire and the Making of America's Vietnam* (New York: Random House, 2012), xii, 262.

3. *The Pentagon Papers*, Gravel edition, vol. 1 (Boston: Beacon Press, 1971), 591–92 (Eisenhower); *U.S. President's Commission* on *Materials* Policy, 5 vols. (Washington, DC: Government Printing Office, 1952); Richard N. L. Andrews, *Managing the Environment, Managing Ourselves: A History of American Environmental Policy* (New Haven, CT: Yale University Press, 1999, 2000), 182–83.

4. Paul A. Kramer, "Power and Connection: Imperial Histories of the United States in the World," *American Historical Review* 116 (December 2011): 1348–91.

5. Wikipedia Commons file photo, Vietnam War Protesters, 1967, http://en.wikipedia.org/wiki/File:Vietnam_War_protesters_1967_Wichita,_Kans_-_NARA_-_283625.jpg.

6. Charles Debenedetti, *An American Ordeal: The Antiwar Movement of the Vietnam Era* (Syracuse, NY: Syracuse University Press, 1990), 95 (quote).

7. Barbara Tischler, "The Antiwar Movement," in *A Companion to the Vietnam War*, ed. Marilyn B. Young and Robert Buzzanco (Malden, MA: Wiley-Blackwell, 2002), 384–402, at 387.

8. Regarding the case for the Progressive Labor Party see "GF" [Grover Furr], "The Rise and Fall of the Anti-Vietnam War Movement in the U.S.," http://msuweb.montclair.edu/~furrg/Vietnam/riseandfall.html.

9. Port Huron Statement of the Students for a Democratic Society, 1962, http://coursesa.matrix.msu.edu/~hst306/documents/huron.html.

10. Martin Luther King Jr., Riverside Church Meeting, New York City, April 4, 1967, http://www.stanford.edu/group/King/liberation_curriculum/speeches/beyondvietnam.html.

11. Howard Schuman, "Two Sources of Antiwar Sentiment in America," *American Journal of Sociology* 78, no. 3 (1972): 513.

12. The Sixties Project, Vietnam Veterans against the War (VVAW), http://www2.iath.virginia.edu/sixties/HTML_docs/Resources/Primary/Winter_Soldier/VVAW_entry.html.

13. Circuit Court of Cook County, IL: *Vietnam Veterans against the War, Inc., Plaintiff, v. Rowland Cordero and the Vietnam Veterans against the War, defendants*, in VVAW, "Beware of VVAW AI," http://www.vvaw.org/about/vvawai.php; Bill Branson, "From the National Office," *Veteran*, http://www.vvaw.org/veteran/article/?id=2205.

14. It produced a large body of work, notably Walter LaFeber's *The New Empire* (Ithaca, NY: Cornell University Press, 1963).

15. Daniel Schirmer, *Republic or Empire: American Resistance to the Philippine War* (Cambridge, MA: Schenkman Publishing Co., 1972); Robert L. Beisner, *Twelve against Empire: The Anti-Imperialists, 1898–1900* (New York: McGraw-Hill, 1968); E. Berkeley Tompkins, *Anti-Imperialism in the United States: The Great Debate, 1890–1920* (Philadelphia: University of Pennsylvania Press, 1970); Richard E. Welch Jr., *Response to Imperialism: The United States and the Philippine-American War, 1899–1902* (Chapel Hill: University of North Carolina Press, 1978).

16. William Appleman Williams, *Empire as a Way of Life* (New York: Oxford University Press, 1980).

17. Arthur Schlesinger Jr., *The Imperial Presidency* (Boston: Houghton Mifflin, 1973), 299–300.

18. Greg Grandin, *Empire's Workshop: Latin America, the United States, and the Rise of the New Imperialism* (New York: Metropolitan Books, 2006), 62.

19. Reagan, Remarks and a Question-and-Answer Session with Southeast Regional Editors and Broadcasters, May 15, 1987, *Public Papers of the Presidents*, 1987, vol. 1, p. 514.

20. Grandin, *Empire's Workshop*, 117.

21. Walter LaFeber, *Inevitable Revolutions: The United States in Central America*, 2nd ed. (New York: Norton, 1993), 327–28 (quote at 327).

22. Ibid., 224, 250, 357; Chicago Religious Task Force on Central America Records, 1982–92, http://digicoll.library.wisc.edu/cgi/f/findaid/findaid-idx?c=wiarchives;view=reslist;subview=standard;didno=uw-whs-m93153; Roger Peace, "The Anti-Contra-War Campaign: Organizational Dynamics of a Decentralized Movement," *International Journal of Peace Studies* 13, no. 1 (Spring/ Summer 2008): 63–83, at 67; Francis Shor, *Dying Empire: U.S. Imperialism and Global Resistance* (New York: Routledge, 2010), chap. 7.

23. "Thirty Years of CISPES Solidarity," at http://cispes30years.org/; Shor, *Dying Empire*, 111; Grandin, *Empire's Workshop*, 139.

24. As Roger Peace states: "In the interest of building a broad based campaign, most Leftists avoided such hot-button terms as 'socialism' to describe the Sandinista experiment and 'imperialism' to describe U.S. foreign policy." In Peace, "Anti-Contra-War Campaign," 70.

25. Christian Smith, *Resisting Reagan: The Central American Peace Movement* (Chicago: University of Chicago Press, 1996), 216.

26. "Remarks at the Annual Convention of the National Association of Evangelicals in Orlando, Florida, March 8, 1983," http://www.reagan.utexas.edu/archives/speeches/1983/30883b. htm; Lawrence S. Wittner, *Toward Nuclear Abolition: A History of the World Nuclear Disarmament Movement, 1971–Present* (Stanford, CA: Stanford University Press, 2003), 120, 261.

27. David Adams, *The American Peace Movements* (New Haven, CT, 2002), 16, http://www. culture-of-peace.info/apm/title-page.html; see also Wittner, *Toward Nuclear Abolition*, 237; "President Says Foes of U.S. Have Duped Arms Freeze Group," *New York Times*, October 5, 1982.

28. Wittner, *Toward Nuclear Abolition*, 184, 320.

29. Francis Fukuyama, "The End of History?" *National Interest*, Summer 1989, at ps321. community.uaf.edu/files/. . ./Fukuyama-End-of-history-article.pdf.

30. Michael Hardt and Antonio Negri, *Empire* (Cambridge, MA: Harvard University Press, 2000), xiv, 189, xv.

31. Naomi Klein, *No Logo* (London: Flamingo, 2000), 57, 112, 162, 172.

32. Ibid., xxi.

33. Amy Kaplan and Donald Pease, eds., *Cultures of U.S. Imperialism* (Durham, NC: Duke University Press, 1993), 16.

34. Quoted in Niall Ferguson, *Colossus: The Rise and Fall of the American Empire* (New York: Penguin, 2004), 6 (Bush); Robert Kagan, quoted in David Norman Smith, "Recognizing Empire: Alienation, Authority, and Delusions of Grandeur" in Jennifer M. Lehmann and Harry F. Dahms, eds., *Globalization Between the Cold War and Neo-imperialism*, Current Perspectives in Social Theory, vol. 22 (Kidlington, Eng.: Emerald Group Publishing, 2006), 72.

35. William Earl Weeks, *The New Cambridge History of American Foreign Relations*, vol. 1, *Dimensions of the Early American Empire, 1754–1865* (Cambridge: Cambridge University Press, 2012).

36. John Lewis Gaddis, *Surprise, Security, and the American Experience* (Cambridge, MA: Harvard University Press, 2004); Ferguson, *Colossus*.

37. Richard Seymour, *American Insurgents: A Brief History of American Anti-Imperialism* (Chicago: Haymarket Books, 2012).

38. Walter L. Hixson, *The Myth of American Diplomacy: National Identity and U.S. Foreign Policy* (New Haven, CT: Yale University Press, 2008), 105.

39. Maureen Dowd, "History Up in Smoke," *New York Times*, April 16, 2003, http://www. nytimes.com/2003/04/16/opinion/history-up-in-smoke.html.

40. Statement by Historians against the War [HAW], April 15, 2009, http://www. historiansagainstwar.org/. "As historically minded activists, scholars, students, and teachers, we stand opposed to wars of aggression, military occupations of foreign lands, and imperial efforts by the United States and other powerful nations to dominate the internal life of other countries. . . . HAW collected more than 2600 signatures on its revised statement, stimulated dozens of campus teach-ins; held two national conferences (2006 in Austin and 2008 in Atlanta); and gained passage by the American Historical Association of the first anti-war resolution in the AHA's history"; American Empire Project, http://www.americanempireproject.com/ americanempireproject.htm.

41. United for Peace and Justice, "UFPJ Unity Statement," http://www.unitedforpeace.org/ufpj-unity-statement/.

42. E.g., "Peace Action," http://www.peace-action.org/allies; DePaul, "Peacemaking, Nonviolence, Justice, and Anti-war Resources," "http://las.depaul.edu/pax/StudentResources/NatlandIntlPeacemakingNonviole/Peacemaking.asp.

43. Adopted as a work in progress at the June 2003 United for Peace and Justice National Strategy Conference, http://www.unitedforpeace.org/ufpj-unity-statement/.

44. *BBC News*, "Millions Join Global Anti-war Protests," February 17, 2003, http://news.bbc.co.uk/1/hi/world/europe/2765215.stm.

45. *BBC News*, "Anti-war Rally Makes Its Mark," February 19, 2003, http://news.bbc.co.uk/1/hi/uk/2767761.stm.

46. Paul Waldman, "Conceived in Delusion, Sold in Deception," *American Prospect*, March 5, 2013, http://prospect.org/article/conceived-delusion-sold-deception.

47. "Remarks by the President on a New Beginning, Cairo University, Cairo, Egypt" (June 4, 2009) at http://www.whitehouse.gov/the_press_office/Remarks-by-the-President-at-Cairo-University-6-04-09; also quoted in Julian Go, *Patterns of Empire: The British and American Empires, 1688 to the Present* (Cambridge University Press, 2011), 1.

48. Ron Paul, "Opposing the Use of Military Force against Iraq," October 10, 2002, http://www.antiwar.com/paul/paul51.html.

49. Bill Kauffman, *Ain't My America: The Long, Noble History of Antiwar Conservatism and Middle-American Anti-Imperialism* (New York: Macmillan, 2008), 9.

50. *Theodore and Woodrow: How Two American Presidents Destroyed Constitutional Freedoms* (Nashville, TN: Thomas Nelson, 2012); blurb at http://www.barnesandnoble.com/w/theodore-and-woodrow-andrew-p-napolitano/1111582450?ean=9781480594975.

51. Thomas E. Woods Jr., "The Anti-Imperialist League and the Battle against Empire," Ludwig Von Mises Institute, December 15, 2006, http://mises.org/daily/2408.

52. Andrew Levine, "A Snare and a Delusion: Ron Paul's Anti-Imperialism," *Counterpunch*, Weekend Edition, January 20–22, 2012, http://www.counterpunch.org/2012/01/20/ron-paul%E2%80%99s-anti-imperialism/.

53. Levine, "Snare and a Delusion."

54. Richard Phillips, "Vernacular Anti-Imperialism," *Annals of the Association of American Geographers* 101, no. 5 (2011): 1109–25, at 1111.

55. John Feffer, "Books: Guarding the Empire from Four Miles Up," *Inter Press Service News Agency*, http://www.ipsnews.net/2012/06/books-guarding-the-empire-from-four-miles-up/.

56. Engelhardt, *Terminator Planet*, quoted in Feffer, ibid.

57. Feffer, "Guarding the Empire."

58. Book Review: *Terminator Planet: The First History of Drone Warfare, 2001–2050*, in *Understanding Empire*, at http://understandingempire.wordpress.com/2012/08/10/book-review-terminator-planet-the-first-history-of-drone-warfare-2001-2050/.

59. On de-territorialization and re-territorialization (first publicized for the discipline of history via Hardt and Negri's *Empire*) see Stuart Elden, *Terror and Territory: The Spatial Extent of Sovereignty* (Minneapolis: University of Minnesota Press, 2009); Elden, "The State of Territory under Globalization: *Empire* and the Politics of Reterritorialization," *Thamyris / Intersecting*, no. 12 (2006): 47–66.

60. David Gianatasio, "Sarcastic Amazon Reviews Take a Darker Turn on Toy Drone's Product Page," *Adweek*, http://www.adweek.com/adfreak/sarcastic-amazon-reviews-take-darker-turn-toy-drones-product-page-146843; and Amazon customer review, December 17, 2012, "Helped

me teach my son about the Imperial forces," http://www.amazon.com/review/RRS9UJ11 66RI3.

61. Pew Research Global Attitudes Project, "Global Opinion of Obama Slips, International Policies Faulted: Drone Strikes Widely Opposed," http://www.pewglobal.org/2012/06/13/global-opinion-of-obama-slips-international-policies-faulted/. See also Nick Turse and Tom Engelhardt, *Terminator Planet: The First History of Drone Warfare, 2001–2050* (New York: Nation Books, 2012).

62. This point is discussed in the conclusion of Gopal Balakrishnan, "Hardt and Negri's *Empire*," *New Left Review* 5 (September–October 2000), http://newleftreview.org/II/5/gopal-balakrishnan-hardt-and-negri-s-empire.

# Contributors

Laura Belmonte is Department Head and Professor of History at Oklahoma State University. She is the author of *Selling the American Way: U.S. Propaganda and the Cold War* (2008) and *Speaking of America: Readings in U.S. History* (2006). She is currently coauthoring *Global Americans: A Transnational History* (forthcoming 2015).

Robert Buzzanco is Professor of American History at the University of Houston. He is the author of *Masters of War: Military Dissent and Politics in the Vietnam Era* (1996) and coeditor, with Marilyn Young, of *A Companion to the Vietnam War* (2002).

Julian Go is Professor of Sociology at Boston University. He is the author of *Empire and the Politics of Meaning: Elite Political Cultures in the Philippines and Puerto Rico during US Colonialism* (2008) and *Patterns of Empire: The British and American Empires, 1688 to the Present* (2011).

Alan Knight is Professor of the History of Latin America at the University of Oxford. He is the author of numerous books on the United States and Mexico, including *US-Mexican Relations, 1910–1940: An Interpretation* (1987) and the two-volume study *The Mexican Revolution* (1986).

Ussama Makdisi is Professor of History and holder of the Arab–American Educational Foundation Chair in Arabic Studies at Rice University. His most recent publications are *Faith Misplaced: The Broken Promise of U.S.-Arab Relations, 1820–2001* (2010) and *Artillery of Heaven: American Missionaries and the Failed Conversion of the Middle East* (2008).

Erez Manela is Professor of History at Harvard University. He is the author of *The Wilsonian Moment: Self-Determination and the International Origins of Anticolonial Nationalism* (2007) and coeditor of *The Shock of the Global: The 1970s in Perspective* (2010) and of *Empires at War, 1911–1923* (2014).

Peter Onuf is Senior Research Fellow, Robert H. Smith International Center for Jefferson Studies, Monticello, and Thomas Jefferson Foundation Professor Emeritus, University of Virginia. Among his many publications are *Jefferson's Empire: The Language of American Nationhood* (2001) and *The Mind of Thomas Jefferson* (2007).

Jeffrey Ostler is Beekman Professor of Northwest and Pacific History at the University of Oregon. He is the author of *The Plains Sioux and U.S. Colonialism from Lewis and Clark to Wounded Knee* (2004) and *The Lakotas and the Black Hills: The Struggle for Sacred Ground* (2010).

Patricia Schechter is Professor of History at Portland State University in Oregon. She is the author of *Ida B. Wells-Barnett and American Reform, 1880–1930* (2001) and *Exploring the Decolonial Imaginary: Four Transnational Lives* (2012).

Jay Sexton is Associate Professor of American History at Corpus Christi College, the University of Oxford. He is the author of *Debtor Diplomacy: Finance and American Foreign Relations in the Civil War Era, 1837–1873* (2005), *The Monroe Doctrine: Empire and Nation in Nineteenth-Century America* (2011), and coeditor with Richard Carwardine of *The Global Lincoln* (2011).

Ian Tyrrell is Emeritus Professor of History at the University of New South Wales, Sydney, Australia. Among his many publications are *True Gardens of the Gods: Californian-Australian Environmental Reform, 1860–1930* (1999); *Transnational Nation: United States History in Global Perspective since 1789* (2007); and *Reforming the World: The Creation of America's Moral Empire* (2010).

# Index